Early Professional Development
for Social Workers

Edited by Raymond Taylor, Malcolm Hill and Fergus McNeill

Published by
VENTURE PRESS
16 Kent Street
Birmingham
B5 6RD
www.basw.co.uk

British Library Cataloguing-in-Publication Data
A catalogue record for this book is available from the British Library

ISBN: 978-1-86178-084-3 (paperback)

Printed by:
Hobbs the Printers Ltd
Brunel Road
Totton
SO40 3WX

Printed in Great Britain

Dedication

This book is dedicated to the staff and students of the Glasgow School of Social Work (GSSW) and to the first Head of the School, Professor Joan Orme. Many of the chapters in this collection began their lives as presentations to the GSSW seminar series. Between 2004 and 2011, the GSSW was a joint School of the Universities of Glasgow and Strathclyde. From 2011, it will reside in the Faculty of Humanities and Social Sciences at the University of Strathclyde.

Contents

List of Tables, Figures and Boxes

Tables

Figures

Boxes

Preface

It gives me great pleasure to write a preface to this book which I hope will make an important contribution to the development of social work in the United Kingdom. This book is published at an important point in the history of the discipline. Social Work is now part of a registered profession in each of the four countries of the United Kingdom and a range of national social work policy initiatives have emphasised the importance of social workers being equipped to operate as autonomous, and accountable, professionals.

Service users need confident social workers who practice with integrity and professional courage and who can be potent advocates for those whom they represent. They also need practitioners committed to their ongoing learning and development at every stage in their careers. The Codes of Practice and Post Registration Training and Learning Requirements (PRTL) are now firmly established and are there to support both professional registration and continuing professional development.

This is an edited book with chapters written by authors with extensive experience of social work practice. The central focus of the book is on the early professional development needs of practitioners. The editors have encouraged contributors to write for a UK readership on a range of social work issues whilst giving proper recognition to the legal and policy differences of England, Scotland, Wales and Northern Ireland. Each country within the UK faces similar challenges, including those problems arising from the current economic climate; however, there is much which can be learned from reflecting on current issues in social work practice and exploring the range of interventions which are being applied in different parts of the United Kingdom.

In relation to workforce issues in particular, across the United Kingdom, individual administrations have formulated new policies and strategies in relation to social work education which have much in common; the expectation that workers will have the skills to work in multidisciplinary teams, are able to use research evidence to inform their practice and have the skills necessary to engage meaningfully with a wide range of service users.

I hope this book will be used extensively by practitioners, managers, social work educators and all those committed to driving up standards and improving social work practice.

Gary Coutts
Convener Scottish Social Services Council
Vice Chair Skills for Care and Development

List of abbreviations

ADHD	Attention Deficit Hyperactivity Disorder
ASP	Adult Support and Protection (Scotland) Act 2007
AWIA	Adults with Incapacity (Scotland) Act 2000
BAAF	British Association of Adoption & Fostering
BASW	British Association of Social Workers
CAF	Common Assessment Framework
CAIRO	Climate Assessment Inventory for Risk and Opportunity
CCP	core correctional practices
CDWC	Children's Development Workforce Council
COSLA	Convention of Scottish Local Authority Services
CPD	continuing professional development
CQSW	Certificate of Qualification in Social Work
CYC	child and youth care
DCSF	Department for Children, Schools and Families
DH	Department of Health
DHSSPS	Department of Health, Social Services and Public Safety
DipSW	Diploma in Social Work
DTTO	drug treatment and training order
EBP	evidence-based practice
EM	electronic monitoring
EPD	early professional development
ESRC	Economic and Social Research Council
FGC	family group conferencing
GP	general practitioner
HDC	Home Detention Curfew
HEI	higher education institution
HNC	Higher National Certificate
IAF	Integrated Assessment Framework
IASSW	International Association of Schools of Social Work
ICT	information and communication technology
IFP	independent fostering provider
IRISS	Institute for Research and Innovation in Social Services
LSCB	Local Safeguarding Children Board
MAPPA	Multi-Agency Public Protection Arrangements
MASC	Modernising Adult Social Care programme
MHCT	Mental Health (Care and Treatment) (Scotland) Act 2003
NHS	National Health Service
NOMS	National Offender Management Service

NOS	National Occupational Standards
NSWQB	National Social Work Qualification Board
NVQ	National Vocational Qualification
OFMDFM	Office of the First Minister and Deputy First Minister
PMLD	profound and multiple learning disabilities
QAA	Quality Assurance Agency
RCA	Radio Corporation of America
SCQF	Scottish Credit and Qualifications Framework
SCR	Serious Case Review
SER	social enquiry report
SiSWE	Standards in Social Work Education
SRAG	Significant Risk Advisory Group
STRADA	Scottish Training on Drugs and Alcohol
SVQ	Scottish Vocational Qualification
TOPSS	Training Organisation for the Personal Social Services
UK	United Kingdom
UN	United Nations
UNCRC	United Nations Convention on the Rights of the Child
US	United States
WORP	Women's Offending Reduction Programme

Notes on contributors

Jane Aldgate OBE is a graduate of Edinburgh University and a trained social worker. She is Professor of Social Care at The Open University and Honorary Professorial Fellow at the University of Edinburgh. Jane has researched and written about a wide range of child welfare issues across the UK, including family support, services for looked-after children and child protection. Recent research includes studies on kinship care and child wellbeing for the Scottish Social Work Inspection. Contemporary co-edited books include *The Developing World of the Child* (2006, Jessica Kingsley Publishers) and *Enhancing Social Work Management: Theory and Best Practice from the UK and the USA* (2007, Jessica Kingsley Publishers). Jane is currently seconded to the Scottish Government's *Getting it right for every child* team as Professional Advisor. She was awarded an OBE in 2007 for services to children and families.

Joy Barlow MBE is the Head of STRADA (Scottish Training on Drugs and Alcohol), a partnership between the University of Glasgow and DrugScope. Before setting up STRADA in 2001, she designed and developed unique residential and outreach services for women dependent on drugs and alcohol with their children, for the Aberlour Child Care Trust in Scotland. She has been a member of the Advisory Council on the Misuse of Drugs, being on the prevention working group that produced *Hidden Harm*. She has also been a member of the Scottish Advisory Committee on Drug Misuse, and is a longstanding advisor to government on substance misuse issues. She has presented and written widely on the impact of parental substance misuse on children, and workforce development. She was awarded an MBE in 1998.

Peter Bates has been part of the National Development Team for Inclusion since 1999, a not-for-profit agency providing consultancy and training for mental health, learning disability and older persons' services. He previously had jobs with the probation service, the employment service, social services, the NHS and audit. In his work with over 130 local services, Peter has combined an understanding of the pressures at the frontline with a persistent dream of good support in healthy communities. He has published 80 items in the areas of employment, disability, empowerment and inclusion and is a Visiting Research Fellow at Staffordshire University.

Denis Bracken is Professor of Social Work at the University of Manitoba where he has been teaching criminal justice social work for over 30 years. He holds postgraduate degrees from the University of Toronto and the London School of Economics (LSE). Current research interests include desistance from crime and urban aboriginal gangs, social work training and community justice, and the criminal justice response to offenders with Foetal Alcohol Spectrum Disorder (FASD). He is the co-author of two reports for the Manitoba Government on working with domestic violence offenders. Denis has been an academic visitor at DeMontfort University, Trinity College Dublin and the Inner City Social Work Program and later Associate Dean in the Faculty of Social Work responsible for Distance Education and undergraduate programmes. Presently he is Rector of St. Paul's College at the University of Manitoba.

Lena Dominelli is Chair of Applied Social Sciences and Associate Director in the Institute of Hazards, Risk and Resilience Research at Durham University. She is currently undertaking research into disaster interventions including the 2004 tsunami and climate change and older people. She has written widely in areas of social work, social policy and sociology. These include over 30 books, the latest of which are *Social Work: Theory and Practice for a changing profession; Women and Community Action* and *Anti-Racist Social Work*. She was President of the the International Association of Schools of Social Work from 1996 to 2004, and received a medal of honour from the French Senate for her contribution to international social work and an honorary PhD degree from the Univesity of KwaZulu-Natal in South Africa.

Jane Donald has a background as a senior manager in the arts heading major initiatives including education, marketing, sales and media relations for Glasgow's Concert Halls and Celtic Connections International Festival. This led to academic roles and she is completing her PhD in the School of Management at the University of St Andrews. Her academic research focuses on creativity, health and organisational studies. She has pursued her commitment to social justice by working for the NHS in East Glasgow on a health equalities programme.

Andrew Eccles is Lecturer and Course Director of the MSc Community Care in the Glasgow School of Social Work. His current area of interest is in ethical considerations around the use of assistive technology; previous research has included evaluating interprofessional working for local government and heath authorities.

Pam Green Lister is a Senior Lecturer in Social Work at the Glasgow School of Social Work. Her main interests are in child protection and social work education. She has undertaken research in child protection for Glasgow and Western Isles Child Protection Committees, Greater Glasgow Primary Health Care Trust and the Association of Chief Police Officers Scotland. Among her most recent and relevant publications are: Stalker, K, Green Lister, P, Lerpiniere, J and McArthur, K: *Child Protection and the Needs and Rights of Disabled Children* (2010, University of Strathclyde Faculty of Education/Sir Halley Stewart Trust); Green Lister, P and McKinnon, M: *Report of the Literature Review of Recommendations of Child Abuse Inquiries in Respect of the Police Force* (2010, Association of Chief Police Officers Scotland) and Green Lister, P: 'Clinical supervision in child protection for community nurses' (*Child Abuse Review* 2005, 14(1), pp 57-72).

Douglas Hamilton, Head of Scotland, Save the Children UK, joined Save the Children in April 2005 and has led on the organisation's policy, advocacy and research work in Scotland. He has recently specialised in issues relating to children's rights and child poverty. Douglas is also a board member of the Scottish Alliance of Children's Rights and One Parent Families Scotland. His previous experience includes policy and research roles with the Scottish Human Rights Centre, Children in Scotland, Barnardo's and COSLA. Douglas studied law as an undergraduate and also completed an MSc in Social Research.

Malcolm Hill, Professor, has researched and written on a wide range of topics concerning children, families and child welfare policies and services. He was one of the founding members of the Glasgow Centre for the Child & Society and served as Director of the Centre until 2005. He has published extensively on child protection and youth crime.

Susan Hunter is a Senior Lecturer in Social Work at the University of Edinburgh where she has primary responsibility for teaching in community care. She is also programme director of the MSc in Advanced Professional Studies (Adult Protection) aimed at qualified practitioners in health and social welfare. Her current research interests include an evaluation of self-directed support in three test sites in Scotland; supported employment and people with learning difficulties; and experiences of detention under the Mental Health (Care & Treatment) (Scotland) Act 2003.

Andrew Kendrick gained his PhD in Social Anthropology from the London School of Economics in 1984. He was a Lecturer and Senior Lecturer in Social Work at Dundee University before he took up the post of Professor of Residential Child Care with the Scottish Institute for Residential Child Care at Strathclyde University. Andrew became Head of Department of the Glasgow School of Social Work in 2006. He has carried out a wide range of research in the field of child care and welfare, with a particular focus on residential child care.

Lee Knifton has an academic background in social science and public health and is a Visiting Lecturer at Strathclyde University. He is involved in numerous research programmes at international, EU, UK and community level, with an interest in mode 2 research approaches in relation to health equity, the health and social impact of stigma and discrimination, and issues around mental health. He is Associate Head of the Mental Health Foundation programmes in Scotland, Health Improvement Lead with NHS Greater Glasgow and Clyde, co-chairs the UK Public Health Association section on mental health, and directs the Scottish Mental Health Arts and Film Festival.

Mark Lymbery is Associate Professor of Social Work at the University of Nottingham. He has published widely on various areas of social work, with a particular emphasis on policy and practice relating to adults. He jointly wrote the acclaimed text *Social Work: An introduction to contemporary practice* (2008, Pearson).

Duncan Mackay qualified as a Social Worker in 1982 and worked in that capacity for seven years in various locations. He became a Senior Social Worker in the former Strathclyde Regional Council, then moved into a planning role to manage production of the first joint community care plan for the Argyll and Clyde health board area. At local government reorganisation in 1996 he moved to North Lanarkshire Council, where he has been Head of Social Work Development for the last seven years. The Council has been at the forefront of implementing the personalisation agenda, where Duncan has led the development of highly innovative approaches to supporting people, community capacity building and commissioning.

Gillian MacIntyre is a Lecturer in the Glasgow School of Social Work, a joint school of the Universities of Glasgow and Strathclyde. Her doctoral thesis explored the transition from childhood to adulthood for young people with learning disabilities. Her research interests are in the areas of learning disability, mental health and social work education

Gill McIvor is Professor of Criminology at the University of Stirling and Co-Director of the Scottish Centre for Crime and Justice Research. Her recent research has focused on alternatives to imprisonment and diversity, with recent projects including the evaluation of the Scottish pilot drug courts, women's experiences of community service and probation, the evaluation of the 218 Project and research on women's experiences after prison in Australia. She has been a member of the Scottish Prison and Community Justice Accreditation Panels, the Getting Best Results Steering Group (aimed at promoting effective work with offenders in Scotland) and a short-life group on services for female offenders convened by the Scottish Executive. Her publications include *Women Who Offend* (2004), *What Works with Women Offenders* (2007, with Rosemary Sheehan and Chris Trotter) and *Working with Women Offenders in the Community* (forthcoming, with Rosemary Sheehan and Chris Trotter).

Fergus McNeill is Professor of Criminology and Social Work at the University of Glasgow. Prior to becoming an academic in 1998, he worked for a number of years in residential drug rehabilitation and as a criminal justice social worker. His research interests and publications have addressed a range of criminal justice issues, including sentencing, community sanctions, ex-offender reintegration and youth justice. His previous books include Reducing Reoffending: Social Work and Community Justice in Scotland (with Bill Whyte, 2007, Willan), Youth Offending and Youth Justice (with Monica Barry, 2009, Jessica Kingsley) and Offender Supervision: New Directions in Theory, Research and Practice (with Peter Raynor and Chris Trotter, 2010, Willan/Routledge).

Graham McPheat is a lecturer based in the Glasgow School of Social Work at Strathclyde University. During this time he has been heavily involved in the MSc in Advanced Residential Childcare and the MSc in Social Work Management. Prior to moving to GSSW Graham worked for ten years as a practitioner and manger in residential child care services in Edinburgh. He has been involved in research looking at recruitment and placement trends in residential childcare.

Mike Nellis is Professor of Criminal and Community Justice in the Glasgow School of Social Work at the University of Strathclyde. He is a former social worker with young offenders and between 1990 and 2003 was closely involved in the training of probation officers at the University of Birmingham. He has written extensively on the changing nature of the probation service, the promotion of community penalties, the significance of electronic monitoring and the cultural politics of penal reform (including the educational use of prison movies and prisoners' autobiographies).

Joan Orme began her social work career as a Probation Officer, working first in Sheffield and then Southampton. Her first academic post at the University of Southampton was specifically for training Probation Officers. She continued in generic social work education, with a specific interest in probation education and training, at Southampton until she took up her post at Glasgow. Joan was appointed the first Professor of Social Work at the University of Glasgow in October 2000 and helped to establish the Glasgow School of Social Work, a joint School of Glasgow and Strathclyde Universities. She was appointed the founding Head of the School in 2003. Her main areas of research have been in workload management, social work practice and criminal justice.

Alison Petch has spent most of her career involved with research and policy, latterly in health and social care. From 1985 to 1993 she worked at the Social Work Research Centre at Stirling University, established to evaluate social work effectiveness. In 1993 she moved to Glasgow University as Director of the Nuffield Centre for Community Care Studies. The work of the Centre focused on the evaluation, promotion and dissemination of community care policy and practice and included research on partnership working and individual outcomes. The opportunity to ensure that the evidence from research was implemented in practice tempted her south in October 2005 to work with **research in practice *for adults***, a partnership agency funded by local authorities. In October 2009 she returned to Scotland as Director of IRISS (Institute for Research and Innovation in Social Services). This focuses on equipping the workforce to deliver effective outcomes for those who access Scotland's social services through the promotion of evidence-informed practice and innovation and improvement.

Neil Quinn has a background in mental health social work and community development and is an academic within the Glasgow School of Social Work. His principal research interest is mental health inequalities and he has published widely on tackling stigma and discrimination in relation to the media, the arts, low-income communities, social work services, workplaces, student mental health and also on cultural beliefs about mental health. He plays a lead role in major European-wide research projects, including the EU-funded ASPEN programme, designed to address the stigma associated with depression across the EU member states. Neil combines his academic role with a practice one, managing an innovative mental health improvement programme within East Glasgow, which tackles inequalities in mental health within schools, workplaces and with asylum seeker and later-life groups. He also chairs a range of groups, including the Glasgow Anti-Stigma Partnership and the Sanctuary programme working with asylum seekers and refugees, and is co-chair of the UK Public Health Association Mental Health Special Interest Group. He is an advisor to the Scottish Government on mental health improvement policy.

Jacquie Roberts has been the Chief Executive of the Care Commission since October 2001. The Care Commission regulates care homes for children and adults, adoption and fostering services, secure units, special residential schools, early years services and care at home and housing support services. A priority for the Care Commission is to drive up all standards of care following a much more person-centred approach. Jacquie worked as a social worker in Oxfordshire in the 1970s. After a period of working as a specialist in child protection research and practice, she moved to Lambeth Social Services Adoption and Fostering Unit. In 1986 she became Project Head of Tayside regional child protection family centre, while continuing research and teaching in child abuse and neglect. She managed children and families services and older people's services in Dundee before being appointed Director of Social Work for Dundee City Council in 1997. Her special interests are: standards, services for older people, child protection and looked-after children.

Denis Rowley has worked in social work, community work and community care for nearly 40 years. He started his career in 'services' as volunteer and then as a Nursing Assistant at Gogarburn Hospital in Edinburgh. This was a life-changing experience and three decades later he had the privilege of locking the door, having overseen the resettlement of over 300 people into better lives in the community. He played a key role in several other similar programmes of service redesign and resettlement. He is currently part-time Director of Equal Futures and also works as an independent consultant in health and social care through Denis Rowley Associates. His current main interest is in the development of approaches that are effective in addressing isolation and loneliness.

Clive Sellick is Reader in Social Work at the University of East Anglia where he is Director of Teaching and Learning. He also teaches on the MA/BA Social Work programmes and the Specialist Child Care Award. His research interest is fostering, especially the role and function of independent fostering providers, and he has conducted four related linked studies between 1998 and 2005. He is the author and joint author of many articles, books and book chapters arising from this research. He has most recently been a part of two research teams engaged in two major studies: of adoption support for birth relatives and contact, funded by the UK government's Department for Children, Schools and Families;

and of care planning for permanence in foster care funded by the Nuffield Foundation. Clive is a former Social Worker, Team Leader and Magistrate.

Laura Steckley began working in residential treatment for adolescents in 1990 in the United States. She moved to Scotland in 1999 and worked in residential childcare until 2003, when she started her current role in education and research.

Irene Stevens worked in a variety of fieldwork and residential settings in the statutory and voluntary sector throughout the 1980s and 1990s, as well as teaching in further education. Before joining the Glasgow School of Social Work, her two last posts were as Unit Manager in a secure unit, and as Head of Social Work Services at a residential school for autistic children.

In January 2001 she joined the Scottish Institute for Residential Child Care (SIRCC). In her current post, she is responsible for practice development literature, co-edits the *Scottish Journal of Residential Child Care* and is SIRCC's Research Manager. In terms of spiritual well-being, Irene has researched and evaluated the use of storytelling in residential care, and has given conference presentations on applying care ethics within the social services. She has published widely on a variety of subjects and has co-authored a book on collaborative practice in residential child care.

Ailsa Stewart is a Lecturer in Social Work at the Glasgow School of Social Work; a joint school of the Universities of Glasgow and Strathclyde. She is a qualified social worker with a background in the voluntary sector. Her research interests are mental health, learning disability and adult protection.

Raymond Taylor is a Registered Social Worker with 25 years' experience in practice, teaching and management. He is a Social Work Manager with a Scottish local authority and an Honorary Senior Research Fellow with the Glasgow School of Social Work. Between 2001 and 2006 he was Head of Learning and Development with the Scottish Social Services Council and worked closely with other UK regulatory bodies and a range of Sector Skills Councils.

Joan E. R. Watson is a part-time tutor for the Glasgow School of Social Work at Strathclyde University, contributing to both qualifying and post-qualifying courses. From 2003 to 2008 Joan was Course Director for the MSc in Social Work Management, during which time she undertook research into social work management education. Prior to 2003 Joan had 28 years' experience at both practitioner and management levels in statutory social work in the Glasgow and South Lanarkshire areas.

Introduction

Raymond Taylor, Malcolm Hill and Fergus McNeill

Social work is a rewarding profession in which use of self, intuition and remaining reflective are central to help bring about positive changes in the lives of service users. The work is frequently complex and emotionally demanding, occasionally dangerous, but also brings many satisfactions. The role requires that practitioners constantly strive not only to develop their knowledge and skills, but also maintain their integrity in situations characterised by confusion, uncertainty and conflicting demands. This book aims to provide an up-to-date overview of key domains in social work. It should be helpful to students and experienced professionals and managers, but is particularly targeted at those who are recently qualified.

The transition from being a student to being a fully qualified practitioner can be daunting in any field of professional practice. Social work is by its very nature especially challenging and the purpose of this book is to help identify and respond to the Early Professional Development (EPD) needs of social workers to help equip them to overcome these new challenges. EPD has the potential to offer social workers (and indeed many occupational groups) consistent support with their development from initial professional training, through induction, into the early part of their professional life. EPD is part of a wider process of Continuing Professional Development (CPD) undertaken by social workers in the initial part of their career. CPD enhances the competence of individual practitioners and consists of a wide range of reflective, and developmental, activities designed to improve an individual's knowledge and skills.

The term EPD, more commonly used within the education sector, is now beginning to be used by some of the regulators of social work in the UK. It refers to development activity that is focused on the needs of any professional group, including social workers, in the first five years of their careers. During this time, drawing on Berliner's (2001) five-stage taxonomy, the newly-qualified social work recruit sets out on a journey which takes them from being a *novice*, to becoming an *advanced beginner* before developing *competence*. Achieving competence enables the practitioner to progress towards *proficiency* and to enter the stage of professional development that allows them to develop the depth of knowledge and range of skills necessary to become an *expert* in their chosen field. This book has been written to provide support and guidance to social workers who are on this lifelong journey.

The importance of ongoing training after qualification to support professional development has been recognised in different ways by each of the four United Kingdom (UK) Care Councils. The General Social Care Council and Northern Ireland Social Care Council, for example, have introduced or are considering a probationary year. In England there are new programmes for newly-qualified social workers. In addition, each Care Council in the UK shares broadly similar requirements for post-registration training and learning. While there is evidence of increasing divergence in the professional formation of social workers in each country of the UK, including the abolition of the General Social Care Council itself, systems of initial professional education still have much in common. Shared standards and expectations include requiring social workers to demonstrate that they can engage meaningfully with service users, operate effectively in interprofessional settings and have a critical understanding of research evidence and its applications.

It is also important to note that developing as a practitioner is not limited to progressing through the different educational systems and frameworks that have been created by the regulatory bodies. Rather, as noted by Tovey (2007), social work is a profession in which both ongoing personal growth and emotional maturity are crucial. These personal qualities are inextricably intertwined with professional development. It is important that individual social workers regularly reflect on and review their work to improve their own direct practice. With experience they will also be increasingly able to help more junior colleagues through informal consultation and support, as well as move into supervisory and managerial roles for those who choose that career path.

As editors we have paid particular attention to the importance of a UK perspective on a broad range of social work issues while also taking account of the distinctive legal jurisdictions and policy priorities of England, Scotland, Wales and Northern Ireland. For over ten years, political devolution within the UK has resulted in the creation of new policies and strategies in relation to education, healthcare, criminal and youth justice and social work. Each UK government has introduced radical changes to the way in which social work is regulated and social workers are educated. In this book we examine these changes within the context of wider policy and practice developments in the UK care sector. These policy changes are now beginning to impact in different ways on the main social work specialisms of childcare, adult services/community care, and criminal justice, as well as education and training.

Practitioners in each country of the UK face similar personal, professional and political challenges; the need to ensure that all children are safe and well; the expectation that we will work effectively with colleagues from other agencies to reduce the incidence of youth crime and the occurrence of child abuse; the desire to improve the quality of life of users of community care services and their carers; and the aspiration that work with adult offenders will result in restitution to victims, the rehabilitation of offenders and safer communities. Each chapter in this book reflects on current practice and policy concerns in social work. Many of the chapters also comment on how well different systems of intervention are working in different parts of the UK.

Structure of the book: chapter by chapter

We have ensured that the book is relevant to the needs of every newly qualified social worker in the UK who, as a result of the requirement for professional registration, is responsible for adhering to the Care Councils' requirements for post-registration training and learning. Where possible, chapters can be used by social workers, or groups of practitioners, engaged in informal staff development activity or enrolled on formal post-qualifying and post-graduate programmes.

The book is divided into four main parts as follows:

1 The Context of Early Professional Development
2 Themes and Issues in Child and Family Social Work
3 Themes and Issues in Community Care
4 Themes and Issues in Criminal Justice

In Part 1 – The context of Early Professional Development – **McIntyre and Orme** focus in Chapter 1 on the implications, for the EPD of newly-qualified social workers, of raising the qualifying level for entry into the profession to an undergraduate degree. This radical change in social work education and training occurred in all four countries of the UK, with different arrangements and requirements. The chapter explores the different models of CPD that have emerged in the UK and contains key messages for social work practitioners.

In Chapter 2, **Bates and Lymbery** argue that changes in the nature and organisation of society have created a new climate for both practitioners and people who use services. The chapter opens with a discussion of the nature of society and notes that concepts of 'risk' and 'blame' have become interconnected and have come to dominate the actions of professionals. The authors argue that social workers need to hold on to a clear and ethical understanding of their work if they are to be able to manage risk and respect and safeguard the rights of service users.

The importance of ethical awareness is reinforced by **Stevens** in Chapter 3 on ethically based, spiritually aware, practice. Stevens invites us to consider that, while we may find ourselves using our skills in a variety of practice settings in the course of our career, one aspect that all of these practice settings will have in common is that we will be working with people who have been identified by society as disadvantaged. We will find that we have power in relation to many of these service users. An understanding of ethics and spirituality may support us in exercising this power wisely. This chapter examines some of the philosophical approaches to ethical practice, and draws on some of the ancient religious philosophical traditions. While the relationship between religion and spirituality is becoming more contested in contemporary literature, Stevens argues that some of the ancient religious philosophies have spirituality at their heart and may have something to contribute to ethical practice in contemporary social work.

In Chapter 4 on management and leadership in social work, **McPheat and Watson** set out what early career social workers can expect from leaders and managers in terms of induction, supervision (including supportive, managerial and developmental functions), the management of motivation and stress and CPD. The chapter draws on a research study that examined the effectiveness of a post-qualifying social work management programme.

In Chapter 5, **Dominelli** reviews developments in anti-oppressive practice. She emphasises the connections between individuals and different parts of society, giving particular attention to the dynamics of personal, cultural and institutional oppression. She describes how these are linked to power, identities and narratives of space and place. Guidance is provided on how to work in an empowering way by responding to individual needs that converge with or diverge from the collective needs of wider groupings based on social divisions.

In Chapter 6, **Mackay and MacIntyre** provide a critical review of personalisation and argue that the relationship between the citizen, the provider and the local authority is changing. The introduction of personalisation has the potential to help service users achieve enriching and fulfilling lives. This change is, however, dependent on social workers using their skills in new and different ways.

In Part 2 – Themes and Issues in child and Family Social Work – **Hamilton** notes in Chapter 7 that child poverty in the UK has decreased somewhat over the last decade, but levels remain substantially above government targets set in the late 1990s. Children living in poverty miss out not only on 'basics' such as food and clothes, but also on activities and social acceptance. Their long term life chances are also adversely affected. Service access can be helped by assistance with not only charges, but also indirect costs for example for travel, appropriate clothing, equipment and materials. Combating poverty is a less prominent feature of social work than 20 years ago, but it remains vital for social workers to aid and advocate for individual families financially and collaborate with community-based organisations.

In Chapter 8, **Green Lister** examines how child protection is increasingly seen as part of a wider system to safeguard children. She notes that policy emphases have swung between an emphasis on investigation potentially leading to emergency measures and more supportive and preventive approaches. Constant reassessment and interpretation of information available are vital in situations of serious and longer-term neglect or abuse. An increasing range of interventions are available to help improve parenting and support children who have been traumatised, although evidence about effectiveness is limited.

In Chapter 9, **Aldgate** reviews national assessment frameworks for children that have been developed in the four jurisdictions of the UK. They espouse broadly similar objectives, but differ in the manner of delivery, especially as regards the degree of standardisation required of local government and the extent of reliance on detailed forms. Another key contrast is between an approach seen as rooted in social work services as in England and Wales and an approach based on universal health and education services as in Scotland, although all attempt to promote shared terminologies and collaboration across agencies.

In Chapter 10, **Kendrick, Steckley and McPheat** compare developments in residential care in the UK with patterns elsewhere. They note that international declarations on residential care have been mixed in tenor, including some references to positive contributions and others to the negative impact of 'institutions', as revealed in abuse scandals. In many parts of Europe, residential care caters for higher proportions of children than in the UK. The education and training of staff in the UK has improved in recent years, but often lacks the coherence and focus of social pedagogy in much of Europe and child and youth care in North America.

In Chapter 11, **Sellick** discusses how services for looked-after children have been transformed in recent years by the development of many new voluntary and private agencies specialising in the recruitment and support of foster carers. Many local authority social workers and managers were initially suspicious of this development, but now most see the independent sector as providing a valuable additional resource. Dangers include dominance by business motivations and crowding out of innovative agencies, but so far the growth in the mixed economy of foster care seems to have heightened placement choice, professionalisation of the service and carer satisfaction.

In Part 3 – Themes and Issues in Community Care – **Roberts** outlines the demographic and attitudinal challenges facing services for older people. In Chapter 12, she argues that coherent policies and strategies are required based on clear principles and human rights, as in children's services. Better support for informal carers is required to achieve better outcomes for older people and enable more people with dementia to avoid placement in an institution. The growing diversity of housing types and supports needs to be developed further with regard to both care in the community and group homes.

In Chapter 13, **Rowley and Hunter** chart the profound changes that have taken place in relation to social work and learning disability. They focus on some of the common challenges that have emerged in policy and practice across the four jurisdictions of the UK. They also reflect on some specific challenges that may be faced by social work practitioners and managers working in this field.

In Chapter 14, **Quinn, Knifton and Donald** consider the way in which mental health inequality serves to reinforce the stigma and discrimination experienced by service users. The chapter introduces the concept of 'personal narratives' and considers whether these are useful to address stigma and discrimination towards people with mental health problems. The themes that form the basis of this chapter – personal narratives and mental health stigma – will be of interest to practitioners concerned with inequality. The authors examine how narratives shape public consciousness and effect change.

In Chapter 15, **Petch and Eccles** explore the policy and practice of partnership working, examining the various partnerships that social workers are encouraged to pursue, but focusing in particular on that between health and social care. They examine the reasons behind the strong push for partnerships over the past decade and the way in which emphasis has been put primarily on procedures, often at the expense of dealing head on with the complexities of implementation on the ground. This provides the context for the contemporary shift in focus to outcomes, where the chapter explores user and carer defined outcomes and considers the extent to which a range of partnerships succeed in delivering the outcomes that users are seeking.

In addressing adult protection, in Chapter 16 **Stewart** describes how the need to protect adults from harm has been a recent development in policy and practice. Legal rights, powers and duties in this area are also scattered across a range of statutes. Stewart cautions against over-simple notions of vulnerability and notes the challenges of balancing rights, risks and duties which often appear to be in conflict.

In Chapter 17, **Barlow** examines the contribution of social workers to the issue of substance misuse. She explores the nature of the links between social work practice and substance misuse; and the benefits to this field of work of the social work discipline and its approach. Barlow also considers the nature of education and training for social workers in substance misuse and emphasises the importance of EPD in substance misuse. She also identifies barriers to good practice and notes how these may be overcome.

In Part 4 – Themes and Issues in Criminal Justice – **McNeill** draws, in Chapter 19, on two literature reviews, one examining how and why people come to desist from offending and the other exploring how and why criminal justice social work's culture has changed in recent decades. As well as noting that change is difficult for both 'offenders' and criminal justice social workers, McNeill notes that the successful negotiation of processes of change or transition depends not just on the motivations of those concerned, but also on their capacities or skills, and on their access to support networks and opportunities.

Continuing the theme of change within the criminal justice field, in Chapter 20 **Nellis** examines the challenges created by the development of electronic monitoring (EM) of offenders in the UK since the 1990s. He examines both the constructive potential of this new form of technology to reduce our reliance on the use of imprisonment (and perhaps to support rehabilitation), and the complex reasons why this potential remains unrealised. In particular, he points to the problems of integrating surveillance (provided by the private sector) with the more rehabilitative traditions and activities of probation and criminal justice social work (within the state sector). He stresses the importance of tackling these problems if EM is to develop beyond merely punitive or surveillance uses.

In Chapter 21, **Bracken** explores criminal justice social work in three countries – Canada, Ireland and Scotland – focusing on questions around training, knowledge, skills and values. Drawing on qualitative research with practitioners in all three jurisdictions, Bracken reports some mixed views from practitioners about developments in practice that draw primarily on psychological research on risk assessment and intervention programmes, sometimes at the expense of professional discretion and broader social work concerns. However, he notes that recent developments both in desistance research and in 'what works' research itself appear to be reconstituting the space where social work knowledge, values and skills have purchase and relevance.

In Chapter 22, **McIvor** looks more specifically at the evidence concerning what works with women who offend. Although she acknowledges that the evidence on this question is still limited, her review suggests not just that women's pathways *into* offending are different from men's, but also that their pathways *out* are different. It follows that interventions with women need to attend to these differences and to adapt if they are to be effective. McIvor points to a growing consensus that services need to be women-focused, accessible, holistic and capable of offering women longer-term support. Returning to one of the messages of McNeill's chapter, she argues that the answers to the questions of how best to develop services (and to enhance justice) can only be found in dialogue between policy makers, practitioners, researchers and, most importantly, women themselves.

References

Berliner, D (2001) *Early Professional Development for Teachers* Oxford: David Fulton Publishers.

Tovey, W (2007) *The Post Qualifying Handbook for Social Workers* London: Jessica Kingsley Publishers.

Part 1

The Context of Early Professional Development

Chapter 1

What a Difference a Degree Makes

Gillian MacIntyre and Joan Orme

Introduction

The focus of this chapter is on the implications for the early professional development (EPD) of newly-qualified social workers of raising the qualifying level for entry into the profession of social work to an undergraduate degree. The introduction of the undergraduate degree as the minimum qualifying level for social work was the most radical change in social work education and training in the United Kingdom (UK) since its inception. The change occurred in all four countries of the UK, albeit with different arrangements and different requirements. Postgraduate routes to qualification in England, Scotland and Wales continued but they too had to meet the country-specific requirements[1].

The raising of the qualifying level came about partly as a response to the death of Victoria Climbié in England and the subsequent analysis of practice and training (Laming, 2003) and partly because of longstanding concerns in the profession and social work academia that the complexities of the work required a degree-level qualification (Orme et al., 2009). The degree is a generic qualification introduced to improve practice in all areas of social work. While in much of the UK, qualification for criminal justice social work is separated from mainstream social work training, in Scotland this is included in the qualifying degree.

The requirements for the degree differed between the four countries and country-specific requirements emerged in Scotland (Scottish Government, 2003), Northern Ireland (NISCC and SSI, 2003) and England and Wales (DH, 2002). All drew on the benchmark statement for social work degrees published by the Quality Assurance Agency (QAA) (QAA, 2000) and the National Occupational Standards issued by the Training Organisation for the Personal Social Services (TOPSS) (TOPSS, 2002). All sets of requirements had prescriptions for curriculum content and the practice learning component of the degree. Of particular significance were:

- the increase in length of training from two years to a minimum of three;
- the increase in the number of days in assessed and supervised practice;
- the lowering of the age at which people could enter the profession; and
- the requirement for students to register with the governing body for social work in the country where they trained and subsequently practised.

These changes were associated with varying levels of change in post-qualifying development in the different countries. However, it is apparent that raising the qualifying level to an undergraduate degree, changes to the teaching content of the qualifying degree and the expectations of assessed practice all have implications for the standards to be achieved at the completion of training. These requirements will inevitably inform the EPD needs of qualifying social workers. As Preston-Shoot (2004, p 670) argues appropriate qualifying education prepares the way for future learning and professional development: 'Social work education, fit for purpose, will enable students to take responsibility for their continuing professional development'.

With the introduction of the degree in England, the Department of Health (DH) commissioned a longitudinal multi-method evaluation to examine the implementation and impact of the new degree in England which commenced in 2004[2]. In 2007, as part of its work to develop the research infrastructure for social work, the Economic and Social Research Council (ESRC) commissioned a UK wide audit of research teaching on social work degrees[3]. This chapter draws on the findings of these projects to explore the implications of the move to degree-level qualification for the EPD of newly-qualified social workers.

Policy development does not stand still, however, and there have been significant discussions and developments around social work education and training since the publication of these documents. For example, in Scotland a major review of social work (Scottish Government, 2006) led to recommendations for legislation, policy and practice, which have implications for the education and training of social workers. In England, another child abuse inquiry, the case of Baby Peter, contributed to the establishment of a Social Work Task Force by the Department for Children Schools and Families (DCSF) to conduct a 'nuts and bolts' review of the profession and to advise on the shape and content of a comprehensive reform programme for social work (www.dcsf.gov.uk/swtf/).

This chapter will therefore reflect on the implications that these developments have for requirements for the education and training to support the EPD of beginning practitioners.

Within social work education, debates have centred on the need for practitioners to be able to synthesise theory and practice. Theory in this context refers to the different subject knowledge (including Law, Sociology, Human Growth and Behaviour) and social work values that are taught on qualifying courses and are applied to skills development. The extent to which practitioners can make decisions on the basis of knowledge acquired through academic learning and knowledge acquired through practice was at the heart of discussions around the requirements for the new degree in England (DH, 2002) when the then minister announced that it should be a 'practical degree'. Social work academics (e.g. Sheppard, 1995; Fook et al., 2000; Sheppard et al., 2000) have explored the extent to which social workers use theory in practice. In recent discussions about social work education and training these debates have also been informed by the need for social work practitioners to be able to draw on a research base to inform practice (Orme and

Powell, 2008). For Preston-Shoot (2004) raising the qualifying level to an undergraduate degree provided opportunities to synthesise theory, research and practice.

While in many ways we argue that such divisions are artificial we, structure our analysis by separating out what we know about the development of theory and practice in qualifying programmes. We use this to help identify the nature of post-qualifying opportunities required to assist the continuous learning and professional development of beginning practitioners. However, in doing this we became aware that discussions about the content and structure of social work education and training, at whatever level, carried assumptions about the role and tasks of social work; assumptions about what practitioners were being prepared for. We therefore also explore the messages from qualifying social work education about expectations of practitioners when they enter the profession.

Theory versus practice?

The introduction of the new degree was welcomed by many as involving a move away from a competence-based approach to practice to one that incorporated underpinning knowledge essential for qualifying workers (Orme, 2001) and would enable newly qualified workers to adopt a 'flexible and intelligent approach to their practice' (Preston-Shoot, 2004, p 670).

Theory

The benchmark statement (QAA, 2000) for undergraduate degrees in social work was clear that social work draws on a number of subjects within the social sciences such as Law, Philosophy, Psychology and Sociology. However, the requirements for social work education in the four countries of the UK have organised this knowledge in slightly different ways. To varying degrees the country-specific requirements reflected the concerns at the time of the benchmark statement about both the knowledge and the skills that beginning practitioners required.

The requirements in England, for example, identify five key areas that have to be covered on qualifying courses:

- Human growth and development, mental health and disability;
- Assessment, planning, intervention and review;
- Communication skills with children, adults and those with particular communication needs;
- Law; and
- Partnership working and information sharing across agencies and disciplines.

(DH, 2002, pp 3-4)

In Scotland, the *Framework for Social Work Education* (Scottish Government, 2003) includes the Standards in Social Work Education (SiSWE), which identify six key roles for social workers (based on the National Occupational Standards [NOS]) and describe the necessary learning foci, underpinning knowledge and high-level transferable skills needed to undertake these roles. The organization of requirements for learning in the SiSWE have been designed to emphasise the balance between professional knowledge, professional skills and ethical practice.

In Northern Ireland, the Northern Ireland Framework Specification for the Degree in Social Work (NISCC and SSI, 2003) also focuses on the six key roles and requires that social work courses promote three main elements of professional development:

- Ethical practice;
- Professional responsibility and accountability;
- Professional competence.

The Northern Ireland framework also summarises the expectations of those who use services and carers of social workers. To be competent against the standards contained in the Framework newly-qualified workers are required to demonstrate that they meet these expectations in practice. They include:

- Communication skills and information sharing;
- Good social work practice;
- Advocacy;
- Working with other professionals;
- Application of knowledge;
- Application of values. (NISCC and SSI, 2003, p 39)

This is an explicit statement in the NI Framework but an analysis of requirements in all four countries highlights these as core themes, to a varying extent. Also, the acknowledgement of the role of service users and carers in the development and delivery of the degree is an expectation in all four countries.

Significantly, the knowledge required is not explicitly theoretical (that is, particular academic theories are not specified) but include: services relevant to users' and carers' needs and circumstances; benefits and direct payments (self-directed support); legislation; and an in-depth knowledge of the users and carers group they are working with. As a pointer for EPD, the Northern Ireland Framework also requires that practitioners keep themselves up to date with all relevant knowledge and information and with the rights of service users and carers. The Northern Ireland arrangements also differed from the other three countries in that registration requirements in Northern Ireland have a 3+1 model. That is, students have to have a year in practice after completing their academic qualification before they can register as a qualified social worker.

What is common within the requirements of the four countries is the way in which they focus on the need for students to acquire theoretical knowledge alongside practical skills in order to develop an awareness of ethical practice. This recognises the complexity of the social work role and the need to develop students' knowledge and skills at a number of levels. The ways in which the requirements were implemented by higher education institutions (HEIs) across the four countries were left open to interpretation.

Initial research into the new degree tended to focus on specific aspects of the degree such as module development or the involvement of service users. Most significantly, this research focused on the process of delivering the degree, not on the outcomes of the learning experience. Earlier research into social work education (Marsh and Triseliotis, 1996) had sought the views of students and employers by asking them to reflect retrospectively on the training experience. Subsequent research into the new degree in England by Blewett and Tunstill (2008), who undertook an audit focused on the views of educators and employers. In this context the evaluation of the England degree commissioned by the DH is important because it sought to achieve a comprehensive perspective by gathering statistical data, interviewing key stakeholders and mapping changes in students' performance.

The evidence from case study sites at HEIs in the DH evaluation found that curriculum requirements were met in a variety of ways. Generally, 'universal' topics that closely linked to the prescribed curriculum for the degree (such as Law and Social Work Values and Ethics) were covered in the first year of the course with topics related more strongly to working in practice settings (such as mental health, assessment, planning and intervention) being covered in the second year and beyond (DH, 2008, p 98). Some concerns were expressed in England that compared to the requirements for the previous qualification – the Diploma in Social Work (DipSW) – there was limited attention to social work values and anti-oppressive and anti-discriminatory practice in the new degree programmes. While this was addressed with specific learning outcomes in the frameworks developed in Scotland and Northern Ireland in England, the DH requirements stated that courses had to ensure that 'the principles of valuing diversity and equalities awareness are integral to the teaching and learning of students' (DH, 2002, p 3). In other words, this was something that should permeate the course. In the words of a student at a case study site in the DH evaluation:

> *The course has pushed like a lot about anti-discriminatory, anti-oppressive practice at every opportunity, but I think that's really good because like we probably all practice like that anyway but now we're aware of actually the reason we are doing it.*

(DH, 2008, p 99)

Perhaps one of the most contentious of the requirements was the one for interprofessional learning. Newly-qualified social workers are increasingly expected to work within inter-professional and multi-professional settings. Debates have focused on the stage at which inter-professional learning should be introduced into the qualifying programme (DH, 2008) and whether it is more appropriate for it to take place in post-qualifying education (Taylor *et al.,* 2006). Despite a number of models for providing classroom-based interprofessional learning, including joint teaching and shared learning, students at the case study sites in the DH evaluation reported that it was their experience on practice placement rather in the classroom setting that had developed their understanding of interprofessional working.

The centrality of research and research teaching within the requirements also differed between the four countries. In England, for example, there is no requirement that beginning practitioners have to have any underpinning knowledge or theoretical skills in research. In Scotland, on the other hand, within the SiSWE there is reference to research in the descriptions of transferable knowledge associated with most of the key roles and in key role four (developing professional competence) the learning focus involves 'evaluating and using up to date knowledge of and research into social work practice' (Scottish Government, 2003, p 36). The Northern Ireland Framework specification also makes reference to the relationship between research and practice by requiring students to: 'Implement plans using a range of methods of intervention, which are knowledge and evidence based' (NISCC and SSI, 2003, requirement B18).

Research teaching within social work education is essential in order to influence the 'culture of practice'. Research teaching (and teaching informed by research) should contribute to the development of the workforce as well as make a contribution to the evidence-based policy and practice agendas (Orme & Powell, 2008). The ESRC audit of research teaching on qualifying programmes (Orme *et al.,* 2008) found that all courses surveyed gave some attention to research and 95 per cent of those offered specific modules in order to develop students' awareness of research and its relationship to professional practice. A noteworthy distinction was made between teaching students to critically appraise and evaluate research and teaching them to undertake research. The ESRC audit suggested that on those courses that taught research methods, a relatively narrow range of methods and designs were taught on research courses in the UK and that all of the teaching was classroom based. As well as time restrictions in an already full curriculum, some social work academics identified a resistance to the use of research among some practice organisations. The ESRC audit concluded that there was a need to engage in discussions about research teaching on qualifying courses and the relationship between research practice and professional standards (Orme *et al.*, 2008, p 195). If research teaching takes place only within the academic curriculum it becomes more difficult to develop links between research and practice. The ESRC audit acknowledged that there needs to be agreement about what level of research awareness or competence should be achieved on completion of a qualifying degree. This will have obvious implications for the EPD of newly-qualified practitioners.

The resistance to use of research in practice learning in some practice organisations leads us now to consider the implications of the practice learning requirements for the new degree for the EPD of newly-qualified workers.

Practice

Two of the main changes associated with the introduction of the degree were the increase in the number of days that students had to spend on practice placement (that had to be divided between two practice settings) and the requirement that students demonstrate their readiness to undertake supervised practice as part of their qualifying studies. These changes were introduced to improve the quality of practice learning and to ensure that practice took a central role within the new degree. The generic element of the degree was embedded in the requirement that students have experience of 'statutory social work tasks involving legal interventions' and of 'providing services to at least two user groups' (DH, 2002, p 3).

Despite these changes, practice assessor respondents to the evaluation of the England degree (DH, 2008) were clear that their expectation of students remained unchanged (from the previous DipSW). Practice assessors reported that two aspects emphasised in the requirements for social work training, namely the emphasis on communication skills and theoretical knowledge, had improved with the introduction of the degree. With respect to the requirement for interprofessional learning, practice assessors noted that placements offered opportunities for "inter-agency working" (DH, 2008, p 132). This is particularly important given the changes taking place in adults' and children's services (in England and Wales) which will require newly qualified social workers to undertake new roles and new ways of working within an inter-agency context. The findings from the DH evaluation led to the conclusion that irrespective of whether in an adults or children's setting, students were equally likely to gain experience of inter-agency working ((DoH, 2008: 133). The implication of this for EPD is that while newly-qualified practitioners might have experienced inter-agency working, they should be given the opportunity to reflect on and develop underpinning knowledge and consider the implications of inter-professional working in the particular setting in which they begin their early professional career. This is particularly important in view of debates around the process of developing a professional identity (see Taylor et al., 2006).

Concerns over the availability of statutory placements and the need to support and develop capacity in the voluntary and private sector resulted in a perception that students may not have adequate experience in particular practice settings prior to qualification. These concerns were further emphasised in the aftermath of the Baby Peter case in England. In its submission to the Social Work Taskforce, the Children's Development Workforce Council (CWDC) argued, from the perspective of employers, that 'the current arrangements for training of social workers are not fit for purpose' (CWDC, 2009, point 21). While not going as far as arguing for a specialist degree in childcare, it articulated a conviction that 'people with insufficient childcare experience should not be permitted to enter into practice'. On the other hand, it might be argued that social work has many domains that are significant in the lives of all service user groups such as mental health issues and students need basic introductions to all of these.

Ensuing policy developments have focused on what should be achieved at qualifying and post- qualifying level and this has implications not only for newly qualified workers but also for managers and mentors. Those employing newly qualified practitioners have a responsibility to ensure that these workers are supported to build on their substantive knowledge and build on their procedural knowledge in particular domains of practice. This is evidenced by the recommendation in the report of the Social Work Task Force (2009, p 8, emphasis original) which acknowledges the need for a national framework which will 'give shape to the more coherent and effective national framework for the continuing professional development of social workers'. The report further recommends that this framework should include a new Masters in Social Work Practice.

Linking theory to practice

Research from nursing has suggested that on first embarking on a professional course, students express a desire to begin practising straight away (Anderson & Kiger, 2007). Focus groups with students as part of the evaluation of the new social work degree in England confirmed this notion, with students initially expressing ambivalence towards the academic elements of the course, stating an anxiety to "get out and practice". Such ambivalence resonated with concerns expressed more generally about the need for a degree-level qualification for social work (DH, 2008, p 182) with resistance being expressed initially by some stakeholders. By the end of the degree course, however, students reflected that their ability to link theory and practice had developed both within the classroom setting and on placement. This was reassuring given their earlier concerns that they would not be able to practise what they learned in the classroom. Significantly, students' understanding of good practice evolved from a belief that social work was about helping people towards an understanding that social work was about empowerment:

> Whenever anyone starts this course and it's 'why do you want to do it [social work]?' 'It's to help people'. And I think this course helps you realize that social work's not about helping people, saving them and making their lives better, it's about – this sounds very corny – it's about empowering them and just providing them with skills so that they can make the changes they need to make themselves.
>
> (Case studies, student focus group, time 2) (DH, 2008, p 183)

Students reported that their understanding of the role of social workers had been enhanced significantly by the involvement of service users and carers in the development and delivery of courses. While service user and carer involvement in the delivery and development of social work education across the four countries had been developing over time it was formalised by the requirements of the new degree.

Readiness for what?

Discussions about curriculum content, practice learning opportunities and the observations on the *purpose* of social work and the role of social workers raise questions about what qualifying programmes are preparing students *for*. Policy initiatives and academic and professional discussions that have focused on what social work is and what it is for have implications for social work education and training and consequently for the EPD of qualifying practitioners .

Role of continuing professional development

The methodology used in the evaluation of the social work degree in England included the use of vignettes to discern changes in the way that students conceptualised their practice during the process of undertaking a degree-level qualification (Orme, *et al.,* 2009). Comparison of the findings with literature on professional development (Benner, 1984; Dreyfus and Dreyfus, 1986; Fook *et al.,* 2000) indicated that, although professional development is not a linear process, the students at the end of their course were assessed as performing as "advanced beginners". This means that they approached situations by applying situational rules (that is, rules or understandings learnt in the classroom) but also by drawing on their concrete experience (that is, experience gained on practice placement). This helped to give a context to their learning, which they then applied to other areas. Evaluation of the vignettes completed by the students at the case study sites in the evaluation of the degree in England suggested that they had greater substantive knowledge (i.e. knowledge about facts, concepts and relationships) rather than procedural knowledge – which is the ability to use substantive knowledge in complex situations. For example, they demonstrated knowledge of legislation and policy. Overall, the progress identified by the evaluation of students' responses to vignettes at the beginning of their studies and again at the end of their course indicated that they were synthesising their learning: "The nature of the changes demonstrated in the vignettes suggested that students had moved from wishing to being a reactive helper to becoming a more reflective and discerning practitioner" (DH, 2008, p 286).

Having said that, students and social work educators felt that employers expected a greater level of knowledge and expertise than was appropriate at the end of qualifying training. Students made a distinction between the level of preparedness achieved through undertaking a qualifying programme and the subsequent complexities of practice (DH, 2008, p 185). Likewise, academic staff felt that by the end of the degree, students were ready to enter the workforce but emphasised that they should be given an opportunity to consolidate their learning upon entering the workforce. Although a survey of directors of social work undertaken as a part of the DH evaluation suggested that only 15% of respondents were dissatisfied with newly qualified social workers (DH, 2008, p 218), employers expected a greater knowledge of agency-specific policy and practice and procedures, which would enable students to take on more complex cases at an earlier stage in their professional career. In Blewett & Tunstill's (2008, p 34) survey of 22 service managers employed at different levels in statutory and non-statutory organisations, the 'overwhelming majority of views expressed could be seen as supportive of the degree'. Academic researchers (such as Marsh & Triseliotis, 1996; Pithouse and Scourfield, 2002) have argued that in qualifying education there is an inherent tension about the purpose of qualifying professional courses. This tension usually occurs between academics who want to provide a generic social work education and employers who want to recruit newly qualified professionals who have the ability to "hit the ground running" and have expertise in one area of work in particular. This tension is exemplified in the response to the Social Work Taskforce by the CWDC:

> we need to look at the output and outcomes of the degree – what tests and measurements can be utilised in order to inform the final assessment so that we are confident that an individual is fit to practise. There may be different approaches, depending on the specialist area of each social worker, but we must be clear that people with insufficient childcare experience specialism should not be permitted to enter into practice.
>
> (CWDC, 2009, point 20)

Having said that, almost all of the respondents in the Blewitt & Tunstill (2008) audit recognised the danger of agencies being unrealistic about the level of practice at which students should be able to work immediately on graduation. However, the fact that students were allocated cases with complex needs was seen to be a response to the high thresholds at which social work teams were working. Thus, lack of confidence in the qualities of the students at qualifying level could be more to do with structural problems rather than inadequacies of qualifying education as a preparation for professional life. Such problems include the fact that agencies carry a high number of vacancies and employers are under pressure because of rising caseloads especially in areas such as child protection. The fact that students in the evaluation of the degree in England expressed some lack of confidence in taking on the role of a professional, was ascribed not to a lack of preparation, "rather, a distinction was made between the level of preparedness achieved from undertaking a professional qualifying programme and the subsequent complexities and uncertainties of professional practice" (DH, 2008, p 185). As one social work educator interviewed in the evaluation of the England degree expressed it:

> *I would like to take part in producing a social worker who is able to hold tensions, to be aware of the tensions of their role and to be able to hold those tensions and also be able to use their reflective processes to both make decisions, support others who are making decisions, but also get support, but also actually have the confidence to be able to build a sense of self-esteem, so that social workers can ask for help when they need it, know when they need to do that and work with others closely and to hold, to keep humanity… for service users to be able to come out thinking: 'well I knew why they were doing what they were doing. I may have hated it but I can't say I didn't know why they were doing what they were doing.*

> (DH, 2008, p 186)

In other words, newly qualified social workers need to have the ability to reflect on what they know but perhaps more importantly, they also need the ability to recognise not only what they do not know but also how to go about finding out. They will require support and mentoring as part of their professional development in order to do this effectively and critically.

The response of the CWDC to the Social Work Task Force and subsequent policy developments precipitated by the Baby Peter case, for example Lord Laming's (2009) report on child protection in England illustrate the ongoing discussions around generic or specialist education and the implications for qualifying and post-qualifying education and training.

Generism v. specialism

Discussions prior to the degree being introduced focused on whether there should be specialist programmes or a more generic qualification. This debate has persisted since the 1970s with the introduction of the Certificate of Qualification in Social Work (CQSW). Major concerns related primarily to whether social work graduates were equipped to work with vulnerable children and families. These concerns have been exacerbated by high-profile media attention which has led to public condemnation.

When the new social work degree was introduced in all four countries of the UK the decision was made to offer a generic programme. As highlighted in the preceding section, the organisation of the degree in all four countries involved compulsory modules all of which included a children and families component. Models allowing students to follow specialist interests have emerged to varying extents, with, for example, some courses offering students the opportunity to undertake a specialist pathway relating to children and families or adult social care in their final year (see DH, 2008). The ambivalence about the specialist/generic debate was indicated by the survey of directors of social work which was undertaken in 2006. Twenty-two out of 47 respondents favoured generic social work education. However, 21 favoured separate programmes for adults and children (DH, 2008, 224), suggesting an almost equal split in opinion.

While there have been differences in the organisation of services between Scotland and England since 1968, recent arrangements for devolution have been accompanied by further differences in social work and social care policies between all four UK countries. For example, the separation of children's and adults' services is proceeding more rapidly in England than in the other countries (Hocking, 2009). Future decisions about qualifying education in relation to these changes will have an impact on the qualified worker's transition into the workforce and their EPD in the different countries. While a generic degree is currently the norm the issues of further specialist training for newly qualified workers entering the workforce continue and have been addressed in different ways in the four countries. One potential model that may allow newly qualified social workers to specialise early in their professional development is the 3+1 model that has emerged in Northern Ireland. This enables newly qualified workers to specialise in a particular area at the end of their degree qualification in their first year in practice and prior to full registration. This occurs with specific supports and learning requirements as it is still part of their professional education.

Likewise, the introduction in 2008 of a pilot of a comprehensive programme of support for newly-qualified social workers (NQSWs) in children and families social work in England recognises the pressures faced by newly qualified workers in this area. The scheme is designed to offer a comprehensive induction schedule through the first year of employment including:

- high-quality supervision and training;
- easy-to-use guidance materials;
- a professional development plan designed to increase confidence and maximise capability.

The support package is designed to ensure that NQSWs receive consistent, high-quality support and that those supervising them are confident in their skills to provide that support. The programme aims to contribute to increasing the number of people who continue their long-term career within children and families social work (see www.cwdcouncil.org.uk/nqsw). Skills for Care is also providing funding for employers in adult services (see www.skillsforcare.org.uk/socialwork/NewlyQualifiedSocialWorker/NewlyQualifiedSocialWorker.aspx).

Significantly, the CWDC argues that there is insufficient emphasis or attention given by many local authorities to their responsibilities towards the training and development of social workers and social care workers in both children's and adults' social services (CWDC, 2009, point 11). It argues that the emphasis is on developing the post-qualifying award but suggests that it is not necessarily fit for purpose in relation to safeguarding because the current post-qualifying framework in England lacks a commissioning strategy and the responsibility for funding, quality assurance and inspection is so diversely spread as to compromise its effectiveness.

In Wales, the Care Council for Wales works closely with the Welsh Assembly Government on the framework of qualifications for the social care workforce and has introduced the Induction Framework 2008, which can be used as a tool for managers to audit the skills, knowledge and experience of new staff, and will help identify their development needs. Also, once qualified, social workers in Wales are expected to maintain and extend their knowledge and skills, and one way of achieving this is by undertaking Care Council approved post-qualifying courses (see www.ccwales.org.uk/qualifications-and-careers/qualifications).

In Scotland, developments for EPD include the rolling out of the Scottish Credit and Qualifications Framework (SCQF). Developed in 2001, this framework had implications for the SiSWE (www.sssc.uk.com) for qualifying education as well as post-qualifying education and training. The aim of SCQF is to be more explicit and provide a national vocabulary about the learning expected of students at different academic levels. It includes twelve academic levels up to doctoral level, each with its own descriptor. Work undertaken to ensure that the SiSWE in Scotland was aligned to the SCQF was evaluated in 2008 by the Institute for Research and Innovation in Social Services (IRISS, formerly SIESWE) (IRISS, 2008). The evaluation specifically addressed the question of academic levels in practice settings. However, the fact that the SCQF has level descriptors for academic qualifications up to doctoral level will also impact on the education and training of newly-qualified social workers in Scotland. But it is some of the questions asked about qualifying level that resonate with the conclusions drawn from the two evaluations that form the basis of this chapter. For example:

- How are research and enquiry skills of a student assessed against the SCQF framework?
- Is this an expectation of practice teachers?

These questions are pertinent to the findings of the ESRC audit of research teaching on the degree throughout the UK that attention needs to be paid to the practice component of qualifying education. The importance of this is reinforced by the lack of attention to research teaching in the proposed arrangements for social work education recommended by the Social Work Taskforce (2009) in England.

Conclusions

Throughout this chapter we have tried to highlight the impact that changes brought about as a result of the introduction of a degree-level qualification in social work will have for newly qualified social workers. We have shown the ways in which the requirements for social work education put in place across the four countries of the UK differ. However, all four countries have recognised the complexity of the social work role by emphasizing the importance of developing students' theoretical knowledge base and skills in order to prepare them for ethical practice. Drawing principally on two research studies (DH, 2008; Orme *et al.*, 2008) we have identified areas of particular significance in the new curriculum for newly qualified social workers relating to anti-oppressive practice, inter-disciplinary working and the use and teaching of research.

Two areas of particular tension have become apparent and raise important questions around the role and purpose of social work education. First, there is a perception that employers expect newly-qualified social workers to be able to "hit the ground running". Our research has suggested that while students feel prepared in terms of substantive knowledge their ability to apply this knowledge in complex, agency-specific situations (procedural knowledge) requires further support and development. Second, questions have been raised about the extent to which a generic social work qualification can prepare students for work with specific service user groups. While this is a complex and politically sensitive debate, what remains clear is that while the qualification is generic, newly qualified social workers will need to develop further service user group-specific knowledge upon entering practice. Early professional development should be seen therefore as a transitional process during which time newly qualified workers should be given the opportunity to further develop and apply their knowledge, with appropriate mentoring and supervision.

The implications of these observations are that, on the basis of the research findings qualifying education should involve both building knowledge of academic subjects and practice experience of the situations social workers deal with. The practice component obviously allows students to apply knowledge. However, the timescales involved in qualifying training and the availability of practice learning experiences mean that the opportunities to apply knowledge are limited. This means that EPD needs to enable beginning practitioners both to develop their knowledge base and to reflect on this and in the specific practice setting in which they are employed.

Induction for newly-qualified social workers should deal with particular policies and procedures with further ongoing support to develop theoretical knowledge in the particular practice setting. As we alluded to above, professional development is not a linear process and therefore opportunities for EPD need to allow newly qualified social workers to move to the next levels of professional development, which include that of expert (Dreyfus & Dreyfus, 1986; Fook *et al.*, 2000). Experts move beyond simply applying situational knowledge and use intuition which involves developing a level of understanding associated with practice wisdom that occurs when making links between cases (Fook et al, 2000). Early professional development needs to create situations and offer supervision to enable practitioners to gain the confidence to identify and make those links.

To add to the complexity, newly qualified social workers should also be given support to develop their own professional identity. In doing so, this will enable them to develop the confidence and status they need to work alongside other professionals within multi-disciplinary settings.

It is also crucial to recognise that knowledge is not a static concept but one that is constantly evolving and changing. Research not only generates new knowledge but also informs and often changes the ways in which we understand existing knowledge. Newly-qualified social workers need to be discerning about research and EPD should ensure that newly qualified workers are supported to develop critical appreciation of research alongside enabling those who are interested to undertake research methods training with a view to developing their skills as practitioner researchers.

We propose therefore that EPD should consist of three main components:

- **Building knowledge** – newly qualified workers should be encouraged to critically reflect on and then build on their existing knowledge. This may involve revisiting particular theories already studied to increase understanding for the particular practice setting. For example, Howe and colleagues (1999) have theorised attachment theory and applied it to childcare practice beyond the basic understandings available through teaching on most social work qualifying courses.
- **Applying knowledge** – professionals need to continue to develop their confidence in applying their existing knowledge to cases, recognising similarities and themes between cases. This will allow them to develop a more intuitive approach to decision making. This has implications for the nature of the supervisory relationship in the early stages of a practitioner's career. Supervisors need to have an overview of the total workload not just for the purposes of allocating work and managing the workload but also to facilitate the worker's reflections on the different cases, making links between them and identifying knowledge that is required to deal with them. This helps to identify the required programme of post-qualifying learning and teaching, which might involve undertaking further reading, exploring websites for research studies, attending seminars, attending short courses or undertaking study for another qualification.
- **Developing knowledge** – alongside this, newly qualified social workers need to be supported to develop new knowledge by undertaking their own research. In some ways this may well develop from the process of applying knowledge. Exploring what is available to help understanding of particular situations will also reveal gaps in knowledge. Research training should underpin all EPD to enable practitioners either as individuals or collaboratively to identify researchable topics and develop research questions.

While these components are to some extent developmental, they also have to take place alongside each other. How this is achieved is a perennial problem for those developing teaching timetables in qualifying education and, in particular, making decisions about when to schedule placements. One way to build knowledge and apply it has been achieved by the requirement in all four countries of the UK for the social work degree to involve service users and carers in the development and delivery of the degree. In the evaluation of the degree in England, students were universally positive about teaching and learning sessions that were led, delivered and/or designed by service users. This suggests that arrangements for EPD and related training and learning opportunities should be similarly underpinned by the involvement of service users and carers.

In concluding this discussion about the implications of a degree-level qualification for EPD the key question remains: what is the most effective way of supporting such development? There are currently four models:

- the Northern Ireland model, which involves extending the period of training into the workforce: newly-qualified professionals undertake a "probationary" year, prior to becoming a fully qualified professional;
- the introduction of a framework such as the SCQF, which introduces standards in terms of what has to be achieved by practitioners in the workforce;
- in Wales the Induction Framework 2008 which can be used as a tool for managers to audit the skills, knowledge and experience of new staff, and help identify their development needs;
- the development of the newly-qualified social worker position within children and families social work in England; this status brings with it particular requirements for supervision and training and a protected workload.

While each of these models has its own advantages and disadvantages, all are significant in terms of providing recognition of the support and training requirements of newly qualified social workers. The models represent an acknowledgement of the demands that are put on newly qualified workers and the complexity of the tasks they face.

Messages for professionals

- Newly qualified social workers need to reflect on their own learning needs.
- Managers need to provide opportunities in supervision and professional development courses to reflect on accumulated and new knowledge that newly qualified workers are gaining in the particular professional setting.
- Early professional development should be underpinned by service user and carer involvement.
- An appreciation of research and opportunities to undertake research training should be viewed as central to the process.

Notes

1 The reforms of social work education led to the cessation of postgraduate routes to qualification in Northern Ireland.

2 The evaluation of the new social work degree qualification in England (2004-07) funded by the DH was undertaken by Shereen Hussein, Jill Manthorpe, Jo Moriarty and Martin Stevens of the Social Care Workforce Research Unit, King's College London; Endellion Sharpe of Sharpe Research; and Kate Cavanagh, Beth Crisp, Pam Green Lister, Gillian MacIntyre and Joan Orme of the Glasgow School of Social Work; with the support of Marie McNay, Evaluation Co-ordinator for the DH and the advice and support of a Reference Group of stakeholders and Advisory Group of people with experience of using services and/or caring. The members of the research team were deeply saddened by the death of their colleague Kate Cavanagh in November 2008.

3 The audit of research teaching in the social work degree (2007-08), funded by the Economic and Social Research Council (ESRC) was undertaken by Joan Orme, Gillian MacIntyre and Sally Paul of the Glasgow School of Social Work; Jan Fook and Jackie Powell of the University of Southampton; and Elaine Sharland of the University of Sussex.

While the chapter draws on the findings of the two evaluations identified, the views expressed in this chapter are entirely those of the authors.

References

Anderson, E and Kiger, A (2007) '"I felt like a real nurse" – student nurses out on their own' *Nurse Education Today* 28(4), pp 443-49 (http://dx.doi.org/10.1016/j.nedt.2007.07.013).

Benner, P (1984) *From Novice to Expert: Excellence and power in clinical nursing practice* London: Addison Wesley Publishing.

Blewett, J and Tunstill, J (2009) *Fit for Purpose? The Social Work Degree in 2008* London: General Social Care Council (www.gscc.org.uk/NR/rdonlyres/07253B5C-D5DA-4926-9E89-F1984E2BFCA0/0/AuditreportfullversionforpressFINAL.pdf).

CWDC (Children's Development Workforce Council) (2009) *Submission to the Social Work Task Force, Department for Children, Schools and Families* London: Social Work Taskforce (www.dcsf.gov.uk/swtf/).

DH (Department of Health) (2002) *Requirements for Social Work Training* London: Department of Health (www.dh.gov.uk/en/Publicationsandstatistics/Publications/PublicationsPolicyAndGuidance/DH_4007803).

DH (2008) *Evaluation of the New Social Work Degree in England, Volumes 1 & 2* London: Department of Health (http://owa.gla.ac.uk/exchweb/bin/redir.asp?URL=http://www.dh.gov.uk/en/Publicationsandstatistics/Publications/PublicationsPolicyAndGuidance/DH_086079).

Dreyfus, H L and Dreyfus, S E (1986) *Mind over Machine: the Power of Human Intuition and Expertise in the Era of the Computer* New York: Free Press.

Fook, J, Ryan, M and Hawkins, L (2000) *Professional Expertise: Practice, Theory and Education for Working in Uncertainty* London: Whiting and Birch.

Hocking, J (2009) 'Similarities and differences in social work practice and the workforce in the four UK countries' *Community Care*, 17 June (www.communitycare.co.uk/Articles /2009/06/17/111813/is-social-work-the-same-after-devolution.html).

Howe, D, Brandon, M, Hinings, D and Schofield, G (1999) *Attachment Theory, Child Maltreatment, and Family Support: A Practice and Assessment Model* London: Routledge.

IRISS (Institute for Research and Innovation in the Social Services) (2008) *New degree, New Standards?* Dundee: IRISS.

Laming, Lord (2003) *The Victoria Climbié Inquiry* London: HMSO.

Laming, Lord (2009) *The Protection of Children in England: A progress report* Norwich: The Stationery Office.

Marsh, P and Triseliotis, J (1996) *Ready to Practise? Social Workers and Probation Officers: Their training and first year in work* Aldershot: Avebury.

NISCC and SSI (Northern Ireland Social Care Council and Social Services Inspectorate) (2003) *Northern Ireland Framework Specification for the Degree in Social Work* Belfast: DHSSPS.

Orme, J (2001) 'Regulation or fragmentation? Directions for social work under New Labour' *British Journal of Social Work*, 31(4), pp 611-24.

Orme, J, MacIntyre, G, Cavanagh, K, Crisp, B, Green-Lister, P, Hussein, S, Manthorpe, G, Moriarty, J and Stevens, M (2009) 'What (a) Difference a Degree Makes: An evaluation of the social work degree in England' *British Journal of Social Work* 39(1), pp 161-78.

Orme, J and Powell, J (2008) 'Building Research Capacity in Social Work: process and Issues' *British Journal of Social Work* 38(5), pp 988-1008.

Orme, J, Fook, J, MacIntyre, G, Paul, S, Powell, J and Sharland, E (2008) *Audit of Research Teaching on the Social Work Degree* Swindon: ESRC.

Pithouse, A and Scourfield, J (2002) 'Ready to practice? The DipSW in Wales: views form the workplace on social work training' *Journal of Social Work* 2(1) pp 7-27.

Preston-Shoot, M (2004) 'Responding by degree: surveying the education and practice landscape' *Social Work Education* 23(6), p 667- 92.

QAA (Quality Assurance Agency) (2000) *Benchmark Statements: Social Policy and Administration and Social Work* Gloucester: Higher Education Authority (www.qaa.ac.uk/academicinfrastructure/benchmark/honours/socialpolicy.asp).

Scottish Government (2003) *The framework for Social Work Education in Scotland* Edinburgh: Scottish Government (www.scotland.gov.uk/Publications/2003/01/16202/17019).

Scottish Government (2006) *Changing Lives: Report of the 21st Century Social Work Review* Edinburgh: Scottish Government.

Sheppard, M (1995) 'Social work, social sciences and practice wisdom', *British Journal of Social Work* 25(3), pp 265-94

Sheppard, M, Newstead, S, Di Caccavo, A and Ryan, K (2000) 'Reflexivity and the Development of Process Knowledge in Social Work: A Classification and Empirical Study' *British Journal of Social Work* 30(4), pp 465-88.

Social Work Taskforce (2009) *Final Report of the Social Work Taskforce* London: Department of Children Schools and Families (www.dcsf.gov.uk/swtf).

Taylor, I, Sharland, E, Sebba, J and Leriche, P (with Keep, E and Orr, D) (2006) *The learning, teaching and assessment of partnership work in social work education* London: SCIE.

TOPSS (Training Organisation for the Personal Social Services) (2002) *The National Occupational Standards for Social Work* Leeds: Skills for Care (www.skillsforcare.org.uk/developing_skills/National_Occupational_Standards/National_ Occupational_Standards).

Chapter 2

Managing Risk in a Risk Averse Society

Peter Bates and Mark Lymbery

Introduction

This chapter will argue that changes in the nature and organisation of society have created a new climate for both practitioners and people who use services. Concerns about risk and how to manage it have become dominant in many areas of life. In some traditional risk management approaches, the person is a passive subject upon whom the assessment is applied, and they may even be absent when key decisions are made (Langan and Lindow, 2004). Such an approach clearly fails to engage the person's own insights and perspectives and is unlikely to motivate them to be an active risk manager or bear responsibility for their own actions. In recognition of this, government seeks a new social contract with its citizens, in which the person[1] bears greater responsibility for themselves, services are personalised and power devolved. As a result, social workers need to hold on to a clear and ethical understanding of what they are doing in managing risk and safeguarding opportunity.

This chapter opens with a discussion of the nature of society, arguing that the related concepts of 'risk' and 'blame' have come to dominate the actions of professionals. It follows by exploring the values and beliefs that lie behind many of our risk management actions. We then explore the interplay between the team climate and risk outcomes and offer some suggestions about how individual social workers can help to build a team climate that supports individuals to stay safe and live well. As the Equalities and Human Rights Commission recently summarised it, 'Care and support has the potential to become a springboard, not simply a safety net, focused on helping people to maximise control over their lives, to make social and economic contributions and to stay safe and well' (EHRC, 2009, p 6).

Risk and blame in British society

Over recent years, Western society has become increasingly preoccupied with risk, gaining such titles as the 'risk society' (Beck, 1992) and even the 'blaming society' (Barry, 2007). Beck (1992) has argued that the primacy of the concept of 'risk' in society is a direct consequence of the nature of society, which he characterises as 'modernity'. In supporting this perspective, Webb (2006) has pointed out the apparent paradox that unparalleled levels of social stability and affluence are accompanied by increasingly acute levels of personal anxiety and insecurity.

Gardner (2008, pp 77-8) neatly summarises the ranking applied to different risks by contemporary Western society, as shown in Box 2.1.

Box 2.1
Features judged high-risk in contemporary Western society

- A single event catastrophe – rather than the same things dispersed over time.
- Novel or unusual risks, especially if we do not understand them and cannot see how to reverse the effects of something going wrong.
- Lack of personal control, especially if we do not choose to engage the risk, and especially if it affects me.
- It is much worse if children are involved or the victim is personally identifiable rather than just a statistic.
- Where the effects generate fear, harm some people in society and benefit others, and are managed by institutions we do not trust or have a poor record of managing this kind of thing.
- Immediate threats loom larger in contrast to those in the future, although we worry about spoiling things for future generations.

Much of what a social worker might encounter could be fitted into this list. While a number of separate contributory factors have been put forward, many have their origins in the nature of neo-liberal governance, where there has been a disintegration of traditional certainties – for example, professional authority (Parton, 1996). Of course, one of the consequences of the decline in trust in professionals' judgements has been a high-profile focus on their decisions. For social work this has resulted in a vicious circle of increased accountability and scrutiny leading to ever-tighter definitions of acceptable actions; in turn this triggers reduced confidence, higher levels of scrutiny and renewed attempts to increase accountability.

As a result, professionals feel that they are likely to be blamed if their decisions lead to unwelcome consequences; as Douglas (1992) has suggested, the close relationship between risk and blame ensures that the search for a supposedly responsible person occurs immediately following an unwelcome event. Consequently, it has been argued that we are a 'risk-averse' society (Scott, 2000), unwilling to countenance the consequences of decisions that result in tragic circumstances; for Furedi (2002) this has involved the creation of a 'new moral order' based on the worship of safety and the avoidance of risk. This is, he argues, deeply problematic, being simultaneously prescriptive, intrusive and anti-humanistic. At the same time, however, workers with adults are enjoined to provide wider opportunities for people to take risks in society (DH, 2005) and are criticised for favouring protection over risk (CSCI, 2008). This creates an impossible tension for social workers to manage: as a result, according to Barry (2007), the social work profession is now lacking in confidence, under-utilises its workers' skills, has become increasingly risk averse, stifles autonomy and lacks support.

In addition, the risk assessment and management strategies that have been developed tend to be overly formalised and mechanistic, based on the notion that risk can be accurately predicted and managed (Parton, 1996): indeed, there is much more emphasis on risk assessment than risk management (Stalker, 2003). This feeds into the anti-humanistic concerns noted by Furedi (2002). We would therefore suggest that it is vital for social workers to develop models of risk management that build on the humanistic traditions of the profession, particularly those that include the voice of the person at its heart – and this is often missing from the literature on risk (Stalker, 2003).

Values-driven risk assessment and management

While social workers need to practice ethically against the backcloth of society's values, they also find themselves employed within organisations that make assumptions about people who use social care services. In childcare, the concern is mostly to protect the person from harm, while in criminal justice it is to constrain the perpetrator in order to protect the community, while people receiving community care services are often viewed as vulnerable. In mental health services this vulnerability is compounded by another level of risk – the level of dangerousness that they are presumed to offer to others (Stalker, 2003). Such assumptions are rarely exposed to scrutiny.

Meanwhile, staff are often preoccupied with policy compliance, and experience conflict between their own values and the organisation's assumptions as no more than a vague sense of unease. However, in pursuance of ethical, reflective practice, it is vital to examine the assumptions about risk that drive local policies and practices. For example, in our reflections we have identified the following negative assumptions that we feel can sometimes influence risk management decisions:

- It is possible to work on the basis that all the negative stereotypes about people who use services are true – that they are incapable, dishonest, dangerous, irresponsible and lack insight. Consequently, when a service encounters one person who is dishonest or dangerous it may turn that single experience into a prohibition that constrains opportunities for all.
- In some settings, despite contrary evidence, staff are assumed to be benevolent and therefore the service is deemed to be safe; by contrast, the public may be seen as malevolent and the community can be considered to be a dangerous place.
- In a parallel development, increasingly suspicion attaches to the motives of members of the public who care for each other's children (Laing, 2009), who sit by the person who has a learning disability in the church or synagogue or who pop round to visit an elderly neighbour.

- If people receiving services are hurt, this may be considered to matter less than hurting a member of the public. Consequently, some agencies may make the error of overlooking this or treating it less seriously than if a member of the general public had been abused. One investigation of disability hate crime found when people reported bullying to staff, only 47% had something done about it (Alcock, 2000).
- If people are assumed not to change, risk is considered to be almost entirely a function of the person's history and internal make-up. As a result, arrangements to manage risk are likely not to take account of the individual or be constructed in a manner that responds to her/his humanity and difference.

These five assumptions commonly lead to three inappropriate responses to managing confidentiality and disclosure while balancing risk and opportunity. These models can be named as 'intrusive', 'binary' and 'tapered' respectively:

- The 'intrusive' model occurs when organisations recognise a risk, and then attempt to manage it by dominating areas of the person's life, either by introducing services or through control and regulation. As a result, instead of the person bearing an appropriate share of responsibility for keeping everyone safe, the service tries to expand its control in a futile attempt to safeguard the person. This increases dependency, inflates expectations and diverts resources away from the people that need the most help.
- The 'binary' model occurs when organisations create a kind of apartheid between all staff, or a group of staff, and everyone else. Their procedures for managing information demonstrate that certain staff are part of the in-crowd, privy to confidential briefings and included in the meetings where risk management decisions are taken. In this scenario, the person is usually kept outside the meeting room, along with their close family members, work colleagues and anyone else that the person likes to meet away from the service. The risk assessment document may even be completed in this way, with decisions made in the unofficial conversation that takes place before the family enter the room, with warnings being passed around within the in-crowd while others are kept in the dark to supposedly comply with data protection requirements.
- The 'tapered' model occurs when people are positioned in a series of concentric circles at varying distances from the epicentre of the risk issue. Those closest to the centre are deemed to have a right to the fullest information and the most power over risk management decisions, while those at greater distances are less well informed and have less influence. While there may be some merit in this 'need-to-know' approach, it tends to become set in stone, rather than being redrawn for every circumstance. For example, close family members often find

themselves closest to the person and at greatest risk, but workers commonly place them in the outer circles, rarely invited to risk management meetings or kept informed about changes in the service that is provided.

Instead of these mistaken assumptions and faulty responses, the goal is person-centred, context-specific risk management. Such an approach will:

- involve the person and the people that know them best as potential experts in keeping themselves and others safe, through balancing obligations towards the wider society with the person's preference to define what they want in life and what safety means to them;
- extend the principle of 'least restrictive intervention' – that any intervention should curtail people's basic rights and freedoms as little as possible – to support aspirations for improved wellbeing, inclusive living in the community beyond services, independence and opportunities to contribute to others, as these will build a safer society for everyone in the long run; this demands risk taking as well as risk minimisation, risk management as well as risk assessment so that people select the most inclusive intervention as well as the least restrictive one;
- ensure that the assessments, interventions, monitoring and controls that are introduced to manage risk are proportionate, both to the scale of the risk being managed and to the distribution of effort between risk management and other interventions, and that staff are able to justify their actions;
- recognise that behaviour is contextual, and that every environment will have formal or informal mechanisms for the assessment and management of risk that will influence what happens there, and so these need to be built into the risk management process for each person in each setting;
- feed learning from each success and failure into a learning culture within social care services so that the organisation's understanding of safeguarding becomes increasingly nuanced and subtle rather than rule bound.

Enhancing inclusion reduces risk

Managing risk in this way is no easy task, and the Scottish Government (2006) policy paper *Changing Lives* concluded that effectively managing risk while encouraging innovative and personalised practice is one of social work's biggest challenges. Staff views of the benefits or risks associated with engaging in community life beyond the service will influence how they respond. Analysis of the circumstances surrounding suicide and homicide has shown clearly that social exclusion increases risk (DH, 2001), and this is endorsed by the Home Office evidence review on criminal reoffending (Harper and Chitty, 2004). The same themes occur repeatedly – homelessness, unemployment, isolation, family breakdown, poor educational attainment and lack of access to support when misusing alcohol or drugs. The curious thing about these findings is the lack of fit between diagnosis and treatment. One might expect that such clear evidence that, say, unemployment and social isolation hugely increase risks, would lead to a corresponding investment in initiatives that promote job opportunities and friendship building. Instead, in the case of the report on mental health, suicide and homicide, recommendations were largely focused on the removal of ligature points, and reducing the volume of medication that people take home from hospital.

Meanwhile, we find that fieldwork staff often say that while promoting inclusive lifestyles may actually be risk reducing, it does not feel like that. This is partly because having a job, for example, may be less risky than being unemployed, but the stress involved in getting a job is considerable and may lead to a substantial, if temporary, increase in problems. The result is that, in many services, living an isolated, boring, under-occupied life is somehow viewed as less risky than trying new things or stepping outside the protective cocoon of services. It is as if we can keep people safe by denying them opportunities.

Team climate and risk management

In the 20 days before the news of Baby Peter's tragic death hit the headlines in autumn 2008, social workers in England made 453 care applications. This contrasts with the 20 days after the announcement, when there were 652 applications (*Community Care*, 2009). Therefore we observe that, although risk management may be theorised as a person-centred process driven entirely and scientifically by the objective assessment of the person's individual circumstances, in reality it is heavily influenced by wider events. This is a key dimension of the 'risk society' (Beck, 1992), noted earlier. Negative media reporting exerts a 'chilling effect', encouraging social workers to wrap themselves in the apparently protective warmth of defensive practice (Parton, 1998) – a natural survival strategy as people read and watch media reports of their failing colleagues.

We conducted a series of explorations into literature, conversations and email exchanges with experts to identify other external factors that might exert an influence over the decision-making process in addition to media reporting of tragedies. While some of these factors affect the whole of society, others are played out within the team, affecting risk management decisions at a local level. Iterations with groups of practitioners distilled this thinking into a team self-assessment questionnaire we called CAIRO – the Climate Assessment Inventory for Risk and Opportunity. This has subsequently been used in a variety of settings as a tool for staff and team development.

CAIRO was set at the level of the team, rather than seeking a measure of the whole organisation, since, as Edmondson (2004) observes, organisational culture is a patchwork quilt rather than a uniform, smooth fabric. The process of creating the instrument was not straightforward, particularly as most work on risk management comes from high-risk environments where the goal is to eliminate all adverse events, such as unnecessary deaths or injuries. Social work shares the goal of eliminating unnecessary adverse events, but crucially recognises the value of positive risk taking to facilitate responsibility and enrich the person's quality of life. As a risk-free environment would tend to create dependency and hence crush the spirit, the government particularly welcomes approaches to practice that provide opportunities for positive risk-taking (DH, 2005).

Within CAIRO there are five subheadings; each is followed by a number of questions, posed as a Likert Scale between two extremes, which contrast the undesirable with the desirable climate, badged 'winter' and 'summer'. The questionnaire takes fifteen to twenty minutes to complete. The five subheadings are as follows:

- The person is at the centre of the risk management process.
- Resources are available to provide support.
- Individual staff take a helpful approach.
- The staff team works well.
- Documentation and recording supports a good process.

Average team scores are compared with overall averages and fed back in a team development day, where the majority of the time is spent exploring actions that the team might take to improve poor scores or maintain good ones. During the day, the team develops an action plan, and progress is reviewed some months later by repeating the questionnaire.

Following through the process with several teams has generated a pool of possible ideas – a bank of climate change technologies – for improving the team climate as it impacts risk management decisions, and a new way to fulfil governance responsibilities, since the 'risk and opportunity climate' in individual teams will have a substantial impact on the quality of service provided to people needing social care. Box 2.2 provides an illustration of the process as it was used in one team.

Box 2.2
Using CAIRO in the addictions team

Managers wished to obtain more information about the team and so CAIRO questionnaires were completed in late September 2009. During the development day in October, the average CAIRO scores were shared with the team. This highlighted a number of areas of concern that made some staff feel uncomfortable, but they drew on the ideas bank and added their own proposals to build an action plan that would address the issues that had been raised.

By March 2010, staff felt that CAIRO had contributed to improvements in the team. In particular, members feel that they share successes more often and have a better culture of listening, reflection and learning from one another. Visiting each other's offices for informal conversation and occasional shared lunches has led to new ideas for service improvements, and the team has found a way to sustain the healthy living project that was in danger of closing, thus keeping a focus on strengths rather than deficits. Despite rumours of cuts in funding levels, staff morale has increased since completing CAIRO, and is noticeably consistent, as people are more open and feel able to discuss their fears and concerns rather than being of low mood and not saying why.

Despite careful explanation, some team members have not made the connection between team functioning and risk management.

The following sections follow the themes used in the CAIRO questionnaire, examining the reasons why they are included, and suggesting ways for individuals and teams to take action and ensure that the team climate is conducive to positive, responsible risk assessment and management.

Person-centred practice

The first section of CAIRO asks team members to rate the extent to which the service is practising in a person-centred way (Bates et al., 2009). This means starting with the whole-life aspirations and preferences of the person, and then, informed by that broad perspective, exploring the person's own insights and possible solutions to problems, rather than relying entirely on professional expertise. Approaches such as the expert patient programme, the recovery movement in mental health, self-advocacy in learning disability and narrative explanations of dementia, engage with the rich archive of experiences that people bring to the safeguarding task.

Applying a person-centred approach to risk management means that social workers look to the person's ideas for keeping safe, rather than just offering their own. It engages with the distinction between feeling safe and being safe. While these two things are quite different, social workers need to pay attention to the person's own sense of feeling safe, both to uncover information about unexpected situations where the person may feel unsafe, and to find out what it means for the person to be safe on their own terms. Because each person has their own repertoire of risk management strategies, the task of social work becomes partly to help people understand themselves well enough to use appropriate strategies that will help to keep everyone safe. Although the foregoing is essentially very simple, we have come across risk assessment documentation that not only contains no record of the person's own perspective, but also even provides no prompt or space on the form to allow such observations to be recorded.

The second key area under this heading concerns organisational support for risk-taking behaviour by people who use the service. Again, this is obviously a limited freedom, but the fundamental goal of promoting independence from services can only be achieved if there is a social contract in which responsibility for actions is shared between the person and the social care agency. Unfortunately, while general talk about the 'dignity of risk' is common, day-to-day management of social care services can easily favour a risk-averse approach, in which workers practise defensively rather than making decisions in which they can justify their approach and support risk taking as well as risk minimisation.

Third, we ask about the use of language and humour under the heading of 'person-centred practice'. While hard-pressed staff can manage the stresses of the job through humour and a host of other strategies, the use of disrespectful nicknames can mask stereotypes and assumptions that inhibit clear thinking. In general, stress will reduce time to plan for risk, increase short-term thinking, reduce mindfulness and creativity, and lead to more risk neglect or risk aversive behaviour.

Resources

Social workers spend much time signposting people to support that is provided by other agencies. If these services are absent, whether through a historic lack of investment in third sector and community activities, through a failure to strategically develop the market and commission a broad range of options or through funding cuts, then this restricts the absolute amount of support and its flexibility, narrowing options for people. For example, some people live far from their home neighbourhood in residential care or hospital because there is a shortage of skilled local expertise or step-down facilities that will ease the transfer back home.

Early piloting of the CAIRO questionnaire suggested that staff find restricted access to resources one of the most challenging aspects of their work, generating scores that stood only just above complaints about the documentation – of which more below. One consequence of this is that people can be inappropriately badged as 'high risk' as a device to obtain help.

Limited resources within the team influence risk-taking behaviour too. If workloads are unreasonably high so that people become burnt out and exhausted, then sickness levels are likely to be high and posts may remain unfilled. As a result the team may lack the full range of professional disciplines, grades and experience. In such circumstances, staff are more likely to try and cope by becoming either risk-averse or reckless.

Improving the quality of life reduces risk, and some people who move from barren, institutional environments to homely, individualised settings and interesting activities leave their dangerous behaviour behind. Risk reduction interventions include the development of different housing options that might include tenancy with floating support, assistants employed by the person themselves through their own personal budget, and day opportunities that are tailored to the person's ambitions and support people to access valued roles and relationships in the community.

Inventiveness is sometimes overlooked as an essential quality of effective social work practice. It counteracts tendencies for risk assessment to be formulaic and mechanical, and becomes increasingly important when responding to people with complex support needs. Effective workers will collaborate with the person, their family and friends to invent a new solution that meets outcome criteria while effective teams will celebrate and nurture that creative spark. Not only will they solve the immediate problem, but they will also challenge the underlying cause of the problem to prevent it from happening again.

In the right environment, new and inexperienced workers can bring strongly held values, (Catlin and Maupin, 2002) and a fresh perspective to offer unexpected solutions. However, this positive trend is at odds with the caution that attends new roles. Markowitz (1952) first studied financial risk and found that people tend to manage it by the portfolio rather than by the individual item. This means that we tend to evaluate the total burden of risk that we are bearing before deciding whether or not to take on a new risky activity. Those new and inexperienced staff, for example, are likely to find that simply coping with their daily responsibilities feels risky as there is a lot to learn and many potential ways in which things might go wrong, and so they will be more cautious than their more experienced counterparts. This will be particularly true for team leaders who are new to the role.

Individual staff

The personality of individual workers affects how they address risk issues and these matters come to a head when limited resources are available to support the person. At its worst, scarcity evokes feelings of fatalism, victim thinking and blame, while for others, risk-taking evokes feelings of exhilaration and working with limited resources stimulates intelligence and creativity. Visitors to the team leave feeling inspired and confident that something worthwhile can be accomplished.

A positive attitude is achieved as people are individually willing to acknowledge the challenges, uncertainties and stresses of managing risk. They utilise team meetings and informal discussions between team members to share their uncertainties or bring forward new information that may change a previous decision, avoiding denial and paralysing uncertainty. Rather than distancing themselves from an emotional connection or over-identifying with the person, they talk about their emotional responses, such as pride in the person's success, sorrow in sharing their failure and helplessness when the person does not accept help; this ensures that they remain in touch with their emotional responses to the pressures of social work (Charles and Butler, 2004).

Not only do staff find the courage to share these uncomfortable feelings, but they also share out the actual work. They are sufficiently aware and assertive to identify times when they are over-burdened and so redistribute risk around other team members as necessary. The team has avoided the 'self-service allocation meeting' and similar arrangements that lead to eager staff repeatedly volunteering until they burn out, while their more reluctant colleagues keep silent, avoid adding to their own workload and negatively diffuse their personal responsibility among their peers. It is worth noting in passing that such unhelpful behaviours can also be played out between organisations, and some inter-agency risk management approaches seem designed to diffuse rather than share responsibility.

It is our view that these qualities can be learned and should not be viewed as fixed personality traits. Indeed, the skills that social workers are presumed to have – communication, reflection, relationship-building and so on (Wilson et al., 2008) – should fit members of a social work team to act in these ways. It is important for practitioners to be aware that they must develop skills that fit them for the team and organisational context within which they work (Eadie and Lymbery, 2002). This is an often-neglected part of an individual's learning, both during and after qualification.

Team working

We have noticed considerable variation between teams in the frequency and reliability of staff meetings and supervision sessions. Furthermore, some of these meetings may be overstocked with organisational matters and monitoring procedural compliance rather than providing opportunities for members to reflect on their practice, test out their judgements and share the burden of risk. Such meetings are more likely to be dominated by information giving or environmental scanning when services are reorganised or reduced and when new laws or procedures come into force.

Constant reorganisation, financial pressures and increasing bureaucratisation can lead teams to abandon work/life balance policies and time in lieu provision as staff miss holidays, ignore the Working Time Directive and go to work when they are sick (Holmes et al., 2009). This creates a culture that expects perfection and then punishes those who fall short, thus encouraging members to be secretive. This reinforces problematic behaviours by individual members (Charles and Butler, 2004): it does not promote healthy accountability and learning in a 'just culture'.

Tragedies or serious untoward incidents remind everyone of what might go wrong, especially if the sensationalist media become involved. Although this can help the team draw back from unsafe practices and adopt a thorough approach, it is more likely to make people defensive and obscure the value of positive risk-taking. At these times, there is a particular value in talking about things that go right, as well as sharing what might go wrong, and healthy teams will take time to learn from what has happened, share success stories and devise ways to quickly recover from the big chill that follows a serious incident. As well as providing simple encouragement, talking about success increases trust and hope, reminding the team of their common purpose, thus reducing risk (Cherniss 1995; Hofmeyer & Marck 2008).

Teams where risk is not well managed sometimes contain members who express strong opinions in ways that others find overly controlling. Those people always get their way as other people give up on the discussion and disagreements are hidden or seen as unacceptable. In contrast, warm relationships in the team mean that members talk to each other about their work and their personal lives, disclose positive emotions such as enthusiasm, encouragement and hope, value dissent and engage in disagreement without becoming adversarial, and correct tendencies such as conformity, polarisation, the shift to risk and the shift to caution within group decision-making processes (Furnham, 2005). Henriksen and Dayton (2006, p 1547) summarise research on the conditions under which staff have a clear understanding of their responsibilities as: people are accountable for specifiable actions, can assess their own performance and change direction when needed, tasks are challenging and engaging, group members are friends and on good terms, and when groups are small and formed of similarly competent members.

Paperwork

There has been an international shift from professional to bureaucratic approaches to social work (Burton and van den Broek, 2008) and we suspect that this has had a disproportionate impact on risk management. As the personalisation agenda shifts control to the person and the marketplace diversifies, shifting services from statutory to independent providers, the quality assurance process becomes more complex and attenuated. We fear that this will lead not only to lengthier documentation, but also to the construction of less accessible documents that make it even harder to include the person as an active partner.

Despite this, the points made earlier about the value of involving the person as an active risk manager in their own life remain true, and the most effective risk management paperwork will be created in partnership with the person, updated with them, and the service will retain a copy while the original remains with the person themselves. Adopting such a practice reminds staff that people have access to statements written about them, that the Human Rights Act protects privacy and demands that information collection should be relevant and proportionate, and that statements need to be respectful and evidence-informed. The 224 staff who have completed the CAIRO questionnaire to date gave this topic (documentation that involves the person) the lowest rating of all 27 questions – they were less satisfied about this aspect than any other dimension of the CAIRO questionnaire.

A particularly interesting part of the CAIRO questionnaire has been to ask staff whether the guidance materials (standard forms, risk management protocols and so on) actually help them to make a better decision. One might expect that effective guidance would press staff to be rigorous and systematic in their approach, with this occasionally leading to 'eureka' moments in which new opportunities are discovered. In general, this is not the case, and staff report that the guidance materials are burdensome rather than insightful, and that tools have replaced rather than supplemented professional judgement. The result is that sometimes the guidelines are neglected, and managers respond with demands for improvements in procedural compliance rather than examining the quality, relevance and practical utility of the guidance itself.

We have shown how individuals and teams need to understand the ambiguous and uncertain nature of many risk assessments in order to harvest the tacit knowledge that comes through continuing curiosity, contradictory evidence and tentative emotional responses. This complexity also needs to be embodied in guidelines; they should not read as if facts can be gathered and conclusions drawn without any uncertainty or worry, as if, once the procedure is complete, staff have discharged all their responsibilities and need trouble themselves no further, apart from watching for new evidence. Given the ambiguous nature of the social work environment, it is quite understandable that social workers might be drawn to the illusory certainty of concrete, mechanistic approaches to assessment and risk management.

Finally, we suggest that there is a connection between data collection systems and risk management. The more that a service reduces human experience to key performance indicators and neglects the human stories that lie behind the statistics, the greater the risk that this will distort perception and judgement, leading to poor risk management decisions. While public services are unlikely to be free of the obligation to collect numbers, a serious focus on narrative accounts may help to humanise the work and improve risk management, as long as these stories are balanced.

Conclusion

It is no simple task to manage risk effectively while supporting people to live as independently as possible, contribute to the wider society and fulfil their personal aspirations. Social workers need to manage risk alongside their duty to respect rights, address need and meet other formal obligations. Therefore, individual social workers, the teams that they work in and the organisations that employ them cannot afford to be complacent. Henriksen and Dayton (2006) wrote powerfully about the forces that lead to the phenomenon of 'organisational silence' whereby very little is said or done in response to significant problems or issues facing an organisation or industry, and Barry's (2007, p 46) international literature review concluded that 'most of social work's current accountability systems are reactive, adversarial and stifle professional autonomy'. Where all staff feel restricted, or compensate by believing that they are delivering above-average work, attributing all successes to their own skill and all failures to external factors, then the truth is clouded.

Instead, assumptions and stereotypes need to be exposed and replaced with ethical decision-making through which the person is engaged as an expert in managing their own life. Team and organisational resources need to be deployed well, and times of stringency faced with determined courage and innovation. Relationships within the team need to ensure that everyone's viewpoint is valued, problems are considered without oversimplification and both success and failure lead to further reflection. Procedures and data processing should support staff in their efforts to deliver a high-quality service that promotes opportunity while keeping everyone safe. Most importantly, much more can be done to increase the contribution of the person themselves to the task of risk management. Many of the issues raised in this chapter can be difficult to discuss openly, but their impact on people's lives can be substantial.

Note

1   In this chapter, when the term person is used, it refers to the person using the service (sometimes called the service user, patient or client). Everyone else is called a relative, staff, friend or colleague as appropriate.

References

Alcock, E (2000) *Living in Fear: The need to combat bullying of people with a learning disability* London: Mencap.

Barry, M (2007) *Effective Approaches to Risk Assessment in Social Work: An international literature review – final report* Edinburgh: Education Information and Analytical Services, Scottish Executive.

Bates, P, Seddon, J and Dowell, A (2009) 'Social inclusion work in mental health: using life domains and the Inclusion Web' in Poll, C, Kennedy, J & Sanderson, H (2009) *In Community, In Practice* Manchester: HSA Press, chapter 11.

Beck, U (1992) *Risk Society: Towards a New Modernity* London: Sage Publications.

Burton, J and van den Broek, D (2008) 'Accountable and Countable: Information Management Systems and the Bureaucratization of Social Work' *British Journal of Social Work* (39)7, pp 1326-42.

Catlin, D W and Maupin, J R (2002) 'Ethical orientations of state police recruits and one year experienced officers' *Journal of Criminal Justice* 30(6), pp 491-8.

Charles, M and Butler, S (2004) 'Social Workers' Management of Organisational Change' in Lymbery, M and Butler, S (eds) *Social Work Ideals and Practice Realities* Basingstoke: Palgrave.

Cherniss, C (1995) *Beyond Burnout* London: Routledge.

CSCI (Commission for Social Care Inspection) (2008) *Safeguarding Adults: A study of the effectiveness of arrangements to safeguard adults from abuse* London: CSCI.

Community Care (2009) 15 January.

DH (Department of Health) (2001) *Safety First: Five-year report of the National Confidential Inquiry into Suicide and Homicide by People with Mental Illness* London: DH.

DH (2005) *Independence, Well-Being and Choice* London: The Stationery Office.

Douglas, M (1992) *Risk and Blame: Essays in Cultural Theory* London: Routledge.

Eadie, T and Lymbery, M (2002) 'Understanding and working in welfare organisations' *Social Work Education* 21(5), pp 515–28.

Edmondson, A (2004) 'Learning from failure in health care: frequent opportunities, pervasive barriers' *Quality and Safety in Healthcare* 13(suppl II), pp ii3-ii9.

EHRC (Equality and Human Rights Commission) (2009) *From Safety Net to Springboard: A new approach to care and support for all based on equality and human rights* London: EHRC.

Furedi, F (2002) *Culture of Fear: Risk-Taking and the Morality of Low Expectations* (revised edition), London: Cassell.

Furnham, A (2005) *The Psychology of Behaviour at Work: The individual in the organization* London: Taylor & Francis.

Gardner, D (2008) *Risk: The science and politics of fear* London: Virgin Books.

Harper, G and Chitty, C (eds) (2004) *Home Office Research Study 291: The impact of corrections on re-offending: a review of 'what works'* London: Home Office Research, Development and Statistics Directorate.

Henriksen, K and Dayton, E (2006) 'Organisational silence and hidden threats to patient safety' *Health Service Research* 41(4), pp 1539-54.

Hofmeyer, A and Marck, P B (2008) 'Building social capital in healthcare organisations: thinking ecologically for safer care' *Nursing Outlook* p 145-51.

Holmes, L, McDermid, S, Jones, A and Ward, H (2009) *How Social Workers Spend their Time: An analysis of the key issues that impact on practice pre- and post implementation of the integrated children's system* London: Department for Children, Schools and Families.

Laing, A (2009) 'Police officer forced to drop childcare plans calls for more Ofsted discretion' *The Telegraph* 28 September.

Langan, J and Lindow, V (2004) *Living with Risk: Mental health service user involvement in risk assessment and management* Bristol: The Policy Press/JRF.

Markowitz, H M (1952) 'Portfolio selection' *Journal of Finance* 7(1) pp 77-91.

Parton, N (1996) 'Social work, risk and the "blaming system"' in Parton, N (ed) *Social Theory, Social Change and Social Work* London: Routledge.

Parton, N (1998) 'Risk, Advanced Liberalism and Child Welfare: The Need to Rediscover Ambiguity and Uncertainty' *British Journal of Social Work* 28(1), pp 5-27.

Scott, A (2000) 'Risk Society or Angst Society? Two views of risk, consciousness and community' in Adam, B, Beck, U and van Loon, J (eds) *The Risk Society and Beyond: Critical issues for social theory* London: Sage Publications.

Scottish Executive (2006) *Changing Lives: Report of the 21st century social work review* Edinburgh: Scottish Executive.

Stalker, K (2003) 'Managing Risk and Uncertainty in Social Work: A literature review' *Journal of Social Work* 3(2), pp 211-33.

Webb, S A (2006) *Social Work in a Risk Society: Social & Political Perspectives* Basingstoke: Palgrave.

Wilson, K, Ruch, G, Lymbery, M and Cooper, A (2008) *Social Work: An introduction to contemporary practice* Harlow: Pearson Education.

Chapter 3

Exploring Ethically Based, Spiritually Aware, Practice

Irene Stevens

Introduction

> *About what am I now employing my own soul?*
> *On every occasion I must ask myself this question.*
> (The Meditations of Marcus Aurelius: Long, 2006, p 72)

When I began to write this chapter I had the good fortune to take a trip with one of the best arbiters of the moral conscience, a Glasgow taxi driver. Inevitably, the conversation got round to football. The driver was complaining about a decision made by a referee the evening before. 'You know,' he said, 'the boy didn't mean to bring the other player down … yes, when you look at it, the decision was within the rules but sometimes it's not just about the rules, it's about doing what's right.' In a nutshell, the taxi driver identified the issue that faces social work practitioners every day.

As a social work practitioner, a question that often arises is 'how do I know what is right in this situation?'. Answers to this question may be helped by an understanding of ethics, which critically examines frameworks of moral reasoning. Also relevant are particular moral codes relating to good or bad behaviour, fairness and honesty. Social work practice is a moral activity and moral activities are those concerned with doing right. I would suggest that this has always been central to social work practice and is becoming more and more pertinent as we move through the twenty-first century.

So where does spirituality come into this? Perhaps more than any other occupation, social work practice in its various forms concerns itself with the whole person in the context of their life. An holistic approach to practice means that we should be engaging at all levels, including physical, social, psychological *and* spiritual aspects. Spirituality can be seen as the person's drive to understand the purpose and meaning of their life. As practitioners, we have this drive as do the individuals, families and communities with whom we work. In this way, it is the common feature of our humanity. It encourages a view of being connected to each other and to the universe, past and present. I would argue that of all the aspects to which a social work practitioner attends in the UK, the spiritual dimension is perhaps the least well understood. This is hardly surprising given the rational-scientific bureaucratisation of social work practice in the UK, and the paucity of teaching about spirituality in social work education (Holloway, 2007). Anecdotally, my experience has been that practitioners feel very uncomfortable talking about 'the S word'! As Crompton said, 'To talk about religion and spirituality is for many people as embarrassing as talking about sex, death and money' (cited in Gilligan and Furness, 2006, p 617). When it comes to making the right decisions, I believe that an understanding of ethics coupled with a spiritual perspective is one way of helping practitioners at post-qualifying level to work through the complex moral dilemmas which face them. Ethical practice lies in doing what is right and a spiritual perspective puts us in touch with the part of our own humanity that we share with every other human being who has ever existed.

As a social work practitioner, you may end up using your skills in any one (or more) of a wide variety of practice settings. The aspect that all of these practice settings will have in common is that you will be working with people who have been identified by society as disadvantaged, and you will find that you have power in relation to that group of people. An understanding of ethical practice and spirituality may help you to use that power wisely. In this chapter I will look at some of the philosophical approaches to ethical practice, including drawing on some of the ancient religious philosophical traditions. The relationship between religion and spirituality is becoming more contested in contemporary literature. While I will discuss this at a later point, suffice to say that some of the ancient religious philosophies have spirituality at their heart and may have something to contribute to ethical practice.

Question: Spend a few moments thinking about your understanding of ethics and spirituality. How would you define these for yourself? Have your feelings and understandings about these concepts changed over time?

An exploration of ethical approaches for social work practice

> What actions are most excellent? To gladden the heart of human beings, to feed the hungry, to help the afflicted, to lighten the sorrow of the sorrowful, and to remove the sufferings of the injured. (A *hadith* [record from the oral tradition] relating to the Prophet Muhammad: Al-Bukhari)

How would you define your job as a social work practitioner? The International Association of Schools of Social Work state that:

> *Since its beginnings over a century ago, social work practice has focused on meeting human needs and developing human potential. Human rights and social justice serve as the motivation and justification for social work action. In solidarity with those who are disadvantaged, the profession strives to alleviate poverty and to liberate vulnerable and oppressed people in order to promote social inclusion.* (IASSW, 2001)

Compare this to the hadith above, which is drawn from the spiritual tradition of Islam. Might it be that this *hadith* describes some of the tasks with which you are involved in practice? The IASSW definition certainly has a degree of resonance with this religious philosophy, which was first recorded over 1,400 years ago.

Social work practice in the UK is underpinned by a particular set of principles that should help define how to approach the activities that are undertaken in its name. These principles include aspects such as dignity and respect. The way in which we put these principles into practice in the UK is laid out in Codes of Practice for all four UK jurisdictions. The fact that social work practice is a moral pursuit is immediately obvious from a cursory reading of the codes, referring as they do to moral categories such as respect, responsibility and protection. In the course of their work at post-qualifying level, social workers will meet situations that raise moral dilemmas for them. For example, what do they do when the rights of service users and carers clash? Moral philosophy gives us a range of options. We will now examine some of these.

Virtue ethics

Virtue ethics emphasise the moral character of the person. The person's ethical stance comes from their practice of the virtuous aspects of their character. The virtues in ancient philosophical tradition are associated with the work of Plato and Aristotle. Plato described four cardinal virtues, which were wisdom, courage, moderation and justice (see Allen, 2006). The key virtues for Aristotle included courage, temperance, gentleness and care (see Ross, undated). A virtue is a disposition that is well entrenched in its possessor, a deep and integral part of their being. Virtues must be accompanied by phronesis or practical wisdom, and they must contribute to *eudaimonia*. The Greek term '*eudaimon*' is composed of two parts: *eu* means 'well' and *daimon* means 'divinity' or 'spirit'. To be *eudaimon* is therefore to be living in a way that contributes to spiritual wellbeing. A virtue must be practised in the conduct of living. When looking at the *hadith* at the beginning of this section, you can see clear links between this ancient Greek tradition and Islamic philosophy, especially the emphasis on the characteristics of 'excellent' actions. In terms of spirituality, the concept of *eudaimonia* is congruent with the drive to understand the purpose of life. Some commentators believe that virtue ethics can be important in helping to inform ethical practice. (McBeath and Webb, 2002; Prior, 2005; Gray, 2009).

Prior (2005) argues that care is a virtue that is highly relevant to social work practice. She suggests that by focusing on traditions, history and 'small narratives' in social work, we are provided with an alternative way to intervene and arrive at morally correct decisions. Think about our taxi driver and his frustration at the inability of rules in helping the referee arrive at the 'right' decision. Instead of defining ethical practice by rules that ought to govern our conduct, virtue theorists advocate the development of character habits. Habits such as care, courage and fairness, used in the pursuit of *eudaimonia*, have great potential to lead us to right outcomes.

Virtue ethics feel congruent with social work practice. They give us some guidance about the traits we need to exhibit as a practitioner. They do, however, have a number of shortcomings. First, the possession of virtues does not help us to deal with some complex moral dilemmas. How does the possession of certain traits help us to come to conclusions about abortion, for example? Second, how do we treat lapses in virtuous behaviour, either in ourselves or in those with whom we work? Last, is there a definitive, culture-free list of virtues, which would reflect the different modes of conduct that each culture values?

Question: Look back at the four Platonic virtues. How might these apply in your practice? Look back at your definition of spirituality. Do any of the Aristotelian virtues link with this?

EXPLORING VIRTUE ETHICS IN PRACTICE

Davy is an elderly man with alcohol-related dementia. He has no family and lives in an area of high deprivation. He still lives at home but is increasingly vulnerable to financial abuse from a variety of people who know when he gets his pension. From a social work point of view he may be a vulnerable adult. The question is whether or not to take an order out, which would remove him to a safer place. To help make this decision, a virtue ethicist would put their virtuous traits into action. Let us take the virtues of wisdom, courage, justice and moderation. Wisdom is a combination of your knowledge plus how you put your knowledge into action. Courage helps you to face difficult or dangerous situations and to act in those situations. Justice is the quality of being fair and morally right in your actions. Moderation is about not acting in extremes. These are some definitions but the important thing for the virtue ethicist is that you *embody* these qualities. The virtues are nothing unless they are practised. You *are* courageous, just, wise and temperate. What would be the courageous, just, wise and temperate action in this instance? You might need to confront Davy and the people who are taking his money (courage). You may think that removing Davy is an extreme act (moderation). You may know that Davy can get access to many types of support that he does not have access to currently (wisdom). You may talk to Davy to decide what he believes is the fairest outcome for him in the situation (justice). These are some aspects of virtuous ethical practice.

Ethics of care

At first sight, it might seem that ethics of care and virtue ethics are the same. However, the key difference is that 'care is not reducible to dispositions within a particular individual, since, by its very nature, care is oriented towards relationships that extend beyond individuals' (Held, as cited in Gray, 2009, p 5). Two of the key theorists in the examination of the ethics of care are Tronto and Gilligan. Tronto (1993) discussed how logic and reason became highly-valued and seen as properties of the public realm of work. Care, feeling and sentiment were relegated to the private realm of home. Gilligan (1982) claimed that she heard a distinctive moral voice among the women who were the subjects of her research. She called this voice the 'voice of care'. This voice emphasised the equal moral worth of all people. The ethics of care reject impartiality, insist on the need to be sensitive to others and emphasise the central place of concern and sentiment. Think of our taxi driver's comment again. While having set rules would imply that the same principles should hold for all people in the same situation, the ethics of care insist that judgements require sensitivity to the particular moral features of each situation. In the case of the football player, the moral features lie in the intention behind the act, not just within the act itself.

Ethics of care is becoming a much more widely debated area, particularly for social work practice in the community. Noddings, *et al.* (1996) indicated that care is not happening unless the person who is cared for actually experiences the feeling of being cared for by a care-giver. Noddings, *et al.* (1996, p 27) are critical of some of the agencies set up to care: 'The fact is that many of us have been reduced to cases by the very machinery that has been instituted to care for us'.

Commentators such as Meagher and Parton (2004) argue that social work practitioners should begin to re-engage with the ideas about care and use the ethics of care as a means to inform their work. However, social work practice in reality also encompasses notions of justice. Justice would suggest that everyone is entitled to the same service. One potential problem, therefore, is that the application of care ethics may lead to different levels of service based on situational and subjective judgements. With no external arbiter, the ethics of care can be experienced as unjust, as noted by Gray and Lovat (2007).

EXPLORING THE ETHICS OF CARE IN PRACTICE

You are running a group for young people at risk. Subita is a 15 year old young person who has been and has been cutting herself and misusing drugs. As a field social worker, you may be involved in assessment, attending reviews, and perhaps making referrals to other agencies such as mental health services. You may, however, also be intervening directly to prevent Subita from harming herself further. Counselling and being physically present and emotionally available to the young person would also be part of your role. Both sets of tasks are about care and both are needed, but they are put into practice in different ways. The feeling of being cared for is usually the most important one for the client so, from a care ethics perspective, you should make sure your practice helps the young person feel cared for. This places a huge emphasis on your relational skills and ability to provide emotional containment stemming from an empathic base.

Consequentialism

Another ethical approach is consequentialism. Practice based on consequentialist ethics would say that the 'rightness' of an action should be determined by the outcome. If the outcome is good for the person, community or society, then it is a right action. Bentham and Mill are probably two of the best-known philosophers in this area. Practice based on consequentialism may be referred to colloquially as 'the greatest good for the greatest number'. In more recent times, Rawls (1971) presented an alternative approach. He sought to identify what choices people would make about the organisation of society, if they had no idea where they would be placed in the social and economic order, that is, they operated from behind a veil of ignorance. Rawls argued that in this circumstance people would adopt the maximin rule, that is, make the choice that produced the best outcome for the least advantaged position. This is a different version of consequentialism, which can be applied to moral dilemmas. Applying consequentialism to moral issues may allow us to develop goal-orientated practice. On the negative side, consequentialism also fits well with 'managerialism', the term used to describe a culture where targets and performance indicators are paramount, with pressures to engineer outcomes to present the most positive picture. While this has become a predominant feature of contemporary social work practice in the UK (Clarke and Newman, 1997; Meagher and Parton, 2004), it has been heavily criticised as not being congruent with social work values.

A more fundamental criticism of consequentialism is how do we know what the consequences are or will be for any particular intervention? Usually we can make an educated guess, considering as many factors as possible. However, we live in a complex, non-linear world. As McBeath and Webb (2002, p 1016) stated, 'social work interactions and their results are often patterned but are not highly predictable'. Actions may have foreseen *and* unforeseen consequences.

Question: Spirituality is about the drive to understand meaning in life, which is something that all practitioners share with the people with whom they work. How does a spiritual perspective fit with consequentialism?

EXPLORING CONSEQUENTIALIST PRACTICE

Chantelle is a young lone mother of three children. She has come to the attention of social services through a referral from the nursery school. The teachers there have concerns about the care and wellbeing of the two children who attend the nursery. Their hygiene is poor and they look underfed and tired. There is some question that the children may be at risk. On visiting, it is clear that Chantelle is having difficulties coping. She is on benefits and living in poor-quality social housing. However, when you see Chantelle with her children, it is obvious that they have a warm and loving relationship. The greatest good for the greatest number would be that Chantelle could be supported to build on her existing love for her children. The practical and emotional supports you put in place would, hopefully, have positive consequences. Alternatively, place yourself, Chantelle and the children behind the 'veil of ignorance'. What decisions would you make from that stance? Would you conclude that the consequences of the family staying together might be good for Chantelle, but not necessarily for the children? From a Rawlsian perspective, your decision should be guided by the best outcome for the least powerful.

Deontology

The final approach we will examine is deontology. If you were taught ethics during your qualifying training as a social worker, this is likely to be the approach with which you have come into contact. Deontology is concerned with our duties and responsibilities to other people. Following a deontological approach, moral conduct consists of following certain rules defined by those duties. Probably the most widely quoted philosopher of this persuasion is Kant. He offered a suggestion for how we should act, called the *Categorical Imperative*. This was based not on what a person may want or desire but on a single principle that he thought should apply in all circumstances. It can be stated as:

> *Act only on that maxim through which you can at the same time will that it should become a universal law.* (Kant, 1964, p 88).

Foundational for Kant were the role of reason, the ability to make moral judgements based on universal principles, and impartiality, viewing each person as an independent rational human being. He believed that no act was, within itself, either right or wrong. For Kant, it was the motive of the person performing the act that dictated its morality. As Gray (2009, p 2) commented when discussing the deontological approach, 'when a social worker respects a client, she does this because it is the right thing to do in terms of professional values and code of ethics'. Feelings or emotions have no particular part in this because they are not reasons to act.

Kant believed that people should be able to develop rules that allow the categorical imperative to be promoted. If the categorical imperative is followed through in each situation where a moral dilemma arose, then what is right in one situation should also be right in every situation. When examining how social work practitioners approach their tasks in the UK context, it becomes clear that their actions are greatly influenced by rule-based ethics. Clark alludes to the rule-based approach in his examples of how social workers should approach dilemmas:

> *Social work is legitimated by state authority. Social workers cannot give priority to their private judgement of client actions over key principles of law and accepted morality.* (Clark, 2000, p 156)

Kant's influence is also seen in Codes of Practice and Charters of Rights. Such instruments are codifications of the categorical imperative. Rule-based ethics also fit well with procedurally-based conceptions of social work practice. The positive aspect of deontological approaches is that they have helped to move practice forward by the setting of standards for practice, and procedures to protect vulnerable people. Yet deontological approaches do not always equate with 'doing right'. To illustrate this, I will return to the conversation with the taxi driver. Unlike the taxi driver, the deontologist may miss the moral point, emphasising the rules but more likely debating the mechanics of the game or the justice of the final result. From a philosophical point of view, the difficulty with practice based on deontology arises in deciding what the rules are and how we know that the rules will lead us to the right action. Also, what if the rules conflict with each other? One answer might be to create a hierarchy of rules, so that if they come into conflict, then one rule has priority over another. This, however, can create a situation where the underlying morals of the situation can become very fluid, which is problematic. It merely replaces one set of rules with another. Also, deontology 'valorise[s] the place of the rational autonomous individual, bound by duty to help others. Care is thus conceived of as rational rather than primarily relational' (Smith, 2009, p 3). Finally, rule-based ethics imply a denial of the aspects of being that are not fully rational: the spiritual, the emotional and the intuitive.

Activity: Having considered these four approaches to ethical practice (virtue ethics, ethics of care, consequentialism and deontology), try to identify which of them resonates most with you. Why do you think that particular way of conceptualising ethics fits best with you? Now think of a moral dilemma you have recently faced at work. Apply each of the four methods and see if you arrive at the same or different conclusions for each.

Personal motivation and public role: Linking ethical practice and spirituality

> *That which the ear can hear but needs no ear to hear. That alone is spirit.*
> *(Kena Upanishad, one of the Hindu scriptures)*
> (Goodall and Zaehner, 1996, p 168)

For me, there is a deep connection between ethical practice and spirituality; that is, between the imperative to do the right thing and the drive to understand the meaning of life and our place in history and the universe. Social work in the UK cannot escape its spiritual roots, both as an occupation with a history based in religious organisations, and as a moral pursuit. Two of the most influential early theorists in UK social work were Biestek and Egan. Felix Biestek (1961), a Jesuit priest, gave us seven principles of individualisation, purposeful expression of feelings, controlled emotional involvement, acceptance, a non-judgemental attitude, client self-determination and confidentiality.

Gerard Egan (1975) emphasised the qualities of openness, honesty, non-judgemental warmth and empathy in our practice. Russon (1997) pointed out the similarity between his helping model and the reflective philosophy of St Ignatius of Loyola, which was developed in the sixteenth century. It has been common in the literature to draw a distinction between religion and spirituality, and to see them as two separate entities. Joseph, as cited in Bullis (1996, p 2) stated that religion is 'the external expression of faith, comprised of beliefs, ethical codes, and worship practices. Religion is based on an organised set of beliefs that there is a spiritual realm beyond our own physical world and this set of beliefs is usually shared by a number of people, giving rise to a communal element. Canda (1988) argued that while spirituality is at the heart of religious practices, it is separate from this. He defined spirituality as 'the human quest for personal meaning and mutually fulfilling relationships among people, the non-human environment and, for some, God' (Canda, 1988, p 243). Mathews (2009, p 4) stated, religion 'is merely one way of expressing spirituality and it is not essential to be a member of a faith group in order to express spirituality'. Holloway (2007) alluded to the problems with this 'spirituality-religion binary' when she pointed out that without some reflection on the religious philosophies, spirituality is barely distinguishable from the way in which traditional 'secular' social work values are articulated. Henery (2003, p.1111–12) went further and argued that the 'spirituality-religion binary' means that 'Ethnic minorities are generally characterised as first religious and only then spiritual. They are, therefore, placed en masse in the disfavoured half of the "spirituality–religion" binary'. Wong and Vinsky (2009, p 1343) argued that the use of the term 'spirituality' out of context of religion has an unspoken 'Euro-Christian ethnocentric and individualistic' bias.

The literature on spirituality in social work has been growing over the past two decades (Canda, 1988; Bullis, 1996; Derezotes, 2006; Gilligan and Furness, 2006; Crisp, 2008; Robinson, 2008; Mathews, 2009). Yet Holloway (2007, p 265) suggests that 'the increased sympathy towards 'spiritual practice' is not as great in social work as it is amongst other human services professions, and that there is continuing inhibition and resistance in the UK in social work education in particular'. So at this point, I would like to ask you to become aware of any feelings you may have about spirituality and its place in social work, and read with an open mind.

When reading the material to prepare this chapter, I was struck by the number of times I read that some principles are self-evident. Here are just two examples:

One would acknowledge that the need for care is necessary to sustain oneself. (Gray, 2009, p 4)

[that a social worker should not be violent, sexually abusive or neglectful to children] I take as uncontroversially true in that it is based on such a broad and deep consensus about human rights that the opposite viewpoint is simply unconscionable. (Clark, 2006, p 81)

53

The question I began to ask myself is *why* are these things taken to be self-evident across cultures and across time? One answer lies in the possibility that there exists within each of us a spiritual dimension, which is deeply embedded within us by the very fact of our humanity. That certain actions are universally 'unconscionable' (like harming a child) says something about what is right and wrong in our ways of relating to other people. This is similar to the times when we have a feeling that something about a situation is 'just not right'. When talking about acts that are 'unconscionable' or about a feeling that something is 'just not right', we often invoke *intuition*; in times of moral conflict, we somehow *know* or *feel* what is right and hence act accordingly. In the managerialist, neo-liberal world of contemporary social work in the UK, feelings and intuitions are often discounted in the face of evidence-based rational-scientific responses. While not dismissing the positive aspects of managerialism (one example of which might be child protection procedures), I would suggest that there is an important place for intuitions and feelings. Further, I would suggest that some of these intuitions and feelings are aspects of spirituality, or a higher-level consciousness. Derezotes (2006) calls this 'transpersonal consciousness' and suggests that it can be developed by contemplation of moral dilemmas (mindfulness), cultivating compassion and by adopting a view of self as part of a body-mind-spirit-universe continuum. Developing transpersonal conscious-ness and allying this to our understanding of ethical approaches to social work interventions can help to aid ethical practice.

I have argued that ethical stance and spiritual perspective are two important aspects of decision-making in social work. Indeed, I would go further and suggest that 'spirituality provides a framework through which ethical reflection can occur' (Robinson, 2008, p 82). Like Robinson, I believe that spirituality and ethics are related to each other. The moral imperative to 'do the right thing' is closely related to our sense of connectedness with the rest of humanity. If we examine the links between religion, spirituality and ethical practice, we see common themes. The five main world religions (the three monotheistic Abrahamic traditions of Christianity, Islam and Judaism, and the two Eastern traditions of Buddhism and Hinduism) are based on ancient philosophies, which explore the nature of right and wrong, as well as laying down guidance on how to pursue happiness. Also, these religions emphasise common points for living the good life. Judaism, for example, gives us the term *hesed*, meaning loving-kindness, which is almost identical to the Buddhist term *metta*. Christianity talks about the need for *compassion* while Islam talks of *rahmah*, and Hinduism talks of *karuna*. *Karuna* and *Rahmah* also mean compassion and the idea of suffering with the other. All of these religions talk about the concept of service, be it to the individual, the family, the wider community or to a higher power. Religious traditions incorporate potent terms that help us to conceptualise spirituality and which are also useful to consider in ethical practice.

Question: Think about your work with non-voluntary service users. Referring to some of the religious terms above, how might they help you to understand and justify your practice with non-voluntary service users?

For you as a qualified social worker, an interesting question to explore briefly is to look at the reasons why you decided to consider social work as a career in the first place. Research on the motivations of students in Scotland across six universities found that students chose social work because it helps those in need. The authors reported that 'the fundamental, underlying motivation for all focus group respondents was to "care for others" (Scottish Executive, 2005, p 3). Clark (2006, p76) put this well when he said that 'welfare professionals have to be personal exponents of the values they presume to trade in professionally; and to do so, they have to be personally committed to values and ways of life that extend well beyond the scope of their contract of employment'. The way in which a qualified social worker conceptualises their job, and how this contributes to their own search for meaning, has clear implications for ethical practice.

Question: Think of an example from your practice where you or another person acted in a way which could be defined as professional but which did not 'feel right'. What was it that made the action 'feel wrong'?

Finally, it is important to consider the meaning of spirituality for those with whom we work. I stated earlier that spirituality is a dimension that exists within us all. Research is clear about the positive contributions of a spiritual dimension to the lives of disadvantaged people (Connor *et al.*, 2003; Daining and DePanfilis, 2007; Robinson, 2008; Jackson *et al.*, 2010). Such contributions include a feeling of connection to culture and community, a way of dealing with loss and grief, an experience of unconditional love from a higher source and the development of a sense of purpose. As I have stated previously, a full assessment of need should include the spiritual dimension. As social workers, it is up to us to find the language within ourselves to relate to and encourage this important dimension of being.

Some concluding remarks

> *The mind of the wise man draws him to the good.*
> *(Katha Upanishad, one of the Hindu scriptures)*
> (Goodall and Zaehner, 1996)

On a personal level, ethically based, spiritually aware, practice can act as a balm for the self through its congruence with personal values. At an organisational level, it can serve as a counterbalance to those aspects of managerialism that are unhelpful in practice. The relevance of ethics and spirituality should be recognised and greater attention should be paid to these, particularly in social work education.

I hope that you are encouraged to examine what Russon (1997, p29) ... refers to as 'closed, prejudiced attitudes to folk, cultural and religious literature sources in order that such sources are accepted ...with more objectivity' ... I agree with her when she asks us to 'be aware of personal as well as academic and scientific prejudice' (Russon, 1997, p29).

In terms of the implications for post-qualifying work, practitioners should not be afraid to act upon their feelings of love, compassion and forgiveness, which are grounded in a spiritual dimension. We are in a privileged position in-so-far as social work now has its own history, narratives, laws and standards. These can give some normative guidance on decision-making. We should, however, also listen to our intuitions and not be afraid to use these as part of ethical decision-making processes. We should engage actively with some of the approaches to ethical decision-making that have described in this chapter and use contemplation and dialogue to help in this process. I would like to finish with a short phrase from McBeath and Webb (2002, p 1033). I think it sums up my own personal attitude to one of the most important aspects of self, which contributes to ethically-based, spiritually-aware practice.

Few people can hush the small voice that tells us what's right.

To this I would add a short phrase from one of the other religious philosophical traditions, which almost echoes these sentiments:

Dear friends you must never become tired of doing right.
(Paul addressing the Thessalonians)
(The Bible)

References

Al-Bukhari, Muhammad ibn Ismail (850) Hadith relating to the Prophet Muhammed (accessed 23 October 2009 at
www.usc.edu/schools/college/crcc/engagement/resources/texts/muslim/hadith/bukhari/)
Allen, R E (2006) *Plato: The republic* New Haven, CT: Yale University Press.
Biestek, F P (1961) *The Casework Relationship* London: Unwin.
Bullis, R K (1996) *Spirituality in Social Work Practice* London: Taylor & Francis.
Canda, E (1988) 'Spirituality, religious diversity and social work practice' *Social Casework* 69(4), pp 238-47.
Clark, C (2000) *Social Work Ethics: Politics, principles and practice* London: Palgrave.
Clark, C (2006) 'Moral character in social work' *British Journal of Social Work* 36(1), pp 75-89.
Clarke, J and Newman, J (1997) *The Managerial State: Power, politics and ideology in the remaking of social welfare* London: Sage.

Connor, K, Davidson, J and Lee, L C (2003) 'Spirituality, resilience and anger in survivors of violent trauma: A community survey' *Journal of Traumatic Stress* 16(5), pp 487-94.

Crisp, B (2008) 'Social work and spirituality in a secular society' *Journal of Social Work* 8(4), p 363-75.

Daining, C and DePanfilis, D (2007) 'Resilience of youth in transition from out-of-home care into adulthood' *Children and Youth Services Review* 29(9), pp 1158-78.

Derezotes, D (2006) *Spiritually Orientated Social Work Practice* London: Allyn & Bacon.

Egan, G (1975) *The Skilled Helper* Pacific Groves, CA: Brooks Cole Publishing.

Gilligan, C (1982) *In a Different Voice* Boston, MA: Harvard University Press.

Gilligan, P and Furness, S (2006) 'The role of religion and spirituality in social work practice: Views and experiences of social workers and students' *British Journal of Social Work* 36(4), pp 617-37.

Goodall, D and Zaehner, R C (1996) *Hindu Scriptures* Berkeley: University of California Press.

Gray, M (2009) 'Moral sources and emergent ethical theories in social work' *British Journal of Social Work* (advanced electronic access, doi: 10.1093/bjsw/bcp104).

Gray, M and Lovat T (2007) 'Horse and carriage: Why Habermas's discourse ethics give virtue a praxis for social work' *Ethics and Social Welfare* 1(3), pp 310-28.

Henery, N (2003) 'Critical commentary: the reality of visions – contemporary theories of spirituality in social work' *British Journal of Social Work* 33(8), pp 1105-13.

Holloway, M (2007) 'Spiritual need and the core business of social work' *British Journal of Social Work* 37(2), pp 265-80.

IASSW (International Association of Schools of Social Work) (2001) Description of social work values (accessed on 15 October 2009 at www.iassw-aiets.org/index.php?option=com_content&task=blogcategory&id=26&Itemid=51).

Jackson, L J, White, C R, O'Brien, K, DiLorenzo, P, Cathcart, E, Wolf, M, Bruskas, D, Pecora, P, Nix-Early, V and Cabrera, J (2010) 'Exploring spirituality among youth in foster care: Findings from the Casey Field Office Mental Health Study' *Child and Family Social Work* 15(1), pp 107-17.

Kant, I (1964) *Groundwork of the Metaphysics of Morals* New York: Harper Row.

Long, G. (Trans) (2006) *The Meditations of Marcus Aurelius* London: Watkins.

Mathews, I (2009) *Social Work and Spirituality* Exeter: Learning Matters.

McBeath, G and Webb, S A (2002) 'Virtue ethics and social work: being lucky, realistic and not doing one's duty' *British Journal of Social Work* 32(8), pp 1015-36.

Meagher, G and Parton, N (2004) 'Modernising social work and the ethics of care' *Social Work and Society* 2(1), pp 10-27.

Noddings, N, Gordon, S and Benner, P (1996) *Caregiving: Readings in Knowledge, Practice, Ethics and Politics* Philadelphia, PA: University of Pennsylvania Press.

Prior, J (2005) 'The virtue ethics of Alistair Macintyre in the context of social care practice', PhD Thesis, Glasgow: University of Strathclyde.

Rawls, J (1971) *A Theory of Justice* Cambridge, MA: Bellnap Press.

Robinson, S (2008) *Spirituality, Ethics and Care* London: Jessica Kingsley Publishers.

Ross, W D (Trans) (undated) *Aristotle's Nichomachean Ethics, Book I, Section 8* (accessed on 25 September 2009 at http://classics.mit.edu/Aristotle/nicomachaen.1.i.html)

Russon, M (1997). 'A "common-sense" approach to reflection' Conference Proceedings, July pp 26-30, Standing Conference on University Teaching and Research, University of London (accessed on 20 November 2009 at www.leeds.ac.uk/educol/documents/00002906.htm).

Scottish Executive (2005) *Insight 23: Motivations for undertaking the new social work degree* Edinburgh: Scottish Executive (accessed on 21 September 2009 at www.scotland.gov.uk/Resource/Doc/77843/0018557.pdf).

Smith, M (2009) *Rethinking Residential Child Care: Positive perspectives* Bristol: The Policy Press.

The Bible (1983) Paul's second letter to the Thessalonians (2Th 3:13) London: Thomas Nelson.

Tronto, J (1993) *Moral Boundaries: A political argument for an ethic of care* London: Routledge.

Wong, Y L-R and Vinsky, J (2009) 'Speaking from the margins: A critical reflection on the 'Spiritual-but-not-Religious' discourse in social work' *British Journal of Social Work* 39(7), pp 1343-59.

Chapter 4

Management and Leadership in Social Work

Graham McPheat and Joan Watson

Key questions

- As a new social worker, what can you expect from your manager?
- How will your transition to your new role and team be managed and your induction handled?
- What will be the purpose and process of supervision?
- How will you be helped to maintain professional motivation and manage stress?
- How will your employer support you to achieve the mandatory requirements concerning your continuous professional development?

Introduction

The need for effective management and leadership in social work services is paramount. The demands placed on social work managers to deliver are significant, particularly so for those new to the role. However, the challenges involved in supporting workers, particularly those new to the profession, to learn and develop such skills has never been greater. This chapter sets out what newly qualified social workers can expect from leaders and managers in terms of induction, supervision (including supportive, managerial and developmental functions), the management of motivation and stress, and continuous professional development. The first section of the chapter details some of the policy context and debates surrounding and impacting on social work today. The second section considers some of the key factors involved in education for social work management and the ways in which managers are supported to develop the skills necessary to support all staff. The final section focuses on how managers are expected to support newly qualified workers within this context and draws on a research study that examined the effectiveness of a post-qualifying social work management programme, providing evidence of how prepared social work managers feel to undertake some of these roles.

The policy context

The challenges for social work in the twenty-first century are many and varied. They include increased and changing expectations of service users and carers (Van

Zwanenberg, 2009; Wilkinson, 2009) and increased partnership working (Douglas, 2009), while new registration and continuing professional development requirements for social work staff have sought to raise standards within the profession (SSSC and IRISS, 2008). A number of high-profile reports, commissioned following the deaths, or long-term abuse, of service users have highlighted the crucial role of leadership and management in modern social work organisations (O'Brien, 2003; Laming, 2003, 2009). These reports all stress the importance of taking account of the changing environment in which social work is practised and highlight gaps in management skills.

A major review of social work services in Scotland took a fundamental look at all aspects of social work, including consideration of the requirements for strong leadership and management to underpin all of the developments emanating from the review. The review concluded that leadership was a concept that was relevant to all workers (Wilkinson, 2009) and that "social work services must develop enabling leadership and effective management at all levels and across the system" (Scottish Executive, 2006, p 94). Other policies (Scottish Executive, 2005) have also underlined the importance of effective management as well as:

- recognising the complexities of leading and managing in social work;
- making a call for a comprehensive framework of educational opportunities for social work managers to prepare managers for their role;
- developing effective leadership and management, with an emphasis on, for example, research-informed practice, inter-professional interagency working and critical decision making and reflection.

An ability to motivate and lead others is identified as a key personal capability required by managers and leaders hoping to promote continuous professional learning (Wilkinson, 2009) while the task of creating a 'learning and performance culture' is identified as a required organisational capability (SSSC and IRISS, 2008). This focus on a learning culture was earlier introduced by Skinner (2005) who recommended that employers examined the steps that could be taken to move towards social service organisations becoming learning organisations.

A number of reports point to the need for new organisational forms to meet the challenges of partnership working with many managers now leading multi-disciplinary, multi-professional teams (Van Zwanenberg, 2009). The inquiry into the death of Victoria Climbié (Laming, 2003) was particularly clear in identifying what it regarded to be severe and systematic failures of management and leaderships at all levels (Cullen, 2009) and such examples serve to highlight the necessity to develop systems of management that can operate effectively across organisational boundaries. The Department of Health (DH, 2000) envisaged that partnership working would lead to major redesign of the care system for England and Wales. As a consequence, in certain areas of England and Wales, health trusts and social service agencies were merged into one joint trust. Grace and Martin (2008, p 12) concluded that "the last decade has seen significant improvements in the performance of English local authorities in terms of ... (an) ability to work in partnership with other agencies", with adult social care services being cited as a particularly good example of an area of improved services.

Scotland has not witnessed such a centrally driven major reorganisation of social work agencies although the "growth of partnership working has sometimes caused traditional service boundaries to become blurred" (SWIA, 2009, p 5). Restructuring has been organised and developed differently with some organisations separating out aspects of services and joining with other resources, such as education (Van Zwanenberg, 2003). This has characterised itself in different ways, ranging from the merging of education and children's social work services departments to the creation of both Community Health and Community Health Care Partnerships.

This involves managers having to increasingly grapple with the challenges of managing the integration agenda with partner agencies and other parts of the local authority and requires certain skills and abilities in multi-disciplinary, multi-professional working (Van Zwanenberg, 2003). Leaders in such settings will be required to demonstrate special characteristics, particularly an ability to work with even more ambiguity than previously existed in more traditional social work settings (Close, 2009). Such challenges will be just as real and relevant in voluntary and independent organisations as in local authorities or other statutory settings. In certain situations this will entail the challenges involved with having a social work manager in a different location or a manager of a different profession closer to hand if you work in a hospital or school. These and other scenarios will involve highly developed communication and negotiation skills to ensure that positive working relationships are developed and maintained.

A requirement to work in partnership is also as pronounced within large single agencies as it is in multi-agency settings. The inquiry into the death of Caleb Ness highlights the imperative of good communication within agencies, as well as between agencies (O'Brien, 2003). Newly-qualified workers will require close support in managing such issues. Such factors serve to reinforce the importance of social work management education and the requirement for managers to be equipped to manage and support newly qualified workers.

Education for social work management

The changing face of management requires a different approach to management education: away from the approaches that assume that management direction and control is linear, to one that embraces the complexities of new and evolving working arrangements, recognising that development will take time and will require sophisticated support (Close, 2009).

Several policy initiatives and reviews (TOPPS England, 2000; Scottish Executive, 2005, 2006) stress the need for a collaborative approach to management education. The

Scottish Executive (2005) placed particular emphasis on the relationship between the employer organisations, universities, the college sector and other education providers to ensure that the needs of the employer organisations for a competent and confident workforce were fulfilled. They highlighted the need for partnership between the further and higher education sectors, employers and Centres of Excellence to undertake the essential role of supporting workforce development in social work agencies.

Van Zwanenberg (2003) suggested that this partnership approach should not only involve social work agencies but should be a multi-agency approach bringing together managers from social work and other related professional groups at key stages in the education process. The focus, according to Van Zwanenberg (2003), should be on the core values of social work, linked to professional standards, building skills in multi-professional/multi-agency working and contributing to both individual and organisational learning. In a more recent report Van Zwanenberg (2005) indicates that partnership education aimed at social work managers should not be the only option on offer, with specific education for social work managers still being appropriate.

Social work managers, mainly qualified social workers, come with a set of values, beliefs and attitudes about how to practise social work, but these do not always provide managers with a framework for managing that practice. The social interaction and networking on social work management education programmes should be designed to encourage a questioning, reflective approach to learning – building from the experience and knowledge that students bring with them to the academic course, but also challenging and encouraging the reframing of ideas. This runs parallel to points made by Skinner (2005) who, while exploring the concept of continuous professional development, highlighted a need to develop reflective practice but went on to say that while this was necessary it was often lacking.

It is also perhaps worth acknowledging that some frontline workers will themselves be thinking of a move into management and others may not want to do so now but may decide to later. As such, it is important for workers to think about how they might prepare for this. Obvious and easily accessible strategies may involve constantly reflecting on the manner in which they experience management and leadership and how effective they assess this to be as well as identifying activities of particular or potential relevance to management and leadership for the their continuous professional development activities.

Social work management support for newly-qualified workers

Newly-qualified social workers will require additional supports as they make the transition from student to practitioner. This chapter now examines some of the ways in which these supports may be delivered and organised. Within this section, reference will be made to a research study that examined the effectiveness of a post-qualifying social work management programme assessed at Scottish Credit and Qualifications Framework (SCQF) level 11, providing evidence of how prepared social work managers feel to undertake some of these roles (Watson, 2006).

Induction

The first few days of a new job can be amazing, with excitement and terror delivered in equal measures. Those starting in a new social work role are likely to feel no different, with any terror often being associated with anticipation regarding levels of professional responsibility, the management of risk and potentially heavy workloads. Good practice would dictate that newly-qualified social workers can and should expect a thorough induction to their new role and team as well as a phased development of their workload. There is a requirement for social workers to increasingly practise in a manner whereby they exercise professional autonomy (Scottish Executive, 2006). This necessitates that all workers be intimately familiar with the complex requirements of their role and for new social workers this process of familiarisation will begin with their induction.

The specific content and organisation of induction will be determined by the nature of the employer and the role in which any new worker is commencing, but there are certain principles that should remain consistent throughout. Induction may be organised by the specific team the new employee is joining or alternatively by a personnel or human resources section. Induction will allow for the transmission of basic information about the organisational structure and details concerning health and safety and other immediately relevant policies and procedures. Starting a new job will involve significant adjustment and an effective induction process should help workers adjust emotionally to their new workplace as well as conveying important cultural messages about what the organisation expects from employees (Torrington et al., 2008). Mullins (2005, p 817) states that an induction programme should: 'be designed to help new members of staff to familiarise themselves with their new environment, to settle easily into their new jobs and to establish harmonious working relationships with other members of staff'. Other literature more specific to social work identifies that the induction process can go beyond some of these more basic functions and allow exploration of the history of the team and its philosophy as well as beginning to find out what the new person can offer the team (Coulshed and Mullender, 2006). It would also be expected that induction would involve a process of socialisation as well as beginning to identify any training and development necessary for the new employee to effectively commence the job.

The ever-increasing requirement for social work organisations to work in inter-disciplinary settings means that social workers have to develop an awareness of not only their own agency but also those they may be likely to interact with. An introduction to other agencies and organisations should start during the induction process. The ability to network was viewed as an important benefit of study by social work managers undertaking management study (Watson, 2006). Consequently, new social workers should expect their managers to aid them with the task of beginning to form their own networks relevant to their new role.

Supervision

It is the task of the social work manager to elicit the best from their staff in order that clients receive the best service possible. The Association of Directors of Social Work (ADSW) and the Scottish Executive identified that when staff experience support that makes them feel valued there are a range of benefits to be gained:

> When staff feel valued and supported they are more easily retained and are off sick less; they will show greater motivation, commitment and flexibility; they will go 'the extra mile' to give of their best to service users; they will be a powerful force to promoting a positive public image of services and service providers. (ADSW and Scottish Executive, 2005, p.2)

Supervision should play a central role in the delivery of this support, although the functions of supervision are more complex than this alone. Different managerial roles will be potentially in tension and will need delicate handling as they require a balance of support alongside ensuring compliance with agency policies or the law. Morrison (2005, p 20) identifies eight distinct tasks for anyone involved in delivering supervision:

- ensuring the supervisee is clear about their roles, responsibilities and accountabilities;
- ensuring that the best interests of the service user are promoted;
- ensuring that the worker meets the agency's objectives and standards;
- ensuring that the worker has a manageable and appropriate workload;
- developing a supportive and positive climate for practice and performance;
- enhancing the worker's development;
- supporting the worker in managing the demands (tasks and emotional) of the work;
- promoting clear communication between the organisation and the worker.

Different frameworks also attempt to set out the main functions or roles of supervision. Kadushin (1976, cited in Hawkins and Shohet, 2000) set out three such functions – *educative*, *supportive* and *managerial*. The educative function is concerned with developing the skills, understanding and abilities of the supervisee and this will be achieved through reflection on and exploration of their work with clients. The importance of this educative function will be familiar to managers who have recently undertaken management training. Watson (2006) identified that social work managers commencing on social work management education indicated that obtaining a theoretical perspective was an anticipated benefit of the venture and by the end of their first academic year, comments from many students emphasised the importance of marrying practice and knowledge. The importance of the supportive function is vital for clients as well as for the supervisee. Effective supervision will respond to how workers engaged in practice may become affected by the distress and pain of the client as well as providing workers with the opportunity to become aware of how this has affected them and how to deal with any reactions. The managerial function reflects a responsibility for quality control. Supervisors may carry responsibility to ensure that the standards of the agency are being upheld as well as having some responsibility to ensure that the work of their supervisees is appropriate and falls within defined ethical guidelines.

The different functions are not totally separate but are combined to provide a comprehensive supervision experience. When discussing supervision, the Support Force for Children's Residential Care (1995, p7) commented that the functions are "intertwined like the strands of a rope". If any strand is weak this impacts on the other strands. "For example, helping staff develop is an effective way of offering them support, and both lead to better work. Like a rope, if one strand is weak, the rope is weak." In different settings and situations some functions will be more prominent than others. It would be hoped for newly-qualified social workers commencing on their career that in the initial stages the supportive function may be more prominent than the others. It is important that new workers engage in their supervision proactively to ensure that they receive the level and type of supervision required. This will require that new workers quickly begin to acknowledge and manage the power dynamics inherent within supervision.

While the potential benefits of supervision may be well-established, it is not always the case that it is delivered as frequently and effectively as it should be. Skinner (2005, p 17) highlighted the importance of reflective practice but went on to detail staff who commented on "the absence, infrequency and poor quality of staff supervision offered and its lack of attention to their developmental needs". Worryingly, following consultation with directors of social work, managers, practitioners and related organisations, she concluded that many staff did not seem to practice reflectively. They cited scarcity of time, lack of adequate staff supervision and lack of recent practice in doing so – the last of these due, they said, to lack of organisational expectation, encouragement and experience. This presents a significant challenge and may come as something of a culture shock for newly qualified workers, fresh from qualifying courses that underline and demand the need for critical reflection. Wilkinson (2009) highlights how continuous professional development is based around personal capabilities that involve self-awareness and self-management; however, barriers to reflective practice will not encourage a climate for learning and will be detrimental to the development of newly qualified workers.

Other factors may also create potential blocks for a new social worker and inhibit their ability to engage in an effective supervisory relationship – such as personal issues, their previous experience of supervision or a difficulty in receiving support (Hawkins and

Shohet, 2000). Often, however, the reasons behind an absence of supervision or its ineffective implementation can involve a lack of agency policies or standards on supervision, inadequate supervision arrangements, poor recording and a lack of prioritised time free from interruptions (Morrison, 2005).

Motivation and stress

The demands of being a newly qualified social worker can be extreme and a key role of a social work manager should be the support offered to help manage the process of transition, providing both motivation and, where possible, minimising stress. Theories of employee motivation are likely to be relevant as managers attempt to encourage best performance by promoting individual autonomy (Hafford-Letchfield, 2009). Social workers are likely to derive motivation from a number of factors, including economic rewards, satisfaction from the nature of the job itself and the social relationships formed within their work settings.

There is an increasing concern about workplace stress and its impact on wellbeing for social work and care staff. Social work managers are in a position to influence the factors that contribute to practitioner stress and wellbeing. The frontline manager has a responsibility for working to maintain systems, structures and cultures that support their staff and protect their wellbeing (Madden, 2007). The Scottish Executive (2006) recognised the need to motivate staff to encourage effective performance when it identified some of the negative experiences of social work staff associated with a blame culture, heavy and inequitable caseloads, demands exceeding resources and constant pressure loaded with crises. Failure to manage this can be a costly process for organisations, the staff within them and their service users:

> Apart from the millions of pounds lost each year studies show that sickness absence, stress and poor general health have a negative effect not only on the performance of the individuals concerned, but on the well being of colleagues and service users. It may also have a negative impact on morale.
> (ADSW/Scottish Executive, 2005, p 46)

Such factors can ultimately lead to organisations losing staff. A review of recruitment and retention conducted by the Audit Commission (2002) found that stress was the single biggest factor cited in the decision of staff to leave public sector organisations. However, it is also important that responsibility is not always placed on individual members of staff experiencing such issues. Coulshed and Mullender (2006) identify how emphasis is often placed on the individual, citing concepts such as emotional exhaustion. However, issues associated with this are often more systemic and there needs to be an awareness of this: *"since stress-related problems rarely appear in only one person at a time, organisations need to examine in what ways their systems might erode their staff's ability to cope"* (Coulshed and Mullender, 2006, p 182).

Skye *et al.* (2003) identify some of the means by which managers can support staff and reduce the likelihood of emotional strain and possible burn-out. Strategies can involve the provision of both a safe and a supportive context to raise work issues, a balance of different types of work, emotional and professional support as well as support to maintain boundaries between different areas of life. Coulshed and Mullender (2006, p 182) comment further on this theme and caution against line managers who have *"unrealistic expectations of what is possible, who give too little supervision and do not use it as an opportunity for praise, and who expect or allow work to seep into non-work time"*. As with the issues of supervision, it is important that new workers engage proactively with their line managers to ensure that they receive the level of support and motivation required. Like with supervision, this will require new workers to quickly begin to acknowledge and manage the power dynamics inherent within their line management arrangements. While aspects of this may be challenging, it is imperative that newly qualified workers begin to take proactive steps to ensure that they receive the necessary support and guidance at the outset of their career so that issues of motivation and stress are managed right from the beginning. In many ways this is also consistent with the expectation of critical self-reflection and development, which runs alongside requirements regarding continuous professional development.

Continuous professional development

Lishman (2002) comments upon how the uncertain and challenging arena of social work requires social workers to continually engage in a process of ongoing personal and professional development if they are to be able to practise effectively. Continuous professional development may take many forms and activities may involve study, training courses, seminars, reading, teaching and any other activities that will advance the development of workers. Importantly, Williams looks past the provision of such opportunities and thinks about the culture within which these are provided:

> CPD is not simply a matter of having flexible opportunities for training and employee development (essential though these are) but is connected intrinsically with the promotion of learning cultures within the workplace, the valuing of knowledge building and skills development and a solid commitment to evidence-based activity.
>
> (Williams, cited in Skinner, 2005, p 3)

Despite being at the very start of their professional social work career, and in many cases fresh from higher education institutions, newly qualified social workers need to engage in continuous professional development activities from the word go, not only for reasons of good practice but also for regulatory purposes. In a Scottish context, newly-qualified workers are required to engage in a minimum of 24 days (144 hours) of continuous professional development activity within the first 12 months of their registration with the Scottish Social Services Council (SSSC). The importance of continuous development cannot be understated and was identified by the Scottish Executive (2006) as a priority issue to be addressed.

Unfortunately, the difficulties involved in achieving some of these targets and requirements are significant. As well as highlighting the central importance of continuous professional development, the Scottish Executive (2006) commented on the requirement for increased investment in personal development across the sector if aspirations regarding lifelong learning are to become a reality. These challenges were highlighted by Skinner (2005) who commented that feedback from staff working in social services indicated that practice in continuous professional development was varied, not only between organisations but also between staff groups within organisations. Some of the difficulties in achieving good practice mirror issues raised by Watson (2006) when evaluating the experience of social work managers studying for a social work management qualification. Difficulties associated with the completion of their studies often involved a lack of support from line managers, assistance with their workload and an absence of dedicated study time.

The process of continuous professional development will not only enhance the practice and knowledge of individual practitioners but also has the potential to benefit the wider organisation. Managers should have a role to play in the development of agency policy, such ideas being consistent with the concepts of learning organisations and organisational learning. Frontline workers can feed into that process, either when consulted by management or when they individually or collectively identify an issue they think the agency has neglected or is not dealing with well. This further reinforces the importance of frontline workers engaging with management in a process of continual development, both as individual practitioners and as an agency.

As a final point it is perhaps worth noting that in their research exploring how organisations in Scotland are tackling the issue of leadership development, Tourish and Pinnington (2009, p 214) highlight the risk of lessons from development programmes not being taken back to the workplace and recommend that formal programmes have to be supplemented by "mentoring, coaching and other interventions designed to sustain deep reflection and ongoing learning in the real world of work". This factor highlights very clearly the need for continuous professional development to sit alongside other effective processes, of which induction and supervision will be vital components.

Conclusions

A number of key reports and policy frameworks contain much content significant to the task of managing and leading social work services. Social work managers require the ability to motivate and recognise the challenges presented by the modern social work landscape of inter-professional and interagency working. Central to this is the requirement to induct, support and supervise newly qualified social workers in an effective manner so as to maximise motivation and minimise stress.

In addition to an expectation that this be a process that employers engage in from the outset, the evidence from various sources (Skinner, 2005; Scottish Executive, 2006; Watson, 2006) suggests that numerous barriers exist, which can impact negatively on the provision of necessary supports – especially adequate supervision and access to meaningful and effective opportunities for continuous professional development. As such it is vital that newly qualified workers are both aware of the supports that they should expect and able to advocate for their provision. Learning and the development of competence and expertise will take time, especially the reflective learning that is required for social work, and effective induction, supervision and continuous professional development will be central to this process.

References

ADSW (Association of Directors of Social Work) and Scottish Executive (2005) *Improving Frontline Services: A framework for supporting frontline staff* Edinburgh: Scottish Executive.

Audit Commission (2002) *Recruitment and Retention: A public service workforce for the twenty-first century* London: Audit Commission.

Close, P (2009) 'From Transition to Transformation: Leading the management of change' in McKimm, J and Phillips, K (eds) *Leadership and Management in Integrated Services* Exeter: Learning Matters, pp 73-92.

Coulshed, V and Mullender, A (2006) *Management in Social Work* (3rd edition), Basingstoke: Palgrave Macmillan.

Cullen, A (2009) 'Leadership and Management: Not losing sight of both' in Van Zwanenberg, Z (ed) *Leadership in Social Care* London: Jessica Kingsley Publishers, pp 54-68.

DH (Department of Health) (2000) *A Quality Strategy for Social Work* London: The Stationery Office.

Douglas, A (2009) *Partnership Working* Abingdon: Routledge.

Grace, C and Martin, S (2008) *Getting Better all the Time? An independent assessment of local government improvement and its future prospects* London: IDeA.

Hafford-Letchfield, T (2009) *Management and Organisations in Social Work* (2nd edition), Exeter: Learning Matters.

Hawkins, P and Shohet, R (2000) *Supervision in the Helping Professions* (2nd edition), London: Open University Press.

Laming, Lord (2003) *The Victoria Climbié Inquiry: Summary Report of an Inquiry* London: The Stationery Office.

Laming, Lord (2009) *The Protection of Children in England: A Progress Report* London: The Stationery Office.

Lishman, J (2002) 'Personal and Professional Development' in Adams, R, Dominelli, L and Payne, M (eds) *Social Work Themes, Issues and Critical Debates* (2nd edition), Basingstoke: Palgrave, pp 95-108.

Madden, R (2007) 'Liability and Safety Issues in Human Services Management' in Aldgate, J, Healy, L, Malcolm, B, Pine, B, Rose, W and Seden, J (eds) *Enhancing Social Work Management: Theory and Best Practice from the UK and USA* London: Jessica Kingsley Publishing, pp 149-78.

Morrison, T (2005) *Staff Supervision in Social Care: Making a real difference for staff and service users* Brighton: Pavilion.

Mullins, L (2005) *Management and Organisational Behaviour* (7th edition), Harlow: Prentice Hall.

O'Brien, S (2003) *Report of the Caleb Ness Inquiry: Executive summary and recommendations: Edinburgh and the Lothian's child protection committee* Edinburgh: The Stationery Office.

Scottish Executive (2005) *National Strategy for the Development of the Social Service Workforce in Scotland 2005-2010: A plan for action* Edinburgh: The Stationery Office.

Scottish Executive (2006) *Report of the 21st Century Social Work Review: Changing Lives.* Edinburgh: The Stationery Office.

SSSC and IRISS (Scottish Social Services Council and Institute for Research and Innovation in Social Services) (2008) *The Framework for Continuous Learning in Social Services* Dundee: SSSC/IRISS.

Skinner, K (2005) *Continuing Professional Development for the Social Services Workforce in Scotland* Dundee: SIESWE.

Skye, E, Meddings, S and Dimmock, B (2003) 'Theories for Understanding People' in Henderson, J and Atkinson, D (eds) *Managing Care in Context* London: Routledge, pp 211-36.

SWIA (Social Work Inspection Agency) (2009) *Guide to Supported Self-Evaluation: Building excellent social work services* Edinburgh: SWIA.

Support Force for Children's Residential Care (1995) *Staff Supervision in Children's Homes* London: Department of Health.

TOPPS England (Training Organisation for the Personal Social Services – England) (2000) *Modernising the Social Care Workforce: The first national training strategy for England* Leeds: TOPPS England,

Torrington, D, Hall, L and Taylor, S (2008) *Human Resource Management* (7th edition), Harlow: Prentice Hall.

Tourish, D and Pinnington, A (2009) 'Learning from Current Trends in Leadership Development in Scotland' in Van Zwanenberg, Z (ed) *Leadership in Social Care* London: Jessica Kingsley Publishing, pp 198-216.

Van Zwanenberg, Z (2003) *Leadership and Management Development in Social Work Services: A report of a research study undertaken by the Scottish Leadership Foundation on behalf of the Scottish Executive* Edinburgh: The Stationery Office.

Van Zwanenberg, Z (2005) *Leadership and Management Development in Social Services Organisations: Short life study.* Edinburgh: The Stationery Office.

Van Zwanenberg, Z (2009) Leadership for 21st Century Social Work in Van Zwanenberg, Z (ed) *Leadership in Social Care* London: Jessica Kingsley, pp 13-26.

Watson, J E R (2006) 'Social Work Management Education in a Changing Context: A case study of an academic social work management course', unpublished thesis, Glasgow: University of Strathclyde.

Wilkinson, C (2009) 'Leadership and Learning: The purpose of a continuous learning framework for social care' in Van Zwanenberg, Z (ed) *Leadership in Social Care* London: Jessica Kingsley Publishing, pp 149-61.

Chapter 5

Anti-oppressive Practice: Its continued relevance in the 21st century

Lena Dominelli

Introduction

British society has become increasingly unequal, a fact not helped by the current fiscal crisis whereby the financial system has been saved at the expense of public expenditures in the welfare sector. These measures have intensified existing structural inequalities that are based on a social system that places profits before people. Poverty, low incomes and reduced access to health, education and the personal social services are the result. This situation is not unique to the UK: poverty is increasing within and between countries, with women and children being the most affected (UNDP, 2009). Such harsh realities make it imperative that social workers who work with excluded and marginalised peoples who bear the brunt of such inequalities promote anti-oppressive and empowering practice wherever they can.

In this chapter I explore the relevance of anti-oppressive social work to today's complex understandings of practice and argue that anti-oppressive practice (AOP) continues to have an important place in a social worker's repertoire of skills for contemporary practice. I base my arguments on the innovations that AOP has brought about in the profession.

Defining oppression and anti-oppressive practice

Oppression is the devaluing of individuals and groups in any or all aspects of their lives. The dynamics of oppression involve a 'superior' or dominant group of people marginalising or denying opportunities to one defined as 'inferior' or subjugated. This binary becomes the tool for 'othering' people by configuring relationships between them as part of the included group (us) or the excluded one (them). Inclusion and exclusion may be based on negative or stereotyped perceptions of others' characteristics, area of residence, behaviour and so on.

I have defined AOP as:

> *a form of social work practice which addresses social divisions and structural inequalities in the work that is done with people whether they be*

users ('clients') or workers and which aims to provide more appropriate and sensitive services which respond to people's needs regardless of their social status. Anti-oppressive practice embodies a person-centred philosophy, an egalitarian value system concerned with reducing the deleterious effects of structural inequalities upon people's lives; a methodology focusing on both process and outcome; and a way of structuring relationships between individuals that aims to empower users by reducing the negative effects of hierarchy.

(Dominelli, 1993, pp 11 and 24)

This definition attempts to engage holistically with the interactive, complex and fluid social relations that feature in people's lives. These are embedded in people's identities or who they are, as they create themselves and are created in and through social relations. A holistic approach to identity enables a practitioner to address all those aspects that are relevant (for example, 'race', gender, age, class, disability, culture and religion) without pitting one against the other or choosing one of these dimensions above another in a hierarchy of oppression. They all become important and have to be addressed at some point, depending on what a particular intervention aims to achieve. Seeing identity as complex and fluid and constructed in and through social relations enables practitioners to respond to an individual as a unique person while at the same time acknowledging that they are part of a wider, socially constructed collective group and take the implications of this position into account when working out how to engage a service user. Hence, it is important to understand both what it means to an individual to be, for instance, a woman or older person, and the structural significance of gender and age. Holistic practice is an integral part of AOP because it enables a practitioner to link the personal with the structural elements of oppression; understand the connections between one aspect of one's life and another; and envisage connections that exist between peoples and one part of a system and another.

Contextualising anti-oppressive practice

AOP has an honourable pedigree in British social work, but it is contested territory and often has practitioners wondering how to realise empowering AOP in the field (Khan and Dominelli, 2000). AOP has featured in the British social work literature since the 1980s and is exemplified in the writings of Dominelli (1991, 1993, 2002a; Braye and Preston-Shoot (1995) and Dalrymple and Burke (1995). AOP in the United Kingdom (UK) arose from the ashes of radical social work (Bailey and Brake, 1975) after it had been taken to task for not addressing a range of social divisions including gender, class, culture, religion, 'race' and ethnicity and for creating a hierarchy of oppressions whereby those who were oppressed competed with each other to establish credentials as the most oppressed individual or group. AOP retains several elements of the radical tradition that it actively promotes. Meanwhile, Ferguson (2008) is seeking to revitalise radical social work for contemporary societies. The items that AOP retains from its radical past include:

- being based on human rights and citizenship;
- seeing individuals as agents in their own lives;
- focusing on structural inequalities;
- promoting empowering forms of practice;
- linking individual growth with that of community development;
- theoretical and practice innovations.

As an inheritor of the radical mantle, AOP also has links to other forms of social work usually associated with a commitment to social emancipation (Freire, 1972) both in the UK and overseas. These include:

- strengths-based social work in the United States (US) (Saleebey, 2001);
- structural social work in Canada (Mullaly, 1997);
- feminist social work in the UK (Dominelli and McLeod, 1989; Dominelli, 2002b);
- anti-racist social work in the UK (Dominelli, 1998);
- black and Africentric perspectives in social work in the UK (Ahmad, 1990; Graham, 2002);
- constructionist social work in the UK (Parton and O'Byrne, 2000);
- critical theory in Australia (Fook, 2002);
- postmodern social work in Australia (Healy, 2002);
- first Nations social work in Canada (Bruyere, 2001; Green and Thomas, 2007);
- Maori constructs in social work in Aotearoa/New Zealand (Tait-Rolleston and Pehi-Barlow, 2001).

AOP's critical stance towards existing social relations have often placed it on a collision course with policy makers and opinion formers who believe that society is best organised as it is and that any failure of individuals to thrive is due to their own personal inabilities and deficiencies in making the most of opportunities afforded to them (see Phillips, 1993, 1994; Pinker, 1993).

The values, knowledge and skills bases of anti-oppressive empowering practice

Egalitarian, social justice-based values

AOP has been embedded in the egalitarian values of social work. These include the following:

- empowerment, sometimes seen as self-determination;
- equality between and among peoples;
- social justice as the basis for recognising claims aimed at righting past wrongs;
- human rights and entitlement to services;
- addressing personal needs and structural inequalities;
- holistic approaches to people and communities.

These values link AOP with what ought to be good practice in general, and can be used by practitioners who feel comfortable with social work's traditional values, but are unfamiliar with the tenets of AOP, to guide the orientation of their work. Practising these values is complicated as each has to be contextualised and interpreted within specific settings before it can be applied. This leaves room for dispute. Additionally, these values have been criticised for being Western-oriented (Yip, 2005) and thereby promoting the forms of exclusion that AOP opposes.

Although AOP is committed to developing emancipatory forms of practice and eliminating inequality in all its forms, it has been critiqued by post-modern theorists for:

- relying on unitary forms of identity that are fixed, unchanging and uniform or what is termed 'essentialist';
- seeking to change society through the medium of professional social work;
- adopting an overtly political position that opposes social injustice in and through practice;
- being naive and idealistic.

These criticisms have to be taken seriously as they can undermine AOP's claims to being on the side of oppressed people and promoting social justice. At the same time, it is crucial not to become so apologetic about its failings that its strengths are ignored, or the apology undermines its capacity to support those in need of allies. For example, I would argue that accepting the charge that AOP values are Western-oriented runs the risk of ignoring the commitment to equality, social justice and empowerment in many other world traditions, even if these are differently expressed. For instance, the ideal of equality has appealed to millions of people in China and elsewhere, so should not be seen as the preserve of the West. After all, Westerners can hardly claim to having implemented equality across the whole of their societies as is witnessed by increasing inequalities under neo-liberalism and the loss of civil liberties to wage a 'war on terror' in the name of national security.

Knowledge and skills for anti-oppressive practice

Practitioners working in empowering ways across difference have a considerable range of knowledge and skills to acquire through training and continuing professional development, keeping up-to-date and becoming aware of the latest research that could improve their practice. The knowledge wheel (see Figure 5.1 below) identifies these in diagrammatic form. Before they can be used, the knowledge, skills and values represented in this Figure have to be *contextualised*.

Figure 5.1: The knowledge wheel for anti-oppressive practice

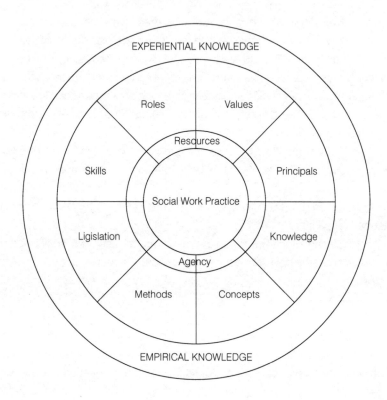

Source: Dominelli (2008)

These skills can be taught in the classroom and on placement where practice can be supervised and individuals supported to become confident and highly proficient anti-oppressive practitioners. Contexutalisation provides the point at which general knowledge and understanding becomes particular or relevant to the specifics of the given situation in which an intervention is scheduled to take place. It requires the practitioner to:

- engage with the service user and work to develop egalitarian working partnerships with them;
- think about that particular person and their circumstances including their social, financial and physical environments;

- understand the wider systems in which their relationships are embedded;
- assess the impact of both the personal and structural dimensions of their lives on the behaviour of that individual (or group or community if that is the practitioner's focus of attention) and those of the people with whom they are relating.

This would include family, religious institutions, social networks and other relationships that are important to that person at that specific juncture in their life. And, it would enable a social worker to find the gaps in people's relationships or their 'social capital' (Putnam, 2000). Social capital exists in three forms – bonding, bridging and linking. A practitioner who can see that family relationships (bonding social capital) need to be extended, can be inspired to engage the service user in creating 'bridging social capital' by developing wider links within their community, or expanding their horizons through 'linking social capital' to create even wider networks.

Contexts tailor a general understanding of a social phenomenon to a specific situation and individual. They cannot be ignored in empowering social relations. Contexts have to be examined and assessed for their specificity and relevance before they can be used. When contextualising practice, anti-oppressive practitioners have to:

- understand the dynamics of oppression – this includes how these are produced and reproduced in personal thought processes, attitudes and behaviours; and how they become embedded in institutional routines and cultural practices and norms;
- appreciate people as complete human beings who live in specific socio-political and historic contexts that require holistic interventions to address their problems;
- become aware of the connections between their own personal beliefs, institutional policies and cultural practices and how these impact upon their relationships with service users and others;
- realise how the dynamics of oppression interact with, feed off each other and change through negotiated interactions with people;
- form alliances to eliminate oppression in both the personal and the structural aspects of social life, including with those outside social work, especially in social policy;
- support claims for human rights, entitlement to services and social justice;
- promote resilience and the capacity of those they work with to take control of their lives.

Realising the above tenets in practice may be difficult. Encountering obstacles can cause practitioners to become disheartened in their work. The dynamics of oppression can be difficult to comprehend and can complicate interventions if they are poorly understood.

They combine both the personal and the structural dimensions of oppression, interacting with each other to reinforce and feed off each other in a constantly moving dance (see Figure 5. 2).

Figure 5.2: Interactive dimensions of oppression

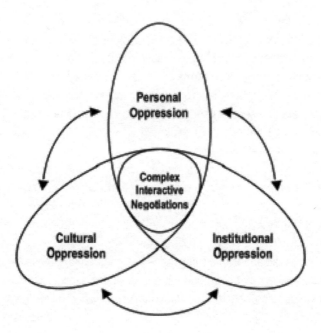

Source: Adapted from Dominelli, L (2008)

An individual will experience personal oppression as a bias or form of discrimination against them individually, based on some aspect(s) of their identity that is used to classify them as inferior or less deserving of opportunities than someone else. Oppression draws on stereotypical responses that do not take account of a person's specific skills, talents or merits. Oppression occurs within institutional settings within which, legislation, policies and routines oppress the individual directly or indirectly, usually as a member of a specific collective group that is deemed inferior or less deserving than others.

These complicated dynamics also call for a sophisticated, holistic approach to various interventions. Figure 5.3 indicates the range of levels, systems, factors and relationships that social workers engage with when promoting holistic, AOP. Interventions that use this holistic chart indicate that the processes of oppression:

  • operate in the interstices of everyday life to integrate personal behaviour with
    the social structures of society and encompass its personal, institutional and

cultural levels and all are implicated in creating oppressive situations and relationships;

- 'other' people through binary dyads that can either include or exclude and marginalise people while undermining their aspirations for a better life;
- normalise people in the dominant group at the expense of those in the subordinate one;
- emphasise commonalities within and across social divides at the expense of diversity among people as this becomes devalued and the categories of insiders and outsiders are created within a population;
- deny people agency and control over their lives in the personal, institutional and cultural domains except for members of the privileged group;
- reproduce inegalitarian social relations throughout society.

Appraising and constantly reappraising these dynamics is crucial for social workers, so they do not draw on stereotypical assumptions about who people are but respond to self-defined specific identities when working with and across diversities. It also enables them to visualise and engage with the multiplicity of roles and aspects of their lives that people combine in one identity and those they choose to present to others depending on what they seek to achieve through a given interaction. By engaging with these complexities, it is possible to avoid 'othering' people or locking them into binary relations that focus on 'those who are like me' (us) and 'those who are different from me' (them) to examine those elements that people have in common with each other and those that are different. For example, a white English practitioner might find that a black British service user with a different ethnic origin shares a love of reggae music that could enable them to connect on the basis of musical tastes and discover what strengths the service user has that might be brought to bear on solving the problems that require social work intervention. In such a situation, music becomes a source of connection that might be more powerful than that accorded to the social worker through formal status as a professional with a legislated right to intervene; and can provide an entry point into understanding the different elements of the service user's life that have resulted in particular difficulties requiring formal attention. Practitioners who understand these dynamics can avoid the pitfalls that complex, constantly changing, oppressive social relationships bring in their wake and thereby combine responding to individual uniqueness while simultaneously locating them in their social context and position as active players in creating the circumstances of their lives.

Figure 5.3: Holistic empowering practice chart

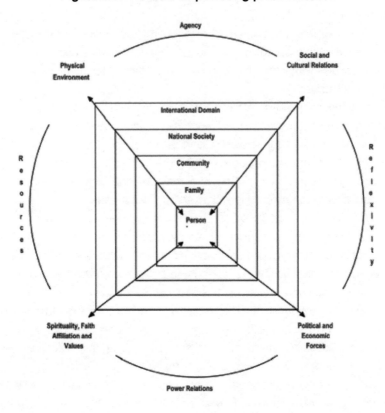

Source: Adapted from Dominelli (2002)

Narratives of belonging, exclusion and power

Identity is associated with feelings of belonging (or not) to a particular space and being accepted as such (or not) and is nurtured by the 'them-us' binary that divides a polity into acceptable and unacceptable groups (Dominelli, 2008). Rejection becomes the basis for social exclusion and perpetuation of oppressive relationships. It can be psychologically as well as socially damaging to individuals and relationships between them.

Narratives of rejection cast the other person as expendable or unnecessary in a particular situation and are indicative of 'power over' relationships where power is assumed to be a zero-sum game in which they can enforce their views. Its assumptions contrast with Foucauldian views of power as multi-faceted, interactive and configured in and through social relationships (Foucault, 1980). 'Power over' relations can occur on any front – 'race', ethnicity, culture, religion, gender, age, class, disability, sexual orientation and so on, individually or in any combination. Seeing power as a zero-sum game forms part of a powerful ideology that enables people to be objectified and cast as insignificant, threatening or less than human. This depiction of other people may even lead to violence against those deemed the objects of other people's actions, and/or inferior.

Other power relations can include those of the 'power to do' something. These are normally associated with agency and the capacity to take control of one's life either individually or collectively through group action, often undertaken with others like oneself. 'Power with' relations imply a sharing of power, which can be used to transcend differences and find common purpose with those unlike oneself in order to act. Thus, the 'power to do' or take action and 'power with' or working in partnership are used in promoting AOP. All of these ways of conceptualising power relations have to be understood by practitioners if they are going to ·act in empowering ways that promote the capacities of service users to act as agents of their own futures.

Figure 5.4 indicates the various narratives or stories that people use to define their sense of space and place and the extent to which they accept or reject others as being part of it. Several of these narratives can coexist with each other and they can also overlap. These spaces are contested places whereby people seek to protect their territory and jostle for ascendancy as in the first two positions (top centre and right, moving clockwise); demand that space is shared by all groups as in the next three positions; and agree to share their space in egalitarian relationships as in the sixth position (clockwise from the top).

Figure 5.4: Narratives of place and space

Source: Adapted from Dominelli (2008)

I now consider an example whereby a zero-sum view of power is used to oppress individuals and groups. I focus on Peter Connelly, otherwise known as Baby P, to demonstrate how adultism was a crucial dynamic that got in the way of social workers understanding what was going on in that particular 'family'. Adultism prioritises the needs and views of adults over those of children and leads to the abuse of power that crosses gender divides (Dominelli, 1989). In Peter's case, there were several forms of oppression and hierarchies of power relations at play. Adultism was one; sexism was another; and poverty was a further one. There were others, but I will limit my discussion to these given time and space constraints because I think they were absolutely crucial to what went wrong. Adultism was influential in configuring Peter as a toddler dependent on the adults in his life to meet his needs. He was expected to be like an adult and jostle for his space in the 'family' in complete contradiction to his actual position as dependent or someone who the adults should have been caring for.

Baby P was murdered in August 2007 at the age of 17 months. His mother, her boyfriend, and her boyfriend's brother were found guilty and sentenced to prison for his death. The child lived surrounded by poverty and violence along with other problems. The boyfriend and his brother were both violent men. Baby P was known to Haringey Children's Department and had been seen 60 times by health practitioners, the police and social workers. Except for one social worker, they did not diagnose Peter as a child who was being abused by his carers at home, even though he had been taken to hospital with serious injuries on a number of occasions.

Adultism enabled the three adults (the mother, her boyfriend and her boyfriend's brother) caring for Baby P to place the fulfilment of their needs above Peter's. They abused their power through the use of violence to ensure that this was how relationships in the household were conducted. Had the social workers involved in this case, understood these dynamics, they could have made certain that they specifically questioned the adults about Peter's care instead of making assumptions about it and taking the adults' words at face value. Had they carried out a holistic anti-oppressive assessment, the practitioners would have been able to see that these adults had their own problems and differentiate between Peter's needs and those of the three adults. They would have sought to address all of these issues, while referring the adults to other services if unable to address these directly themselves. A holistic approach would have assisted the social workers constantly to ask themselves, who was the 'client' they were trying to serve? Recognising their different positions within the family and taking account of power hierarchies between them would have highlighted the importance of not using the same social worker to engage with all members of one 'family'.

In this holistic assessment, the social workers would have been able to uncover the sexism that gave the men power over the mother and dictated how she ran her life. This would have included that of being subservient to their wishes on a gender basis – a matter that the men reinforced with power, including using force. The mother's fear of being without a man in her life would have meant that she would be psychologically subservient and submit to her boyfriend's demands, doing whatever would please him to keep him with her. Earlier, this man's use of gender violence extended to raping a two-year-old girl. As these sexist dynamics would interact with those embedded in adultism, Peter's needs would come a poor second to this man's. These four lived in poverty. For them, the environment became a constraining factor that would have compounded their difficulties and limited their aspirations for themselves and Peter. Understanding the structural configuration of the family and the dynamics of their interpersonal interactions as people with individual needs would have enabled practitioners to see that at moments of stress, Peter would have been deemed a nuisance or expendable as the adults struggled to meet their own needs.

A social worker who understood how power dynamics in these relationships served to exclude Peter from being considered as a person with rights and entitlements on the same basis as the powerful ones in his 'family' circle would have been better able to protect his interests, advocate for him and remove him from an unsafe situation. This would have facilitated their accountability for Peter's well-being and made it easier for practitioners to discharge their duties and not conflate Peter's needs with those of the adults in the relationship. It would have also assisted in the allocation of resources to the family on a differentiated basis that prioritised Peter's needs without neglecting those of the mother and the two men in her life. An approach that acknowledged the presence of sexism in this 'family' would have meant that the mother's need to escape an abusive relationship would have been highlighted and she could have been empowered to obtain help too. The men also required assistance, particularly that which would teach them how to relate to other people – men, women and children – without having to abuse their power to negotiate the fulfilment of their needs.

Working in empowering, anti-oppressive ways

AOP draws on a practitioner's capacity to think holistically, reflectively and creatively in using their professional judgement; look for connections between what is known and not known; think of appropriate ways of working with service users that do not rely on stereotypes; examine and investigate the specificities of a particular situation rather than simply ticking boxes; and be innovative in meeting people's needs with the resources to hand. Nothing would be taken for granted; everything would be questioned and explored for its ramifications in what was done or not done. A critical reflective and reflexive stance is crucial in understanding how to address diversity and difference, especially those elements that a practitioner might be unfamiliar with, or hesitant about. For example, a practitioner who lacks confidence to work with, say, a Muslim service user and feels that they have reached an impasse in knowing what to do, should identify resources that will help them get beyond this blockage without undermining the person's right to receive an appropriate service or their dignity. These resources range from support from colleagues and a supervisor who might be more knowledgeable about this particular skilled area of work, making links with Muslim organisations to see what resources might be accessed and undergoing further training in handling diversity and difference so that they feel confident in working with those receiving services, regardless of the basis of their difference.

Training can provide guidelines and these could be useful in a variety of circumstances and in identifying how to make the most of the resources at hand. An illustration is provided by the 'substitution strategy' whereby a practitioner can use a simple 'what if' question to reflect on their behaviour in a particular situation (Dominelli, 2008). For instance, the social worker could ask: 'What if this person were like me, a white working-class British man, would he think/act in the same way? How is what I am doing or saying different or is it the same? Am I being paralysed by fear of doing the wrong thing? How do I empower myself in this situation? Who do I go to for help if I am stuck?'.

Another useful way of thinking about this situation is to examine similarities and differences between people, focus on their needs and highlight those that they have in common and those that are different. This would build on the substitution strategy that relies on a practitioner substituting a person from the 'them' or excluded category with one in the 'us' or included category to reflect on the dynamics of oppression and/or empowerment that are being enacted in a particular situation. This can be conceptualised as individuals and groups 'X' (the excluded one) and 'Y' (the included one). This conceptualisation is generalisable in that it can be used to reflect on any group, regardless of whether the identity being considered is based on 'race', ethnicity, culture, religion, sexual orientation, disability, gender, class or other social division. This approach should reveal those elements that people have in common, those that converge and those that diverge from one another.

A starting point is that of exploring both common and different needs. Those needs that people have in common can provide the basis for looking at which ones each individual has to have fulfilled and enables the practitioner to give attention to how this might be done without pitting the needs of one group against another. Drawing on international instruments such as the Universal Declaration of Human Rights (UDHR), which all countries that are members of the United Nations (UN) including the UK have signed and incorporated into national legislation; can be helpful in achieving such aims. For example, Articles 22 to 27 of the UDHR refer specifically to general human needs such as food, clothing and shelter. In addition, these specifically highlight education, health and the personal social services, which social workers are constantly negotiating in responding to service users' claims for assistance (George, 2003).

I have created Figure 5.5 on convergent and divergent needs, which enables practitioners to examine these in a systematic manner and reproduce it below. It depicts the different points at which social workers negotiate needs that are common, convergent and divergent across and within groups at both individual and collective levels. The different needs can be plotted on this chart and enable the social worker to make comparisons between the services that are needed and those that are offered to different types of groups. Plotting these on the chart can be done as an exercise whereby the practitioner reflects on the implications of different choices that they *might* make before they actually deliver them in practice. In this way, they can also look at the 'fit' between different claims on their resources and the demands for them. If used before delivering a service, adjustments can be made as the discussions with the service user develop.

Figure 5.5: Converging and diverging needs

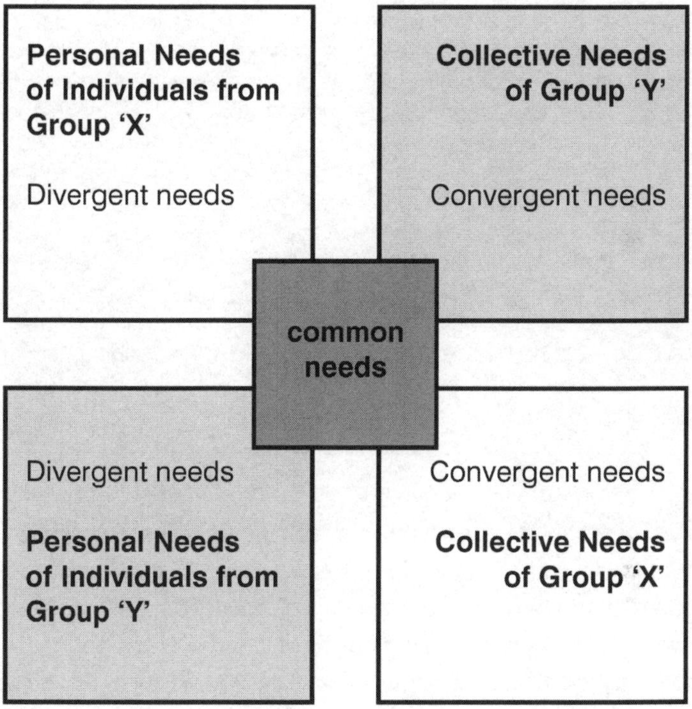

Personal Needs of Individuals from Group 'X' Divergent needs	Collective Needs of Group 'Y' Convergent needs
	common needs	
Divergent needs Personal Needs of Individuals from Group 'Y'	Convergent needs Collective Needs of Group 'X'

Source: Adapted from Dominelli (2008)

Box 5.1 is a case study that can be used to explore issues raised by AOP.

Box 5.1
Case study: respecting older people within acceptable professional boundaries

Gwen was an 80-year-old white woman with limited mobility and mild dementia. She had a good relationship with her social worker. And, unlike many of her friends, whose social workers changed every few months, Gwen had had the same one for five years. Gwen felt she had developed a good relationship with her social worker, a middle-aged white woman called Jane. She looked forward to 'fussing' over Jane, making her sponge cakes for tea. Jane was fond of Gwen, but she did not like her giving her tea and cakes whenever she went to see her. She was also worried that Gwen was becoming dependent on her. But she didn't want to alienate her.

Gwen was coping well with the deterioration in her health and she loved to feel that she was still a useful member of society and could offer something to those who cared for her. However, when Jane came to see her one day, she had laid out a sumptuous tea – cucumber sandwiches, crumpets, a lovely sponge cake and a pot of tea. Jane looked at the spread and tried hard to cover her irritation at Gwen spending her limited cash in this way, especially when she felt that she could not partake of the spread.

Jane's predicament shows how different perceptions of a situation can produce ethical dilemmas and conflicting outcomes for social workers. Jane is trying to maintain her professionalism by drawing limits or boundaries around what she deems acceptable behaviour when it comes to accepting hospitality. A cup of tea and piece of cake is alright. More food than that is not. Jane does not think about this situation from Gwen's point of view. Thus, she does not believe that she is being oppressive in her approach towards Gwen. However, Gwen wishes to show her appreciation of the support that Jane has offered her over the years. She has taken pleasure in preparing this spread and saved up to make it possible. Gwen finds Jane's failure to grasp her viewpoint oppressive. Even though she realises that Jane is a social worker exercising power associated with her status as a practitioner and operating within the constraints that her position imposes on her to behave professionally, Gwen feels offended by Jane's reaction. She feels her dignity and right to treat people as guests in her own home has been undermined. This upsets her.

Gwen's response indicates that she felt that Jane had denied her agency and the space within which to self-define her actions or act as she saw fit. These are important elements in AOP. Jane has to find a way of refusing the hospitality without offending

Gwen's sense of dignity and capacity to give back or thank someone for doing their job well. Intriguingly, the question to be asked of Jane is how she had handled Gwen's desire to thank her long before their relationship reached this point. For example, had she unintentionally indicated that she assumed tea and cakes would always be there for her instead of seeing them as a special treat that she could recognise as a token of Gwen's appreciation? An important thing would have been for Jane to reflect on this ritual and check that she and Gwen were working on the same page.

This case also indicates that long-standing relationships can get in the way of maintaining professional boundaries. However, adhering to their maintenance in simplistic ways like Jane did can become oppressive and damage a worker's relationship with a service user. Avoiding such conflicts can occur through a sensitive understanding of the complex power dynamics that are being played out in the situation, or they can be handled in a bureaucratic manner. Preventing the formation of such attachments and the ensuing conflict of interests that can arise is one reason why managers prefer to rotate social workers on a regular basis, and underscores a bureaucratic response to the issues raised. On the other hand, research has identified that service users value continuity (Dominelli *et al.,* 2005; Beresford *et al.,* 2008). These insights can be used to promote an AOP that builds service user capacity and accords them dignity and agency in their conduct.

Questions for further consideration regarding the case study

1   Consider the conflicting values that are evident in this situation.
2   How you would take control of the situation and re-establish more appropriate professional boundaries in the relationship? In your discussions, consider the context in which Gwen lives as well as the interaction between her and the social worker.
3   Would you allow Jane to continue being Gwen's social worker?

Conclusions

Promoting AOP is complicated and not necessarily straightforward. But it continues to be extremely important. It asks social workers to think about the whole person and respond to all forms of oppression that they might be experiencing, regardless of their source. Thus, gender, 'race', ethnicity, age, class, disability, religion, culture or any other aspect of identity can be taken on board without losing sight of the specificity of each. This means recognising that there are common dynamics that operate in all forms of oppression while their contexts and the particularities of each specific situation have to be distinguished so that they can be addressed appropriately and sensitively. An empowerment approach to practice requires social workers to think carefully about what they are doing, the contexts in which they are operating and the power relations that they are embedded within. To make the best use of their skills as anti-oppressive practitioners, it helps if they can:

- reflect on social inequalities and take action to eradicate these in their own practice;
- undertake individual and collective actions that will help to eliminate inequalities in society more widely in their personal, institutional and cultural dimensions;
- undertake research to acquire the evidence that highlights the social construction of inequality and marginalisation and regularly update their knowledge about the latest research findings;
- mobilise individuals and communities to challenge the perception that oppression is an inevitable part of life;
- help people to understand how oppression works by deconstructing it and exposing how its dynamics keep people in their place as controlled 'subjects';
- articulate egalitarian social relations that are controlled by those involved in them working in partnership with each other;
- form alliances to eliminate systemic inequalities in both social work practice and throughout the social order.

Questions for further consideration and discussion

- Why is anti-oppressive practice necessary in a society that claims to be democratic and egalitarian?
- Consider the relevance of your identity when you are meeting people who are similar to you and when you are meeting those different from you.
- How can you become empowered to feel more confident when working in empowering, anti-oppressive ways?
- How would you deal with multiple sources of oppression so as to avoid creating a hierarchy that prioritises one source of oppression over the others?
- How would you identify the training that you might need to empower yourself in working in accordance with the tenets of anti-oppressive practice?

References

Ahmad, B (1990) *Black Perspectives in Social Work* Birmingham: Venture Press.

Aubrey, C and Dahl, S (2006) 'Children's voices: The views of vulnerable children on their service providers and the relevance of services they receive' *British Journal of Social Work* 36(1), pp 21-40.

Bailey, R and Brake, M (1975) *Radical Social Work* London: Edward Arnold.

Beresford, P, Croft, S and Adshead, L (2008) '"We Don't See Her as a Social Worker': A Service User Case Study of the Importance of the Social Worker's Relationship and Humanity' *British Journal of Social Work* 38(7), pp 1388-407.

Braye, S and Preston-Shoot, M (1995) *Empowering Practice in Social Care* Buckingham: Open University Press.

Bruyere, G (2001) 'Making Circles: Renewing First Nations Ways of Helping' in Dalrymple, J and Burke, B (1995) *Anti-Oppressive Practice: Social care and the law* Buckingham: Open University Press.

Dominelli, L (1991) 'Anti-oppressive practice' in Dominelli, L, Patel, N and Thomas Bernard, W (eds) *Anti-Oppressive Paradigms for Practice* Sheffield: Sociological Studies, Sheffield University.

Dominelli, L (1993) *Social Work: Mirror of Society or Its Conscience? Inaugural lecture*, Department of Sociological Studies, Sheffield University, 26 May.

Dominelli, L (1996) 'Deprofessionalising social work: Equal opportunities, competence and postmodernism', *British Journal of Social Work* 26(2), pp 153-75.

Dominelli, L (1998) 'Anti-Racist Practice and International Social Work', published as 'Culturally Competent Social Work: A Way Towards International Anti-Racist Social Work?' in Guttierez, L, Zuniga, M and Lum, D (eds) (2003) *Education for Multicultural Social Work Practice* Alexandria, VA: Council on Social Work Education, pp 281-94.

Dominelli, L (2002a) *Anti-Oppressive Social Work Theory and Practice* London: Palgrave Macmillan.

Dominelli, L (2002b) *Feminist Social Work Theory and Practice* London: Palgrave Macmillan.

Dominelli, L (2004a) 'Practising Social Work in a Globalising World' in Tan, N T and Rowlands, A (eds) *Social Work Around the World III* Berne: IFSW.

Dominelli, L (2004b) *Social Work: Theory and Practice for a Changing Profession* Cambridge: Polity Press.

Dominelli, L (2008) *Anti-Racist Social Work* (3rd edition), London: BASW/Palgrave Macmillan.

Dominelli, L, Lorenz, W and Soydan, H (eds) (2001) *Beyond Racial Divides: Ethnicities in Social Work Practice* Ashgate: Aldershot.

Dominelli, L and McLeod, E (1989) *Feminist Social Work* London: Macmillan.

Ferguson, I (2008) *Reclaiming Social Work: Challenging Neo-Liberalism and Promoting Social Justice* London: Sage Publications.

Fook, J (2002) *Social Work: Critical theory and practice* London: Sage Publications.

Foucault, M (1980) *Power/Knowledge: Selected Interviews and Other Writings, 1972-77* New York: Pantheon Books.

Freire, P (1972) *Pedagogy of the Oppressed* Harmondsworth: Penguin.

George, S (2003) 'Globalizing rights?' in Gibney, M J (ed) *Globalizing Rights* Oxford: Oxford University Press.

Graham, M (2002) *Social Work and African-Centred Worldviews* Birmingham: Venture Press.

Green, J and Thomas, R (2007) 'Learning Through Our Children, Healing for Our Children: Best Practice in First Nations Communities' in Dominelli, L (ed) *Revitalising Communities in a Globalising World* Aldershot: Ashgate.

Healy, K (2000) *Social Work Practice: Contemporary Perspectives on Change* London: Sage Publications.

Healy, L (2002) *International Social Work: Professional Action in an Interdependent World* Oxford: Oxford University Press.

Khan, P and Dominelli, L (2000) *Social Work and Globalisation: A Report* Southampton: CISCODEV and Social Work Studies, Southampton University.

Laming, Lord (2009) *The Protection of Children in England: A Progress Report* London: DCSF.

Mullaly, R (1997) *Structural Social Work* Toronto: McClelland and Stewart.

Parton, N and O'Byrne, P (2000) *Constructive Social Work: Towards a New Practice* Basingstoke: Palgrave.

Phillips, M (1993) 'An Oppressive Urge to End Oppression' *The Observer*, 1 August.

Phillips, M (1994) 'Illiberal Liberalism' in Dunant, S (ed) *The War of the Word: The Political Correctness Debate*. London: Virago.

Pinker, R (1993) 'A Lethal Kind of Looniness', *The Times Higher Educational Supplement*, 10 September.

Saleebey, D (2001) 'Practising the Strengths Perspective: Everyday Tools and Resources', *Families in Society* 82(3), pp 221-22.

Tait-Rolleston, W and Pehi-Barlow, S (2001) 'A Maori Social Work Construct' in Dominelli, L, Lorenz, W and Soydan, H (eds) *Beyond Racial Divides: Ethnicity in Social Work* Aldershot: Ashgate.

UNDP (United Nations Development Programme) (2009) *The Human Development Report, 2009* New York: UNDP.

Yip, K S (2005) 'A Dynamic Asian Response to Globalisation in Cross-Cultural Social Work' *International Social Work*, 48, pp 593-607.

Younghusband, E (1978) *Social Work in Britain, 1950-1975* London: Allen and Unwin.

Chapter 6

Personalisation and the Role of the Social Worker

Duncan Mackay and Gillian MacIntyre

Introduction

Defining personalisation

The language of social work has often adopted words that sound as though they should be familiar and widely understood, but invite different interpretations amongst those who use them. A recent example of this is 'personalisation'. 'Personalisation' is a relatively recent term that has, in a short space of time, become the 'big idea', the dominant ideology in social policy that has attracted support from successive Westminster governments. In Scotland, too, it has received ministerial endorsement through adoption of the recommendations of *Changing Lives: The 21st century review of social work* (Scottish Executive, 2006), which stated: 'Increasing personalisation of services is both an unavoidable and desirable direction of travel for social work services'. In order to trace the historical development of the concept we need to look at its emergence across the United Kingdom (UK) but first it is necessary to outline what we mean by personalisation.

Personalisation has been, to date, a contested concept. Some argue that it is a concept that fits coherently with the ethos and values of best social work practice. Others suggest that it is an essentially consumerist vision that excludes the most marginalised people in our communities. In simple terms, the definition of personalisation given by the Scottish Government is: 'It enables the individual alone, or in groups, to find the right solutions for them and to participate in the delivery of a service. From being a recipient of services, citizens can become actively involved in selecting and shaping the services they receive' (Scottish Government, 2008, p 10).

In England, the Department of Health (DH) has outlined personalisation as being about 'the way in which services are tailored to the needs and preferences of citizens. The overall vision is that the state should empower citizens to shape their own lives and the services they receive' (Prime Minister's Strategy Unit, 2007, p 33). From a social work perspective, this can be interpreted as being about enabling people we work with to get the best possible life. People should be supported to achieve choice and control over their own lives and – as a logical extension – should be able to maximise choice and control over any support they may need in order to achieve a good life. Both of the definitions appear to make an assumption that personalisation is about exerting influence or control over services. While this may be the case for many people, it should not be assumed that the only way to achieve a good life is through the use of formal and organised social services.

The emergence of personalisation as a distinct concept is often attributed to Charles Leadbetter and the publication of *Personalisation through Participation* in 2004. He argued for a 'new script' for public services, describing the concept of "co-production" whereby people were viewed as active participants operating in partnership with public agencies in order to define their own needs and choose the support they require to meet these needs, rather than operating as merely passive recipients of processes and services.

Leadbetter has been criticised for seeking to apply a consumerist approach to public services. Ferguson (2007), for example, argues that personalisation is an acceptance of the marketisation of social work that promotes rather than challenges the de-professionalisation of social work practice. Others see the potential of personalisation to bring about radical change from the current position where 'professional and resource allocation and power are aligned on one side, with professionals defining the problem as well as authorising and implementing the solution' (Hunter and Ritchie, 2007, p 14). Whilst acknowledging that co-production is not a "magic fix", Hunter and Ritchie see it as an important way to tackle "some of the deep-rooted malaise in the contemporary human service system" provided it is supported by an "underpinning world view" and not viewed as a "technical bolt-on to an existing service system" (Hunter and Ritchie, 2007, p 14).

Why personalisation?

The growth of the personalisation agenda has its roots in two very different camps. It can be attributed in part to the work of the independent living movement, which has been defined as:

> ... *disabled people of all ages having the same freedom, choice, dignity and control as other citizens at home, at work, and in the community. It does not mean living by yourself or fending for yourself. It means the rights to practical assistance and support to participate in society and live an ordinary life.* (Equality and Human Rights Commission, 2009, p9)

The independent living movement emerged in the 1960s from a climate of civil rights activism in the United States (US). It did so because people with disabilities were deeply frustrated by the barriers they experienced in trying to achieve the modest aims outlined above. The language is strikingly similar to that of personalisation, where ideas of choice and control are prominent.

Personalisation can also be viewed as an important part of the wider modernisation agenda in social work and social care. Although this agenda has taken different forms across the UK, what is common across all four countries and indeed across Europe is growing pressure on existing provision alongside the anticipated growth in future demand as a result of changing demographics and particularly the projected increase in older people (Newman *et al.,* 2008). This will be exacerbated by financial pressures, which require financial cuts to public services. Such is the need for change that it is no longer enough to simply "do more of the same for less" (Scottish Executive, 2006). Arguably what is required will involve a significant cultural shift in the way in which support is provided to individuals and the role of social work within that process. The modernisation agenda in England has resulted in an increased emphasis on individualisation and on user directed and controlled services. The focus has increasingly been on changing the role of adult social care service users from passive recipients of services to managers of their own support as exemplified in the Green Paper *Independence, Well-being and Choice* (DH, 2005) and *Our Health, Our Care, Our Say* (DH, 2006).

Focusing on needs and outcomes for individuals and their carers by working in partnership to promote choice and control is an undoubtedly positive development, particularly when one considers the argument that traditional social work (or at least some aspects of it) had lost its way somewhat. Some services were designed in ways that required people to fit in with what was on offer rather than the other way around. Instead of supporting people to be connected or reconnected to their own communities, people were brought into services that were considered to be the most appropriate way to meet their needs. Day centres were created for older people, people with physical disabilities, people with learning disabilities and people with mental health problems. Often, perversely, they excluded people with the highest levels of need as the staffing ratios weren't adequate to meet those needs.

Day centres for older people were equipped with hairdressers instead of supporting people to get their hair done at the same hairdresser they had used all their lives, where they caught up with the gossip and mixed with their peers. Such services were even subsidised to make them more attractive. People were bussed out of their own communities to attend social work centres, disregarding the fact that people had a wide range of needs, interests and aspirations. Although some services succeeded in becoming more inclusive as envisaged in a range of policy documents such as *The same as You?* (Scottish Executive, 2000) and *Valuing People* (DH, 2001), others made only cosmetic changes. Instead of working with people in their own lives and communities they visited 'the community' on outings. People were taken ten-pin bowling because it was a fun, ordinary activity but this often took place when the facility opened at ten in the morning when no other bowlers were there.

Inflexible building-based services, and the identification of these services to meet needs, resulted in them being filled (not necessarily with people who had the highest needs) and the consequent creation of waiting lists. Capital was frequently invested in more of the same instead of equipping community centres and libraries with adult changing facilities and swimming pools with mobile hoists, facilitating inclusion and challenging stigma. There were major increases in funding for social work between 1998 and 2008 but too often this was invested in congregated, albeit smaller-scale, services.

Personalisation turns this thinking on its head. It makes clear that we need to work with the person concerned to identify what would constitute the best possible life. For all of us this usually relates to factors such as where we live, having relationships, making a contribution, having an income to make choices, having hopes and dreams; achieving changes in our life over time. Truly personalised approaches to meeting need will always include the people who are important to the individual concerned. Most of us choose to share our lives with others, but we make conscious choices in this respect. They are not usually arrangements imposed on us with other people we may not know or like, or who happen to share a similar label.

What Leadbetter (2004) describes as "co-production" is about true collaboration or partnership with people in identifying individual outcomes and how these may be achieved. By identifying intended outcomes we can assess the extent to which our intervention has been successful in achieving those outcomes. If we do not, we are more likely to measure outputs, for example how many hours a week of home care should continue to be provided.

No one would deny that an increased emphasis on choice and control is an important development, in keeping with the original aims of the independent living movement. Advocates of this approach may, however, view with concern any attempts to position personalisation as key to achieving required public sector savings, not because personalisation is not capable of achieving more efficient use of resources but because it increases the risk of being discredited if perceived as driven primarily by fiscal motives.

Developments in the personalisation agenda

The language of personalisation is often presented in confusing ways where terms like 'self-directed support', 'individual budgets' and 'direct payments' are used interchangeably or even in ways that are directly contradictory. If we think of personalisation as a broad concept – a way of thinking and working that enables people to maximise choice and control over their lives – self-directed support is best viewed as the term used to describe how people may exercise choice and control over any support they may require to lead a good life.

A defining feature of self-directed support is the concept of an individual (or personal) budget, informed by some form of supported self-assessment. It is the transparent upfront allocation of a resource (which in turn requires adoption of a resource allocation system) that enables people to make meaningful choices about how that resource may be used, and the extent to which they wish to assume control over all or some of the identified resource. While a direct payment is one of the ways – and often a good way – of doing this, it requires people to assume direct control over the resource, which not everyone wants to do. If direct payments are delivered in a single dimension and not available as part of a wider system of self-directed support, there is little choice over the extent to which people exercise control over the resource itself. It is effectively all or nothing, which is fine, but only for those who wish to exercise full control. Furthermore, if it is not part of a system of self-directed support, it does not fundamentally change what has been described as the 'gift' relationship between councils and citizens, that is, the social worker assesses your needs and tells you at the end of it what you get in the form of a financial 'gift' (which may be set at rates so low as to inhibit meaningful purchasing power).

In a system of self-directed support, people can still take all or some of the identified resource (which they have been part of determining through a co-production process, and know before any support or services are introduced) as a direct payment; they can place all or some of it with a third party such as an appointee or guardian to exercise on their behalf (legislation varies in the UK over the legalities of such arrangements); or they can simply be aware of it as a virtual budget but have no desire to control it and receive directly provided or commissioned support.

While recognising the evolution of this wider context, it is important not to minimise the impact of direct payments, which perhaps provided the first clear evidence of a shift towards increasing choice and control by the citizen. Direct payments were introduced in Scotland, England and Wales in 1997 as a result of the Community Care (Direct Payments) Act 1996. Originally, local authorities were able to make cash payments to service users under the age of 65 with physical or sensory impairments, learning disabilities or mental health problems. This was later extended to include people over the age of 65, 16- and 17-year-olds and parents of disabled children (Pearson, 2006). However progress has been relatively slow and the uptake of direct payments by different service user groups has been variable.

The use of direct payments can bring many positive benefits (see, for example, Pearson, 2006; Riddell et al., 2006) including greater independence and control. It can also be cost effective as work by Heywood and Turner (2007) has shown. Set within a wider system of self-directed support it is probably too early to predict what impact this will have on numbers of people who elect to take their individual budget as a direct payment. It seems reasonable, though, to assume that the more people know what their individual budget is and the more they are engaged in serious discussions about how they may use it, numbers of direct payments will continue to grow.

In Control

It was, perhaps, the fact that so few people with learning disabilities were able to access direct payments, or generally exercise their rights as citizens, that prompted one of the key developments that frames our thinking on personalisation. Duffy (2003) wrote Keys to Citizenship following his experience of running a provider organisation for people with learning disabilities, then working with a Scottish local authority to develop different approaches to the ways people with learning disabilities could be supported and included to be full citizens in their own communities.

This work was the precursor to 'In Control' – an approach that pioneered the concept of an individual budget. Duffy's considerable achievement was in changing attitudes towards people with learning disabilities to be adopted by the (Westminster) government across the community care spectrum. His work arguably helped to build a bridge from "service-land" to ordinary life that had often become fractured, driven by a growing preoccupation with process and the measuring of performance against outputs. It also informs what is an essential characteristic of personalisation, that is, that it is not simply about social work services but is concerned with approaches that enable people to achieve a good-quality life – a life generally characterised by active citizenship, inclusion and participation, and connectedness to the people and places that are important to them.

This work influenced further policy development in England, including the testing of individual budgets. The DH commissioned an evaluation of the individual budget pilot sites (Glendinning et al., 2008), prior to rolling out the process across England. Individual budgets were broadly welcomed by service users and carers. It was acknowledged that they offered people greater control over their daily lives and people generally welcomed the support provided and the ways in which it was delivered (Glendinning et al., 2008). There were important differences by service user group, however, with older people reporting significantly lower psychological well-being after receiving an individual budget while those with mental health problems reported a significantly higher quality of life. People with physical disabilities reported greater satisfaction and a higher quality of care (Glendinning et al., 2008).

Significantly, little difference was found in relation to the cost of care funded by individual budgets and those funded by conventional means. The average cost was £280 per week for an individual budget compared with £300 for a conventional care package. Again there were significant differences by service user group. Despite this, and the arguably premature timing of the evaluation, the DH in England committed to this approach as the way forward, with targets in place for 30% of those eligible to have an individual budget by 2011 (Prime Minister's Strategy Unit, 2007). There are no explicit targets in place across the rest of the UK. A national strategy for self-directed support in Scotland was launched in November 2010 and there is consultation on the need for future legislation.

The common thread across this pattern of policy development is an emphasis on organising support in ways that enable people to take control of their lives and fulfil their role as citizens. This approach fits well with emerging national policy on outcomes such as (in Scotland) the development of National Outcomes Measures and Single Outcome Agreements. Likewise, the work of the Scottish Government Joint Improvement Team in developing a tool for measuring user-defined outcomes (the Talking Points approach) demonstrates a shift of focus away from process to outcomes in relation to both assessment and commissioning of services (Miller *et al.,* 2008).

Working in partnership – the process of self-directed support

The process of self-directed support involves genuine partnership working between the local authority, citizens and their families and friends, and, potentially, a range of providers from the statutory, voluntary and private sectors. The focus needs to be on agreeing what needs require to be met; identifying the resource available to meet those needs; engaging in discussion as to how the resource can be used; and defining mutually agreed outcomes to be achieved with the use of those resources.

The first stage – assessment – is the statutory duty of local authorities, which will also apply some form of criteria to determine eligibility for support. A personalised approach, however, recognises that most people will be able to identify their own needs, although some may require more support than others to do this. This process of supported self-assessment does not replace a local authority's legal obligations but should properly form a key part of the assessment of need.

People deemed eligible for support are then allocated an indicative budget. Put somewhat crudely the formula used relates needs to points and points to cash. Implementation of these arrangements is hugely variable across the UK at present – in some parts it is still embryonic – and there is no unified system within or across the four countries. Once the budget is identified the person is advised of the amount that they have to "spend". The social work role then involves discussing how they may wish to use the indicative resource to meet the intended outcomes. As described previously the resource can be drawn down as a direct payment, all or in part, allocated to a third party to manage on their behalf or left as a virtual budget where the person does not wish to exercise any direct control over the funding.

There are potential barriers that may inhibit applying this approach. The eligibility criteria used by a local authority may be set so high that only people at, or near, crisis are deemed to qualify for support. The more this is likely to be the case, the less likely people may be to wish to engage in discussions about controlling their own resources. The funding allocated to meet eligible needs may be too low to meaningfully enable the person to meet their needs, or may be substantially lower than the value of any service currently or previously provided. There may be inadequate support provided to the person to exercise their responsibilities as an employer, or budget holder. There may also be difficulties bringing other funding streams into the individual budget other than those from social work (such as those from health or leisure services).

Despite the barriers, self-directed support offers a different way of working with people to achieve outcomes in their lives that may not be reached through more traditional approaches.

Further challenges in implementing the personalisation agenda

Role of social worker – reframing of the social work task

Successful personalisation requires a significant cultural shift from an approach that has been characterised as 'for you' (and sometimes applied as 'to you') to become 'with you' with the aim of becoming 'by you'. It also requires recognition that most people (and the people closest to them) know their own needs well, although some may need some assistance to think through how these needs can best be met.

Broadly speaking, social workers are in two camps when it comes to the personalisation agenda. There are those who believe that these changes afford them greater opportunities to exercise their social work skills by freeing them up to build relationships and provide support. There are others who feel that these changes will result in a de-skilling of the profession, requiring social workers to operate as nothing more than brokers advertising particular services. However, Leadbetter and Lewis (2005) have suggested that the social work role will be more akin to that of personal advisor, counsellor or support worker. Manthorpe et al. (2009) have argued that the situation may be more complex as although professionals may be enthusiastic about the concept of personalisation per se they may feel insecure about their new role. These fears might relate to finding the space to work in new ways and are likely to be exacerbated by continuing uncertainties in relation to the role of social work with adults more generally (particularly in England) (Manthorpe et al., 2009).

The individual budget pilots suggest that the social work role will continue to change and may initially relate to picking up the pieces until things bed in or to providing a service until others become available before moving on to a safeguarding role (Glendinning et al., 2008). This may lead to role conflict and social workers may find themselves with the twin pressures of responding to individual need on the one hand and safeguarding adults at risk of harm on the other. This tension is likely to exist whichever model is adopted. Evidence from the US has suggested that staff are likely to take on a counselling or consultant role assisting people to think through and plan their support and review their expenditure (Manthorpe et al., 2009). They are also likely to monitor quality and provision of services being provided to meet needs.

Training and workforce issues

Consideration of the pre- and post-qualifying professional development implications for social workers of this new approach is crucial. Learning opportunities need to be created that enable social workers to develop their existing skills and abilities while also providing practitioners with the confidence to change the culture of some existing social work practice, in particular the formulaic approach that has tended to characterise assessment and care management. Arguably, this is less evident in work with children and families where there is less focus on securing a service to meet a need as the 'service' is often the social worker's relationship with the family.

As increasing numbers of people choose to assume control over all or some of their individual budgets, local authorities need to ensure that they have direct access to sufficient expert advice, whether to exercise their responsibilities as an employer or in the financial requirements of managing a budget. This raises questions in terms of who should provide this support – whether it should be social work services, other organisations or through some form of collaboration (Manthorpe et al., 2009). The level of funding made available to individuals must take account, not simply of a person's support needs, but also the costs associated with this area of activity.

Commissioning

Successful personalisation is not simply a matter of addressing knowledge or skills deficits. It requires local authorities to exercise their strategic commissioning responsibilities in different ways.

Social work practitioners need more than their own skills to support people to maximise self-reliance. They need to draw on partnerships with universal services such as education, leisure and health in order to promote inclusion and participation. They also need to be able to access a range of enabling approaches, some of which may include formal services, at least for a period of time in someone's life. This means investment both in intensive alternatives to institutional care and also in preventive approaches that may not always be social work funded. Best practice examples of the latter include supported employment, peer support networks such as Key Ring (or its Scottish counterpart Neighbourhood Networks), support for carers that anticipates future issues as well as facilitating tangible support at times of greatest need, and Choose Life initiatives in suicide prevention.

Personalisation is about enabling people to make a journey from client-hood to active citizenship. It requires social workers to play a role in community capacity building by working with football clubs, taxi drivers, volunteers, employers, time-banking schemes, arts organisations and transport providers. It means changing employment policies so as not to exclude people who are marginalised.

Where formal services are required the service should be planned, designed and funded around the person. This requires significant change in relation to commissioning and procurement practices. The challenge for many local authorities is how to disinvest from services that are not currently delivered in these ways, and also on complying with procurement directives that were designed to secure furniture rather than support.

Legitimate use of resources

Social workers are concerned to ensure that funds are used and administered lawfully.

There are complex ethical issues relating to, for example, the payment of family members or friends taking on the role of personal assistant. In England, the Association of Directors of Adult Social Services (ADASS, 2009) has produced guidance – *Personalisation and the Law: Implementing Putting People First in the current legal framework* to ensure that funds are administered fairly and within the boundaries of the law. The individual budget pilots revealed staff concerns around judging what could be viewed as legitimate and appropriate for social care. Is paying for a holiday or gym membership for example an acceptable use of funds? (Glendinning *et al.*, 2008). It may well be, provided it can be demonstrated to be an effective use of public funds to achieve mutually identified outcomes.

Managing risk

It can be argued that the principles of personalisation can be applied to all people, including those where statutory duties relating to protection apply or where the person concerned is an unwilling participant, like some people in the justice system for example. It does not diminish those public protection responsibilities, and there are clearly circumstances where the risks posed by an individual to others or themselves cannot be compromised by their own right to self-determination. That is not new. Social workers working in child protection, with people with severe mental health problems or with dangerous offending behaviour have always had to exercise professional judgement in such matters. Even when intervention is mandatory there can still be a dialogue on how this is best managed and delivered to ensure the desired outcome for an individual (Scottish Government, 2009).

Sound risk assessment and management is founded on defensible decision making, which is in turn based on knowing a person well. More personalised approaches to the assessment of risk explore the perceptions of the person concerned, and those who know them best, and are not disproportionately reliant on professional views, expressed by people who do not always have sufficient knowledge of the individual or who rely too heavily on the use of static risk assessment tools. As argued by Bates and Lymberry, in Chapter 2, social work is founded on relationships with individuals. It is well placed to play a key role in the assessment and management of risk.

Personalisation does, though, present different challenges in how this is exercised. Issues such as the employment of family members or neighbours without Criminal Records Bureau (disclosure) checks for example may become a significant issue with the potential for harm or the risk of financial exploitation (Glendinning *et al.*, 2008). However, personalisation should mean not imposing blanket regulations or restrictions. Instead, recognition is given to the fact that there are many circumstances where people can make such judgements safely and appropriately. There will also be circumstances where there is a role for social work services to intervene, for example in the field of adult protection.

Conclusions

There is an increasing expectation that social work will be practised in highly personalised ways. This creates additional challenges. Personalisation is based on outcomes, and success is therefore more difficult to measure than simply counting outputs. A personalised approach is, however, more likely to result in a better quality of life for individuals and helping organisations to evidence strategic indicators such as shifts in the balance of care. This is a transition that needs to be well managed and founded on skilled social work practice. It will be difficult to navigate this journey at a time of major public sector efficiency savings.

There is one certainty arising from the Personalisation Agenda – that of a changed relationship between citizen, provider and local authority. It is this changed relationship that has the potential to be empowering, enriching and fulfilling for both the person concerned and also for the social work practitioner.

Key messages for early career professionals

- Assessment should focus on strengths, abilities and potential as well as on needs. Needs should not be seen as deficits that always need to be addressed by services.
- Formally identifying mutually agreed outcomes at the conclusion of an assessment will enable informed review and the basis for measuring success.
- Well-informed judgements about risk are founded on the relationship the social worker has with a person and cannot be solely predicated on the basis of static risk assessment tools.

References

ADASS (Association of Directors of Adult Social Services) (2009) *Personalisation and the law: Implementing Putting People First in the current legal framework* London: ADASS.

DH (Department of Health) (2001) *Valuing People* London: HMSO.

DH (2005) *Independence, Well-being and Choice* London: HMSO.

DH (2006) *Our Health, Our Care, Our Say* London: HMSO.

Duffy, S (2003) *Keys to citizenship* Birkenhead: Paradigm.

Equality and Human Rights Commission (2009) *Ready for Action: Key issues and disabled people's priorities for independent living* March, Glasgow: EHRC.

Ferguson, I (2007) 'Increasing user choice or privatizing risk? The antinomies of personalization' *British Journal of Social Work* 37(3), pp 387-403.

Glendinning, C, Challis, D, Fernandez, J, Jacobs, S, Jones, K, Knapp, M, Manthorpe, J, Moran, N, Netten, A, Stevens, M and Wilberforce, M (2008) *Evaluation of the Individual Budgets Pilot Programme: Final Report* London: Department of Health.

Heywood, F and Turner, L (2007) *Better outcomes, lower costs. Implications for health and social care budgets of investment in housing adaptations, improvements and equipment: A review of the evidence* London: Office for Disability Publications.

Hunter, S and Ritchie, P (2007) *Co-production and Personalisation in Social Care: Changing Relationships in the Provision of Social Care* London: Jessica Kingsley Publishers.

Leadbetter, C (2004) *Personalisation through Participation* London: Demos.

Manthorpe, J, Jacobs, S, Rapaport, J, Challis, D, Netten, A, Glendinning, C, Stevens, M, Wilberforce, M, Knapp, M and Harris, J (2009) 'Training for Change: Early days of Individual Budgets and the implications for social work and care management practice: a qualitative study of the views of trainers' *British Journal of Social Work* 39(7), pp 1291-305.

Miller, E, Whoriskey, M and Cook, A (2008) 'Outcomes for users and carers in the context of partnership working: from research to practice' *Journal of Integrated Care* 16(2), pp 19-27.

Newman, J, Glendinning, C and Hughes, M (2008) 'Beyond modernisation? Social care and the transformation of welfare governance' *Journal of Social Policy* 37(4), pp 531-57.

Pearson, C (ed) (2006) *Direct Payments and the Personalisation of Care* Edinburgh: Dunedin Academic Press.

Prime Minister's Strategy Unit (2007) *Putting people first: a shared vision and commitment to the transformation of adult social care* London: HM Government.

Riddell, S, Ahlgren, L, Pearson, C, Williams, V, Watson, N and MacFarlane H (2006) *The Implementation of Direct Payments for People Who Use Care Services* Scottish Parliament Health Committee Report, SP Paper 624, Edinburgh: Scottish Parliament.

Scottish Executive (2000) *The Same as You? Review of services for people with learning disabilities* Edinburgh: HMSO.

Scottish Executive (2006) *Changing Lives: The 21st century review of social work* Edinburgh: HMSO.

Scottish Government (2008) *Personalisation:A shared understanding* Changing Lives Service Development Group, Edinburgh: HMSO.

Part 2

Themes and Issues in Child and Family Social Work

Chapter 7

Child Poverty in the UK: Issues and answers

Douglas Hamilton

Introduction

As part of early professional development it is important that social workers have an understanding of the social and political context that impacts on the everyday experience of their service users. This chapter provides some discussion of child poverty in the UK given that the context of poverty strongly increases the likelihood of contact with social services, even though this may not be made explicit at referral (Cunningham and Cunningham, 2007). The impact and reality of child poverty on children's life experiences is so pervasive that it can often be overlooked when a particular case requires a focus on specific family difficulties and/or care issues. It is also necessary to consider that the experience of poverty is not the same for everyone. A severe and persistent experience of child poverty will usually have the most pronounced impact on growing up and future life chances, but short-term or episodic poverty has adverse effects too. The aim of this chapter is to provide an opportunity for practitioners to consider the links between child poverty and a range of outcomes for children, and to reflect on what impact that may have on practice.

Child poverty in the UK

In March 1999, the then Prime Minister, Tony Blair, made a commitment to end child poverty within a generation. The aim of the United Kingdom (UK) Government was to eradicate child poverty by the year 2020, a target that is now enshrined in law as a binding duty on government by the Child Poverty Act 2010. Devolved administrations in Scotland and Northern Ireland are also committed to action under the Act, and similar provisions are applicable in Wales through the Children and Families (Wales) Measure 2010.

Eradication of child poverty is defined in the Act using four targets covering:

- relative poverty;
- combined low income and material deprivation;
- persistent poverty;
- absolute poverty;

Defining and measuring child poverty is a complex and contentious matter and there is no universal agreement on a perfect measure (DWP, 2003). The headline measure that is most often used is the relative measure of child poverty (household income below 60% of the UK median before housing costs).

According to this relative measure of child poverty there were 2.9 million children in the UK living in poverty in 2007/08 (DWP, 2009), a reduction of about half a million children since 1998/99. Given that the government's own targets were to achieve a 25% reduction by 2004/05 and a 50% reduction by 2009/10, it is apparent that progress has been made but is considerably behind schedule. Between 1999 and 2004 the previous upward trend in child poverty rates was reversed, but this stalled in the subsequent five years. It has been suggested that the initial reduction was due to policies such as improved benefits and tax credits making an impact on a minority of low-income households who were easiest to help, while other measures are going to be required for the longer term-targets to be met (Hirsch, 2006). The rates of child poverty vary quite considerably across different regions and nations of the UK. Inner London has by far the highest rate of child poverty, more than double the rates of the South East and East of England (CPAG, 2008). The current rates of child poverty in the UK are still high compared to other countries. In European terms, the UK is ranked 24th out of 26 countries based on child wellbeing indicators related to material resources (CPAG, 2009).

The impact of child poverty

The high level of child poverty in the UK tells us that it is a significant issue but it only begins to hint at the effects that child poverty has on experiences of childhood and future life chances. Money is at the heart of any discussion of poverty and, to start with, it is important to consider issues such as income adequacy. However, the impact of poverty goes beyond a lack of material resources and therefore this section also considers the links between poverty and a range of other issues that affect children.

The definition of poverty provided by Townsend (1979, p 31) is of individuals, families or groups whose 'resources are so seriously below those commanded by the average individual or family that they are, in effect, excluded from ordinary living patterns, customs and activities'. While most people are content to use this definition as a starting point, it has always raised the question of how you come to any agreement on what an acceptable standard of living is in the UK, and how much money you would need in order to afford that standard.

In 2008, the Joseph Rowntree Foundation published a report setting out a Minimum Income Standard based on what members of the public thought was the minimum level of income that individuals and families require in order to participate in society (Bradshaw et al., 2008). The standard was calculated on the basis of requirements that included food, clothes, accommodation, utilities, fuel, household goods, personal goods and services, transport, and social and cultural activities. According to this measure, in 2008, a couple with two children needed £370 per week (after income tax and excluding housing and childcare costs). A family in receipt of out-of-work benefits would only reach about two thirds of this level. All of the 2.9 million children classified by government statistics as living in poverty are in households that have incomes below this standard.

Based on this analysis, it is clear that a lack of financial resources means that children living in poverty do not have access to the material goods or opportunities that the public think are a necessity for growing up in the UK. Parents are therefore forced into tough choices about which necessities they or their children must do without. In a 2006 survey by Save the Children, a quarter of low-income parents said that their child missed out on basics such as fresh fruit, essential shoes and clothes, and a warm home (Save the Children, 2006). In addition to children missing out, the same report found that 91% of low-income parents said that they often went without to make sure that their child had enough. Two-thirds of parents reported going into debt to make ends meet. This affects relationships with partners and their children and often has an impact on the parent's health.

At the end of the day, you end up going without, under-nourishing yourself. Obviously you under-nourish yourself because you never under-nourish your children. It ends up making you ill, and what happens to your children when you're ill? You just have to get on with it. It makes it harder.

(Tony, parent quoted in Lister and Strelitz, 2008 p 9)

The stresses of this hard-pressed financial situation for parents are exacerbated further by the fact that the poorest households often have to pay more for basic goods and services. They do not have the purchasing levels to access lower-cost gas and electricity rates, insurance, banking and credit facilities. A low-income household can pay up to 150% more for essential large items such as an oven bought on credit and 10% more on gas bills paid by pre-payment meters rather than direct debit. All in, this can add up to a 'poverty premium' of £1,000 a year, meaning that an already stretched income has to go further on essential items than the average household budget (Save the Children, 2007).

The impact of poverty on the experience of childhood goes beyond the financial and material pressures faced in the home. Ridge (2006), drawing on her own and others' research with children, has shown how poverty affects their lives not only through 'going short' as regards food, clothes and household basics. Their range of activities is also often severely restricted. At school they may well be unable to afford to go on trips or pay for materials supporting their education. Some feel ashamed that they cannot dress like peers or have felt picked on because 'we didn't have enough money' (Ridge, 2006, p 28). On the other hand, children commonly seek to help themselves through paid errands and work, while peers and relatives may help out with the costs of activities.

Children's access to and enjoyment of services provided by the voluntary, public and private sectors are significantly affected by poverty. A research study on the impact of poverty on children's experiences of services found that affordability in terms of entrance fees and the cost of travel, equipment or a uniform is one of the most significant influences on service access and use (Wager *et al.,* 2007). However, the study also showed how a combination of low household income and living in an area of deprivation further reduces the ability of children and young people to access a range of services. Concerns about safety, limited local service provision and transport difficulties are more pronounced in the most deprived areas. This is compounded by the more restricted availability of safe, attractive open spaces for children in such neighbourhoods. Children therefore have fewer opportunities to learn and socialise which leads to longer-term impacts on their lives. It is the cumulative impact of a series of missed opportunities for children living in poorer households that is identified as being of particular significance. The layering of financial and spatial inequalities means that young people from lower-income households who are growing up in deprived areas have the poorest access to both formal services and informal spaces. Hence, there is a need for greater awareness among service providers about the impact of poverty on children and the importance of assisting with indirect as well as direct service costs.

In addition to the impact of poverty on the experience of childhood, it is also clear that poverty has an extreme impact on future life chances. Despite some improvements between 1999 and 2009, there remain significant inequalities in children's' health and education outcomes across the UK (MacInnes *et al.,* 2009). Children growing up in poverty are more likely to have lower levels of literacy and numeracy and leave school with few qualifications. Poverty also has a demonstrable impact on indicators such as low birth weight, dental health and underage pregnancies. It is not just physical health that is affected: 21% of children growing up in families where no parent has ever worked end up with some sort of mental disorder compared to 5% from better-off households (ONS, 2005). Research from Scotland has shown that a child born in Calton in Glasgow, one of the most deprived areas in the UK, can only expect to live to 54 and is three times as likely to suffer from heart disease and four times more likely to be hospitalised than a child in the city's prosperous western suburbs. A girl born in poverty in Scotland today can expect to die 11 years earlier than a girl born in a better-off family. A boy can expect to die 17 years earlier (NHS Scotland, 2004).

Severe and persistent child poverty

In any discussion about child poverty, it is important to recognise that some children are growing up in poorer households than others. Of the millions of children living in poverty, some will live in households that have an income close to the 60% median income threshold and others will be much further away.

Research has identified that approximately 1.7 million children in the UK are living in severe poverty (Save the Children, 2010). Between 2004/05 and 2007/08 the proportion of children living in severe poverty rose from 11% to 13%. Using a combined income and deprivation measure, Save the Children has been identifying and tracking progress on tackling severe child poverty since 1997 (Adelman *et al.,* 2003; Magadi and Middleton, 2005, 2007). Although there have been reductions in the overall number of children living in poverty in that period, there has not been a similar decrease in the number of children living in severe poverty (Strelitz, 2008). The implication is that policy measures introduced since 1997 have not had as much impact on those children living in the poorest households.

The risk factors associated with living in severe child poverty are similar to those for general poverty but are more pronounced. For example, 44% of children living in severe poverty have a mother with no qualifications compared to 31% of children living in non-severe poverty, and 62% of children in severe poverty have no parent in paid employment compared to 42% of children living in non-severe poverty (Magadi and Middleton, 2007). A particular area of concern from the 2007 report was the finding that a significant proportion of children living in severe poverty were living in households where benefits and tax credits were not being claimed, suggesting that more needs to be done to ensure that the poorest families are getting all the money that they are entitled to.

Besides differences in the severity of poverty, its duration is also important. Some households move in and out of poverty for one or more short episodes, while for others the experience is constant year after year. Children growing up in persistent poverty are more likely to live in poor housing, experience longstanding illness or disability, be in trouble with the police and lack multiple deprivation items (Strelitz, 2008). The negative consequences are most pronounced among children living in poverty that is both severe and persistent.

The causes of child poverty

The prevalence and impact of child poverty in one of the richest economies of the world raises questions as to the causal factors that create this situation. McKendrick and Dickie (2007) outline four broad circumstances that are often thought to cause of poverty:

- *Individual behaviour:* This is drawn from social stereotyping with a common perception of the 'feckless poor'. This analysis suggests that individuals have created this situation for themselves and do nothing about it. Although there is something intuitive about this analysis, it does not take into account the structural forces that impact on individuals. It is also not adequate in explaining the large and fluctuating number of low-income households in the UK.
- *Social factors:* Some of the main social factors that lead to or exacerbate poverty are grouped under four headings: Lifecycle, Families and households, Social, and Place. The authors are careful to point out that poverty levels cannot be simply explained by the changing composition of families (including the rise of lone-parent households), but that there is a combination of social factors that are shared among social groups that make them more susceptible to

experiencing poverty and create barriers to moving out of poverty. Examples of some of the social factors are to do with gender, work status, ethnicity and disability.

- *Political factors:* This recognises that poverty levels are affected by government action or inaction, as a result of political choices and strategies. Government decisions in relation to policy areas such as benefits, taxation, and employability strategies all have a direct influence over levels of poverty. For example, over the past few years there has been a reduction in the numbers of children and pensioners living in poverty as a direct result of political choices, but a similar benefit has not been experienced by working-age childless households, which has not been a priority area of government focus.
- *Economic factors:* The macro-economy sets the economic conditions for the country and this undoubtedly has an impact on jobs and the availability of material resources. However, a purely economic analysis does not explain why child poverty exists in periods of economic growth.

It is recognised that some or all of these factors may be at play in individuals' lives and that solutions to ending child poverty need to take account of each of the four perspectives.

The social work response to child poverty

The reality behind the statistics outlined above is encountered on a daily basis by social workers in their practice. Child poverty provides the context in which many children are facing a range of other challenges that affect their welfare and future life chances. Children who are looked after come mainly from low-income households, while poverty is a major factor in child abuse (Kirton, 2009).

Cunningham and Cunningham (2007) provide a useful discussion about the role of social work in relation to poverty. They suggested that social work as a profession largely developed out of attempts to address the needs of those living in poverty but that over time the profession has lost sight of the vital role it has to play in tackling poverty. While many people still enter the profession with the intention of making a positive impact on the lives of people living in poverty, the reality of day-to-day practice makes it harder to take an approach that is about alleviating poverty. This is a challenge that is central to debates about the role of the social work profession and how social workers reconcile their own ideological beliefs with those of their employers.

This is not an issue that is unique to social workers in the UK. Allan (2006, p 68) recognises that, in Australia, while social 'workers in the field recognise the complex problem of poverty, they are not involved in addressing it'. Her view is that an individualised case-based approach to intervention and policy means that consideration of the impact of structural issues, such as poverty, is minimised.

There is undoubtedly scope within an individualised approach for social workers to address issues of poverty in their casework. A task-centred practice approach is focused on service users working in partnership with social workers to learn new methods of problem solving. Workers using this approach aim to find practical solutions to address issues such as finance and housing (Cunningham and Cunningham, 2007). Direct assistance in relation to welfare and benefits advice and applications is one way in which social workers can make a direct impact on the household income. Some social workers are reluctant to get too involved in income and expenditure issues but Manthorpe and Bradley (2001, p 286) argue that an ignorance of finance is both 'untenable and unprofessional'.

Although interventions that address the financial concerns of a household are useful, they will not be sufficient in addressing the wider factors that contribute to that family living in poverty. Social workers are in a privileged position of having information and insight into individual family circumstances that few other professionals can come close to. From that position, there come opportunities for advocacy on behalf of individual service users and more broadly on behalf of groups of people.

Individual advocacy can be seen within the context of an interagency approach that attempts to provide a more holistic response to an individual's needs that cuts across many of the social factors that cause and exacerbate poverty. An ability to advocate on behalf of a parent or child and assist them in relation to work, training, education or childcare can enable other agencies to take a more targeted approach that ensure that those most in need are being identified and assisted. Given that those families experiencing severe poverty are those that also face the most barriers to service provision (Strelitz, 2008), the role of social workers in facilitating access could be very significant as part of a more coherent approach to addressing severe child poverty. As Dickens (2009) acknowledges, there will be times when a sticking plaster is just what is needed but there also needs to be an understanding of the 'bigger picture' of poverty and inequality. This understanding will assist social work practitioners to identify new opportunities and partnerships that can help their service users.

Based on the information and insight gained from individual cases, social workers collectively are in a position to be powerful advocates for the poor within their own agencies, their local areas and at a national level. Collective action from social workers can be focused on then tackling the structural causes of poverty that, on an individual case basis, create frustrating and seemingly insurmountable challenges. Since the heyday of community social work and local patch teams in the 1980s, there has been a trend away from 'collective and welfare oriented approaches' (Barry and Hallett, 1998, p 8). However, Manthorpe and Bradley (2001, p 286) suggest that 'managing to champion the interests of the most disadvantaged may be the one distinctive and enduring contribution of social work'. A social work that is more 'politically and socially engaged' and that recaptures a more 'radical spirit' (Lymbery, 2001) points to the central role that the profession should play in efforts to end child poverty. Supporting the development and activities of neighbourhood organisations and groups provides one means of putting this into practice (Jordan with Jordan, 2002).

Taking the steps to end child poverty

As a result of the legislation referred to at the start of this chapter, the UK and devolved governments as well as other public authorities have statutory duties to develop and implement strategies to end child poverty. The Child Poverty Act 2010 sets out some of the 'building blocks' that will need to be addressed in those strategies: employment and skills; financial support; health, education and social services; housing; and the promotion of social inclusion. It remains to be seen how effective this measure will be in a period of severe constraint on public spending following the financial crisis of 2008-09.

It is clear that eradication of child poverty will require a wide-ranging approach that has already been reflected in the strategies adopted by the UK and devolved administrations over the last decade. However, it is also clear that a much bolder approach is required in order to speed up the rate of process. If the 2020 target is to be reached then the next ten years will require four times the level of progress achieved since 1997 (Hirsch, 2008). According to Hirsch, the most critical areas for substantial additional investment are childcare, skills and an improved tax and benefits system. He argues that the only chance of success is to reduce worklessness, raise benefits and improve working parents' incomes.

The powers to make change to end child poverty are spread across a number of levels of government and service providers. The Act provides the opportunity for a more co-ordinated approach and it will be important that different departments work closely together to ensure that policy development in one area compliments what other agencies are doing. This is particularly relevant for the devolved administrations that do not have control over key decisions in relation to tax and benefits.

Future administrations may prioritise different policy solutions and different ways of measuring and defining child poverty. However, one thing that can be said for certain is that the voices and the stories of those families living in poverty will need to be heard in order to inform the decisions that will be made. The poorest children will require powerful advocates on an individual and collective basis, and social workers can play a vital role in providing that advocacy.

Key questions to consider in practice:

- what effect does poverty have on the service users that I work with?
- what is the scope within my existing practice to assist individual service users in addressing the causes and impacts of poverty in their own lives?
- what opportunities are there to advocate collectively on behalf of the poorest children in my area?
- what scope is there to work with local families and organisations such as welfare rights agencies, credit unions and community businesses on a neighbourhood basis?

References

Adelman, I, Middleton, S and Ashworth, K (2003) *Britain's Poorest Children: Severe and persistent poverty and social exclusion* London: Save the Children.

Allan, J (2006) 'Whose Job is Poverty? The Problems of Therapeutic Intervention with Children who are Sexually Violent' *Child Abuse Review* 15(1), pp 55-70.

Barry, M and Hallett, C (eds) (1998) *Social Exclusion and Social Wor,* Lyme Regis: Russell House Publishing.

Bradshaw, J, Middleton, S, Davis, A, Oldfield, N, Smith, N, Cusworth, L and Williams, J (2008) *A Minimum Income Standard for Britain: What people think* York: Joseph Rowntree Foundation.

CPAG (Child Poverty Action Group) (2008) *Child Poverty: The Stats – Analysis of the latest poverty statistics* London: CPAG.

CPAG (2009) *Child Wellbeing and Child Poverty: Where the UK stands in the European table* London: CPAG.

Cunningham, J and Cunningham, S (2007) *Sociology and Social Work* Exeter: Learning Matters.

Dickens, J (2009) *Social Work and Social Policy* London: Routledge.

DWP (Department for Work and Pensions) (2003) *Measuring Child Poverty* London: DWP.

DWP (2009) *Households Below Average Income 1994/95-2007/08* London: DWP.

Hirsch, D (2006) *What Will it Take to End Child Poverty?* York: Joseph Rowntree Foundation.

Hirsch, D (2008) *What Will it Take to End Child Poverty in 2020?* York: Joseph Rowntree Foundation.

Jordan, B with Jordan, C (2002) *Social Work and the Third Way* London: Sage Publications.

Kirton, D (2009) *Child Social Work Policy and Practice* London: Sage Publications.

Lister, R and Strelitz, J (2008) '"Everyone needs money": the voices of parents who have too little' in Lister, R and Strelitz, J (eds) *Why Money Matters: Family income, poverty and children's lives* London: Save the Children.

Lymbery, M (2001) 'Social Work at the Crossroads' *British Journal of Social Work* 31(3), pp 369-84.

MacInnes,T, Kenway, P and Parekh, A (2009) *Monitoring Poverty and Social Exclusion 2009* York: Joseph Rowntree Foundation/New Policy Institute.

Magadi, M and Middleton, S (2005) *Britain's Poorest Children Revisited: Evidence from the BHPS (1994-2002)* CRSP Research Report 3, London and Loughborough: Save the Children and CRSP, Loughborough University.

Magadi, M and Middleton, S (2007) *Severe Child Poverty in the UK* London: Save the Children.

Manthorpe, J and Bradley, G (2001) 'Managing finances' in Adams, R, Dominelli, L and Payne, M (eds) *Critical Practice in Social Work* Basingstoke: Palgrave.

McKendrick, J and Dickie, J (2007) 'Factors leading to Poverty' in McKendrick, J H, Mooney, G C, Kelly, P and Dickie, J (eds) *Poverty in Scotland 2007* London: CPAG.

NHS Scotland (2004) *Healthy Life Expectancy in Scotland* Edinburgh: NHS Scotland.

ONS (Office for National Statistics) (2005) *The Mental Health of Children and Young People 2004* London: ONS.

Ridge, T (2006) 'Childhood poverty: a barrier to social participation and inclusion' in Tisdall, E K M, Davis, J M, Hill, M and Prout, A (eds) *Children, Young People and Social Inclusion,* Bristol: The Policy Press.

Save the Children (2006) *Hard Times* London: Save the Children.

Save the Children (2007) *The Poverty Premium: How poor households pay more for essential goods and services* London: Save the Children.

Save the Children (2010) *Measuring Severe Child Poverty in the UK* London: Save the Children.

Strelitz, J (2008) *Ending Severe Child Poverty* York: Joseph Rowntree Foundation.

Townsend, P (1979) *Poverty in the United Kingdom* London: Allen Lane.

Wager, F, Bailey, N, Day, R, Hamilton, D, Hill, M and King, C (2007) *Serving Children: The impact of poverty on children's experience of services* Edinburgh: Save the Children.

Chapter 8

Safeguarding and Protecting Children in the UK

Pam Green Lister

Introduction

The safeguarding and protection of children has become a major public concern. In social work, child protection has come to dominate work with children and families. Social workers are faced with working with the tension between minimising harm to children and promoting their welfare. While there is increasing specialism in child protection work, social workers working in adult care, for example in the fields of offending, substance misuse and mental health, need to have an understanding of child protection issues and their role in child protection, as the service users they work with may be parents/carers or in other positions that bring them into direct contact with children, and whose actions may impact on the welfare of children. Being a lead professional in a child protection case for the first time can be a daunting experience. However, the emphasis in policy and guidance across the United Kingdom (UK) is on multi-professional and multi-agency working. It is not expected that a single individual takes crucial decisions, rather decisions are made by a team of professionals and frontline workers are supported by supervisors. It is important that lead professionals seek specialist guidance and support both within and outwith their agency.

The UK policy context

In the last ten years there has been a shift in childcare policy across the UK. In the late 1990s the key debate among policy makers, researchers and practitioners was with regard to the relationship between child protection and child welfare. Corby (2006, p 166) describes the movement in the 1990s as a 'considerable backlash against the intrusion of child protection in social work. Parton (1996, p 5) argues that there was an 'over-emphasis on forensic concerns, with too much time being taken on investigations, and a failure to develop long-term co-ordinated treatment, counselling and preventive strategies'. The preoccupation with measuring risk, with reference to performance indicators and the associated apportioning of blame, was considered to be the dominant discourse, which resulted in professional judgement being subsumed under managerialist performance measurement. The reaction described above was not against protecting children but rather against the way that child protection policy had come to be framed with an emphasis on formalised action and legal interventions at the expense of family support.

Corby argues that following the recommendations of the Laming report (Laming, 2003), the changes brought about by the *Every Child Matters* Green Paper (HM Treasury, 2003) and the Children Act 2004 resulted in a transformation of childcare services in England and Wales, and suggests that the 'general tenor' of these changes holds for Scotland and Wales (Corby, 2006, p 160). England and Wales saw the formation of childcare trusts and Local Safeguarding Children Boards (LSCBs) which aim to give 'an extra, special, and mandated space to keep children safe' (O'Brien *et al,,* 2006, p 386). *The Framework for the Assessment of Children in Need and their Families* (DH, 2000) provides detailed procedural guidance responding to and monitoring referrals of child abuse. In Scotland, the emphasis of policy turned to the protection of children as being everyone's duty (Scottish Executive, 2002), and the Getting it Right for Every Child programme was launched in 2005 (Scottish Government, 2005). In Northern Ireland, similar 'Working Together to Safeguard Children' policy and guidance was introduced (DHSSPSNI, 2003). The term 'safeguarding' is increasingly used in preference to 'child protection' because it embraces a wider range of actions and a broader range of children (Broadhurst *et al.,* 2009).

The most fundamental shift in policy in all four countries' policy was the emphasis on universal provision for *all* children by *all* professionals. O'Brien *et al.* (2006, p 378) argue that as a result of this refocusing 'the objective of keeping children safe became intertwined with promotion of children's well being in its broadest sense'. This universalist approach is evidenced in the outcome dimensions of the *Every Child Matters* and *Getting it Right For Every Child* programmes. The *Every Child Matters* report specifies five areas: staying safe; being healthy; enjoying and achieving; making a positive contribution; and economic well-being. The outcome measures for *Getting It Right for Every Child* are eight areas of well-being for children: healthy, achieving, nurtured, active, respected, responsible, included and safe. Prevention of harm, characterised by early intervention is a cornerstone of the safeguarding policy agenda.

The new measures have been broadly welcomed and viewed as a way forward to address the concerns of the over-concentration on child protection investigations (Corby, 2006). The emphasis on multi-agency responsibility, along the entire safeguarding spectrum, also begins the process of addressing the failures of interagency and interprofessional communication identified in inquiry reports into child deaths and Serious Case Reviews (SCRs) (Brandon *et al.,* 2008). However, a growing critique has developed of this all-encompassing approach, with concerns expressed about the unintended consequences of the developments. On the one hand, there are concerns that the universalist approach will result in more children being drawn into the statutory system, resulting in increased surveillance and intrusion into people's lives (Garret, 2003). On the other hand, it is feared that the universal nature of provision, with the concentration on prevention of longer-term risks for children living in multi-problem families, might result in professionals losing sight of child protection issues (Hayes and Spratt, 2009). Furthermore, in England and Wales the relationship between the 'over-arching children's trusts' and the strategic partnership of LSCBs is not entirely clear. O'Brien *et al.* (2006, p 393) warn that 'Balancing keeping children safe within such a universalist approach is structurally complex at a delivery level, … and emotionally demanding'.

Key features of the assessment process in safeguarding and protecting children

There are key features of the early stages of the assessment process in safeguarding and protecting children, which are common for all social workers: awareness and recognition; gathering and interpreting of information and initial decision making.

Awareness and recognition

Being aware of how child abuse may manifest itself and being able to then recognise that a child may be unsafe is a core skill in assessment in childcare. The safeguarding of children can be seen as a continuum with preventive measures being used at one end of the continuum for children seen as in need, rather than at risk, and protective measures at the other end of the continuum where children are clearly identified as at risk of harm. However, from their analysis of SCRs, Brandon *et al.* warn that:

> In most cases child protection did not come "labelled as such" [and]staff working in early intervention are working within the safeguarding continuum not in a separate sphere of activity … Most children who die from abuse or neglect are not at the child protection end of the safeguarding continuum at the time of the incident. Rather they are children who have additional or complex needs who do not always come within the ambit of children's social care. (Brandon *et al.*, 2008, p 313-4)

The 'signs and symptoms' of child abuse are widely known (see, for example, Corby 2000) and a range of child and family characteristics in cases of child abuse have been identified. Family characteristics include: neglect; intergenerational abuse; domestic abuse in the family; substance misuse by parents or carers; learning disability; a lack of social support networks; mental health issues; house moves or poor housing conditions; and a lack of understanding of the vulnerability of older children living in a household is a further cause for concern (Brandon *et al.*, 2008; Devaney, 2008).

A key finding in inquiry reports and SCRs, is that children who have been killed or seriously harmed are rarely unknown to social services. Similarly, Brandon *et al.* (2008) found that 83% of families who had been involved in SCRs had been previously known to social services. These findings suggest that families have multiple contacts with social services and have been referred to social services on a number of occasions prior to the serious incident. They indicate that multiple referrals are a strong indicator that serious abuse *may* be taking place. The majority of research with regard to re-referrals has been undertaken in the United States (US). In his summary of this research, Forrester (2007) found that re-referrals to agencies were more likely where: caregivers had a history of abuse; the abuse had started at an early age; children had development delays; the child had spent a period of time in emergency foster placements; there was evidence of parental substance misuse and/or domestic abuse; and there had been multiple victims in one family. Re-referrals were more likely to be with regard to neglect than physical or emotional abuse. Forrester suggests that although a re-referral is not necessarily a 'bad' outcome (p 20), practitioners and frontline managers should be aware of the factors associated with multiple referrals when taking the decision to close a case. Consideration should, therefore, be given to longer-term allocation, with specialist assistance in identified areas. This strategy would ease the burden on initial assessments.

Gathering and interpreting of information

The gathering of information in safeguarding and potential child protection situations is complex. As Munro (2005) argues, collecting sensitive information from distressed, hostile and angry families requires highly developed interviewing skills, adapted to interviewing all members of the family. A range of frameworks have been produced to assist professionals in the assessment process. For example, in the UK the Framework for the Assessment of Children in Need and their Families (DH, 2000), the Common Assessment Framework (CAF) and the Integrated Assessment Framework (IAF) (Scottish Executive, 2005) identify a comprehensive range of areas from which information concerning a child and their situation may be obtained. The first of these provides five dimensions of direct work with a child during assessments: seeing the child, observing them, engaging with them, talking with them and doing activities with them (Bell and Wilson, 2003). Professionals working together would assess the following areas of a child's life: health, education, emotional and behavioural development, identity, family and social relationships, social presentation and self-care skills.

The Common Assessment Framework (CAF) used in England and Wales, is a standardised assessment tool for use by all professionals in their initial assessment of the needs of children and is intended to provide 'a simple process for the assessment of a child's needs and strengths' in the context of the family and the wider environment (DfES, 2006). It may be completed online or on paper, and parents and children can make comments on the framework and give consent to the sharing of information. Brandon *et al.* (2006, p 397) suggest that its introduction signals a move from 'dealing with the consequences of difficulties to preventing things from going wrong in the first place'. The CAF pro-forma provides workers with text boxes in which to provide an assessment summary of the strengths and needs of children (health and learning), parents and carers, and family and environment. Workers are asked to consider the extent to which each element of the framework is appropriate, to base comments on evidence and to record any major differences of opinion. The Scottish Integrated Assessment Framework (Scottish Executive, 2005) provides similar guidance on the process and content of assessment, with the aim of bringing together and analysing information from a variety of sources to 'guide appropriate action' (p 5).

The advantages of these assessment frameworks is that they offer workers a substantive 'checklist' to consider and a framework for drawing together information from a variety of sources. Millar and Corby (2006) found evidence that the CAF is useful in facilitating open and clear communication, as information held by agencies is made explicit and aims of any intervention are made clear. Their research showed that the CAF can be used in a nurturing and trusting way. Brandon *et al.* (2006) found that a range of practitioners thought the CAF to be an important tool in multi-agency assessment processes and a good basis for formulating relationships with parents.

However, a growing critique of the frameworks has developed since their inception. One concern is that the frameworks do not address the social and economic contexts of assessment with regard to parenting. Garret (2003) argues that the frameworks police those who are socially marginalised. He critiques the tools that compliment the Framework for the Assessment of Children (DH, 2000) as being based on no evidence of efficacy. He describes a Strengths and Difficulties tool as 'patronising' (p 454) and one that encourages 'potentially pre-emptive and inaccurate diagnostic labelling' (p 453). Garret considers the diagnostic categories to be subjective and accusatory, citing categories of missed medical appointments and non-constructive use of spare time (p 538). White *et al.* (2009, p 1206) concerns are that the structure and format of the CAF 'disrupts the temporal and narrative display of information … [so] that there are no opportunities for the writer to provide a chronological perspective, nor to tell a story, nor to characterise the child or parent'. So, while information is *presented* explicitly, it is difficult for the worker to convey deeper understandings and interpretations of situations, based on professional judgement.

Furthermore, the development of these frameworks has coincided with the increased use of information and communication technology. This has resulted in shared electronic databases and assessments. While these address, in part, the issues of timeous communication of information and the flagging of early concerns between agencies, and assist the technical management of data, all of which have been of concern in inquiry reports, they create new concerns with regard to confidentiality and security (Garret, 2005; Munro, 2005).

The CAF has therefore potential to assist or obstruct comprehensive, interagency assessments. Brandon *et al.* (2006) identify what factors help or hinder the use of the CAF. They identify enabling factors as:

- enthusiasm at grassroots and management levels;
- a view that the assessment will benefit families;
- a history of good multi-agency working;
- a willingness to learn from others;
- an existing information technology system;
- clear structures;
- good training, support and supervision.

They identify hindering factors as:

- lack of agency join up/conflict of interests;
- lack of professional trust;
- a mismatch of vision and practice;
- confusion and muddle regarding processes;
- gaps in confidence and skills;
- lack of support and anxiety about workloads and new ways of working.

It has been argued that the emphasis on gathering information in childcare assessments was a key concern of the 1990s and it is the interpretation of that information to create understanding which is a current policy and practice concern. As Munro states:

> The type of information used in child abuse investigations consist rarely of simple verifiable facts, but more often of descriptions of human actions. These involve interpreting the meaning of the observed behaviour to the actor, and what inquiries have repeatedly demonstrated is how much of the relevant information is ambiguous open to interpretation as sinister or benign. (Munro, 2005, p 380)

Interpretation requires drawing on theoretical knowledge and research for example theories of causation and effect of abuse (Corby, 2000; Taylor and Daniel, 2005; Doyle, 2006) and, as will be discussed below, personal and practice experience and supervision.

Thresholds for intervention

Thresholds for intervention, within and between agencies, are key influences in initial decision making in safeguarding children and in the decision as to whether or not to proceed to investigation. In their third national evaluation of SCRs, Brandon *et al.* (2008) identified a number of key factors that influenced decisions to intervene or to provide services. A central concern is the influence that child or parent cooperation has on the decision to provide a service. Examples were found of a service not being provided because a young person had refused to cooperate and social work services had 'exhausted their helping strategies (p 322). Where lack of co-operation was accompanied by hostility, for example, from parents with a history of violence, it was considered that workers' ability to make judgements were 'severely hampered' (p 323). Parental disguise of their non-compliance also 'wrong footed' workers (p 323) and prevented or delayed intervention. A further theme identified by the researchers was that of 'Professional avoidance or neglect and start again syndrome' (p 324). Cases were found where, although the threshold for intervention had been achieved, 'agencies appeared to avoid or rebuff parents through closing cases, reassessing, referring on, or through a succession of different workers' (p 324). A pattern emerged of workers developing a strategy of dealing with the overwhelming nature of neglect by putting aside knowledge of the past, ignoring past difficulties, and focusing on the present. This strategy is exemplified by parents who had had a long-term history of child neglect, being referred to short-term programmes such as parenting classes, rather than decisions being made that 'enough is enough and the child or children should not remain at home' (p 324). These strategies need to be regarded in the agency context. Brandon *et al.* (2008) reported that inquiries frequently mentioned absences of frontline and managerial staff, as a result of either ill-health or unfilled vacancies, which resulted in non-completion of core assessments, and lack of support for staff in decision making.

Platt's (2006) research into threshold decisions offers further explanations as to the criteria affecting decisions to intervene, He found that referrals were assessed with reference to five factors: specificity, severity, risk, parental accountability and corroboration (p 4). Social workers decided to respond with a child welfare response, as opposed to a no further action one, where parents could be held accountable, possible risks were present and the evidence was corroborated. The decision to move to the next threshold – a child protection investigation – was influenced by the specificity of the harm to the child and the workers' interpretation of the seriousness of the situation based on current information or previous patterns of behaviour. Platt argues that these reasoning devices 'are more complex than the notion based on a simple threshold', based on 'the concept of a straightforward continuum of abuse', and that a more holistic understanding is required (p 15).

Investigation

Formal investigation into potential child abuse may take place prior to an assessment being made – for example a referral requiring urgent action – during the assessment or post initial assessment where causes for concern are identified. The guidelines used for investigation across the UK are broadly similar. In England, Wales and Northern Ireland, the respective Working Together and Framework for the Assessment of Children in Need documents incorporate fixed timescales for inquiries from referral to investigation, child protection case conference, registration, core assessment and review (DH, 2000;

DHSSPSNI, 2003, 2008; DfES/DH, 2004; WAG, 2005; DfES 2006). In Scotland the process is similar although there are no fixed timescales for investigations (Scottish Executive, 2005). The investigations are multi- disciplinary and involve multi-professional information sharing, strategy meetings and decision-making meetings such as a child protection case conferences. They are informed by Local Safeguarding Children Boards/Safeguarding Children Boards/Area Child Protection Committee guidelines and procedures. Useful summaries of key legislation and policies are provided by Jowitt and O'Loughlin (2005, pp 43-58) and Hothersall (2008, pp 119-29). The emphasis in all guidance is on the importance of inter-professional and interagency communication, the lack of which has been a key criticism of child abuse inquiries and SCRs.

Longer-term interventions

Following child protection investigations, where concerns remain about needs and risks, a choice needs to be made about how to work in the longer term with the child and the family. The type of intervention depends somewhat on the statutory status of the child. The following summary of the range of interventions applies mainly, but not exclusively, to children who remain with family/carers in the community, although some interventions, such as individual therapeutic child-focused approaches could apply to children in foster and residential settings. The interventions described are drawn largely from UK-based literature, with some examples given of evaluations of interventions from Australasia, Europe and the US, where they are more relevant to social work in the UK.

COMMUNITY-BASED FAMILY SUPPORT PROGRAMMES

The UK policy emphasis on preventative and early intervention has resulted in a range of programmes based on supporting children and families in the community. Although these programmes are aimed at socially excluded and deprived children and families 'in need', families who have been assessed under child protection procedures might still be considered to be suitable to be referred to these programmes. Indeed, one programme evaluation has found that there has been a move from the programme providing universal provision to more specialised provision aimed at addressing risk rather than need (Tunstill and Hughes, 2004). The Sure Start National Child Care Strategy is a prime example of this broad-based intervention. Sure Start aims to support all families with children under the age of 5, but is also available for families in which there are older children. The support offered includes dedicated family centres, home visiting, intensive health visiting, child-care, health advice, and educational support from a range of professionals. Sure Start and similar programmes have been found to be effective in providing home support, assisting with advocacy, family ill-health and social networking (Tunstill and Aldgate, 2000); better parenting and social functioning for non-teenage mothers and improvements in child well-being, family well-being and parental well-being in connection with the child (Artaraz *et al*, 2007). However, the programmes are less successful in addressing the issue of social deprivation (Tunstill and Aldgate, 2000) or developing parental social networks (Artaraz *et al.,* 2007).

PARENTING PROGRAMMES

Parenting programmes have been developed to address a range of parenting issues from concerns with regard to early parenting, poor parenting skills, problematic behaviour in children and preventing or responding to parental abuse. Typically they are concerned with changing parental and/or child behaviour and their broad aims are to increase responsive parenting, appropriate monitoring and consistent disciplining. The programmes may take the form of individual sessions, group programmes, self-help text-based or online programmes or a mixture of these methods and involve discussion, practice exercises, observation of skills and homework tasks. They may be offered universally in a community, targeted at 'at-risk' families, for example where there is parental substance misuse, or they may be implemented at a tertiary level where parents have already abused a child (Cunningham *et al.,* 2009). Cunningham *et al.* (2009), in their evaluation of large-group community-based parenting programmes, find that there is some evidence that the programmes reduce physical abuse and that they are effective in reducing substantiated abuse and neglect. Barlow *et al.*'s (2002) systematic review of individual- and group-based programmes targeted at parents where there is a high risk of abuse or neglect, find that there is some evidence to indicate that the programmes are effective with regard to physically abusive parenting but not with regard to neglect. The low uptake and high departure rate is a further disadvantage of these programmes (Quinton, 2004). There is a lack of literature on the effectiveness of such programmes in the field of sexual abuse. It is likely that this is because parenting interventions with regard to sexual abuse are likely to be concerned with the education and support of the non-abusing parent in order to keep their child safe.

Family Group Conferencing

Family group conferencing (FGC) was developed in New Zealand (Marsh and Crowe, 1998) and has subsequently been developed across the UK (see Barnsdale and Walker, 2007, for the development in each country). The aim of FGC is to bring together all relevant family members, including extended kin and where appropriate significant non-relatives, in order to identify issues, discuss actions and agree an action plan. The conference is facilitated by an independent co-ordinator. In England and Wales, guidelines have been produced by the Family Rights Group (FRG *et al.,* 2007) As well as being used to help make decisions in relation to permanency planning, contact and youth offending, they are also used when children are considered in need of being safeguarded from significant harm (FRG, 2007). The Family Rights Group provides reports of evaluations of FGC. However, the use of FGC in cases of child protection varies in different countries. Although many case examples have been cited where an FGC has produced positive change, sometimes in unpromising circumstances, there is no conclusive evidence from controlled evaluations of the effectiveness of this method of intervention (Barnsdale and Walker, 2007).

Therapeutic interventions for children who have been abused

Corby (2000, p 198) reviewing a range of international studies a decade ago, argued that 'direct forms of treatment and therapy [with children] have been found to be lacking' as intervention following abuse and neglect has tended to focus on working with parents on their behaviour. However, both practice and evaluation have developed since then. Therapeutic child-focussed work with children who have been abused may take a variety of forms. Doyle (2006) describes a range of therapeutic approaches from individual work, group work and family therapeutic work, and provides advice on the content, duration and focus of therapy sessions. She emphasises the need to establish trust, explore emotions, counter misconceptions and establish protective strategies with children. Evaluation of the effectiveness of direct therapeutic work with children is mixed. For example, Jackson et al.'s (2009) evaluation of a therapeutic service focusing on the emotional and mental health needs of children who have experienced abuse and neglect evidences the value of taking a trauma and attachment perspective within a broader ecological approach. Outcomes for children were measured using a Trauma Symptom Checklist for Children and a Social Network Map. Becker-Weidman and Hughes (2008) report on the effectiveness of a specialised dyadic-developmental psychotherapy approach for children with complex trauma following abuse, which involves direct work with children and family therapy work. In his ten-year research update into therapy for children who have been sexually abused, Putnam (2003) found that cognitive-behavioural therapy of the child and non-abusing parent appears to be the most effective treatment of trauma following sexual abuse, although he argues that larger-scale and longitudinal studies are required in this area.

Supervision in child protection work

Inadequacies in supervision in child protection work have been consistently emphasised in child protection inquiry reports (Laming, 2003). Laming (2009, p 32) described 'Regular high quality organised supervision [as] critical' yet also often not provided. He emphasised that typically frontline staff had too much personal responsibility and that 'anxiety undermines good practice' (2009, p 4). He characterised good supervision as 'open and supportive, focussing on the quality of decisions, good risk analysis and improving outcomes for children rather than meeting targets (2009, p 32).

The key features of good supervision have been described as:

- regular and scheduled: both parties need an opportunity to prepare for it;
- documented: there needs to be a clear audit trail;
- supportive: issues such as workload, stress, safety in dangerous situations and the emotional effect of difficult cases should be addressed;
- probing and challenging: cases should be discussed in detail to ensure that all issues have been covered;
- non-adversarial: a blame culture will lead to defensive behaviour and the cover-up of omissions;
- skilled: line managers need to be fully trained in supervision skills.

(*Community Care*, 2009)

Brandon *et al.*'s (2006, p 405) analysis of the use of CAF found that in high-quality forms, practitioners had received good supervision and support with regard to gathering information, completing the form, developing skills for follow-up, report writing and 'sharing information with other professionals and negotiating skills'. White and Featherstone (2005) also emphasise the importance of supervision to aid inter-professional communication.

The specific challenges of supervision in child protection work are discussed by Cooper (2005) with reference to the Laming (2003) report. Cooper notes that the report highlights what did not happen in supervision but makes little reference to what did happen. He argues that supervision must always address the 'difficult psychological and emotional transactions that child protection work necessarily involves for staff – if they are doing their jobs properly' (2005, p 8).

While supervision should be supportive, it also needs to be probing and challenging so that social workers reflect critically on their assessments and decisions, and are helped to be open to new interpretations of situations. Cooper (2005) warns that abusing parents may be adept at avoiding or misleading parents. Similarly, Munro (2005, p 282) is concerned that inquiries have shown how 'professionals can hold onto their beliefs despite a growing amount of evidence that looks with hindsight, compelling proof of abuse. Thorough supervision with a skilled supervisor would begin to address the difficulties professional find in analysing parents' behaviour and in adopting fresh perspectives.

Conclusion

This chapter has provided an overview of the current policy issues with respect to child protection across the UK. It has discussed the key features of the assessment process of children and families, where there is concern with regard to a child, with reference to findings from inquiry reports and research. The main policy documents guiding a child protection investigation have been identified. Examples of longer-term interventions have been discussed and the importance of good-quality supervision at all stages of the child protection assessment process has been stressed.

In order to prepare for working in the field of child protection, one should ask:

- what do I need to learn?
- where can I find the information?
- how do I prepare myself emotionally for the work?
- what supports do I need in place?

References

Artaraz, K, Thurston, M and Davies, S (2007) 'Understanding family support provision within the context of prevention: a critical analysis of a local voluntary sector project' *Child and Family Social Work* 12(4), pp 306-15.

Barlow, J, Coren, E and Stewart-Brown, S (2002) 'Meta-analysis of the effectiveness of parenting programmes in improving maternal psychosocial health' *British Journal of General Practice* 52(476), pp 223-33.

Barnsdale, L and Walker, M (2007) *Evaluating the Sse and Impact of Family Group Conferencing* Edinburgh: Information and Analytical Services Division, Scottish Executive Education Department.

Becker-Weidman, A and Hughes, D (2008) 'Dyadic developmental psychotherapy: an evidence-based treatment for children with complex trauma and disorders of attachment' *Child and Family Social Work* 13(3), pp 329-37.

Bell, M and Wilson, K (eds) (2003) *The Practitioner's Guide to Working with Families* Basingstoke: Palgrave Macmillan.

Brandon, M, Howe, A, Dagley V, Salter C and Warren, C (2006) 'What appears to be helping or hindering practitioners in implementing the Common Assessment Framework and lead professional working' *Child Abuse Review* 15(6), pp 396-413.

Brandon, M, Belderson, P, Warren, C, Gardner R, Howe, D, Dodsworth, J and Black, J (2008) 'The Preoccupation with Thresholds in Cases of Serious Injury through Abuse and Neglect' *Child Abuse Review* 17(5), pp 313-30.

Broadhurst, K, Grover, C and Jamieson J (2009) 'Introduction: Safeguarding Children?' in Broadhurst, K, Grover, C and Jamieson, J (eds) *Critical Perspectives on Safeguarding Children* Chichester, Wiley Blackwell, pp 1-16.

Community Care (2009) 'Whatever happened to child protection?', 23 April.

Cooper, A (2005) 'Surface and depth in the Victoria Climbié report' *Child and Family Social Work* 10(1), pp 1-9.

Corby, B (2000) *Child Abuse: Towards a knowledge base* (2nd edition), Maidenhead, Open University Press.

Corby, B (2006) 'The Role of Child Care Social Work in Supporting Families with Children in

Need and Providing Protective Services – Past, Present and Future' *Child Abuse Review* 15(3), pp 159-77.

Cunningham, C E, Bremner, R and Boyle, M (2009) 'What makes parenting programmes effective? An overview of recent research' *Research to Practice Notes* Australia: New South Wales Government.

Devaney, J (2008) 'Inter-professional working in child protection with families with long-term and complex needs' *Child Abuse Review* 17(4), pp 242-61.

DfES (Department for Education and Skills) (2006) *The Common Assessment Framework for Children and Young People: Forms* London: DfES (www.dcsf.gov.uk/everychildmatters/resources-and-practice/TP00004/; accessed 19 May 2010).

DfES and DH (Department for Education and Skills and Department of Health) (2004) *National Service Framework for Children, Young People and Maternity Services* London: DH (www.dh.gov.uk/en/Healthcare/Children/NationalServiceFrameworkdocuments/index.htm; accessed 19 May 2010).

DH (Department of Health) (2000) *The Framework for the Assessment of Children in Need and their Families* (www.dh.gov.uk/en/Publicationsandstatistics/Publications/PublicationsPolicyAndGuidance/DH_4008144; accessed 19 May 2010).

DHSSPSNI (Department of Health Social Services and Public Safety in Northern Ireland) (2003) *Co-operating to Safeguard Children* Belfast: DHSSPSNI (www.dhsspsni.gov.uk/show_publications?txtid=14022; accessed 19 May 2010).

DHSSPSNI (2008) *Understanding the Needs of Children in Northern Ireland: Guidance* Belfast: DHSSPSNI (www.welbni.org/index.cfm/go/publications/key/6832628E-09E1-D43F-4F0E0109B9D314BD:1; accessed 19 May 2010)

Doyle, C (2006) *Working with Abused Children* Basingstoke: Palgrave Macmillan.

Forrester, D (2007) 'Patterns of re-referral to social sciences: a study of 400 closed cases' *Child and Family Social Work* 12(1), pp 11-21.

FRG (Family Rights Group), Department for Education and Skills and Welsh Assembly Government (2006) *Family Group Conference Toolkit* London: FRG (www.frg.org.uk/fgc_toolkit.html; accessed 19 May 2010).

Garret, P M (2003) 'Swimming with Dolphins: the New Assessment Framework, New Labour and New Tools for Social Work with Children and Families' *British Journal of Social Work* 33(4), pp 441-63.

Garret, P M (2005) 'Social work's "electronic turn": notes on the deployment of information and communication technologies in social work with children and families' *Critical Social Policy* 25(4), pp 529-53.

Hayes, D and Spratt, T (2009) 'Child Welfare Interventions: Patterns of Social Work Practice' *British Journal of Social Work* 39(8), pp 1575-97.

HM Treasury (2003) *Every Child Matters* Green Paper, Cm 5860, Norwich: HMSO.

Hothersall, S J (2008) *Social Work with Children, Young People and their Families in Scotland* (3rd edition) Exeter: Learning Matters.

Jackson, A, Frederico, M, Tanti, C and Black, C (2009) 'Exploring outcomes in a therapeutic service response to the emotional and mental health needs of children who have experienced abuse and neglect in Victoria' *Australia Child and Family Social Work* 14(2), pp 198-212.

Jowitt, M and O'Loughlin, S (2005) *Social Work with Children and Families* Exeter: Learning Matters.

Laming, Lord (2003) *The Victoria Climbié Inquiry* London: The Stationery Office.

Laming, Lord (2009) *The Protection of Children in England: A Progress Report* London: The Stationery Office.

Marsh, P and Crowe, G (1998) *Family Group Conferencing in Child Welfare* Oxford, Blackwell.

Millar, M and Corby, B (2006) 'The Framework for Assessment of Children in Need and their Families – a basis for a therapeutic encounter' *British Journal of Social Work* 36(6), pp 887-99

Munro, E (2005) 'What tools do we need to improve identification of child abuse' *Child Abuse Review* 14(6), pp 374-88.

O'Brien, M, Bachmann, M, Husbands, C, Shreeve, A, Jones, N, Watson, J and Shemilt, I (2006) 'Integrating children's services to promote children's welfare: Early findings from the implementation of Children's Trusts in England' *Child Abuse Review* 15(6), pp 377-98.

Parton, N (1996) 'Child protection, family support and social work: a critical appraisal of the Department of Health research studies in child protection' *Child and Family Social Work* 1(1), pp 3-11.

Platt, D (2006) 'Threshold decisions: How social workers prioritise referrals of child concern' *Child Abuse Review* 15(1), pp 4-18.

Putnam, F W (2003) 'Ten-year research update review: child sexual abuse' *Journal of the American Academy of Child & Adolescent Psychiatry* 42(3), pp 269-78.

Quinton, D (2004) *Supporting Parents: Messages from Research* London: DfES.

Scottish Executive (2002) *It's Everyone's Job to Make Sure I'm Alright* Edinburgh: Scottish Executive (www.scotland.gov.uk/Publications/2002/11/15820/14009; accessed 17 May 2010).

Scottish Executive (2005) *Getting it Right for Every Child: Proposals for Action* Edinburgh: Scottish Executive (www.scotland.gov.uk/Publications/2005/06/20135608/56098; accessed 17 May 2010).

Taylor, J and Daniel, B (2005) *Child Neglect: Practice Issues for Health and Social Care* London: Jessica Kingsley Publishers.

Tunstill, J and Aldgate, J (2000) *Services for Children in Need: from Policy to Practice* London: The Stationery Office.

Tunstill, J and Hughes, M (2004) 'Family support at the centre: family centres, services and networks' in Quinton, D (ed) *Supporting Parents: Messages from Research* London: Jessica Kingsley Publishers.

WAG (Welsh Assembly Government) (2005) *National Service Framework for Children, Young People and Maternity Services* Cardiff: WAG (http://wales.gov.uk/topics/childrenyoungpeople/publications/nsfchildrenyoungpeoplem aternity/?lang=en; accessed 17 May 2010).

White, S and Featherstone, B (2005) 'Communicating misunderstandings: multi-agency work as social practice' *Child and Family Social Work* 10(3), pp 207-16.

White, S, Hall C and Peckover, S (2009) 'The descriptive tyranny of the Common Assessment Framework: technologies of categorization and professional practice in Child Welfare' *British Journal of Social Work* 39(7), pp 1197-217.

Chapter 9

Ensuring that Every Child Really Does Matter

Jane Aldgate

Introduction

From the very early days, social workers have drawn on knowledge and observations to make professional judgements about how best to help children and families. As far back as 1917, Mary Richmond successfully created a model for social casework incorporating what today we call the ecological approach to assessment (Richmond, 1917). This takes into account the whole of a child's world, including the child, family and the surrounding environment.

This chapter considers briefly what constitutes assessment in child and family social work, the processes that it involves and some of the key theories that are used across the United Kingdon (UK). It then describes the *Framework for the Assessment of Children in Need and their Families* (DH *et al.*, 2000a) implemented in England and Wales, the UNOCINI framework in Northern Ireland and the *Getting it Right for Every Child* assessment and planning system in Scotland, and ends with a discussion of the strengths and weaknesses of having national frameworks, where 'one size fits all'.

What is assessment?

Traditionally, assessment has been seen as a process, not an event. Meyer (1993, p 2) suggests that assessment is a complex skill. It is:

> The thinking process that seeks out the meaning of case situations, puts the particular case in some order and leads to appropriate interventions ... Assessment is the intellectual tool for understanding the client's psycho-social situation, and for determining 'what's the matter?'

Meyer goes on to outline the process of assessment in five steps:

1 Exploration;
2 Inferential thinking;
3 Evaluation;
4 Problem definition;
5 Intervention planning. (Meyer, 1993, quoted in Austrian, 2002, p 204)

These steps are echoed in the various assessment frameworks and systems used in the UK. The actual process of conducting the assessment, including the relationship between service user and worker, is seen as being as important as the outcome (Shemmings and Shemmings, 2001; Rose, 2009).

The contemporary knowledge base for assessment

There are many contemporary theories that underpin assessment in child and family social work. These have evolved over time and some are subject to some degree of social construction. For example, fashions about the best ways to care for young infants have varied over time, disability has moved from a medical to a social model (French and Swain, 2002) and the application of psychological theories about child development has moved from a model diagnosing deficits to one that emphasises strengths (Aldgate, 2006) and resilience (Daniel and Wassell, 2002; Seden, 2002). The interplay between child and environment in ecological theory has, however, remained an integral part of assessing the well-being of children and families for over two decades (Walker, 2002; Aldgate *et al.* 2006).

Children's rights and assessment

Children's legislation since 1989 in the UK, including the Children Act 1989, the Children (Scotland) Act 1995 and the Northern Ireland Children's Order 1995, has embraced the United Nations (UN) *Convention on the Rights of the Child* (UN, 1989), emphasisng the rights of children to be consulted about decisions affecting their lives. Legislation also makes connections between eligibility for services and the well-being of children. Three out of the four UK countries have based their assessment models around similar concepts of children 'in need'. Children are defined as 'in need' if their health and development are impaired or likely to be impaired without the provision of services. The fourth, Scotland, includes a similar definition of children in need in its core statute, but its assessment framework applies to all children, stressing the merits of early intervention.

Moving towards national frameworks for assessment

Prior to the 1980s, assessment was very much a matter for individual workers and their organisations. The first government practice guidance that attempted to provide a framework for assessment was issued in England and was intended for children where there were child protection issues (Gray, 2002). The comprehensive assessment guidance published by the Department of Health (DH: DH,1988) was familiarly known as the 'Orange Book' and much used, but 'practice in assessments was widely variable' and often 'too mechanistic' (Gray, 2002, p170). Also, a growing concern arose about the narrow interpretation of children in need in England as covering only children in need of protection (Aldgate and Tunstill 1995; DH, 1995).

The Framework for the Assessment of Children in Need and their Families in England and Wales

England and Wales led the development of national frameworks for assessment. They took a step forward to produce a framework for all children in need, including but not restricted to those who required child protection services. It was decided to build on the materials for the assessment of looked-after children, which had been developed in the early part of the 1990s, adding two other major domains alongside that of children's developmental needs, namely parenting capacity and the child's wider world to provide a full picture of a child's ecology. England and Wales were both jointly involved in this development.

The prototype English assessment rramework was underpinned by several key principles:

Assessments:
- are child centred
- are rooted in child development
- are ecological in their approach
- are a continuing process not a separate event
- ensure equality of opportunity
- involve working with children and families
- build on strengths as well as difficulties
- are inter-agency in their approach to assessment and the provision of services
- are grounded in evidence based knowledge. (DH *et al.,* 2000, p 10)

These provided the foundation for the development of frameworks in the other countries, incorporating principles and values, building on research findings and stressing service user participation (Rose and Aldgate, 2000; DH 2001).

The framework emphasised the value of the ecological approach to assessing children and families and that children will flourish best if all agencies recognise the part they can play in contributing to good outcomes. In both England and Wales, the framework was accompanied by extensive guidance on its use (see DH *et al.,* 2000a; NAW, 2000). Practice guidance included an exposition of the knowledge base of the framework (DH, 2000). Subsequently, there have been several key publications and training packs to help implementation (see, for example, Horwath, 2001; Aldgate *et al.,* 2006; Horwath, 2009)).

It was always the intention that the framework should be inter-disciplinary. It was owned and published by several government departments concerned with children's well-being:

the DH, the Department for Education and Skills and the Home Office. Unfortunately, however, because the framework grew out of the materials for looked-after children, it has been unable to escape its legacy of being viewed as belonging to and being led by social services. This has hindered its application as a genuine multi-agency assessment framework.

A framework for children in need or at risk?

It was very much the intention that use of the framework could apply to any child in need, including those with child protection concerns and environmental problems alongside children who have health or educational difficulties (Rose, 2009). One major area of criticism of the assessment framework has been the omission of risk as a separate category. Calder and Hackett (2003) believe that a needs-led approach could lead to underestimating risks, while Davies (2008, p 33) believes that the assessment framework 'is not an appropriate tool for investigative work'. Scotland is attempting to reconcile these problems in emphasising both risk and need (Aldgate and Rose, 2008; Scottish Government, 2008).

Framework or practice tool?

The assessment framework was just that, a *framework* for assessment, planning action and review, very much in line with classic assessment models, like that developed by Meyer (1993) described earlier. It was never intended to be used mechanistically, as a checklist, and it was expected that practitioners would use the framework judiciously, according to the individual problems within which they were presented.

Recognition that the framework might require more detailed practice tools to support assessments led to the publication of accompanying scales and questionnaires, designed to help assess special aspects of children's well-being (DH *et al.*, 2000b). Many of these have been widely used, not only in practice but also in research and practice evaluation (see, for example, Aldgate *et al.*, 2007). This has been a useful development that has helped workers to see the value of bringing different sources of information to their ecological assessment.

If that had been the end of the story, it might have enabled an easier implementation but policy makers took the view that workers needed some specific help with deciding how much or how little assessment they undertook. They divided the assessment processes into an initial assessment to be completed within seven days and a core assessment to be completed within 35 days (Rose, 2009). The underlying good intention of timescales was to prevent children waiting for help for a long time. Prescriptive tools were developed to assist practitioners to gather information on a standardised form. These measures combined to create a procedural way of approaching assessment. Unfortunately, the complexity of these changes and the accompanying idea of meeting targets have tended to override the quality of the assessment in some cases.

In spite of imposing complex forms on the gathering of information within the framework, there has been little guidance for workers on how to make sense of the often extensive information they have gathered, except for three useful pages on analysis in the original guidance (DH *et al.*, 2000a, pp. 54-7).

A new interdisciplinary outcomes-led approach and the integrated children's system

In 2003, the Westminster Government published its Green Paper, *Every Child Matters* (HM Government, 2003), which set out its interdisciplinary approach to the well-being of children and young people from birth to age 19. The paper introduced the idea of prescribing desired outcomes for children's services and well-being indicators. It was expected that these would focus professional activity on achieving these across all agencies. The government aspiration was for all children to be healthy, stay safe, enjoy and achieve, make a positive contribution and achieve economic well-being. Wales published its own version in 2004, *Children and Young People, Rights to Action* (WAG, 2004). This went further than *Every Child Matters* in detailing seven indicators for children's well-being, drawn from the *UN Convention on the Rights of the Child* (UN,1989), including a child's right to be free from poverty. The Children Act 2004 strengthened this holistic, interdisciplinary approach to helping children in England and Wales.

The *Every Child Matters* agenda led to the introduction of a second and separate assessment framework in England in 2006, The Common Assessment Framework (HM Government, 2006), developed by a different arm of government. Wales has not adopted the Common Assessment Framework, while Scotland and Northern Ireland have rather different multi-agency approaches. The Common Assessment Framework was designed to strengthen early identification of problems by a range of agencies beyond social work and provide a means by which all agencies could identify and share concerns. There have, unfortunately, been difficulties in some local areas in developing protocols for sharing information from health or education except where a child is formally 'looked after' by the local authority, when statutory requirements about children's well-being come into play. Such barriers to co-operation undermine the principles of early identification and early intervention intended by both frameworks.

A further complication has been introduced through the Integrated Children's System (Cleaver *et al.,* 2008) designed to bring together all the different frameworks and provide a coherent process of recording from first contact to planning and review, supported by an electronic case record system. However, implementing a national information and communications technology (ICT) system has placed considerable demands on agencies and individual workers. It is yet another challenge and diversion for workers away from the actual purpose and processes of assessment.

While it is helpful for practitioners to use a common language in assessment, they now have to grapple with what is in effect a three-part assessment system, the Common Assessment Framework, plus the initial and core assessments of the Assessment Framework along with complex and demanding forms and procedures that have been issued nationally. This has led some to question whether the aims of providing a framework to promote therapeutic work as originally suggested in the guidance accompanying the original Assessment Framework have been sabotaged to 'embody an ethos of bureaucratic regulation with stultifying effects on social work' (Millar and Corby, 2006, p 887). Although there needs to be some acknowledgement that a new system takes time to bed down, evaluations of the framework remain variable (DH and Cleaver, 2003; Cleaver and Walker, 2004; Ofsted 2008).

The UNOCINI Assessment system in Northern Ireland

Northern Ireland has implemented a distinctive assessment framework. In 2006, the newly established Office of the First Minister and Deputy First Minister (OFMDFM) published its ten-year strategy (OFMDFM, 2006), stressing long-term outcomes as in England and Wales and Scotland. Northern Ireland has expanded the five *Every Child Matters* indicators to reflect the Northern Irish context and recent turbulent history. It wants its children to be 'Healthy, Enjoying, Learning and Achieving, Living in Safety with Stability, Experiencing Economic and Environmental Well-being, Contributing Positively to Community and Society, and Living in a Society which Respects their Rights' (OFMDFM, 2006, p 7).

This strategy paper provides the rationale for developments in assessment. An earlier review of existing assessment systems by Bunting (2004) had pointed out the variation across the different Northern Irish Health Care and Social Services Boards and recommended a unified system for all of Northern Ireland.

In 2007, the Department of Health, Social Services and Public Safety (DHSSPS) introduced for consultation a new standardised assessment process for children in need within all Health and Social Services Trusts, broadly following the principles and ideas behind the assessment framework in England and Wales. Another influence was a DHSSPS child protection inspection report in 2006, which had recommended 'enhancing professional practice, multi-disciplinary and interagency work' (DHSSPS SSI, 2006, p 2). After extensive consultation with staff in Health Care Trusts and other agencies, the new Northern Irish assessment framework was introduced: *Understanding the Needs of Children in Northern Ireland*, known as UNOCINI. Extensive guidance was published to support its implementation (DHSSPS, 2008).

The UNOCINI framework is based on similar theory and knowledge to the framework in England and Wales, stressing children's development in an holistic way. As in Wales, it places an additional emphasis on being compliant with the UN *Convention on the Rights of the Child* (UN, 1989). It is an outcome-based model. The heart of the assessment framework has twelve domains covering different aspects of children's ecology. As in the other UK countries, the model stresses the use of a common language for all agencies. It is, however, very much a social services-led model, but set within Northern Ireland's unique system of joint Health and Social Services Boards.

Although assessment is made up of children's needs and risks, the model is service led, as children are grouped to fit with different kinds of service response. Four different levels of need are recognised:

- Level 1: Base population
- Level 2: Children with additional needs
- Level 3: Children in need
- Level 4: Children with complex and/or acute needs (DHSSPS, 2008, p 15)

There are four potential phases to the assessment process, with guidance offered on when it is appropriate to move to the next level of assessment. These are:

- Agency appraisal and preliminary assessment;
- Referral to social services;
- An initial assessment;
- A pathway assessment. (DHSSPS, 2008, p 17).

The fourth phase assigns children to different pathways, according to the degree and nature of service involvement. Children will then receive services according to whether they fit a Family Support Pathway, a Child Protection Pathway or a Looked-after Children Pathway. Appropriate forms are provided to aid the assessment process.

At the time of writing no clear evaluation of the system has been reported. It remains to be seen whether, as in England and Wales, the complexity of the form filling and bureaucracy will get in the way of practitioners being able to act in a timely and proportionate way or will be seen to provide a helpful, structured model of assessment, as is the intention.

Getting it right for every child – Scotland's approach to assessing children

Getting it Right for Every Child (Scottish Executive, 2005) is the key Scottish policy on assessment and planning. It reinforces a tradition that local authorities have had the scope to develop systems and practice according to local need. Scotland has always had its own legislative powers in relation to children and families. Since the 1960s these have been rooted in the Kilbrandon model of social justice (Kilbrandon, 1964). Where compulsory powers are needed to protect children, the welfare-based Children's Hearing system has always had a philosophy of including children and families in decision-making about children's well-being. Devolution has preserved and heightened differences between Scotland and England.

Scotland's strategic plan for children, published as *For Scotland's Children* in 2001 (Scottish Executive, 2001), predated *Every Child Matters*. The Scottish strategy focused on achieving the best possible outcomes for all children by agencies working together, as in the other countries. There was a strong emphasis on children's rights, as in Wales and Northern Ireland. *For Scotland's Children* was distinctive in addressing the role of universal services in early intervention by introducing the idea that every child should have a 'named individual' in health or education, who would be a point of contact for children and families and who could activate help on their behalf.

Getting it Right for Every Child was introduced as part of the reform of Children's Hearings in 2005. It introduced the equivalent of the *Every Child Matters* indicators of well-being, that all Scotland's children should be safe, healthy, active, nurtured, achieving, respected, responsible and included (Scottish Executive, 2005). The approach has since been refined and has become the transformational change vehicle for all children's services. It is more than an assessment framework. It provides a philosophy and way of working for all practitioners across all children's services, and is designed to help every child. Assessment and planning are just parts of the unified approach to offering help across all sectors. More than in the other countries of the UK, *Getting it Right for Every Child* explicitly stresses multi-disciplinary application of the assessment framework. The same system is used by single agencies or agencies working together. It begins in the universal services of health and education but also applies to targeted help, including additional educational support, social work and services for children who are in need of compulsory measures. Scotland's Children's Hearing system includes a wide spectrum of children at risk, from those in need of care and protection to children who have committed offences, all of whom come under the *Getting it Right for Every Child* umbrella.

The Scottish assessment system places an emphasis on values and principles that include children and families in the helping process rather than procedures. These have been translated into *Getting it Right for Every Child's* ten core components, which can be applied in any setting and any circumstance. They provide a benchmark from which practitioners may apply the approach to their areas of work. They set very high aims and only implementation will test their robustness in practice:

1 A focus on improving outcomes for children young people and their families based on a shared understanding of well-being.
2 A common approach to gaining consent and sharing information where appropriate.
3 An integral role for children, young people and families in assessment, planning and intervention.
4 A co-ordinated and unified approach to identifying concerns, assessing needs, agreeing actions and outcomes, based on the well-being indicators.
5 Streamlined planning, assessment and decision-making processes that lead to

the right help at the right time.

6   Consistent high standards of co-operation, joint working and communication where more than one agency needs to be involved, locally and across Scotland.

7   A Lead Professional to co-ordinate and monitor multi-agency activity where necessary.

8   Maximising the skilled workforce within universal services to address needs and risks at the earliest possible time.

9   A competent and confident workforce across all services for children, young people and their families.

10 The capacity to share demographic, assessment, and planning information electronically and within and across agency boundaries through the national eCare programme where appropriate. (Scottish Government, 2008, p14).

In January 2006, a two-year Pathfinder was established in the main city of one large authority (Highland) with a plan for extension across the country by 2011. Implementation is being done gradually, with Community Planning Partnerships opting in as they are able. The government has taken a low-key approach, believing that it is better to win hearts and minds by persuasion rather than by legislation, so there is no equivalent of the Children Act 2004 as in England. There are, however, targets for local authorities in the form of single outcome agreements between local authorities, the government and the Convention of Scottish Local Authority Services (COSLA, 2009). Full implementation will depend in part on this partnership and COSLA's role in supporting *Getting it Right for Every Child*. This could be a strength or a hindrance. It is as yet too early to judge.

The government has concentrated on recommending changes in practice and culture, as well as urging Community Planning Partnerships to streamline their systems but it has left alone the organisational structures of each local authority that provide the governance for implementing *Getting it Right for Every Child*. This could be helpful in targeting local issues but might also lead to councils cherry picking the areas in which they partially implement *Getting it Right for Every Child* rather than going for a whole-systems change approach.

Working closely with the Highland Pathfinder between 2006 and 2008, the Scottish Government has developed a *Practice Model* that all practitioners can use either on a single agency or multi-agency basis to assess, plan, take action and review children's progress. The Practice Model is evidence based, as in the other countries of the UK, using an ecological, whole-child approach, stressing resilience and strengths as well as vulnerabilities. It can be used by any agency and is not led by social work services as has become the custom in England. Assessment is seen as the means to provide help for children and families that is timely (early intervention), proportionate (as much or as little assessment and help as is needed), and puts children and families at the centre (by seeking their views and accommodating their circumstances) (Scottish Government,

2008).

The Practice Model is based around the eight areas of well-being in the national vision for children described earlier, that children should be: safe, healthy, achieving, nurtured, active, respected, responsible and included. Any practitioner, as well as children and their families, can use these well-being indicators as an *aide memoire* to identify concerns, to help formulate a Child's Plan either in a single agency or on a multi-agency basis and to measure outcomes after a review of progress has taken place. The Scottish system expects every practitioner to take responsibility for providing help, reprising the title of the Child Protection Audit and Review, *It's everyone's job to make sure I'm alright* (Scottish Executive, 2002). There are five questions every practitioner should ask if they have concerns about a child:

- What is getting in the way of this child's well-being?
- Do I have all the information I need to help this child or young person?
- What can I do now to help this child or young person?
- What can my agency do to help this child or young person?
- What additional help, if any may be needed from others?
  (Scottish Government, 2008, p 24)

A national form for recording concerns is being developed based on the experience from Highland Pathfinder. Apart from this, there are no fixed templates for professionals to use in more detailed assessments and it is left to individual agencies to decide if they want to use   standard forms. Neither are there timescales set for completion of assessment, indicative of the attitude of the Scottish Government towards valuing the skills and judgement of professionals. This means that   much will depend on the responsibility of everyone to understand and implement practice. There is an emphasis on agencies streamlining meetings and bureaucracy, as well as making sure that every child who needs help has a single plan. Again, change will depend on the will of councils to change systems rather than tinker with what already exists.

In cases where needs are straightforward, a plan can be put in place using the well-being indicators and it is expected that agencies will co-operate on a basis of trust without elaborate referral systems. If agencies need further information, practitioners can use the child-centred assessment triangle to gather information, supplemented by any specialist reports. This is adapted from the assessment triangle in the England and Wales assessment framework with one major difference. It looks at assessment from the perspective of the child, for example, 'What do I need from the people who look after me?', and is called the *My World Triangle*. This can be used by any agency. It now has been incorporated into the handheld maternal health record that midwives and other health professionals use with mothers. It is especially helpful for agencies working together on more complex cases of need and risk. Learning from the problems that social workers have had in England in analysing information gathered round the Assessment

Triangle, Scotland has added into its practice model a *Resilience Matrix* to help practitioners make sense of information they have gathered (see Scottish Government, 2008).

The Highland Council now applies *Getting it Right for Every Child* throughout children's services. It was aligned the Practice Model with its child protection procedures. Children in need of care and protection, looked after children, children who have offended and others who need compulsory measures, will be assessed through the same model (Stradling *et al,*. 2009). Most importantly, they will have a Child's Plan. Where legislation demands certain actions, as where a child may need an educational support plan, this will be incorporated into an overarching plan. When two or more agencies are working together, a *lead professional* is appointed, who can be from the agency most appropriate to the child's needs. This could be health, education, social work or the voluntary sector. A significant feature of the Highland implementation has been to introduce the recommendation in *For Scotland's Children* (Scottish Executive, 2001) that every child should have a named individual (now called a *named person*) in health or education who is a contact point for early intervention.

Computer systems are being developed nationally to help in the sharing of information, but this will be on a need-to-know basis, and each agency will keep its own records of the child. Scotland has decided to go for systems that are as simple as possible and avoid the problems of the English Integrated Children's System.

At the time of writing, a comprehensive external evaluation of implementation in the Pathfinder in Highland by the University of Edinburgh is beginning to show significant improvements in the delivery of children's services, beyond what might have been expected in such a short timescale. Many service users are getting a more appropriate, timely and proportionate service. The named person is effective in identifying unmet need at an earlier stage. More children and young people with concerns or unmet needs are receiving appropriate and proportionate support within universal services or are receiving targeted interventions for shorter periods of time. This includes using the early warning system identified through concerns to provide effective early intervention, reducing targeted support from social work. The quality of the information being shared across children's services has improved significantly. There has also been a significant reduction in the number of care and protection concerns referred to the Children's Hearings in the Highland Pathfinder as a result of more effective screening and more evidence-based decision-making. Police and children's services are working more closely together. Social work, the schools and health have had to produce fewer reports for the Children's Hearings. Observations have shown that planning meetings address the needs of the whole child (Stradling *et al.,* 2009; MacNeil and Stradling, 2010).

The evidence from Highland shows that the ideals of *Getting it Right for Every Child* are beginning to be translated into reality. Questions remain as to whether, in a time of cutbacks in public services funding, there will be the will and resources to make such major changes everywhere. Will child protection investigations be prioritised above early intervention and prevention and will the enhanced role for the universal services that is beginning to occur be at risk? Above all, will it be possible to sustain the inclusive attitude towards children and families in assessment and planning? Such an approach does demand radical changes in attitudes, communication skills and time.

Conclusion

The development of assessment frameworks in each of the UK countries has similar goals: to improve outcomes for children and to provide evidence-based templates for assessing children. They all aim to provide a common language for use by practitioners working with children and families. In spite of this, the directions taken by England and Wales, Northern Ireland and Scotland in implementing the frameworks are very different. Of them all, Scotland has aimed to be streamlined in its approach, having an inclusive approach that takes in all children, not just those in need. It stresses early intervention in all agencies, with an evidence-based *aide memoire* assessment framework that leaves judgement and decisions in the hands of the professionals in partnership with children and families. It is embedded in a way of working that has demanded changes in culture, systems and practice. Will the chief executives and professionals live up to the challenge? Northern Ireland has an elaborate system based on categorisng children in need, which, although providing structure for professionals, seems to go against a children's right approach. England and Wales started with excellent intentions to have a framework any agency could use but have found it difficult to escape from its social work origins. The application of the framework seems mired in complexity, with detailed forms and several confusing parts to the system, driven by targets. It will be several years before we will know if any of these 'one size fits all' approaches can work. What will undoubtedly influence what happens are the skills, knowledge and attitudes of the professionals. Time will tell whether assessment frameworks can work, and if they do, which kind of assessment framework best supports achieving the best outcomes for children.

References

Aldgate, J (2006) 'Children, development and ecology' in Aldgate, J, Jones, D P H, Rose, W and Jeffery, C (eds) *The Developing World of the Child* London: Jessica Kingsley Publishers, pp 17-34.

Aldgate, J and Rose, W (2008) *A Systematic Practice Model for Assessing and Managing Risk* Edinburgh: *Getting it Right for Every Child Team* (Scottish Government).

Aldgate, J and Tunstill, J (1995) *Making Sense of Section 17: Implementing Services for Children in Need within the Children Act 1989* London: The Stationery Office.

Aldgate, J, Jones, D P H, Rose, W and Jeffery, C (eds) (2006) *The Developing World of the Child* London: Jessica Kingsley Publishers.

Aldgate, J, Rose, W and McIntosh, M (2007) *Changing Directions for Children with*

Challenging Behaviour and their Families: Evaluation of Children 1st Directions Projects Edinburgh: Children 1st (www.children1st.org.uk/publications/publications.html)

Austrian, S G (2002) 'Guidelines for Conducting a Biopsychosocial Assessment' in Roberts, A R and Greene, G J (2002) *Social Workers' Desk Reference* Oxford: Oxford University Press, pp 204-8.

Bunting, L (2004) *Assessment of Children in Need in Northern Ireland* Belfast: NSPCC Northern Ireland Policy and Research Unit.

Calder, M C and Hackett, S (2003) 'The Assessment Framework: A Critique and Reformulation' in Calder, M C and Hackett, S (eds) *Assessment in Child Care: Using and developing frameworks for practice* Lyme Regis: Russell House Publishers, pp 3-60.

Cleaver, H and Walker, S with Meadows, P (2004) *Assessing Children's Needs and Circumstances: The Impact of the Assessment Framework* London: Jessica Kingsley Publishers.

Cleaver, H, Walker, S, Scott, J, Cleaver, D, Rose, W, Ward, H and Pithouse, A (2008) *The Integrated Children's System: Enhancing Social Work and Inter-Agency Practice* London: Jessica Kingsley Publishers.

COSLA (Convention of Scottish Local Authorities) (2009) *Concordat between the Scottish Government and Local Government* Edinburgh: Scottish Government (www.scotland.gov.uk/Resource/Doc/923/0054147.pdf).

Daniel, B and Wassell, S (2002) *Assessing and Promoting Resilience in Vulnerable Children: 1. The Early Years; 2. The School Years; 3. Adolescence* London: Jessica Kingsley Publishers.

Davies, L (2008) 'Reclaiming the Language of Child Protection: Mind the Gap Family Support Versus Child Protection: Exposing the Myth' in Calder, M (ed) *Contemporary risk assessment in safeguarding children* Lyme Regis: Russell House Publishers, pp 25-39.

DH (Department of Health) (1995) *Child Protection: Messages from Research.* London: The Stationery Office.

DH (1988) *Protecting Children: A Guide for Social workers Undertaking Comprehensive Assessment*, London: The Stationery Office.

DH (2000) *Assessing Children in Need and their Families: Practice Guidance* London: The Stationery Office.

DH (2001) *The Children Act Now: Messages from Research* London: The Stationery Office.

DH and Cleaver, H (2003) *Assessing Children's Needs and Circumstances: The impact of the Assessment Framework, Summary and Recommendations* London: The Stationery Office.

DH, Cox, A and Bentovim, A (2000b) *The Family Pack of Questionnaires and Scales* London: The Stationery Office.

DH, Department for Education and Employment and Home Office (2000a) *Framework for the Assessment of Children in Need and their Families* London: The Stationery Office.

DHSSPS SSI (Department of Health, Social Services and Public Safety, Social Services Inspectorate) (2006) *Our Children and Young People: Our Responsibilities* Report of Inspection of Child Protection Services in Northern Ireland, Belfast: DHSSPS SSI.

DHSSPS (2008) *Guide to Understanding the Needs of Children in Northern Ireland, UNOCINI* Belfast: DHSSPS SSI.

French, S and Swain, J (2002) 'The Perspective of the Disabled Person's Movement' in Davies, M, (ed) *The Blackwell Companion to Social Work* (2nd edition), Oxford: Basil Blackwell, pp 394-400.

Gray, J (2002) 'National Policy on the Assessment of Children in Need and their Families' in Ward, H and Rose, W (eds) (2002) *Approaches to Needs Assessment in Children's Services* London: Jessica Kingsley Publishers, pp 169-94.

HM Government (2003) *Every Child Matters*, Cm 5860, London: The Stationery Office.

HM Government (2006) *Common Assessment Framework for Children and Young People: Practitioners' Guide* London: Department for Education and Skills.

Horwath, J (ed) (2001) *The Child's World* London: Jessica Kingsley Publishers.

Horwath, J (ed) (2009) *The Child's World* (2nd edition), London: Jessica Kingsley Publishers.

Kilbrandon, Lord (chair) (1964) *The Kilbrandon Report, Children and Young Persons, Scotland: Report by the committee appointed by the Secretary of State for Scotland* Edinburgh: The Stationery Office.

MacNeil, M and Stradling, R (2010) *Getting it Right for Every Child: Evaluation briefing 6* Edinburgh: Scottish Government.

Meyer, C H (1993) *Assessment in Social Work Practice* New York: Columbia University Press.

Millar, M and Corby, B (2006) 'The *Framework for the Assessment of Children in Need and their Families* – A Basis for 'Therapeutic' Encounter?', *British Journal of Social Work*, 36(6), pp 887-99.

NAW (National Assembly for Wales) (2000) *Assessment Framework for Children in Need and their Families* Cardiff: NAW.

OFMDFM (Office of the First Minister and the Deputy First Minister) (2006) *Our Children and Young people: Our pledge: A ten year strategy for children and young people in Northern Ireland 2006-2016* Belfast: OFMDFM.

Ofsted (2008) *Safeguarding Children: The third joint chief inspectors' report on arrangements to safeguard children* London: Ofsted.

Richmond, M (1917) *Social Diagnosis* New York: Russell Sage Foundation.

Rose, W and Aldgate, J (2000) 'Knowledge Underpinning the Assessment Framework' in Department of Health, *Assessing Children in Need and their Families: Practice Guidance*, London: The Stationery Office, pp 7-15.

Rose, W (2009) 'The Assessment Framework' in Horwath, J (ed) *The Child's World* (2nd edition), London: Jessica Kingsley Publishers.

Scottish Executive (2001) *For Scotland's Children*, Edinburgh, Scottish Executive.

Scottish Executive (2002) *It's Everyone's Job to Make Sure I'm alright* Edinburgh: Scottish Executive.

Scottish Executive (2005) *Getting it Right for Every Child,* Edinburgh, Scottish Executive.

Scottish Government (2008) *A Guide to Getting it Right for Every Child* Edinburgh: Scottish Government.

Seden, J (2002) 'Underpinning Theories for Assessment of Children's Needs' in Ward, H and Rose, W (eds) (2002) *Approaches to Needs Assessment in Children's Services,* London: Jessica Kingsley Publishers, pp 195-216.

Shemmings, Y and Shemmings, D (2001) 'Empowering children and family members to participate in the assessment process' in Horwath, J (ed) *The Child's World* (2nd edition), London: Jessica Kingsley Publishers, pp 114-28.

Stradling, B, MacNeil, M and Berry, H (2009) *Changing Professional Practice and Culture to Get it Right for Every Child: An Evaluation of the Development and Early Phases of Getting it right for every child in Highland: 2006-2009* Edinburgh: Scottish Government.

UN (United Nations) (1989) *Convention on the Rights of the Child* Geneva: UN.

Walker, J (2002) 'The Human Life Cycle: Partnership and Parenting' in Davies, M (ed) *The Blackwell Companion to Social Work* (2nd edition), Oxford: Basil Blackwell.

WAG (Welsh Assembly Government) (2004) *Children and Young People, Rights to Action* Cardiff: Welsh Assembly Government.

Chapter 10

Residential Child Care: Learning from International Comparisons

Andrew Kendrick, Laura Steckley and Graham McPheat

Introduction

Over recent years, residential child care has come under increased scrutiny, and there has been marked ambiguity in policy debates about its roles and functions within the range of child welfare services. Considerable concern has been expressed about the institutional abuse identified in countries around the world. Questions have been asked about the effectiveness of residential care in comparison with alternative services. The often difficult experiences of children and young people leaving residential care – particularly those leaving care to independence – have raised questions about policies and practice. The ongoing focus on the importance of the family and family-based care settings has been contrasted with the 'institutional' nature of residential care. These discussions have played out in different ways across the world. It is the aim of this chapter to highlight the main issues to see what lessons can be learnt from comparison with residential care in other countries. The potential scope of this endeavour is huge and we have therefore had to be selective in the examples used, but we hope to contribute to the positive development of residential care.

International comparison of policy and practice can challenge assumptions and bring contrasting perspectives to similar social problems and solutions (Francis et al., 2004; Peters 2008). It highlights the very different issues that residential services may have to address in diverse social contexts. In an increasingly globalised world, international comparison can also guide us with developments in our own countries, as with residential care of unaccompanied asylum-seeking children in the United Kingdom (UK) (Kendrick, 2008a).

The diversity of residential child care across the countries of the world cannot be underestimated, nor the often rapid pace of change (Courtney and Iwaniec, 2009). Nevertheless, it is important that overarching trends in residential child care are recognised. For example, in the developed world there has been a move away from large-scale, institutional care to smaller, residential provision, and to foster care and community services (although these trends are not necessarily uniform across countries). The issues addressed by residential care also vary widely. In certain countries, residential provision has developed in response to problems such as disaster relief, caring for the orphans of AIDS, and addressing widespread poverty and deprivation. In other countries, the focus is much more on child protection, offending behaviour and family welfare. Models of care differ widely, from large-scale institutions providing basic care and education for children to specialist, small-scale provision offering therapeutic services. Standards and quality of residential provision are at different stages of development, as are the education and training of residential child care workers.

Underpinning this diversity of provision, however, it is important to acknowledge the underlying principles of the United Nations Convention on the Rights of the Child (UNCRC). While there are serious debates to be had about the impact of cultural, social and economic contexts on the provision of residential child care, the UNCRC makes clear statements about children's rights to provision, participation and protection, and we will locate residential child care in this children's rights framework.

Issues in international comparison

While international comparison can provide us with useful lessons and help us question the way in which we approach residential services and practice, we must also acknowledge significant difficulties in such comparative analysis.

There is a lack of comparable cross-national statistical information, particularly in the developing world. Colton and Williams (2002) noted the dearth of adequate information in Europe on basic questions such as the number of children entering and leaving residential care each year. Courtney and Iwaniec (2009, p xiii) comment that "the nature and availability of historical and empirical literature on residential care varies considerably from country to country". Interpretation of this information is made difficult by the use of differing terms and definitions; and the different meanings attached to similar practice. Cameron and Moss (2007, p 23) highlight the difficulties posed by language in their research on care work in Europe, and state that it is difficult to find a satisfactory solution to this problem. The definition of residential child care is problematic in itself, and the different models of care emphasise this. The overlap between residential care and other forms of institution – such as hospitals, boarding schools and penal establishments – will vary according to local context.

Another important issue is that the context of residential care also varies widely in terms of political history, economic arrangements, and legal and administrative frameworks (Colton and Hellinckx, 1993; Sellick, 1998). Residential care cannot be considered in isolation from these wider factors and it is sometimes problematic to work out the full implications for residential policy and practice. This also means that markedly different populations of children and young people use residential care in different countries. This may be most obvious in the use of residential care in the developing world for very young children, but even comparison of residential care in the countries of Western Europe identifies significant differences in the residential care population (Francis, et al., 2004; Cameron and Boddy, 2008).

Given these issues, we must be at least a little cautious when we look to apply the knowledge and practices from other countries to our own residential child care settings (and *vice versa*).

International statements on residential child care

As well as establishing more general rights to participation, protection and provision, the UNCRC (United Nations Convention on the Rights of the Child) makes relevant comments in relation to children in state care. Article 3 sets out that the best interests of the child shall be the primary consideration in all actions concerning children, and that "institutions, services and facilities responsible for the care or protection of children shall conform with the standards established by competent authorities, particularly in the areas of safety, health, in the number and suitability of their staff, as well as competent supervision" (UNCRC).

In addition, Article 19 of the UNCRC stresses that all children should be protected from abuse and neglect "while in the care of parent(s), legal guardian(s) or *any other person who has the care of the child*". Article 20 goes on to state that a child deprived or removed from his or her family environment "shall be entitled to *special protection* and assistance provided by the State" (UNCRC, emphasis added). These articles have particular pertinence in relation to the evidence of abuse in residential care that has emerged over recent years (Kendrick, 1998). Article 25 establishes the right of a child who is placed for the purposes of care, protection or treatment to have their circumstances periodically reviewed. These, then, should be established rights for children in residential care across the world.

However, ambiguity about the role of residential child care in the provision of services for children and young people is apparent in two international statements: the *Stockholm Declaration on Children and Residential Care* (2003) produced by delegates to the second international conference on children and residential child care; and the *Malmö Declaration* made by delegates of the 1986 International Federation of Educative Communities (FICE) conference.

The earlier *Malmö* Declaration highlighted the move from large institutional residential settings to new models of 'community' residential care that are treatment-oriented, interdisciplinary and interacting more positively with parents, social networks, neighbourhood and community.

> *Care in residential settings must continue to provide a positive atmosphere and a comprehensible environment for those who live in them, giving them the opportunity to create their own network of dependable social relationships.* (Malmö Declaration, 1986)

The later Stockholm Declaration in contrast stated that:

There is indisputable evidence that institutional care has negative consequences for both individual children and for society at large. These negative consequences could be prevented through the adoption of national strategies to support families and children, by exploring the benefits of various types of community-based care, by reducing the use of institutions, by setting standards for public care and for monitoring of the remaining institutions. (Stockholm Declaration, 2003)

The Stockholm Declaration therefore calls on governments to "restructure the system of public care in order to diminish the use of institutions, develop alternative care approaches and strengthen effective community-based preventive and protective social services". While the Malmö Declaration contrasts institutional settings with new models of residential care, the Stockholm Declaration treats all residential care as institutional and contrasts this with family settings. Courtney, Tolev and Gilligan (2009, p 191) suggest that:

a casual reader of the Stockholm Declaration on Children and Residential Care might easily conclude that the nations of the world had declared as a goal a definitive end to a centuries-long period in which dependent children had lived in group settings away from family and that a clear road map existed to a future that would be free of residential care.

(Courtney, Dolev and Gilligan, 2009, p 191)

Now, there is much in the Stockholm Declaration to be commended and supported, including the emphasis on a rights-based approach to children in public care, the need to adopt standards for public care and proper monitoring arrangements. Indeed, we support development of effective family-based and community-based services for children and young people. However, we must agree with Anglin and Knorth (2004, p 141) when they counter that 'for many young people … good residential care is not a last resort, but rather a preferred and positive choice when their developmental challenges indicate the need for it'.

As we will see, these two Declarations reflect the ambiguities and tensions in the practice of residential child care across the developed and developing world.

Residential care in international contexts

International Trends in Residential Child Care

Courtney, *et al.* (2009) stress that the pathways and development of residential child care in different countries of the world result from the interplay of a series of economic, political, ideological and cultural factors in conjunction with what they term 'precipitating events' such as abuse scandals or disease. Economic development creates the demand for residential care because of the breakdown in family and community structures. It can also create the supply of residential care because of economic surpluses that go into public welfare services, although "the relationship between national prosperity and the use of residential care is complicated by the fact that nations can invest their wealth in very dissimilar ways" (Courtney, *et al.*, 2009, p 193). Political, religious and cultural factors also play a significant part. Religious organisations have been central in the development of residential care, sometimes through colonial or foreign religious organisations. These have played a significant part in the most negative uses of residential care in relation to the relocation and resocialization of indigenous populations, for example in Australia, the United States (US) and Canada (Miller, 1996; Ainsworth and Hansen, 2009). Broader cultural norms can affect the balance between the use of residential care compared to foster care. For example, traditional views of the family in Japan have led to the predominance of residential over foster care – in 2007, less than 10 per cent of children in state care were in foster families (Ocheltree, 2010). Political ideology can most readily be identified in the development of institutions in the communist states of Eastern Europe after 1945, and attempts to move away from institutions with the breakdown of communist states (Courtney, *et al.*, 2009).

'Precipitating events' such as disaster and disease have had a significant impact on the development of residential care in some areas: "the worldwide HIV/AIDS epidemic has been one of a number of contributors to the demand for residential care in some places and may prove to be a decisive factor in others" (Courtney, *et al.*, 2009, p 199; see also Morantz and Heymann, 2010). While such events may be drivers for the increase of residential care, other factors have resulted in a reduction. Abuse scandals have negatively affected the development of residential care in a number of countries, More positively, the increasing focus on family involvement in residential child care has been another important factor in driving forward agendas for change (Hill, 2000; Shaw and Garfat, 2003; Barth, 2005).

Developments in the UK

The focus of this chapter is on international comparison, but a feature of the UK is that social work and child care is a devolved matter, and residential child care has developed differently across the four nations of the UK. Mirroring trends in other countries of the developed world there have been significant changes in residential child care across the UK. Most significant, perhaps, is the marked reduction in the size of the sector across all the countries – linked to the shift towards a preference for a family setting and the concerns raised by inquiries about residential care (Mainey *et al.*, 2006; Kendrick, 2008b; Bullock and McSherry, 2009). However, there are marked differences too. The sector in England and Wales has seen a marked increase in private provision, so that in 2004 almost two thirds of residential establishments were owned privately. In contrast, there were no privately owned establishments in Northern Ireland, and few in Scotland. Here the majority of establishments are run by the statutory sector (Mainey *et al.*, 2006; see also Bullock and McSherry, 2009).

All four jurisdictions have seen an increasing focus on improving the quality of residential care provision. Services must be registered with care commissions, and they are subject to regular inspection against national care standards. The workforce has to be registered, and there are standards of conduct and practice and codes of practice. The councils are empowered to discipline individuals and, ultimately, remove them from the register (Mainey *et al.*, 2006; Kendrick, 2008b).

An important difference among the countries of the UK is the qualification standards of residential child care staff. In England, Wales and Northern Ireland, the minimum qualification for care workers is the National Vocational Qualification (NVQ) 3 in Caring for Children and Young People, while in Scotland care workers need to hold both a Scottish Vocational Qualification (SVQ) or NVQ, and a Higher National Certificate (HNC) or equivalent. Managers in Northern Ireland must hold a Diploma in Social Work (DipSW), those in England, Scotland and Wales a DipSW or S/NVQ 4 (Campbell, 2006). Interestingly, in practice Northern Ireland has a much higher proportion of qualified staff, with half holding a professional social work qualification (Campbell, 2006).

Residential child care in the developed and developing worlds

The factors that have led to the decreasing use of residential care in the UK, have led to a similar trend across the developed world (Colton and Hellinckx, 1993; Sellick, 1998; Hellinckx, 2002; Courtney and Hughes-Heuring, 2009). As we saw above, in countries such as Australia, Canada and the USA, the role of residential care in the forced assimilation of indigenous peoples has also had significant repercussions for the use of residential care. This has included the marginalisation of residential child care – 'what is left of the residential care systems arouse suspicions and a sense that they are no more than a necessary evil' (Hellinckx, 2002, p 76). Ainsworth and Hanson (2009, p 147) argue that in Australia, this has been taken to such an extreme that: 'Australian children and young people who might well have been placed by child care and protective services in residential programs are in desperate circumstances when foster care fails, as no other alternatives exist'.

Use of residential care, however, varies widely. In the US, about one fifth of abused and neglected children are in residential care (Courtney and Hughes-Heuring, 2009). In Europe, in some countries such as Norway and the UK, most children and young people are placed in foster care. In others, such as Denmark, France and the Netherlands, there is a more equal balance in the two types of provision. However, in Southern, Central and Eastern Europe, residential care is predominant, although del Valle *et al.* (2008) note the rapid recent changes in residential provision in Spain. Even within countries there can be wide regional variations (Colton and Hellinckx, 1993; Sellick, 1998). Moreover, trends are not uniform. Knorth (2002) notes that in the Netherlands, despite explicit government policy to reduce the use of residential care, provision increased by more than 10 per cent between 1991 and 1999. Sellick (1998) highlights the much slower pace of change in Central and Eastern Europe.

The issues involved in comparing residential child care provision are equally pronounced when the focus moves from the developed to the developing world. Similarly, the tensions reflected in the Malmö and Stockholm Declarations remain evident. From some of the literature available what is perhaps most apparent is the wide variability in provision and the dominant role of ideology and 'precipitating events' in influencing this.

In many developing countries, the largest child welfare problem is that of orphaned children and much of the residential provision that exists, along with other kinship and community-based responses, is a direct consequence of disease, notably HIV/AIDS (Maundeni, 2009; Stout, 2009; Morantz and Heymann, 2010), natural disasters such as the South Asian tsunami of 2004 (Wanat et al., 2010) and war (Wolff and Fesseha, 2005). Although the extended family is considered the best place to care for children, social and economic changes and the large increase in the number of orphaned children caused primarily by HIV/AIDS have resulted in recent growth in residential provision (Maundeni, 2009; Stout, 2009). There has been a significant involvement of non-governmental organisations (NGOs) in the establishment and delivery of residential provision in Africa. This is mirrored in other parts of the world, particularly in countries such as Cambodia where political and social upheaval has left a continued legacy of orphaned, abandoned and vulnerable children (Emond, 2010). However, as exemplified in the Malmö and Stockholm Declarations, there is continued disagreement regarding the role of residential care. There is concern that residential establishments are developed inappropriately, with a lack of quality, which damages children's development and jeopardises their rights (UNICEF, et al., 2004; Swales, et al., 2006).

The attitudes in Botswana and elsewhere that oppose residential care contrast with the history of countries such as Brazil. Here there is a long-established tradition of residential provision, albeit one which is being increasingly questioned as a consequence of a shift in attitudes regarding the rights of the child (Rizzini and Rizzini, 2009). Significantly, recent research conducted in Cambodia, Ethiopia, India, Kenya and Tanzania concluded that in terms of health, emotional and cognitive functioning and physical growth, outcomes were no worse for institutionally-based children than those experiencing community living (Whetten et al., 2009). Wolff and Fesseha's (2005) study of Eritrean war orphans takes us back to the Malmö and Stockholm Declarations. This research compared the outcomes for children in four settings: home-reared children with their own mother; reunified orphans and their host mother; orphans in small group homes with their host mother; and orphans in a large institution. Those placed in smaller group homes had fewer signs and symptoms of emotional distress and greater adaptive skills not only compared to those in orphans but also those who were reunified. Indeed, they had fewer symptoms of emotional distress than home-reared children. While acknowledging that this was an expensive option, Wolff and Fessaha (2005, p 482) conclude that: 'a dedicated society raised on principles of self-reliance can create humane, sustainable, and culturally appropriate programs of residential group care at the community level that do not depend primarily or exclusively on the technical guidance and financial support of international relief agencies'.

Ways of understanding the work of residential child care

While residential child care is located under the broader umbrella of social work in the UK, in many European countries people who work in residential child care are trained as, and consider themselves to be, social pedagogues – a distinct discipline from social work. Social pedagogy can be defined as the education of children in the broadest sense (Petrie et al., 2006), promoting "wellbeing through broadly based socio-educational strategies" (Smith & Whyte, 2007, p 6).

In Australia, New Zealand, North America, South Africa and some parts of South America, residential child care falls within the child and youth care (CYC) profession, which is also a discipline distinct from social work. CYC can be defined as the development of relationships with children in their lifespace, and in the context of those relationships, helping them to "find different ways to live – ways … less painful for them and those in their lives" (Garfat, 2009, p 57).

Shared ideas among all three of these traditions are not new, although wider contexts of globalisation and technology appear to be increasing the volume of collaborative, "cross-fertilized" thinking and writing about residential child care practice. The most dominant and overarching of themes across the traditions is the centrality of relationships to good practice. Relationships have long been seen as the heart of residential child care practice in the UK (Ward, 2007), and the "conscious use of relationships between the Social Pedagogue and the young people" has been identified as the "essence of social pedagogical practice" (Bengtsson et al., 2008, p 9). Similarly, CYC has historically located relationships with children and their families at the centre of practice. As the field has developed, notions of providing therapeutic relationships have evolved to a more sophisticated form of *relational practice*. From a CYC perspective, relational practice is more than a worker simply having a good relationship with a child or family member; it involves the joint, explicit focus on the experience and maintenance of that relationship, and offers prototypes for future relationships (Garfat, 2008).

A second theme dominant across the three approaches is lifespace. Keenan (2002, p 221) refers to lifespace work as a "therapeutic discipline of its own" involving deliberate use of everyday activities and events in children's living space (Smith, 2005).

Relationships and lifespace work are not ends in themselves, but serve broader aims. CYC and social pedagogic traditions emphasise the overall development of the child as the ultimate aim (Coussee et al., 2008; Phelan, 2008). In the UK, the potential for relationships and activities within the lifespace to promote children's resilience has become an important focus (Gilligan, 2008), resonating with the strength-based approaches in CYC literature (Rudolph & Epstein, 2000).

Provision of reparative experiences has been an explicit purpose of relationship-based practice and lifespace work in the UK (Ward, 2007). Garfat (2004) highlights the numerous opportunities within the lifespace for CYC practitioners to engage in a process of co-creating meanings, with children. This meaning-making work can, for instance, begin to repair internal working models that construct all relationships as exploitative, hurtful or inevitably abandoning.

The very similar concepts of therapeutic containment (Bion, 1962) and holding environments (Winnicott, 1965) have been applied to lifespace work in a more holistically repairing way (Woodhead, 1999). These concepts illuminate how significant disruptions to early care experiences impede children's cognitive and emotional development. Many of these children experience enduring difficulties with managing their feelings and behaviour as a result, affecting most realms of their lives. Therapeutic containment and holding environments offer organising frames for understanding how relationships and lifespace work can be comprehensively utilised to enable children to overcome the impact of early trauma and deprivation, helping them to regain developmental ground.

For those doing lifespace work with children who have experienced trauma and deprivation, the establishment and maintenance of developmentally enhancing, reparative relationships makes significant demands on the self. An emphasis on the importance and challenges of 'presence', an elusive but necessary quality that practitioners must maintain in order to connect with children, runs across all three traditions (de Oliveira & Montecinos, 1998; Kruegar, 1999; Ward, 2007). A focus on self-awareness (Ricks, 1989) and reflective practice (Ruch, 2005b; Petrie et al., 2009) also dominates discussions about how the use of self is understood. Pedagogic traditions offer a simple, tripartite model for understanding use of self called the 'Three Ps': the private, the personal and the professional (Bengtsson et al., 2008). This is a useful shift away from more dichotomous constructions of a personal/ professional divide that can inhibit authenticity and spontaneity within relationships. The previously mentioned concepts of containment and holding environments have also been applied to understanding staff needs (Ruch, 2005a), highlighting the strong emotions provoked by the work and offering ways of understanding and addressing their impact.

Therapeutic communities provide an illustrative, international example of an approach to understanding the work of residential child care that integrates the above-mentioned themes. While there are various definitions of therapeutic communities, Ward (2003) argues that all can be thought of as a specialised version of group care for traumatised children and their families, where the focus is on enabling all of the community's members to realise their potential to help and be helped. Key elements include:

- a commitment to individual therapeutic relationships with children; an emphasis on groupwork for decision making and therapeutic gain;

- a utilisation of everyday interactions in the lifespace for therapeutic communication;
- an engagement with areas of the child's life outside of the lifespace, including family, education and health, towards addressing the whole development of the child;
- a commitment to full systems of support for staff;
- the use of psychodynamic frameworks (often alongside behavioural or cognitive approaches) for understanding and organising direct practice and the complex systems that surround it. (Ward, 2003, p 34)

Across the UK, staff have indicated a desire to be more involved in therapeutic work with the children they care for (Kendrick, 2006); the therapeutic community approach integrates these shared ways of understanding the work of residential child care into a coherent, focused model.

Conclusion

This chapter aimed to review international trends, debates and issues in residential child care policy and practice, in order to learn lessons and question the assumptions about current practice in the UK. While there have been common factors that have affected the development of residential care across different countries, there are also clear differences in professional approaches. We have seen that there is a continuing ambiguity about the role of residential child care in most countries which has led to significant changes over recent years. The negative experiences and poor outcomes of children and young people, along with a focus on the primacy of the family, have led to an anti-residential care bias, which has had varying impact on the development of policy and practice. This has perhaps been most striking in the evidence from Australia where the reduction of the residential sector has led to major consequences for the experience of children and young people (Ainsworth and Hansen, 2009). This parallels the experience in the UK during the 1990s when certain local authorities attempted to get rid of their residential provision (Kendrick, 1995).

In this regard, it is important to refute the claims of the Stockholm Declaration, which imposes such a negative perspective on the role of residential child care, focused as it is on 'institutional environments'. However, it is also clear that the future role of residential child care requires the adoption of a much more focused and theoretically driven approach to working with children and young people. We must certainly learn the lessons of the past in terms of the abuse that has occurred in residential child care settings around the world, and drive forward the improvement of quality and standards in residential child care. We have therefore identified some key aspects of working with children and young people in residential child care which draw on the different contexts and history of residential care across the world. The most dominant themes of relationships and lifespace provide powerful mediums for enhancing development, promoting resilience and providing reparative experiences. Theoretical frames of therapeutic containment and holding environments bring these themes together, and therapeutic communities are offered as an example of a comprehensive approach that applies them.

While we cautioned in the introduction about the problems of imposing models from other countries into local contexts, we have found a convergence of themes and issues that are highly relevant to the development of practice of residential care. In doing this we hope to build on the debates about particular professional and organisational identities in order to focus on the development of day-to-day practice with children and young people. This is a challenge in the developed world and even more of a challenge in the developing world. However, only in this way do we think that the misconceptions and negative perspectives about residential care can be overcome, and the sector move forward in a positive way for the benefit of all those children and young people who need it.

References

Ainsworth, F and Hansen, P (2009) 'Residential programmes for children and young people: their current status and use in Australia' in Courtney, M E and Iwaniec, D (eds) *Residential care of children: Comparative perspectives*, Oxford: Oxford University Press.

Anglin, J and Knorth, E (2004) 'Competing declarations on residential care for children and youth – Stockholm versus Malmö: international perspectives on rethinking residential care', *Child & Youth Care Forum* 33(3), pp 141-49.

Barth, R P (2005) 'Residential care: from here to eternity' *International Journal of Social Welfare* 14(3), pp 158-62.

Bengtsson, E, Chamberlain, C, Crimmens, D, & Stanley, J (2008) *Introducing Social Pedagogy into Residential Child Care in England* London: NCERCC/SET.

Bion, W R (1962). *Learning from Experience* London: Karnac.

Bullock, R and McSherry, D (2009) 'Residential care in Great Britain and Northern Ireland: Perspectives from the United Kingdom' in Courtney, M E and Iwaniec, D (eds) *Residential Care of Children: Comparative perspectives* Oxford: Oxford University Press.

Cameron, C and Boddy, J (2008) 'Staffing, training and recruitment: Outcomes for young people in residential care in three countries' in Kendrick, A (ed) *Residential Child Care: Prospects and Challenges* London: Jessica Kingsley Publishers (pp 210-225).

Cameron, C and Moss, P (2007) *Care Work in Europe: Current understandings and future directions* London: Routledge.

Campbell, A (2006) 'Qualifications and training' in Mainey, A and Crimmens, D (eds) *Fit for the Future? Residential care in the United Kingdom* London: National Children's Bureau.

Colton, M and Hellinckx, W (eds) (1993) *Child Care in the EC: A country-specific guide to foster and residential care* Aldershot: Arena.

Colton, M and Williams, M (2002) 'Residential care: last resort or positive choice? Lessons from around Europe – Editor's note' *International Journal of Child & Family Welfare* 5(3), pp 66-74.

Courtney, M E and Hughes-Heuring, D (2009) 'Residential care in the United States of America: past, present, and future' in Courtney, M E and Iwaniec, D (eds) *Residential Care of Children: Comparative perspectives*, Oxford: Oxford University Press.

Courtney, M E and Iwaniec, D (eds) (2009) *Residential Care of Children: Comparative perspectives*, Oxford: Oxford University Press.

Courtney, M E, Dolev, T and Gilligan, R (2009) 'Looking backwards to see forwards clearly: a cross-national perspective on residential care' in Courtney, M E and Iwaniec, D (eds) *Residential Care of Children: Comparative perspectives* Oxford: Oxford University Press.

Coussee, F, Bradt, L, Roose, R and Bouverne-De Bie, M (2008) 'The emerging social pedagogical paradigm in UK child and youth care: deus ex machina or walking the beaten path?' *British Journal of Social Work* (advance access), bcn147.

de Oliveira, W and Montecinos, C (1998) 'Social pedagogy: presence, commitment, identification and availability' *Teaching Education* 9(2), pp 61-7.

del Valle, J F, Bravo, A, Alvarez, E and Fernanz, A (2008) 'Adult self-sufficiency and social adjustment in care leavers from children's homes: a long-term assessment' *Child & Family Social Work* 13(1), pp 12-22.

Emond, R (2010) 'Caring as a moral, practical and powerful endeavour: peer care in a Cambodian orphanage' *British Journal of Social Work* 40(1), pp 63-81.

Francis, J, Kendrick, A and Poso, T (2004) 'On the margin: residential child care in Scotland and Finland' *European Journal of Social Work* (10)3, pp 337-52.

Garfat, T (2004) 'Meaning making and intervention in child and youth care practice' *Scottish Journal of Residential Child Care* 3(1), pp 9-16.

Garfat, T (2008) 'The inter-personal in-between: an exploration of relational child care practice' in Bellefeuille, G and Ricks, F (eds.) *Standing on the Precipice: Inquiry into the creative potential of child and youth care practice* Alberta: MacEwan.

Garfat, T (2009) 'Barbarians on the horizon: reflections on the advent of evidence-based practices in child and youth care' *Relational Child and Youth Care Practice* 22(4), pp 56-64.

Gilligan, R (2008) 'Promoting resilience in young people in long-term care: The relevance of roles and relationships in the domains of recreation and work' *Journal of Social Work Practice* 22(1), pp 37-50.

Hellinckx, W (2002) 'Residential care: last resort or vital link in child welfare' *International Journal of Child & Family Welfare* 5(3), pp 75-95.

Hill, M (2000) 'Inclusiveness in residential child care' in Chakrabarti, M and Hill, M (eds) *Residential Child Care: International perspectives on links with families and peers* London: Jessica Kingsley Publishers.

Keenan, C (2002) 'Working in the Lifespace' in Lishman, J (ed) *Handbook of Theory for Practice Teachers in Social Work* London: Jessica Kingsley Publishers.

Kendrick, A (1995) 'The integration of child care services in Scotland' *Children and Youth Services Review* 17(5-6), pp 619 -35.

Kendrick, A (1998) 'In their best interest? Protecting children from abuse in residential and foster care' *International Journal of Child & Family Welfare* 3(2), pp 169-85.

Kendrick, A (2006) 'Working with children and young people' in Mainey, A and Crimmens , D (eds) *Fit for the Future? Residential Child Care in the United Kingdom*. London: National Children's Bureau.

Kendrick, A (2008a) 'Black and minority ethnic children and young people in residential care' in Kendrick, A (ed) *Residential Child Care: Prospects and Challenges* London: Jessica Kingsley Publishers, pp 121-34.

Kendrick, A (ed) (2008b) *Residential Child Care: Prospects and challenges*, London: Jessica Kingsley Publishers.

Knorth, E (2002) 'Residential child and youth care in the Netherlands: developments and challenges' *International Journal of Child & Family Welfare* 5(3), pp 84-95.

Kruegar, M (1999) 'Presence as dance in work with youth' *Journal of Child and Youth Care* 13(2), pp 69-70.

Mainey, A, Milligan, I, Campbell, A, Colton, M, Roberts, S and Crimmens, D (2006) 'Context of residential child care in the United Kingdom' in Mainey, A and Crimmens, D (eds) *Fit for the Future? Residential child care in the United Kingdom* London: National Children's Bureau.

Maundeni, T (2009) 'Residential care for children in Botswana: the past, the present and the future' in Courtney, M E and Iwaniec, D (eds) *Residential Care of Children: Comparative perspectives* Oxford: Oxford University Press.

Miller, J R (1996) *Shingwauk's Vision: A History of Native Residential Schools* Toronto: University of Toronto Press.

Morantz, G and Heymann, J (2010) 'Life in institutional care: the voices of children in a residential facility in Botswana' *AIDS CARE*, 22(1), 10-16.

Ocheltree, J (2010) Foster children in Japan, *Metropolis*, Issue 826 (http://metropolis.co.jp/features/global-village/foster-children-in-japan/).

Peters, F (ed) (2008) *Residential Child Care and its Alternatives: International perspectives*. Stoke on Trent: Trentham Books.

Petrie, P, Boddy, J, Cameron, C, Wigfall, V and Simon, A (2006) *Working with Children in Care: European perspectives* Maidenhead: Open University Press.

Petrie, P, Boddy, J, Cameron, C, Heptinstall, E, McQuail, S, Simon, A *et al.* (2009) *Pedagogy: A holistic, personal approach to work with children and young people, across services*, Briefing paper update, 200,. London: Thomas Coram Research Institute.

Phelan, J (2008) 'Building developmental capacities: a developmentally responsive approach to child and youth care intervention' in Bellefeuille, G and Ricks, F (eds) *Standing on the Precipice: Inquiry into the creative potential of child and youth care practice* Alberta: MacEwan.

Ricks, F (1989) 'Self-awareness model for training and application in child and youth care' *Journal of Child and Youth Care* 4(1), pp 33-41.

Rizzini, I and Rizzini, I (2009) 'Children and youth in institutional care in Brazil: Historical perspectives and current overview' in Courtney, M E and Iwaniec, D (eds) *Residential Care of Children: Comparative perspectives* Oxford: Oxford University Press.

Ruch, G (2005a) 'Reflective practice in contemporary child-care social work: the role of containment' *British Journal of Social Work* 37(4), pp 659-80.

Ruch, G (2005b) 'Relationship-based practice and reflective practice: holistic approaches to contemporary child care social work' *Child & Family Social Work* 10(2), pp 111-23.

Rudolph, S M and Epstein, M H (2000) 'Empowering children and families through strength-based assessment' *Reclaiming Children and Youth* 8(4), pp 207-9.

Sellick, C (1998) 'The use of institutional care for children across Europe' *European Journal of Social Work* 1(3), pp 301-10.

Shaw, K and Garfat, T (2003) 'From front line to family home: A youth care approach to working with families' *Child & Youth Services* 25(1/2), pp 39-53.

Smith, M (2005) *In Residence No 2: Working in the lifespace* Glasgow: Scottish Institute for Residential Child Care.

Smith, M and Whyte, B (2007) 'Social education and social pedagogy: reclaiming a Scottish tradition in social work' *European Journal of Social Work* 1(1), pp 1-16.

Stout, R (2009) 'Residential care in South Africa: changing the perspective from social welfare to social development'in Courtney, M E and Iwaniec, D (eds) *Residential Care of Children: Comparative perspectives* Oxford: Oxford University Press.

Swales, D, Geibel, R and McMillan, N (2006) *Applying the Standards: Improving quality childcare provision in East and Central Africa.* London: Save the Children.

UNICEF, UNAIDS and USAID (2004) *Children on the Brink: A joint report of new orphan estimates and a framework for action* (www.unicef.org/publications/files/cob_layout6-013.pdf).

Wanat, S, Whisnant, J, Reicherter, D, Solvason, B, Juul, S, Penrose, B and Koopman, C (2010) 'Coping with the challenges of living in an Indonesian residential institution' *Health Policy*, doi:10.1016/j.healthpol.2010.01.001

Ward, A. (2003) 'The core framework' in Ward, A, Kasinski, K, Pooley, J and Worthington, A (eds) *Therapeutic Communities for Children and Young People*. London: Jessica Kingsley Publishers.

Ward, A (2007) *Working in Group Care: Social work and social care in residential and day care settings* (2nd edition), Bristol: The Policy Press.

Ward, A, Kasinski, K, Pooley, J and Worthington, A (eds) (2003) *Therapeutic Communities for Children and Young People*. London: Jessica Kingsley Publishers.

Whetten K, Ostermann J, Whetten R A, Pence B W, O'Donnell K, *et al.* (2009) 'A comparison of the wellbeing of orphans and abandoned children ages 6-12 in institutional and community-based care settings in 5 less wealthy nations' *PLoS ONE*, 4(12), p 8169, doi:10.1371/journal.pone.0008169.

Winnicott, D W (1965) *The Maturation Process and the Facilitating Environment*
London: Hogarth Press.

Wolff, P H and Fesseha, G (2005) 'The orphans of Eritrea: what are the choices?' *American Journal of Orthopsychiatry* 75(4), pp 475-84.

Woodhead, J (1999) 'Containing care' in Hardwick, A and Woodhead, J (eds) *Loving, Hating and Survival: A handbook for all who work with troubled children and young people* Aldershot: Ashgate Arena, pp 2-21.

Chapter 11

The Rise of Independent Foster Care

Clive Sellick

Introduction

The focus of this chapter is on the development of the independent foster care sector in the United Kingdom (UK), which has been one of the main developments in services for looked-after children over the past twelve or so years. A chapter of this length can only provide a snapshot of this subject. However, a synthesis of the foster care research literature can be found elsewhere which locates the role and functions of voluntary and private sector fostering agencies within a wider foster care context (Sellick, 2006a). Most information about independent foster care relates to England and Wales, but two empirical studies gathered data from across the four countries of the UK (Sellick and Connolly, 2001, 2002; Sellick and Howell, 2003, 2004).

   The reasons for the significant growth in the independent foster care sector will be explored in this chapter and the changes in policy direction that have impacted on practice will be considered. This chapter will also review current challenges for fostering services, which are likely to determine the future of child placement services for looked-after children and their foster carers and social workers. To begin with, what are independent fostering agencies or providers (IFPs)? 'These organisations assess, approve, train and supervise foster carers and provide, for payment, foster placements and therapeutic and educational services to local authorities for children and young people in their care or accommodation' (Sellick, 2006b, p 1346). The organisations include those that are registered as voluntary, not-for-profit, agencies as well as those registered as private, for-profit, organisations. Although the majority of looked-after children are still fostered by local authority carers, a growing number, as we shall see, are cared for by those who have been assessed and approved by non-public sector IFPs.

From a public to a mixed economy of provision

Since the early days of post-war welfare provision, particularly from 1948, fostering children in care was largely organised directly by local authorities although significant numbers of voluntary and private agencies provided residential child care. However, for more than a decade, foster care in England and Wales, and to a lesser extent in Scotland and Northern Ireland, has ceased to be an almost exclusively public sector activity. Two main factors have accounted for this: first, the economic realities of supply and demand associated with changing policy and practice and second, a shifting welfare ideology in the UK. Throughout the UK, fostering has largely replaced residential care provision as the principal placement of choice for looked-after children. The most recently published government figures in England, for example, record that less than 10 per cent of looked-after children were placed in secure units, children's homes and hostels and that the majority of these were teenagers (DCSF, 2009).

With the significant growth in the use of foster family care, most local authorities have experienced considerable difficulties in finding an adequate supply of foster carers. In addition, local authorities across the UK have always had to face financial constraints so that ideals about having available a range of options when placing a child are often challenged by the need to minimise foster home vacancies. Two studies at the end of the 1990s, one in England and one in Scotland, found evidence of a significant shortfall in local authority approved foster carers. In a study by Waterhouse (1997), English local authorities at this time were only able to offer a placement of choice (that is, more than one) to children aged below 10 years in 20 per cent of cases but this fell to a mere 3 per cent for older children and young people. In Scotland, 30 per cent of foster placements were not the first choice of the children's social workers and in 14 per cent of cases no placements were available at all within local authorities (Triseliotis et al., 2000).

As a direct consequence of the shortfall in public sector placement provision, local authorities began to purchase placements from IFPs (nearly all of the English councils that responded to the Waterhouse et al. study did so, although at that stage only modestly and generally as an emergency measure). As local authorities continued to do business with IFPs, in the purchasing of placements and related therapeutic and educational services, these agencies grew rapidly as Table 11.1 demonstrates. These are agencies registered with Ofsted and its predecessors and most are based in England. However, a number of these will also have bases elsewhere in the UK and be registered and inspected by equivalent agencies in those countries.

Table 11.1 The growth of IFPs

Year	Number of IFPs
1993	11
1998	62
2001	90
2006	253
2009	289

The significant growth spurt in the five years between 2001 and 2006 was due to two main factors: the overall policy drive towards commissioning children's services from non-governmental organisations including IFPs and, as we shall see below, the impact of the Care Standards Act 2000, which in England and Wales authorised privately registered IFPs to approve foster carers in the same manner as voluntary and local authority fostering agencies.

This expansion in provision from the independent sector has been encouraged by government policy throughout most of the New Labour era. Speaking to directors of social services departments in 2001 the then-Secretary of State said: 'For too long in my view, there has been a stand off in the relationship between the statutory, private and voluntary care sectors. There should be no ideological barriers getting in the way of best care for vulnerable people' (DH, 2001). This aspiration became policy through the notion of public sector commissioning of private and voluntary sector services. A taskforce was appointed by the government to encourage partnership arrangements between sectors having recognised that 'few local authorities are able to provide, in house, all the services needed by looked after children in their area' (DfES, 2005, p 1).

In line with this policy shift, programmes designed to modernise child welfare, including child placement, provision have included a commitment to what has become termed 'the mixed economy of foster care' (Sellick, 2007). In their national survey of IFPs Sellick and Connolly (2001) found that almost 80 per cent of agencies at that time were registered as voluntary, non-profit-making, ones. However, as a result of legal changes brought about by the Care Standards Act 2000, all fostering agencies became entitled to approve and register their foster carers. Until then only fostering agencies in the public and voluntary sectors were permitted to do so. The foster carers attached to agencies registered as private, for profit, organisations only gained official approval to foster individual, named children on behalf of the local authority in which the children were in care. The impact of the Care Standards Act on the status of non-public sector fostering agencies was significant so that by the middle of the decade, 89 per cent of IFPs had become registered as private agencies (Sellick, 2007). Of these, most are managed by their owners or directors, many of whom have a social work and foster care background. Other agencies have been acquired by private equity companies using venture capital and this development will be considered later in this chapter when the distinction between collaboration and competition is discussed. A former director of the British Association for Adoption & Fostering (BAAF) in Scotland set out the dangers that voluntary providers have already faced in the new world of formalised local authority commissioning:

> *While the larger agencies within the sector, such as Barnardos and NCH, have the strength, financial power and wisdom to retain adequate space for innovative projects, smaller agencies are becoming increasingly preoccupied with meeting their contract specifications, with little room for manoeuvre. For these agencies, the barriers to entry into the welfare market*

have been removed, but the option of exit from the market has also been removed from their control. The result may be stifled growth and lack of innovation. (Giltinan, 2002, p 55)

The impact and practice implications of this trend, especially in respect of private equity providers, will be examined at the end of this chapter.

As the number of IFPs has grown, so too has the proportion of fostered children who are placed in the independent, as opposed to the public, sector. Table 11.2 below shows, by referring to government figures for children looked after by English local authorities (DCSF, 2009), that one quarter of these children are now placed with foster carers attached to IFPs.

Table 11.2: The growth in the percentage of children placed in IFPs

Year	Percentage placed
2001	11%
2005	19%
2007	23%
2009	25%

It is evident from these figures that IFPs have become an established part of the foster placement sector in the UK. Indeed, when children placed with kinship foster carers are excluded, somewhere in the region of one-third of children are placed with 'stranger' foster carers in the independent sector. The rest of this chapter examines three stages in the development of IFPs. It then goes on to anticipate a fourth stage before concluding with a discussion of key issues.

Stage 1: Filling the placement void – but at a price

As we have seen, the shortfall in fostering placements that affected most local authorities in Britain from the mid-1990s forced these councils to purchase, often at short notice, placements from independent fostering providers. This unplanned, and unbudgeted, activity, was referred to generally as 'spot-purchasing' whatever placements were available, when needed, and on a generally emergency basis. Almost no local authorities at this time had entered into formal arrangements with IFPs for the provision of foster placements and related therapeutic and educational services (Sellick, 1999). Instead, local authority managers tended to resist all such transactions unless absolutely necessary because of both financial and ideological reasons. IFPs were variously described as charging 'Rolls Royce' or 'golf club' fees and accused of making a profit opportunity out of children. One local authority manager gave expression to his experience of purchasing IFP placements when he said he was 'being taken for a mug' (Sellick and Connolly, 2002, p 107). As IFPs grew both in number and in size, some local authority social work staff and foster carers were being attracted to transfer to these agencies and this too caused resentment from local authority staff who accused IFP managers of 'poaching' social workers and foster carers, which in turn created much mutual distrust between public and independent fostering agencies.

Thus, easy trust and mutuality were generally lacking between local authority and IFP staff. Local authority managers were content to purchase from and work with staff of established voluntary child care organisations such as Barnardo's and other smaller charitable agencies for the provision of adoption, fostering and residential child care services. However, most were very wary of engaging with what they viewed as the private sector in foster care despite the IFPs national study's finding that as many as 80 per cent of these agencies were registered as voluntary, not-for-profit agencies (Sellick and Connolly, 2001, 2002). In practice it became apparent that the registration status of IFPs made little difference to how their own staff viewed their principles and value base. All of the 55 IFPs in the national study defined their purpose in at least one of three ways: to promote foster children's welfare and development; to deliver high-quality services; and to provide a trained and competent foster carer workforce (Sellick, 2002). In subsequent discussions with a number of IFP managers it also became clear that those in both the private and non-profit sectors were ploughing back significant amounts of their income into service development to give practical expression to these principles (Sellick, 2006b).

Stage 2: Innovations in foster carer support and services for children

As IFPs continued to expand, many began to develop innovative and readily available services for the fostered children and young people as well as placement-related support services to their workforce of approved foster carers. In an early evaluation of one large IFP the researchers discovered a range of educational services including advocacy by an agency-appointed educational liaison officer and an onsite school as well as regular child-centred counselling sessions. Alongside these foster carer support services, including regular respite, dedicated out-of-hours social work support and supervision, training and higher fees, had also been put in place (Sellick, 1999; Sellick and Connolly, 1999). The setting up of services for the children and young people's education and counselling anticipated, and in many cases influenced, subsequent, public sector child and adolescent mental health services and educational developments for looked after children introduced over time through several government policy directives (DH, 1998; DFES, 2004).

A number of studies over many years have recorded high rates of expressed satisfaction by IFP foster carers in response to these child and carer focused support services (DH, 1995; Sellick, 1999; Kirton *et al.,* 2003). A recent study of the views and experiences of children and their foster carers in one large, not-for-profit IFP in England has continued to find very high rates of satisfaction from foster carers with the level and variety of support they received from the agency (Broad, 2008). Connected to this, and unlike local authority fostering agencies, IFPs were experiencing high levels of retention with one study finding that five times as many foster carers were joining as were leaving these independent agencies (Sellick and Connolly, 2001, 2002). Among these were certain kinds of carers previously under-represented in local authorities such as actively and equally engaged male foster carers and those with relevant qualifications in social work, teaching, nursing or youth work (Sellick and Connolly, 2001, 2002).

These changes in organisation and practice have been accompanied by alterations in attitude. Although local authority social workers in the UK have been steeped in post-war public sector practice, those with direct experience of placing children with IFP carers have reported very positively for some time on the services provided and the co-operation they have received from the IFP social workers and foster carers (Sellick, 1999; Sellick and Connolly, 2001, 2002; Sellick and Howell, 2003, 2004). A similar picture has emerged elsewhere in Northern Europe. Dellgran and Hojer (2005) explored the views of almost 2,000 Swedish social workers and social work students about the privatisation of social work. Here too social workers valued good practice and services for the children and families they were responsible for, irrespective of the status of its providers. As these researchers commented: 'When the focus is shifted from welfare state activities in general to specific social work services, the impact of ideology seems to diminish' (Dellgran and Hojer, 2005, p 57).

The contemporary common wisdom that IFPs were leaching or poaching local authority trained, approved and experienced foster carers was not substantiated by the research knowledge. At the time of the national survey, two thirds of IFP foster carers had not transferred from local authorities and were often new to fostering. Many had been able to seriously consider becoming foster carers because the IFP fees and other service conditions represented the equivalent of a living wage, which was not commonly available from local authority fostering allowances. Rather than poaching foster carers, IFPs could be viewed more accurately as rearing them or, to mix the metaphor, were creating new pools of potential carers as opposed to over-fishing from existing stock.

Stage 3: Working together to plan, purchase and provide

Further research began to show that many more local authorities and IFPs had begun to develop collaborative working practices at both senior management and operational levels to identify need, plan service responses and determine costs (Sellick, 2006b). In some cases these public and independent (both private and voluntary) agencies were engaging in joint ventures related for example to foster carer recruitment and training or in the development of decision-making protocols for fostered children in particular localities (Sellick, 2005). In a study of commissioning, one IFP manager illustrated this developing world of inter-sector co-operation and the challenges this presented by saying:

> There has to be this element of trust. If we say we will do something then we do it. The local authority has to see that it's in their best interest to work with us because we provide a good service. They should not feel threatened by us and they have to give up a bit of their control and power too, just as we do, that's what partnership and compromise are about.
>
> (Sellick, 2005, p 7)

One study's review of foster care commissioning explored the notion of 'relational contracting' in business and applied this by testing those factors which were reported to underpin satisfactory and effective working relationships between local authority and IFP staff (Sellick, 2006b). This study suggested that building these relationships over time, where a partnership emerged based on mutual trust, was the cornerstone of effective business delivery. The spirit rather than the letter of legal and contractual arrangements was of central importance and enabled 'fostering managers to operate within a community of mutual interest rather than through individual arrangements where self-interest and opportunism predominate' (Sellick, 2006b, p 117).

Stage 4: Collaboration or competition?

As noted above, IFPs are increasingly turning from owner managed to private equity companies which have invested considerable sums of venture capital. These are accountable to shareholders rather than trustees and compete to provide placements purchased by local authorities. These companies often invest substantial sums of borrowed money into new or struggling companies. They do so as a short-term venture with the objective of obtaining sufficient profits to repay debt and to reinvest elsewhere (Cheffins and Armour, 2007). As the IFP share of the foster care market has grown to one-third of all children fostered by non-relatives (DfSF, 2009) the scale of the income derived has become a very attractive business case for the private sector. This is particularly so in view of the recent rise in children entering care and needing foster placement.

An unlikely source provides a useful way of seeing whether the mixed economy of foster care provision brings with it a promising opportunity for collaborative or relational contracting or whether there are risks within this new world of substantial private sector fostering provision for children in public care. Beyond social work and foster care practice, analogies from a text on trees about the impact of new growth have both relevance and resonance. The first example describes innovation providing wider benefits: 'Alders in particular create nitrogen and are able to improve the soil significantly and so benefit the whole forest. They are excellent pioneers – and in particular are pressed into service for soil reclamation' (Tudge, 2005, p 203). A second example paints a more cautionary picture in explaining that 'It is the stock in trade of parasites to seize new opportunities very rapidly indeed' (Tudge, 2005, p 361).

Early public sector perceptions of IFPs as parasites have increasingly given way to a more positive alder-like image. A third possibility occurs in the same book. 'Mutualism' is a form of symbiosis that benefits both partners in a relationship. For example, bacteria attaches itself to the bark of a tree. Tudge (2005, p 259) writes: 'This is symbiosis of the mutually beneficial kind, known as mutualism: the tree provides the bacteria with sugars, which they absorb; and the bacteria in turn provide soluble nitrogen, which the tree would otherwise lack'. Tudge also explains that the flowers of fig trees are pollinated by small black wasps whose larvae feeds on the fruit: 'without the wasps, the figs could not reproduce, and so would die out, and without the figs, the wasps could neither reproduce nor feed' (2005, p 331). Without local authority fees, IFPs could not have established themselves and without IFP placements, local authorities would not have found enough foster carers for children and young people to support the policy of placing children in family rather than residential care. The parallels may be inexact but what the botanists call mutualism, others call relational contracting (Sellick, 2006b). However, will the new mass of private equity IFPs behave in a predatory manner as Tudge warns in the parasite scenario, seizing profit opportunities rather than offering innovation and collaboration? After having established themselves so successfully, are these agencies becoming a kind of ivy on the face of fostering or a Leyland Cypress 'which grows so fast and casts the shadow that causes so much suburban strife?' (Tudge, 2005, p 107).

Conclusion: key issues and challenges for the future

The nationwide growth of IFPs, and the significant proportion of looked-after children fostered by their carers, is clear evidence of the existence of a mixed economy of foster care in the UK. However, many uncertainties and risks remain. These are related to key issues such as the outcomes for these children, the satisfaction and retention of their foster carers, the status and service provision of their fostering agencies and the costs and commissioning arrangements of their local authorities. These are considered below.

For at least the past decade, governments across the UK have been pushing for better outcomes for children in public care, and particularly those related to placement stability and educational performance (DfES, 2004). Placement choice, additional educational and therapeutic provision for children and support services for their foster carers have certainly been factors associated with IFPs. It is important to acknowledge here that it is very difficult, in separate research studies of differing methodologies and sample sizes, to achieve meaningful comparisons of children's outcomes where their care experiences have been affected by factors such as the length, frequency and types of placement.

However, bearing in mind the clear policy drive towards the provision of foster care from the independent sector over the past decade, remarkably few outcomes studies have provided hard evidence that children fostered in these agencies are 'healthier, better educated, more secure or better planned for' (Sellick and Connolly, 2002, p 119). One study of interim outcomes for children in one large IFP (Farmer *et al.*, 2007) found that many children were not secure twelve months after placement and 38 per cent of the children and 29 per cent of their foster carers 'did not know how long the placement would last and most were not expecting their foster home to be permanent' (Selwyn *et al.*, 2008, p 13).

Although, as we saw above, foster carers and social workers have consistently reported very positively about IFPs, will this degree of satisfaction and related retention be compromised by the impact of private equity? One senior manager of a voluntary IFP certainly sees this risk:

> *The fact that over a third of fostered children in the independent sector are now with agencies owned by private equity companies should be of great concern. Private equity has one primary motive and that is to maximise the return on investment. With pressures on fees from commissioners and more competitive contracting processes with local authorities they can only do this by reducing costs and increasing capacity. This means more workloads for staff and aggressive acquisitions of smaller providers, neither of which result in good outcomes for children in care.* (TACT, 2007)

Alongside these uncertainties and risks, research evidence from elsewhere (for example Barber, 2002; Unruh and Hodgkin, 2004) points to threats to service innovation and diversity. In parts of Australia and the US where all public sector fostering, adoption and residential childcare services were outsourced to the private and voluntary sectors, researchers have echoed the concerns of Giltinan (2002) above in commenting that 'once contracts are let, the supplier becomes a monopolist for a long enough period of time that other nonprofits can be eliminated from effectively competing for future bids' and later that 'in most areas the services delivered are less, not more, diverse' (McCarthy-Snyder and Allen, 2003, pp 28-9).

IFPs and the numbers of children and young people fostered by their carers have expanded significantly with agencies almost tripling in number in the eight years between 2001 and 2008 and children placed more than doubling during the same period. Although there are huge variations between local authorities and countries in their usage of the independent fostering sector, all public welfare agencies, throughout the UK, are now engaged in a mixed economy of foster care provision.

Commissioners, providers and users of foster placements and related services are finding themselves in a new world where the only real certainties are related to an ever-changing landscape of cost constraints, a mixed economy of provision and constantly developing policy initiatives. Legal frameworks do differ across the UK and even within countries local authorities and IFPs practice differently. The significant differences between England, Northern Ireland, Scotland and Wales in respect of their populations, size, national and local governance, law and traditions are of real relevance to policy implementation and the development of practice in foster care. Again, a chapter of this size prohibits a detailed discussion of the impact of different regulations and standards within the UK but these differences are significant. For example, in Scotland the law prohibits local authorities from placing children with foster carers registered with private for-profit agencies (Scottish Commission for the Regulation of Care, 2007) thus requiring these agencies to think creatively in order to practice north of the border. However, there are some clear patterns and trends: of more children being placed with IFP foster carers; of the dominance of a few very large provider agencies, which increasingly operate across the UK; and of the growth of private equity investment in services delivered to the public sector. The need to try and ensure that these developments are guided by concern with children's best interests and that more evidence is gathered about impact on outcomes and satisfaction will remain at the heart of these issues.

Questions

- Will local authority and IFP staff and carers put aside ideological considerations and collaborate more readily in respect of children's needs?
- Will further studies attempt to measure outcomes for both IFP-fostered children and those placed with local authority foster carers?
- What might be the effect on foster carer and social worker satisfaction, both in IFPs and local authorities, in an era of reduced public sector services and increasing numbers of children needing placement?
- Will dissatisfied foster carers move more often between IFPs or back to local authorities? What impact may these moves have on placement stability?
- Will local authorities be required to commission their children's services more widely from outside the public sector?
- In an era of considerable public cost constraints, will local authorities be able to afford to commission so widely from the private and voluntary sectors?
- Will a small number of very large IFPs dominate foster care provision and if so, will fewer agencies mean less diversity and innovation in fostering services?

References

Barber, J (2002) 'Competitive tendering and out-of-home care for children: the South Australia experience' *Children and Youth Services Review* 24(3), pp 159-74.

Broad, B (2008) *Aspirations: The views of children and their foster carers* London: The Adolescent and Children's Trust and London South Bank University.

Cheffins, B and Armour, J (2007) *The Eclipse of Private Equity*, Working Paper No. 339, Cambridge: Centre for Business Research, University of Cambridge.

Dellgran, P and Hojer, S (2005) 'Privatisation as professionalisation? Attitudes, motives and achievements among Swedish social workers' *European Journal of Social Work* 8(1), pp 39-62.

DCSF (Department for Children, Schools and Families) (2009) *Children Looked After in England Year Ending 31st March 2008* London: Department for Children, Schools and Families.

DfES (Department for Education and Skills) (2004) *Every Child Matters: Change for Children,* London: DfES.

DfES (2005) *Looked After Children Taskforce/Commissioning* London: DfES.

DH (Department of Health) (1995) *Independent Fostering Agencies Study* London: Social Services Inspectorate, HMSO.

DH (1998) *Quality Protects: Transforming Children's Services,* London: The Stationery Office.

DH (2001) Alan Milburn's Speech to the Annual Social Services Conference, 19th October.

Farmer, E, Selwyn, J, Quinton, D, Saunders, H, Staines, J, Turner, W and Meakings, S (2007) *Children Placed with FCA: Experiences and progress 12 months on* Bristol: Hadley Centre for Adoption and Foster Care Studies, University of Bristol

Giltinan, D (2002) 'Child care at the end of the millennium' in Hill, M (ed) *Shaping Childcare Practice in Scotland* London: BAAF.

Kirton D, Ogilvie, K and Beecham, J (2003) *Remuneration and Performance in Foster Care* Canterbury: University of Kent at Canterbury and Department of Health.

McCarthy-Snyder, N and Allen, M (2003) 'Managing the uneasy partnership between government and nonprofits: lessons from the Kansas Child Welfare Privatization Initiative', Presentation at the 25th Annual Research Conference of the Association for Public Policy Analysis and Management, Washington, DC, 6 November.

Scottish Commission for the Regulation of Care (2007) *The Quality of Fostering and Adoption Services in Scotland* Dundee: Care Commission.

Sellick, C (1999) 'Independent fostering agencies: providing high quality services to children and carers?' *Adoption and Fostering* 23(4), pp 7-14.

Sellick, C (2002) 'The aims and principles of independent fostering agencies: a view from the inside' *Adoption and Fostering* 26(1), pp 56-63.

Sellick, C. (2005) 'Opportunities and Risks: models of good practice in commissioning foster care' *British Journal of Social Work*, Advance Access, published 6 December, pp 1-15.

Sellick, C (2006a) 'From famine to feast, a review of the foster care research literature' *Children and Society* 20(1), pp.67-74,

Sellick, C (2006b) 'Relational contracting between local authorities and independent fostering providers: lessons in conducting business for child welfare managers' *Journal of Social Welfare and Family Law* 28(2), pp 107-20.

Sellick, C (2007) 'Towards a mixed economy of foster care provision' *Social Work and Social Sciences Review* 13(1), pp 25-40.

Sellick, C and Connolly J (1999) *A Description and Evaluation of the Work of the Midland Foster Care Associates* Norwich: Centre for Research on the Child and Family, University of East Anglia.

Sellick, C and Connolly J (2001) *National Survey of Independent Fostering Agencies* Norwich: Centre for Research on the Child and Family, University of East Anglia.

Sellick, C and Connolly J (2002) 'Independent fostering agencies uncovered: the findings of a national study' *Child and Family Social Work* 7(2), pp 107-20.

Sellick, C and Howell, D (2003) *Innovative, Tried and Tested: A Review of Good Practice in Fostering*, Social Care Institute for Excellence Knowledge Review 4, Bristol: The Policy Press.

Sellick, C and Howell, D (2004) 'A description and analysis of multi-sectoral fostering in the United Kingdom' *British Journal of Social Work* 34(4), pp 481-99.

Selwyn, J, Saunders, H and Farmer, E (2008) 'The views of children and young people on being cared for by an Independent Foster Care Provider' *British Journal of Social Work*, Advance Access, pp 1-18.

TACT (2007) 'The importance of placing children above profit', Press Release (www.tactcare.org.uk/news)

Triseliotis, J, Borland, M and Hill, M (2000) *Delivering Foster Care* London: British Association for Adoption and Fostering.

Tudge, C (2005) *The Secret Life of Trees* London: Allen Lane Penguin Books.

Unruh, J and Hodgkin, D (2004) 'The role of contract design in privatization of chills welfare services: the Kansas experience' *Children and Youth Services Review* 26, pp 771-83.

Waterhouse, S (1997) *The Organisation of Fostering Services: A study of the arrangements for delivery of fostering services in England* London: National Foster Care Association.

Part 3

Themes and Issues in Community Care

Chapter 12

Getting it Right for Older People

Jacquie Roberts

Age will only be respected if it fights for itself, maintains its own rights, avoids
dependence and asserts control over its sphere as long as life lasts.
Cicero, 44BC

Introduction

It was so long ago that Cicero in 44 BC expounded passionately and thoughtfully about
how to achieve a better old age, that it seems to have taken far too long for social welfare
in the UK to return to a similar philosophy. Social work with older people needs to be
founded on the human rights of every individual, no matter what their level of
dependence on others. It is heartening that most recent policy and legislative
developments across the UK reflect this thinking. But the challenge to individual
practitioners and their employers is how to adapt practice and implement changes to
health, care and other systems for older people when services have been embedded in
well-intentioned traditions of protectionism and institutionalisation. Goffman (1961) wrote
powerfully about the negative impact of institutions on people with mental health
problems. Since the middle of the last century, childcare philosophy has embraced the
centrality of the uniqueness of each child, driving services away from large institutions
towards smaller, more specified provision. Younger adults with learning and physical
disabilities have been very successfully decamped from large hospitals to have a normal
place in the community. Older people are adults, too, and its about time that the same
policies, guiding principles and philosophies are applied to services for older people.
Social work needs to play an active part in this transformation.

Guiding principles and philosophy and recent UK developments

International human rights

Human rights principles are central to any planning for social welfare systems for older
people. The United Nations (UN) Declaration of Human Rights (1948) makes it clear that
all signatories have "reaffirmed their faith in fundamental human rights, in the dignity and
worth of the human person and in the equal rights of men and women and have
determined to promote social progress and better standards of life…". This has been
well exemplified across the UK. The Older People's Well-being Monitor for Wales (WAG,

2009) sets out a "milestone" research project that will guide the work of the Welsh Assembly Government and partners in planning for an ageing society. The focus is on five broad aims of well-being that are derived from the UN principles. They are:

- Dignity and social inclusion;
- Material well-being;
- Participation;
- Health and care;
- Self-fulfillment and active ageing.

In the UK government's Green Paper on adult social care (DH, 2009a), the emphasis is on the affordability of a social welfare system for an ageing population. Nevertheless, the document clearly spells out a commitment to a system that is "fair" and "universal, underpinned by national rights and entitlements".

In Scotland, a cross-party group of politicians and other interested parties published a charter of rights for people with dementia and their carers (Alzheimer Scotland, 2010b). The charter is guided by a human rights-based approach, emphasising participation, accountability of those responsible, non-discrimination, empowerment and legality in all decisions made.

As the care regulator in Scotland, it has been most helpful to have human rights-based principles set out in the Scottish Government's National Care Standards for all services, not just those for older people. Specifically, the six guiding principles are *dignity*, *privacy*, *choice*, *safety*, *realising potential*, and *equality and diversity* (www.carecommission.com). By taking a rights-based approach to regulation, we can focus on outcomes for older people and demand increased participation by service users, their families, carers, friends and advocates.

A growing overt declaration to recognise the rights of older people is also being matched by the creation of commissioners, advocates or champions for older people. There are such designated posts in all UK countries apart from Scotland. Whether such posts, which separate older people from all other adults, promote the inclusion and equality of the older citizen is still open for debate, but it does demonstrate a recognition that older people's rights may well have been neglected previously.

Codes of Practice and Ethics

So what does this emphasis on the underlying fundamental principles of human rights mean to the individual practitioner? It should help provide a benchmark by which to check one's practice in individual cases. The Code of Ethics of the British Association of Social Workers (BASW, 2002) begins with spelling out the key principles of respect for human dignity, worth, human rights and self-determination. The social care workforce regulators also set out in their UK Codes of Practice for all social service workers a primary obligation "As a social service worker, you must protect the rights and promote the interests of service users and carers". It is particularly helpful for the individual practitioner that the Codes of Practice are inextricably linked with the Codes of Practice for social service employers, requiring them to ensure the conditions, training and support for social service workers to adhere to their Codes of Practice (www.sssc.org.uk).

Personalisation

Although I still struggle with the word "personalisation" because it is not a term that every lay person would understand, the drive towards more individual, person-centred planning is strongly determined by human rights principles and is having a gradual positive influence on re-thinking services for older people. As Charles Leadbeater (2004, p 20) wrote, personalisation is "an entirely new organisational logic" – "designing solutions from the ground up" and "promoting greater capacity for self-management and self-organisation". For the individual practitioner, personalisation means thinking about the person first and about their care and support in an entirely different way. It means starting with the person's strengths, preferences and aspirations, ensuring that they are at the centre of designing, choosing and controlling what support or care they need. Although, the broad concept is not new, as clearly demonstrated by the quotation from Cicero at the beginning of this chapter, the new formulation challenges practitioners and organisations alike because of the previous dominance of "assessing and meeting needs" enshrined in the NHS and Community Care Act 1990. In Chapter 4 of this book, Duncan Mackay and Gillian MacIntyre write in more detail about what can be achieved through personalisation. It is important here to emphasise that a person-centred rights-based approach is the only way to a successful delivery of social work for older people.

Carers

For nearly every individual request for social work intervention there will be unpaid, informal carers who are vital contributors to the whole system of support for older people. Very often the carers are older people themselves and may be hidden from the formal care network. The most comprehensive study of carers in Scotland in 2006 (Scottish Executive, 2006b) estimated that there are just under 700,000 unpaid carers for older people, 25% of whom are providing more that 50 hours of care per week and 20% of the whole population of carers are over the age of 70.

The Scottish Government's commitment in 2010 to increasing the number or respite hours/days available to carers is one sign of a growing awareness of the need for this vital population to be supported. Carers, too, need respect and to be an integral part of any assessment, not to dominate the solutions, but to work in partnership with the helping agencies and the individual needing care. How often are carers' assessments properly undertaken with this philosophy in mind and, indeed, how often is a carer's assessment offered as a meaningful part of the multi-agency approach? It is important to strike a cautionary note. The fact that these unpaid volunteers are an essential part of the solution to demographic challenges should not be exploited. Too often this could be heard as "the current level of service is unaffordable … your country needs you!". The UK Green Paper (DH, 2009a) tries to avoid such an implication by making the following statement: "Families cannot cope alone, and we believe that the state must play its role". A social worker may often feel that the main obstacle to the right solution for an older person in need is the family's fear that they will be left alone to cope. There is, however, a growing recognition of carers' rights. The English Carers' Strategy for 2008-2011 (DH, 2008a, p 9) states that carers will be "respected as expert care partners" with "access to integrated and personalised services … to support them in their caring role". The individual social work practitioner therefore needs their own person-centred approach to be matched by a commitment at a multi-agency organisational level, which goes beyond rhetoric.

Twenty-first Century challenges

The challenges of old age are universal and timeless. Old age is inevitably characterised and often caricatured by loss, reduction in capacity and disengagement in all spheres, social, physical, psychological and financial. What is striking is how differently people travel through the journey defined as "old age", leading to the conclusion that any assumptions about needs could be ageist.

In every part of the UK, there is now a clear recognition of the demographic challenges facing the population. Predictions vary, but, for example, it is estimated that in Scotland the 75+ population will have risen by 23% from 2008 to 2018 and by 84% by 2033. In the same 25-year period, the number of people aged 60-74 is projected to increase by 33%. (General Register Office for Scotland, October 2009). There is a gradual improvement in the health status of older people, so many older people will not make demands on services, but given the parallel projected increase in the number of people with dementia, the UK is facing a major challenge in how to plan and fund social welfare for older people when they need it.

All UK governments have published policy documents highlighting the demographic challenges but they all run the risk of designating the growing proportion of older people as a problem for the rest of society, thereby shaping policies driven by fear of overwhelming costs and demand, rather than doing the right thing for older people and recognising their contribution to society.

Some important modelling work has been undertaken by Scottish Government officials, who predict that if services for older people continue to be designed and planned the way they are now, then Scotland will need a new 600-bed hospital built every three years for the next 20 years, it will need a new 50-bed care home built every two weeks for the next 20 years, a £2.8 billion investment will be required to maintain the current level of sheltered housing and, in ten years time, virtually all school leavers will need to enter employment in the care sector. As this would require a 22% increase in the health and social care expenditure at a time when the country needs a reduction in public expenditure, then a crisis is looming. As the apocryphal Chinese proverb puts it, it is time for social work to turn this crisis into an opportunity to promote the rights of older people and their carers. Not only does there need to be change at the multi-agency organisational level, but also individual social work practitioners need to move away from the more bureaucratic "care management" type approach to a more rights-based personalised approach. Malcolm Carey (2003) has described how care management has led to less time being spent with the people needing social work help and can even unwittingly promote inequalities.

The challenge of dementia

When people are honest about old age, it is the prospect of ending their years with dementia that makes them most fearful. Caring for a loved one with significant dementia must be one of the most personally challenging tasks anyone can face. Population projections for the rise in the number of people with dementia are increasingly adding to fears of a "tsunami" or "demographic time bomb". Most recent estimates of the number of people across the UK with moderate to severe diagnosed and undiagnosed dementia are just under 900,000, with an estimated 1 in 5 prevalence rate for people over the age of 85, rising to more than 1 in 3 people over the age of 90 years (Alzheimer's Research UK, 2010). In Scotland it is projected that by 2031 there will be a 75% increase in the number of people over 65 with dementia, which is a diagnosis that seems to determine a far greater chance of receiving institutional care. Alzheimer's Scotland (2008) has estimated in 2008 that the proportion of people in care homes with dementia in Scotland is 65%. In contrast, the Scottish Government estimated in 2006 (Scottish Government, 2006) that 5.2% of the population receiving home care were diagnosed with dementia.

In order to tackle the overall challenge of providing good social welfare for older people, clearly if we get it right for people with dementia, we will get it right for everyone. As Alzheimer's Research UK (2010) points out, there can be a huge financial, social and emotional impact on the family and the community when an individual is diagnosed with dementia, and yet the investment in researching how best to help and support people with dementia is woefully lacking. It is helpful that senior representatives of the health professions are now lobbying for better care of people with dementia. I quote from an editorial in the *British Medical Journal*:

> "Until recently dementia was viewed as a living death about which little could be done beyond custodial care".
>
> (Downs & Bowers, 2008, pp 225-6)

It is encouraging that this editorial ends with a rallying cry to doctors to return to the rights and principles that I began with in this chapter:

> *"In planning care and support, doctors need to pay as much attention to the essential human worth of a person with dementia and their retained capacity for relationships, pleasure, communication and coping as they do to deficits and dysfunction".* (Downs & Bowers, 2008, pp 225-6)

For social workers, like healthcare professionals, a number of questions arise. Does an older person with dementia always have to be institutionalised? Is the breakdown of the home setting the result of haphazard and unreliable support? Is there another way to plan services to provide protection for the older person with dementia and the necessary support for the family/carers? Indeed, it is possible, as suggested in a leaflet by Alzheimer Scotland (2010a) for older people and their carers, to access much more personalised care through "self-directed support", a helpful term to cover both direct payments and individualised budgets.

In a publication by the Care Commission and the Mental Welfare Commission for Scotland (2009), *Remember, I'm Still Me*, it was spelt out just how poor the quality of life can be for people with dementia in care homes. In a detailed study of people with dementia in 30 care homes across Scotland, it was found that only 24% of a sample of 182 residents had an adequate record of their life history, half of the total sample of residents in the 30 homes *never* went outside and many people who had been prescribed psycho-tropic drugs never had their medication reviewed. If the care for people with dementia were to be more determined by the philosophy and principles set out at the beginning of this chapter, we might be making fewer mistakes.

Philosophy into Practice

Throughout the UK there are coherent and comprehensive strategies for promoting the welfare of children and young people. For example, the Scottish Government strategy of *Getting it Right for Every Child* (Scottish Executive, 2006) underpins all policy developments in public services for children. This strategy spells out that "families and professionals in Scotland are expected to have a part to play in ensuring that each child is: safe, healthy, active, nurtured, achieving, respected responsible and included" (2006). To have an effective strategy for older people we could simply replace the word "child" with "older person". This is not to deny the reality of old age, but to avoid the possibility that reduced physical capacity dictates all other aspects of an older person's life. Rather, as Cicero argued in 44BC, make old age "a seductive combination of increased wisdom and decaying powers". A strategy for older people today should ring loudly with the message "you still matter" and so should any social work assistance on an individual level.

Another parallel with policies for children is the current emphasis on early intervention. Yes, it is vital for society to invest in the younger generation, but I would also argue that society would gain enormously from policies that anticipate the increasing needs of the older generation and put in place strategies for helping them become less dependent. The Scottish Government and COSLA (2008) have committed to an Early Years and Early Intervention Framework which promotes "a fundamental shift away from dealing with symptoms of inequality" (Scottish Government & COSLA, 2008, p iv Forward) and "rebalances our focus towards identifying and managing the risks that perpetuate inequality" (p iv Forward). Exactly the same approach should apply to providing services for and with older people. Indeed, such early intervention thinking underpins the English strategy document for adults of all ages where experience from partnerships for older people has shown that "there is a need for interventions which address the whole population of older people – not just the 15% who come into contact with social services" (DH, 2008b, p9). It is in this context that social workers should tailor their own interventions and maximise the resources in families and communities. The 2009 English framework rests on:

- citizenship rights;
- neighbourhoods and communities;
- information;
- healthy lifestyles;
- practical support;
- early intervention;
- enabling;
- community support for people with long-term conditions;
- institutional avoidance;
- timely discharge.

It is therefore vital for all frontline social work practitioners to reflect on their own level of intervention, if, indeed, any intervention is needed. As highlighted in a background paper for the Scottish 21st Century social work review, Kerr *et al.* (2005) make it clear that social work should be wary of any assumption of intervention by virtue of a person's age. The authors cite Smales *et al.* (2000) analysis of the social worker's distinctive role: where no-one knows what the answer is, where relationships are complex and where there is a high degree of risk. The main functions of a social worker could be assigned to the following categories:

- information giver;
- counsellor;
- advocate;
- assessor of need;

- care manager and, unfortunately;
- rationing agent and agent of social control.

Starting with the individual and using the rights-based approach, the social worker can most helpfully use the older person's and their network's contribution and strengths to tap into a rich system of support, with a focus on maintaining independence for as long as possible. It is, nevertheless, vital that the independence sought is determined by the older person themselves because there can be dangers of imposing views of independence that risk leading to social exclusion, as described by Plath (2008).

If planners, commissioners, practitioners and regulators of services for older people, continue to think only in the current way about the design of services around passive recipients, we will fail a whole generation. Readers are referred to SCIE (2009) Research briefing on "co-production", a concept which emphasises that people are not passive recipients of services, but have assets, experience and expertise that can help improve services. It is not an "off-the-shelf" model of service provision or a single magic solution but requires a transformation in thinking about power, resources, partnership, risks, expertise and outcomes.

Social work as part of a wider system – a systemic approach

On both an organisational and an individual level, the solution to getting it right for older people lies in embracing a whole-system approach. All current government strategies for older people acknowledge that planning for an ageing society cannot be restricted to the health and care systems. Income maximisation, housing design, transport policies and life-long learning initiatives all play a vital part. Indeed, social work services for older people are less in demand when universal service provision is good. The recent multi-agency inspection reports on older people's services in Scotland (SWIA, 2008) have shown clear evidence that good outcomes for older people depend on good, close collaboration between social work and a broad range of other agencies. Good strategic planning in any geographical area requires a joint approach, well informed by estimates of population need, morbidity and clear financial information.

There are some promising developments in different parts of the UK that are driving forward "integrated care" initiatives for older people. For example, in Durham Dales, an initiative is drawing together district nursing, social work, allied therapies, transport and fuel poverty services, to simplify access and to promote faster delivery of services. In Norfolk, NHS Norfolk, Norfolk County Council and a commissioning group of GP practices have come together to establish fully integrated local health and social care teams to provide personalised care for older and vulnerable people. The specific objectives of this project include the reduction of institutional placements in hospital and care homes, as well as increasing staff and user satisfaction rates (DH, 2009b). The solution to the challenge of getting it right for older people clearly rests on a willingness to break down organisational boundaries and work together.

In Scotland, it is being increasingly acknowledged that the housing sector has a major part to play in the strategic planning for older people. A report to ministers on reshaping care for older people (Joint Improvement Team, 2009, p 11) has stated quite clearly that "strategic planning in the housing sector is not sufficiently connected with planning by health and social care, so respective needs, priorities and budgets are not aligned". This situation has to change if the UK is to deal with the demographic challenges it faces. Specifically, the report recommends making housing needs of older people a higher priority in local housing strategies along with better design of new houses, better resourcing of adaptation and small repairs services, development of new extra care housing, public assistance to older homeowners and private landlords and better working relationships with health and social care.

Social work needs to tackle the challenge on both an organisational and an individual level. The principles behind older citizens' rights should link with a real commitment to break down organisational boundaries and different thinking about the way services are designed. On an organisational level, there is an urgent need to design a comprehensive all-agency "system of caring", which is based on older people's wishes to remain in their own homes for as long as they can. It requires the whole-system approach mentioned earlier, with commitment and investment from health, housing, social work, welfare benefits, transport and universal community services. The system should be specifically designed to give unpaid informal carers a break. The whole-system approach should combat older people's social isolation and help them preserve a sense of significance as well as continuity. Such a system does need strong public support from those who do not yet need care. What and how does the whole population want to invest in a social welfare system that cares for and values the older citizen? These questions are now being asked of the public at a policy level in all parts of the UK.

Because the integration of health and social care is only part of the solution, any social worker worth their salt should be thinking broadly about the range and continuum of services that would assist their clients achieve a better old age. It should start with the information giving, advocacy task. As choice and control are at the heart of the new agenda to reform services for older people, information, advice and advocacy services are vital and should lead to far greater independence and self-management. As pointed out by Horton (2009), older people need a common dataset and information about universal services as well as health and care, which, in turn, will provide opportunities for frontline staff to learn from each other and other geographical areas.

Care homes for older people: the default option?

It is for all these reasons of promoting rights, personal strengths and a more comprehensive multi-agency approach that it is essential to challenge, both at an organisational and an individual level, whether care homes for older people should be the default option. Individual social workers are still brought in by other agencies, notably health, when decisions have already been made informally that the "only solution" for an older person (and often their overburdened carer) is to seek an admission to a care home. Every social worker brought in at this stage needs to question hard this default option. They also need to be empowered by their organisation to work with multi-agency, person-centred solutions. Likewise, strategic planning and commissioning should challenge whether care homes are too often built in as the only solution.

Can care homes really meet the personalisation agenda?

Providing imaginative person-centred care for frail older people, particularly those with dementia, requires a full understanding of all the health and care issues, superb leadership and a very skilled and committed frontline workforce. The Care Commission's (2010) report on the first full year of grading provides evidence that top-quality standards across the board are available in only 6.8% of all Scotland's care homes for older people. That contrasts with 15% of care homes for children, 25% of day care for children and 23.5% of housing support services. A valiant attempt has been made by the Social Care Institute for Excellence (SCIE) and the Registered Nursing Home association (2010) in a 'personalisation briefing' to encourage care homes in how to develop their services to support their residents as individuals, to move away from a "task-driven" model of care in order to support self-determination and independence, "where the person is at the centre of what they do" (p 4). Even so, this document contains the statement "where care is funded by local authority commissioners, early intervention to maintain health and well-being is generally not made available through nursing home care" (p 3). This is too accepting of the status quo. Research has shown that the reason for admission to care homes in 90% of cases is due to ill-health (Bowman et al., 2004) and the proportion of people in care homes with higher dependency needs is reported to have risen. It could be argued that these people used to be resident in hospital wards and therefore their move to a community setting is a great success. However, one must question whether the move to a care home, often made immediately after a medical crisis, is really what the older person perceives to be "Hobson's choice". At these times of crisis when carer arrangements have broken down, older people and their families are not at their strongest or most selective. There can be a strong push for an older person to leave hospital and families can struggle with guilt. It is probably putting consumers in their weakest position to make what might be the most important decision for the rest of their life. Older people need time, support and flexibility when working out how best to maintain their independence and achieve their maximum potential. It should be seriously questioned why people have to commit to an "institution" for ever just because they are old and frail. We no longer accept this state of affairs for younger adults, where there is a clear policy across the UK that people should maintain their own household and be valued as citizens and members of the community.

Diversification of the care home sector

On an organisational level, there is much that could be changed to make sure that the care home sector fits into the overall system of care provision. Lessons could be learnt from the hospice movement. Hospices are no longer simply places where people "go to die". They provide very varied services, including care at home and day care. They are increasingly designed around the person, allowing that person as an individual to choose the services that will help them and their family to manage the consequences of a terminal illness, while maximising their dignity, choice and quality of life. Everyone dies. One way of introducing diversity and a different way of thinking about care of older people is to dramatically increase the options available for older people as they approach death and provide more intensive home-based services.

Care homes are increasingly being acknowledged for their capacity to manage "end-of-life" care. Indeed, there are now national standards in Scotland for non-specialist palliative care for people who live in care homes (Scottish Partnership for Palliative Care and the Scottish Executive, 2006), although care homes have some way to go in training their staff to meet these standards as illustrated in a Care Commission (2008) report on end-of-life care in care homes. A sensitive service during bereavement and end of life is highly valued by relatives who write to the Care Commission praising the spiritual, emotional and nursing care given by the care home to their loved one, enabling them to die peacefully in their own bed, without the distress of being admitted to hospital. Above all, the families value the care and attention they receive to stay with their loved one during the final days.

Larger care homes could alternatively become post-hospital rehabilitation or "maximising potential" units. Rather than becoming a person's alternative permanent home these units could be designed to provide a bridge to return home, giving an older person much more time to adapt and build up strength. As over 70% of care homes are run by the private and voluntary sector, the planning and commissioning of a such a change, which requires business security, needs a comprehensive health and care commissioning strategy.

Care homes could contribute to a system where more highly skilled peripatetic nursing staff could attend to older people wherever they live. Partnerships between local health and community care services and care homes have already developed in some areas, but the strategy is patchy and could be much more energetically pursued. It would lead to far fewer unnecessary hospital admissions for frail older people.

Other community-based measures

In Scotland there are at least 80,000 places in housing support for older people, but a review of sheltered housing in Scotland (Scottish Government, 2008) highlighted the difficulty in having a national strategy for sheltered and extra care housing because of the enormous diversity of current and planned provision across Scotland. Extra care housing was noted to be expensive, but very popular. Should this option only be available to the moneyed classes? Current providers of care homes could, with the right encouragement, develop both housing support, and extra care housing as part of an overall comprehensive provision, using expert staff to form relationships and provide care for older people who might stay in the actual care home only for respite or only in their latter months.

In Chapter 18, Andrew Eccles describes the benefits and the ethical dilemmas behind telecare and assistive technology. Nevertheless, the last twenty years of information technology developments have demonstrated that lives can be transformed by technology to aid quality living. It provides innovative approaches and enhances people's independence in ways not formerly dreamed of, some of which are listed in the Scottish Government's Telecare Strategy, 2008-10 (Joint Improvement Team, 2008). The challenges are for individual practitioners to keep up to date with the creative possibilities these developments have to offer, to raise public awareness and, most importantly, to lobby local partnerships to mainstream telecare within local service planning.

An encouraging study by Carers Scotland found that "even with limited technical support, some carers had found telecare life-changing, and most acknowledged that it was life-enhancing" (Carers Scotland, 2009, p 39). The report recommends that telecare needs to become an integral part of community care and carer assessments and awareness needs to be raised at both a national and a local level.

Another issue for reshaping services for older people, which was made sharper by the recent serious economic downturn, is pensioner poverty. No universal welfare system for older people would work without a universal benefit system based on fairness. There are many options for approaching the funding of services for older people, some of which are being spelt out in the UK strategy documents, but suffice it to say that individual social workers should never fail to seek to maximise older people's income in order to enhance their independence and purchasing power. Whether or not the UK has a system of free personal care, there is still not enough creative thinking around pensioner income and funding for care. A good example of a new approach to maximising an older person's income is that set out by Terry and Gibson (2010). By asking and answering the question "Can equity release help older home-owners improve their quality of life?", the authors describe three equity release pilot schemes. The key features of the schemes are:

- the involvement of the local authority;
- the availability of relatively small sums of money that can be drawn on demand;
- minimising the risk of an adverse effect on entitlement;
- ensuring that the financial solutions other than equity release are well examined.

If we transfer some of these ideas to casework on an individual level, then social workers should feel empowered to undertake meaningful, person-centred assessments alongside their health and housing partners. What level of respite and for whom would help an older person maintain their own home? Have small-scale practical solutions or technical adaptations been fully considered? Are there other more creative alternatives, such as the equivalent of childminding or short-term fostering that are planned around the individual? What stimulating experiences would fulfil an older person's sense of achievement and purpose, in order to reduce any sense of loss or worthlessness? What contact with other members of the community would break down social isolation and give an older person a sense of significance? As Cicero said, all those centuries ago, "An older person is well advised to favour the society of promising young people". Social workers have a strong part to play in helping an older person build or rebuild their links with the community, including vital inter-generational alliances.

Conclusion

The twenty-first century policy and practice implications for social work with older people depend on an unerring commitment to the philosophy that old age is not one negative state that applies universally to every human being. The rights of individuality and participation should underpin attempts to ameliorate any problems that may be the consequence of old age. This philosophy is fundamental to the ethics of social work. By adhering to that philosophy, social work should avoid being side-tracked by economic drivers to treat older people in batches and should prevent institutional design of services that fit the providers' rather than the consumers' preferences. The impact of the ageing phenomenon, which is unique to every individual, can then determine broader design of services and the actual delivery of care to each person.

As social workers engaged in the profession in the early twenty-first century, it is worth continuously asking whether services are being fitted around the individual or whether the individual is being fitted into standard services. Each older person belongs to a family and community, even if there are few evident. It is worth asking whether we have lost the importance of this context by dividing the delivery of services into children's and community care services. It is through positive intergenerational alliances that a better-quality older age will be achieved. How do we ensure that older people, when isolated by various unavoidable communication barriers, still retain the place they choose in the community and the family, being valued for their unique worth? How can social work pursue this agenda and move away from processing older people through bureaucratic assessments in order to access support for daily living? How do we make sure that older people are not pigeon-holed and that their needs and attributes are assessed properly and comprehensively? This is the expectation for children in need and the same standards should apply to older people. Getting it right for every older person is just as important for social work as getting it right for every child.

References

Alzheimer's Research UK (2010) *Dementia 2010* Oxford: Health Economics Research Centre, University of Oxford (www.alzheimers-research.org.uk).

Alzheimer Scotland (2008) 'Number of people with Dementia in Scotland' Edinburgh: Alzhemer Scotland (www.alzscot.org/pages/statistics).

Alzheimer Scotland (2009) 'Charter of Rights for people with Dementia and their Carers in Scotland' Edinburgh: Alzheimer Scotland (www.dementiarights.org).

Alzheimer Scotland (2010b) *Charter of Rights for People with Dementia and their Carers in Scotland* (www.dementiarights.org).

Alzheimer Scotland (2010a) *Taking Charge: A short guide to self-directed support for people with dementia and their carers* Edinburgh: Alzheimer Scotland.

BASW (British Association of Social Workers) (2002) Code of Ethics for Social Workers (www.basw.co.uk).

Bowman, C, Whistler, J and Ellerby, M (2004) 'A national census of care home residents' *Age and Ageing* 33(6), pp 561-66.

Care Commission (2008) *Better Care Every Step of the Way: Report on the quality of palliative and end of life care in care homes for adults and older people* Dundee: Care Commission (www.carecommission.com).

Care Commission (2010) *Making the Grade? Results from the first year of grading registered services* Dundee: Care Commission (www.carecommission.com).

Care Commission and Mental Welfare Commission for Scotland (2009) *Remember, I'm Still Me. A joint report on the quality of care for people with dementia living in care homes in Scotland* Dundee: Care Commission (www.carecommission.com; www.mwcscot.org.uk)

Carers Scotland (2009) *A Weight Off My Mind: Exploring the impact and potential benefits of telecare for unpaid carers in Scotland* Glasgow: Carers Scotland (www.carerscotland.org).

Carey, M (2003) 'Anatomy of a care manager' *Work, Employment & Society* 17(1) pp 121-35.

Cicero, M T (44BC) 'On old age' in *Selected works* (trans. Michael Grant), London: Penguin Books.

DH (Department of Health) (2008a) *Carers at the Heart of 21st Century Families and Communities: A caring system on your side, a life of your own* London: DH (www.dh.gov.uk).

DH (2008b) *Making a Strategic Shift to Prevention and Early Intervention* London: DH (www.dh.gov.uk).

DH (2009b): 'Integrated Care Pilots and Introductory Guide' DH/Commissioning/Integrated Care Gateway Ref 12641

DH (2009a) *Shaping the Future Together*, Green Paper. London: HM Government (www.dh.gov.uk).

Downs, M and Bowers, B (2008) 'Caring for people with dementia' *British Medical Journal* 336, pp 225-6.

Goffman, E (1961) *Asylums: Essays on the condition of the social situation of mental patients and other inmates* London: Penguin Social Sciences.

Horton, C (2009) *Creating a Stronger Information, Advice and Advocacy System for Older People* York: Joseph Rowntree Foundation (www.jrf.org.uk).

Joint Improvement Team (2008) *Seizing the Opportunity: Telecare Strategy 2008-2010* Edinburgh: JIT (www.jitscotland.org.uk).

Joint Improvement Team (2009) *Reshaping Care for Older People: Wider planning for an ageing population – housing and communities* Edinburgh: JIT (www.jitscotland.gov.uk).

Kerr B, Gordon J, MacDonald, C and Stalker, K (2005) *Effective Social Work with Older People* Scottish Executive Social Research, Edinburgh: Scottish Executive (www.scotland.gov.uk).

Leadbeater, C (2004) *Personalisation Through Participation: A new script for public services* London: Demos.

Plath, D (2008) 'Independence in old age: the route to social exclusion?' *British Journal of Social Work* 38(7) pp 1353-69.

SCIE (Social Care Institute for Excellence) (2009) *Research Briefing 31: Co-production: an emerging evidence base for adult social care transformation* London: SCIE (www.scie.org.uk).

SCIE and the Registered Nursing Home Association (2010) *At a Glance 20: Personalisation briefing: implications for nursing homes* London: SCIE (www.scie.org.uk).

Scottish Executive (2006a) *Plans for the Implementation of Getting it Right for Every Child proposals* Edinburgh: Scottish Executive (www.scotland.gov.uk).

Scottish Executive (2006b) *The Future of Unpaid Care in Scotland: Care 21 report* Edinburgh: Scottish Executive (www.scotland.gov.uk).

Scottish Government (2006) Statistics release, Scotland: Home Care Services.

Scottish Government (2008) *Review of Sheltered Housing in Scotland* Edinburgh: Scottish Government (www.scotland.gov.uk/publications).

Scottish Government and COSLA (Convention of Scottish Local Authorities) (2008) *Early Years and Early Intervention: A joint Scottish Government and COSLA policy statement* Edinburgh: Scottish Government (www.scotland.gov.uk).

Scottish Partnership for Palliative Care and the Scottish Executive (2006) Making Good Care Better: National practice statements for general palliative care in adult care homes in Scotland (www.palliativecarescotland.org.uk).

Scottish Social Services Council (2003) 'Codes of Practice for Social Services workers and employers' (www.sssc.uk.com).

Smale, G, Tuson, G and Statham, D (2000) *Social Work and Social Problems: Working Towards Social Inclusion and Social Change* Basingstoke: Palgrave Macmillan.

Social Work Inspection Agency (2008) *Multi-agency Inspections of Older People's Services* Edinburgh: SWIA (www.swia.org.uk).

Terry R and Gibson R (2010) *Can Equity Release Help Older Home Owners Improve Their Quality of Life* York: Joseph Rowntree Foundation.

WAG (2009) *Older People's Well-being Monitor for Wales*. Cardiff: WAG (www.cymru.gov.uk).

Chapter 13

Creating 'Better Lives': Learning Disability, Early Professional Development and Social Work

Denis Rowley and Susan Hunter

Introduction

While social work practice within the statutory sector has seen the replacement of its traditional role in casework by care management, the requirement for sustained and indeed lifetime support for many people with learning difficulties has maintained the centrality of person-centred work for social workers in this specialty. Further, the equality and social justice agenda in learning disability policy sits well within social work professional values and practice despite the increasingly managerialist tendencies of some sectors. That social work has lead roles in both community care and safeguarding service development for people with learning disabilities, places the profession in a key position as both champion and guardian. The changes have been profound, and the challenges fundamental to our understanding of the place of people within our society and how we engage with them in creating 'better lives'.

In this chapter we have in mind qualified practitioners who have experience in a range of social work practice but are new to the field of learning disability. The potential choice of aspects of practice for inclusion is considerable. So we have chosen to focus on some of the common challenges that have emerged in policy and practice across the four jurisdictions of the United Kingdom (UK), together with some issues absent from these documents that are reflected in important aspects of our own practice. We conclude with a reflection on some specific challenges that may be faced by social work practitioners and managers.

Policy context

In this chapter we will draw primarily on Scotland's policy context although we will refer to differences across the UK where relevant. Greig (2008) suggests that the UK enjoys policies that are 'remarkably progressive' and a source of 'envy' in other countries. He identifies their strengths as being rooted in rights, inclusion and citizenship perspectives. Since their introduction, services for adults with learning disabilities have seen the closure of large hospitals and institutions in favour of community living arrangements; increasing emphasis on getting people into work; providing access to mainstream services in health and leisure; and consulting with people and their families in direct and serious ways hitherto unknown in public service development. The intent of all these policies is to increase the choices and control available to people who rely on services.

While targets for learning disability hospital closure have been broadly met (although less so in Northern Ireland), a review of progress within England shows a mixed picture of achievement and a 'wide gap between rhetoric and reality, between aspiration and experience' (Whitehead *et al.*, 2008, p 5) with deficits particularly in advocacy, employment/daytime activity, hate crime, transport, parents with a learning disability and access to healthcare and services that take into account the needs of people with complex needs. These themes are replicated across the four jurisdictions although it seems that progress in Northern Ireland has been much slower and dominated by service-led rather than person-centred ideas (Mansell, 2008). Mansell concludes that policies are at different stages of development and although they have a number of clear 'commonalities', there are also some significant differences across the nations. There are three main factors underlying the common challenges across the jurisdictions:

- demographic pressures;
- ideological and political changes, including wider generic policy shifts and the emergence of personalisation;
- Changing and increased expectations of people with learning disabilities and their unpaid family carers.

Demographic Pressures

UK studies suggest that twenty people in every 1,000 have a mild or moderate learning disability and three to four people in every 1,000 have a severe or profound disability. On this basis, it is estimated that there are around 120,000 people in Scotland with learning disabilities. Of these, about 80,000 are adults over the age of 16. About 30,000 are people with complex needs who require a lot of support. For Scotland, *The Same As You?* (Scottish Executive, 2000) predicted a 1% increase in the population of people with learning disabilities year on year over a ten-year period. Local experience and national research suggest that this was an underestimate. This is true for both the increase in overall numbers and, of greater significance, the growth of those with complex needs requiring high levels of care. This appears to be a UK wide demographic phenomenon.

Ideological and political changes, including wider generic policy shifts and the emergence of personalisation

As well as the changes dictated by *The Same As You?* (Scottish Executive, 2000) and its equivalents in England, Wales and Northern Ireland (DH, 2001; Northern Ireland

Executive, 2005; WAG, 2007), other, wider health and social policy shifts have also influenced the style and direction of services for people with learning disabilities. Thus, services for people with learning disabilities have been influenced by the emphasis in many generic policy documents of such factors as:

- improving health and wellbeing through prevention and effective treatment and support;
- breaking down barriers between services and promoting partnership working;
- promoting the meaningful involvement of service users, carers and the public;
- raising the quality of services while maximising value for money;
- updating structures to focus collaboration around local populations; and not least of all,
- personalisation of services and the development of individual budgets.

In Scotland, people with learning disabilities and their families still embrace the vision set out in *The Same As You?* and the equivalent documents in the other parts of the UK, but are tired and frustrated by lack of progress in achieving that vision. They see no good reason why these things should not be happening in people's lives. For a considerable time now, government policy has also emphasised enabling people to be full citizens as much as meeting their care needs. Shona Robison, Minister for Public Health, has stated that the Scottish government was seeking:

> *transformational change ... in social care ... to move it away from traditional service models based on the needs of providers and commissioners, to support models that empower individuals.*
>
> (quoted in Lothian Learning Disability Strategy Report, 2008, p 30)

User choice and control is therefore to be a central principle of government policy and its implementation one of the main strategic goals.

Changing Lives: Report of the 21st Century Review of Social Work (Scottish Executive, 2006) was produced following a number of high-profile incidents where social work practice was criticised. A series of recommendations were made that intended to improve areas of cooperation and partnership working. This was with the intention of promoting participation, and understanding each individual in the context of their own community and family.The *Changing Lives* report states that: "Personalisation is driving the shape of all public services, with a growing public expectation that services will meet their needs, helping them achieve personal goals and aspirations" (2006, p 9) and goes on to say that services must be organised in ways that enable people to use them effectively, recognising the needs, strengths and aspirations of people and their families. To do this it is suggested that services must:

- have simple, reliable and fair means of accessing services;
- make sure that assessment involves people, using self-assessment where appropriate, building on aspirations to produce clear actions;
- recognise unpaid carers as partners in the provision of care;
- make sure that people moving between different parts of the care system have smooth transitions;
- make sure that services are provided from premises that are fit for purpose;
- test out the application of individualised budgets with different groups of people, then use the learning to change services.

In our view there is some tension between the Scottish Government's promotion of personalisation, increased demand for services and the introduction of new tendering processes that appear to place emphasis on achieving the lowest possible price. *The Same As You?* had previously supported the development of Direct Payments. Recommendation 5 states that "Anyone who wants direct payments should be able to have them, and local authorities should be included in the list of possible providers" (Scottish Executive, 2001, p 24). Despite this, and despite the recommendations of *Changing Lives*, the uptake of Direct Payments has generally remained low in Scotland, possibly due to a lack of cohesion between local authorities and government departments and the lack of accessible information available to people with learning disabilities and carers.

The most significant of the new initiatives to explore different methods of individualised funding or self-directed support is *In Control.* This has been adopted faster and more fully in England than in Scotland where there continues to be an emphasis on the purchase of arranged services as well as the employment of personal assistants. *In Control* is a national programme aimed at changing the organisation of social care so that people who need support can take more control of their own lives and fulfill their role as citizens. It draws on many separate positive developments – person-centred planning, care management, single shared assessment, direct payments, a focus on outcomes, protection of vulnerable adults, regulation of services, eligibility criteria, standards, advocacy and brokerage. Since 2003 this model has been influencing a slow but steady transformation of the social care system in England into a system of self-directed support. Central to the model is a belief that it really helps people to be in control of their support if they know how much money they can spend on it.

With the *In Control* model people who are entitled to support make their own initial determination of their needs using self-assessment. A funding model, which seems fair and reasonable to meet people's needs, is developed locally. Service users have a clear indication of their entitlement and are offered a choice of how their funding will be managed:

- directly by an individual;
- payment to a third party;
- payment to a Trust;
- payment to an organisation; or
- payment to an Individual Support Fund.

Planning in this self-directed support model is individualised with help available for service users to make creative use of the community resources available if they wish to plan their own support needs.

The emergence of an emphasis on self-directed support will necessitate new approaches to care management. An approach that places service users at the centre of decision-making is essential and connections with independent advocacy will if anything become more important.

Increased expectations of people with learning disabilities and their unpaid family carers

People with a learning disability, and their carers, are now better organised to express their views and contribute to service development and to strategic planning. Policy changes and user and carer expectations now mean that more people expect and demand small person-centred services. In addition, service users and carers have a right to involvement in decisions and have more access to effective independent advocacy.

Some significant challenges for services

In the remainder of this chapter we will focus on some areas of service and support that present particular challenges throughout the UK, including:

- support for older people with learning disabilities;
- support for people with profound and multiple learning disabilities;
- support for people with learning disabilities who have mental illness and/or behaviour that challenges services;
- support for people with learning disabilities who commit criminal offences;
- support for people with learning disabilities who are parents.

Older People with learning disabilities

It is clear that one of the most significant changes we can anticipate is a significant growth in the older age group. Like the rest of the population, people with learning disabilities have benefited from improvements in public health and standards of living. This has resulted in increases in longevity and demand for services. The average life expectancy for people with a learning disability has increased and in particular the life expectancy of people with Down's Syndrome has risen from 9 years in 1928 to over 40 years in the 1980s (Wilkinson *et al.*, 2006) and by 2001 it had been noted that some will live into their sixties.

Older people with Down's Syndrome are at significantly higher risk than older people (with or without learning disabilities) of developing dementia. Compared with the older population in general, for people with Down's syndrome:

- the onset of dementia is earlier and the incidence is higher (2% at 30 years, reaching 54% at 60 years);
- the presentation is different (featuring behavioural changes more than memory loss);
- the rate of deterioration is more rapid (1-9 years).

These phenomena have clear implications for policy and practice.

In the light of improving but still low levels of recognition among professionals and families, there is a need for increased knowledge and training. The good practice standard of sharing diagnosis of dementia in the wider ageing population (Gilliard *et al.*, 2005), has not extended to people with learning disabilities but is crucial in ensuring that people affected can be supported to make informed choices and decisions about their future lives as soon as possible (Stalker *et al.*, 1999; Wilkinson and Milne, 2005).

Family carers are an important source of information in achieving early recognition. They may report changes in personality, increased agitation and changes in sleeping patterns before memory and cognitive changes. This cluster of changes can be particularly stressful for carers (Watchman, 2007). Family carers of people with learning disabilities are much older (40% are over 60 years old). They have had a life-long commitment to supporting the individual possibly associated with 'satisfaction' in what they have achieved as much as 'burden'; and as they age, an element of reciprocity and even 'role reversal' may come to characterise the relationship with their son or daughter. Any social work intervention needs to take into account the family's caring history and values in making any transition arrangements or undertaking long-term care planning.

Best practice in learning disability has emphasised the importance of accessing mainstream services. However, people with learning disabilities placed in old-age settings are likely to be much younger than other residents (55 years versus 85 years) and such a decision can be seen to place unwelcome restrictions on people who may have led inclusive lives. This has resulted in learning disability services trying to support people 'in place' as they age.

Given that dementia, let alone learning disabilities combined with dementia, has only recently been given dedicated policy and practice attention in the UK, it is unsurprising that *The Same As You?* (Scottish Executive, 2000) and *Valuing People* (DH, 2001) did not address the challenges arising from increasing numbers of individuals with Down's syndrome and dementia. However, we have the beginnings of a systematic approach to good practice for supporting people with learning disabilities and dementia in the form of the Edinburgh Principles (Wilkinson and Janicki, 2002).

People with profound and multiple learning disabilities (PMLD)

Despite the clear demographic data about the increase in numbers, there has been a limited focus on people with PMLD. This needs to be addressed because improvements in medical technology are leading to a significant increase in the number of adults with PMLD in the future. The PMLD Network has stated that there is a serious lack of understanding of the numbers and needs and that this has resulted in poor planning and monitoring of the support they receive. Adults with PMLD are a relatively small, easily identified group with significant needs for care and support, yet despite these needs, they and their families have often not been provided with services to adequately meet them.

In *Raising Our Sights*, Mansell (2010) estimates that in England there are currently 16,000 people with PMLD. The number of adults with profound intellectual and multiple disabilities is estimated to increase by on average 1.8% each year to 2026, when the total number would be just over 22,000 people. However, the report also notes that:

Access to services is becoming an increasing problem. Families report cuts in services, difficulties in getting an assessment and the tightening of eligibility criteria for essential services, despite their needs staying the same or, in many cases, worsening. (Mansell, 2010, p 5)

People with PMLD experience a range of significant health needs that bring them into frequent contact with healthcare services. The range and complexity of health needs experienced by this group increase with the severity of learning disability. As a consequence of their impairment the majority of people with PMLD have severe sensory difficulties and severe communication difficulties, which can impact on their quality of life. There can be challenges for many people with learning disabilities when accessing general health services, but these difficulties are exacerbated for those with PMLD. Undertaking health assessments with people with PMLD can prove difficult due to their frail physiology, and communication difficulties. As a result of such difficulties in assessment and diagnosis, mental illness, and developmental disorders such as Autism Spectrum Disorder often go unrecognised in this group.

Young people with PMLD may remain isolated from their peer groups as they go through the child to adulthood transition phase. There is currently a lack of appropriate daytime facilities for people with PMLD that takes account of their complex health needs.

People with learning disabilities who have mental illness and/or behaviour that challenges services

We know from research that the overall prevalence of mental health problems in people with a learning disability is significantly higher than that of the general population, with most studies pointing to a prevalence rate of somewhere between 30 and 50%. For reasons that we do not yet fully understand, particular conditions have a higher prevalence among people with learning disabilities. For example while only 1% of the general population develop schizophrenia, we know that approximately 3% of people with a mild learning disability do. Rates of depression and anxiety are also higher. There is an increasing awareness too, of how Attention Deficit and Hyperactivity Disorder (ADHD) can affect people long into adulthood. Emerson's (2001) definition of behaviour that challenges services is widely used. He defines it as is:

> Culturally abnormal behaviour of such intensity, frequency or duration that the physical safety of the person or others is placed in serious jeopardy, or behaviour which is likely to seriously limit the use of, or deny access to ordinary community facilities. (Emerson, 1995, pp 4-5)

Recent studies suggest that between 12 and 17% of people with a learning disability will display behaviour that is challenging to services. Approximately 40-60% of these will show more severe problems, including physical aggression, self-injury and destructiveness towards the environment. Challenging behaviour is more likely to be presented by men, especially in the age range 15-35, in those having a more severe intellectual disability; and in those who have additional sensory impairment.

People who present these challenges to services need to be treated with respect and as individuals. Services should adopt a person-centred planning approach to designing support and should avoid a blame culture where the person with the learning disability is considered responsible for the problem. In order to ensure that services are client specific and designed to meet the needs of the service user, person-centred planning should be adopted among all services providing for people with complex needs. To ensure quality and equity of specialist support services there needs to be consistency of approach.

There is an emerging pattern of people with learning disabilities and complex care needs being the subject of out-of-area placements due either to a breakdown in current local services or to a complete absence of services locally that can respond to their specific needs. The high cost of individualised support arrangements, combined with budget restrictions, has also seen the re-emergence of congregate services, albeit in apparently more benign forms such as new versions of core and cluster services. Social workers need to be alert to the reinvention of the institutions we have spent several decades replacing with more personal and individualised support arrangements.

People with learning disabilities who commit criminal offences

The Same As You (Scottish Executive, 2000) made specific reference to people with learning disabilities who offend and recommended that further work needed to be undertaken in relation to:

- people with learning disabilities who come into contact with criminal justice services as perpetrators;
- people who have perpetrated inappropriate acts but where criminal justice services have not been contacted.

One of the challenges faced when planning and developing services for people with learning disabilities who come into contact with the criminal justice system, or who are at risk of doing so, is the limited data available on the exact numbers falling within this group. Estimates of the numbers across Scotland suggest that there are some 2,500 individuals with learning disabilities and forensic problems, a proportion of whom might require access to specialist services ranging from outpatient and day services through to prison and secure facilities.

It is recognised that people with learning disabilities experience risk factors that make them vulnerable to antisocial behaviours that can result in contact with the criminal justice system. More men than women with learning disabilities demonstrate offending behaviour and there has been a limited focus on women with learning disabilities.

The assessment of the risk of potential reoffending is important, particularly where there is a history of violent and sexual offences. It is important that these risk assessments have been validated and they are viewed as only part of a more comprehensive assessment. There is a need to have in place multi-agency protocols and procedures. There is also a clear need to continue to develop and research the effectiveness of risk assessments to ensure that there is robust evidence to support planning and importantly decisions that restrict an individual's liberty or lifestyle.

In Fife, the Significant Risk Advisory Group (SRAG) has for some years been an integral part of the forensic services. It plays a central role in directing the management of care of offenders with learning disabilities. This multidisciplinary group comprises representatives from the health service, local authority and criminal justice service and has representation from service providers involved in the care of individuals. Broadly, the function of the group is to review and advise on the development and implementation of care plans for offenders with learning disabilities living in community settings. The identification of potential risks associated with individual service users is undertaken and strategies integrated within their care plan are implemented by service providers. Changes to care plans can only be made following a review by the Significant Risk Advisory Group (SRAG) and it is an integral part of service-level agreements that participation and compliance with treatment and care plans will occur. The SRAG arrangements foreshadowed the current arrangements for Multi-Agency Public Protection Arrangements (MAPPA) that were introduced to manage 'high tariff' offenders such as sex offenders. There has been some discussion about extending MAPPA to embrace both child and adult protection committees. They remain separate for the moment but there is overlap and co-operation between them. In the meantime, SRAG continues to operate in parallel to MAPPA so that 'lower tariff' offenders who might also be deemed vulnerable adults are systematically reviewed and supported.

People with learning disabilities who are parents

We do not know how many adults with learning disabilities are also parents. Estimates are variable due to a lack of consistent definitions of learning disabilities and uncertainty about the numbers of adults not known to services although one study (Emerson *et al.*, 2005) found that 7% or 1 in 15 adults in the large sample were parents.

The emerging profile of parents with learning disabilities in the literature is a recent phenomenon. As institutions are replaced by community living and there are changing expectations, individuals aspire to be parents as well as householders and employees.

What we do know is that parents with learning disabilities are disadvantaged when they come in contact with the public childcare system (McConnell *et al.*, 2002; Swain and Cameron 2003; Elvish *et al.*, 2006). Booth has claimed that presumptions of incompetence result in decisions to remove a disproportionately high number of children from parents with learning disabilities (Booth and Booth, 2003). Also they are more likely to lose their children to state care and despite the policy emphasis on kinship care, their children are less likely to be placed with extended family members (Booth *et al.*, 2005). We also know that service silos that separate children and families' teams from adult services teams, mean that parents are unlikely to get support in their own right from workers experienced in adult disability services, but much attention from childcare and indeed child protection workers inexperienced in working with disability. The gaps between maternity, health and children's services further fragment support. The importance of early and appropriate support therefore is crucial to safeguarding the wellbeing of children and protecting the rights of parents under the Human Rights Act 1998 and disability discrimination legislation.

Partnership between health and social services lies at the heart of providing effective support to adults with learning disabilities as they make the transition to parenthood. Good practice guidelines (DH and DfES, 2007; Scottish Consortium for Learning Disability, 2009) set out some of the dilemmas for professionals in this area.

McGaw and Newman (2005) challenge the recurrent and persistent theme in the literature that it is a 'self-evident truth' that people with learning disabilities cannot be adequate parents and should be discouraged from doing so. To what extent should one group of parents be expected to earn the right and to be required to demonstrate competence to become parents when other groups of adults, at risk or otherwise, are not? This remains a contested area where professional knowledge and understanding is less well developed and where there is an increasing need for sound assessment and decision making that neither disadvantages parents nor fails to benefit children.

What do people with learning disabilities need and want?

People with learning disabilities themselves and their family carers share a vision of "a good life" (Etmanski, 2000). Not surprisingly, a good life for people with learning disabilities is not much different from that aspired to by other citizens:

- having a home;
- having loving relationships with family and friends;
- controlling the basic elements in their lives;
- attaining sufficient financial means to live with dignity;
- pursuing their dreams and passions; and
- making a contribution.

A survey of the impact of *The Same As You?* (Curtis, 2006) found that what matters most to people with learning disabilities is getting their own home, having friends and being able to go out more. They also want to make sure that they stay in contact with family and they keep the support that is essential to their independence. They enjoy socialising and they hope for new experiences. The biggest worry that people have for the future is the death of their parents, showing that individuals need to be involved with their families in planning for the future.

For the vast majority of people, a life lacking in relationships precludes living a good life. Indeed, it can be argued that lack of reciprocal social connections is virtually a matter of life and death. We know from research on social capital that individuals who have strong social networks are more likely to have positive outcomes than those who do not. Positive outcomes include:

- greater well-being and ability to cope;
- increased trust;
- improved recovery from illness;
- better ability to deal with transitions.

And yet there are obstacles at every stage for people with learning disabilities in forming relationships. People with learning disabilities say they need more opportunities to meet and spend time with people with similar interests in groups and other social activities, to go to more places to meet new people and to have time to get to know people and talk to them. Some people need help with arrangements and others lack opportunities to meet people their own age or go out at night. These findings confirm that more priority needs to be given to enabling people with learning disabilities to have opportunities to socialise and meet others through schemes that support the creation and development of real reciprocal relationships as opposed to befriending. There are a number of new initiatives that are addressing these problems. For instance, *Dates 'n' Mates* in Scotland (and its equivalent *Stars in the Sky* in England) is a dating agency/friendship matching service run by people with learning disabilities. The voluntary organisation, *Equal Futures*, helps families to build lifelong circles of support in which an individual's allies get together to coordinate efforts to help. Circles of support are not formal structures. They can meet to listen, share ideas, help solve problems and plan how to help – and to have fun! Crucially, they do not consist of "befrienders". Rather, circle members are friends who are there because they want to be there for the person. Their contribution is personal, not professional.

Circles of support are especially potent in tackling the very real problems of social isolation among older families. Evidence suggests that people with learning disabilities living with older carers are particularly prone to loneliness and isolation. In research carried out in Edinburgh in 2008 by EDG, 50 out of 52 older carers interviewed said that their relative had no social contact other than family. The two who said that their relative had good social contact both had circles of support through *Equal Futures*.

It is clear that even those people with learning disabilities in very supportive settings can suffer social exclusion. They tend to have limited circles of support and a very real paucity of reciprocal relationships. This problem can be addressed by strengthening relationships with local communities; by building on the resources they have, helping members of the community to make contact with each other; and by helping people with learning disabilities to become active members of their local and global community.

Reinders (2002, p 2) suggests that we need to consider inclusion as being a wider agenda than one in which people with learning disabilities are able to take up their rights and fill valued social roles. Ensuring that people are taken seriously as citizens is not necessarily the same as taking them seriously as human beings. Inclusion in community life requires that one is participating in the lives of others, and to be participating in other people's lives, one has to be accepted and appreciated by them. In a sense, 'Community is the experience of sharing ones life with people'. Reinders goes so far as to say that in the long run people with learning disabilities may depend on the strength of their social networks much more than on their individual rights.

Through a community-oriented person-centred approach, it is possible to have up-to-date plans for each person that incorporate efforts to build and maintain informal support networks, in this way enabling citizenship, personal networking, decision making, inclusion and involvement in the local community.

Community engagement is concerned, firstly, with providing opportunities for people to learn through taking part in opportunities that would not otherwise be available to them, and second, with involving people in collective effort so that they gain confidence in their own abilities and their ability to influence decisions that affect them.

By adopting a community development-based approach such as asset-based community development (Kretzmann and McKnight, 1997), building enduring circles of support, and using new computer-based safe social networking models such as *Tyze*, it is possible to:

- equip people with skills and competencies which they would not otherwise have;
- realise existing skills and develop potential;
- promote increased self-confidence;
- promote people's ability to take responsibility for identifying and meeting their own, and other people's, needs;
- encourage people to become involved in their community and wider society in a fuller way.

Six years on from *The Same As You?*, NHS QIS (2006) found that improvement in the uptake of carers' assessments was limited by the fact that many people who cared for a person with a learning disability did not have a social worker. Some carers suggested that carers' assessments could be delegated to voluntary organisations that already provide advice and information to family carers of people with learning disabilities.

As far back as 1999, the consultation report *If You Don't Ask You Don't Get* (Stalker, *et al.*, 1999) noted how consistent user and carer views have been. It concluded that service planners need to respond to users' and carers' views by:

- setting up more friendship schemes and 'community connectors';
- increasing social and recreational opportunities for young people;
- offering better choice and availability of short-term breaks;
- setting up a range of work initiatives, such as co-operatives, social firms and supported employment;
- creating more person-centred services and diversified housing and support options;
- ensuring that all those eligible for community care or carers' assessments are offered one;
- exploring the potential for a wider use of direct payments by people with learning disabilities;
- greater development of citizen advocacy schemes;
- publishing more information in community languages;
- offering more support for the siblings of disabled children;
- improving long-term planning to address adults' future support needs.

Most of this is still true today…

Conclusion – striking a balance between autonomy and protection

A characteristic theme in contemporary learning disability policy and practice generally has been the promotion of autonomy and empowerment for a group of people who historically have been denied participation in and control of decision-making in their lives. Some of this has come about as a result of living segregated lives in institutions. In a rapidly industrialising society that placed value on cognitive competence, the origins of these establishments lay in the tangled ideas of both protecting society and protecting the individuals themselves.

More recent policies, exemplified by the closure of the learning disability hospitals, have attempted with some success to promote the rights of people with learning disabilities to an 'ordinary life' – in their own homes, in the community, in jobs, with friendships, leisure activities and choice about how they live their lives.

With increasing community presence, choices and freedoms, have also come new and different risks of exploitation – financial, sexual or physical – and more generally abuse in the form of bullying and harassment. While it is well documented that the institutions presented their own risks (Martin, 1985; Stanley et al., 1999; Butler and Drakeford, 2003) solutions were available to services to intervene protectively once the abuse was recognised. Within the community, especially where people are living in their own homes, as opposed to care homes, such intervention is complex, and requires sophisticated skills and understanding.

The challenge is to both support autonomy and independence and protect vulnerable adults at risk of harm in an agency and policy context that is risk averse and has limited resources at its disposal. In the past, unlike child protection, the legislative underpinnings for intervention in the lives of vulnerable adults had been relatively underdeveloped. However, we now have a raft of legislation and policy guidance in all jurisdictions that has been either modernised or introduced to permit professional intervention in the lives of adults with a mental illness (Mental Health Act 2007; Mental Health (Care & Treatment) (Scotland) Act 2003) who do not have capacity to make decisions for themselves (Mental Capacity Act 2007; Adults with Incapacity Act (Scotland) 2000) or who are at risk of harm (No Secrets 2000 (reviewed in 2009); In Safe Hands 2000 (reviewed in 2010); Adult Support & Protection (Scotland) Act 2007). In Scotland the guidance arrangements for safeguarding that apply to the rest of the UK have been given legislative force through the Adult Support and Protection Act 2007. This requires public bodies to co-operate and provides for intervention in the lives of adults who are regarded as having capacity, where there is evidence of 'undue pressure' from a third party that can be substantiated in court.

It has been argued that 'risk assessment' has replaced assessment of 'welfare' needs in social work practice (Waterson, 2002). In other words, as a result of shrinking resources that have raised eligibility thresholds and managerialist practices to increase public accountabilities, social workers especially in statutory sectors have found their work focused increasingly on risk assessment and management (Titterton, 2005; Barry, 2007) with arguably reduced professional autonomy. This places social workers at the nexus of increasing expectations, more opportunities for intervention but limited resources to support their interventions.

Striking a balance between rights, risks and protection in professional decision-making is one of the major challenges confronting social workers practising in this field today. Much of the literature on risk focuses on negative connotations of 'harm' and on 'risk-averse' agency cultures that are sensitive to the way that risk issues are amplified by the media. The greatest challenge to good practice for practitioners, however, is in developing skills, knowledge and confidence in what has become known as 'positive risk taking' (Titterton, 2010) and 'defensible' decision-making (Baker and Wilkinson, 2010).

Before proceeding to the concluding questions and challenges for practice, it is worth reflecting on whether what you have read in this chapter is what you expected to read about developments in the learning disability field. We hope that the chapter has persuaded you that extraordinary changes have taken place as a consequence of the vision of champions from families, services and government and from activists themselves. The pace of change is quick, the challenges are constantly evolving and there are always battles to be fought and sometimes won. It is not a field of practice for the faint-hearted but the rewards, professional and personal, are incomparable as people who rely on our services move from getting better services to better lives.

Questions and challenges for practitioners and managers

(a) Matching aspirations to resources
- There is a significant tension between the high aspirational nature of the policies in the UK and the fear of risk taking at manager and frontline practitioner levels. How can you as a social worker maintain idealism and a commitment to social justice?
- How do you maintain these high policy ideals and enable people to live a good life?
- How can you shift power and enable real choices?
- How can you resist the development of new forms of congregate services in times of economic restraint?

(b) Responding to changes in demography
- How can you get the support you will need in order to develop the knowledge base required to deal with changing needs – particularly those related to ageing, physical health needs and the ability to resist reinstitutionalisation when psychiatric problems or dementia occur?

(c) Remaining person centred and outcomes driven
- How can you develop person-centred practice that supports individuals to lead their lives to their fullest potential by adopting a strength - rather than deficit - based approach in decision-making?
- How can you engage in outcomes oriented practice in work with both people with learning disabilities and carers?
- Can you insist on using appropriate assessment tools like Talking Points, the Scottish outcomes approach?
- How can managers create and sustain productive links between person-centred planning and wider care management processes, especially outcomes-oriented assessment and service commissioning?

(d) Working in partnership
- How can you foster partnership not only across specialist and mainstream service providers but also across advocacy groups?
- What do you need to do to gain support to challenge the boundaries between elder care, mental health and learning disability services?
- How can your work be informed by the views of carers and users of services, which reaches beyond consultation to collaboration and co-production?

(e) Addressing risk assessment and risk management
How can you strive to maintain a balance between positive risk-taking and risk-averse practices in your work with people with learning disabilities and their families?
- Can you insist on using tools such as PRAMS (Person-Centred Risk Assessment and Management System; Titterton 2005) and the Risk Assessment and Protection Plan (Joint Improvement Team, 2007) that assist professionals to assess, manage and review risk situations in a systematic, multi-agency and dynamic way?

References

Baker K, and Wilkinson, H (2010) 'Professsional risk taking and Defensible Decisions' in Kemshaw, H and Wikinson, B (eds) *Good Practice in Risk assessment and Risk Management*, Volume 3, London, Jessica Kingsley Publishers.

Booth, T, Booth, W and McConnell, D (2005) 'The Prevalence and Outcomes of Care Proceedings Involving Parents with Learning Disabilities in the Family Courts' *Journal of Applied research in Intellectual Disabilities* 18(1), pp 7-17.

Booth T and Booth W (2003) 'Self Advocacy and Supported Learning for Mothers with Learning Difficulties' *Journal of Learning Disabilities* 7(2), pp 165-93.

Butler, I and Drakeford, M (2003) *Social Policy, Social Welfare and Scandal: How British Public Policy is Made* Basingstoke: Palgrave Macmillan.

Curtice, L (2006) 'How is it going: A survey of what matters most to people with learning disabilities in Scotland today', Glasgow: SCLD/Enable.

DH (Department of Health) (2001) *Valuing People: A New Strategy for Learning Disability for the 21st Century* London: Department of Health.

DH and DfES (Department of Health and the Department of Education and Skills) (2007) *Good practice guidance on working with parents with a learning disability* (www.dh.gov.uk/en/Publicationsandstatistics/Publications/PublicationsPolicyAndGuidance/DH_075119).

Dickson, K, Emerson E and Hatton C (2005) 'Self-reported antisocial behaviour: prevalence and risk factors amongst adolescents with and without intellectual disability' *Journal of Intellectual Disability Research* 49, pt11, pp 820-26.

Elvish, J, Hames, A, English, S and Wills, C. (2006) 'Parents with learning disabilities: an audit of referrals made to a learning disability team' *Learning Disability Review* 11(2), pp 26-44.

Emerson, E (1995) *Challenging Behaviour: Analysis and Intervention in People with Learning Disabilities* Cambridge: Cambridge University Press.

Emerson, E (2001) *Challenging Behaviour: Analysis and Intervention in People with Severe Intellectual Disabilities* Cambridge: Cambridge University Press.

Emerson, E, Malam, S, Davies, I and Spencer, K (2005) *Adults with Learning Disabilities in England* Lancaster: Lancaster Centre for Disability Research, University of Lancaster.

Etmanski A, (2000) *A Good Life – For You and Your Relative with a Disability* Vancouver: Planned Lifetime Advocacy Network.

Forensic Mental Health Services Managed Care Network (2004) Report for the Learning Disabilities Service Working Group, Carstairs: Forensic Network Team (www.forensicnetwork.scot.nhs.uk).

Gilliard, J, Means, R, Beattie, A and Daker-White, G (2005) 'Dementia care in England and the social model of disability: lessons and issues' *Dementia* 4(4), pp 571-86.

Greig R (2008) 'Editorial', Themed Issue 'Planning Challenges for UK Learning Disability Services', *Tizard Learning Disability Review* 13(3).

Joint Improvement Team (2007) 'Working Together to Improve Adult Protection. Risk Assessment and Protection Plan: Formats and Explanatory Notes', August, Edinburgh: Scottish Government, Joint Improvement Team.

Kretzmann, J and McKnight, J (1997) *Building Communities from The Inside Out: A Path Towards Finding and Mobilising a Community's Assets* Chicago, IL: ACTA Publications.

Lothian Learning Disability Strategy Report to the Strategy Review Group (2008) Edinburgh: NHS Lothians.

Mansell J (2008) 'Learning Disability Policy and Practice in the UK' *Tizard Learning Disability Review* 13(3) pp 12-14.

Mansell J (2010) *Raising Our Sights: Services for adults with profound intellectual and multiple disabilities* Canterbury: Tizard Centre, University of Kent.

Martin, J P (1985) *Hospitals in Trouble* Oxford: Wiley Blackwell.

McConnell, D, Llewellyn, G and Ferronato, L (2002) 'Disability and decision-making in Australian Care Proceedings' *International Journal of Law, Policy and the Family* 16(2), pp 270-99.

McGaw, S and Newman, T (2005) *What Works for Parents with Learning Disabilities* Ilford: Barnardo's.

NHS Quality Improvement Scotland (2006) *Learning Disability Services: National Overview*, February, Edinburgh: NHS Quality Improvement Scotland.

Northern Ireland Executive (2005) *Equal Lives: Review of Policy and Services for People with a Learning Disability in Northern Ireland* Belfast: Northern Ireland Executive.

Reinders, J S (2002) 'The good life for citizens with intellectual disability' *Journal of Intellectual Disability Research* 46(1), pp 1-5.

Scottish Consortium for Learning Disability (2009) *Scottish Good Practice Guidelines for Supporting Parents With Learning Disabilities* Glasgow: SCLD (www.scld.org.uk/data/asset/file_850_Scottish_Good_Practice_Guidelines_for_Supporting_Parents_With_Learning_Disabilities.pdf).

Scottish Executive (2000) *The Same as You? A Review of Services for People with Learning Disabilities* Edinburgh: The Stationery Office.

Scottish Executive (2006) *Changing Lives: A review of Social Work in Scotland in the 21st Century* Edinburgh: The Stationery Office.

Stalker, K, Duckett, P and Downs, M (1999) *Going with the Flow: Choice, Dementia and People with Learning Difficulties* York: Joseph Rowntree Foundation.

Stalker, K, Cadogan L, Petrie, M, Jones, C and Murray J (1999) *If You Don't Ask, You Don't Get. A review of services for people with learning disabilities: Views of people who use services and their carers.* Edinburgh: SHS/CRU.

Stanley, N, Manthorpe, J and Penhale, B (1999) *Institutional Abuse: Perspectives Across the Life Course* London: Routledge.

Swain, P and Cameron, N (2003) '"Good Enough Parenting": Parental Disability and Child Protection' *Disability and Society* 18(2), pp 165-77.

Titterton, M (2005) *Risk and Risk Taking in Health and Social Welfare* London: Jessica Kingsley Publishers.

Titterton, M (2010: forthcoming) *Positive Risk Taking with People at Risk of Harm Vol 3* London: Jessica Kingsley Publishers.

Watchman, K (2007) 'Dementia and Down's Syndrome: The Diagnosis and Support Needed' *Learning Disability Practice* 10(2), pp 10-14.

Waterson, J (1999) 'Redefining Community Care Social Work: Needs or Risk Led Welfare' Health and Social Care in the Community 7(4), pp 376-79.

WAG (Welsh Assembly Govermnment) (2007) *Statement on Policy and Practice for Adults with a Learning Disability* Cardiff: Welsh Assembly Government.

Whitehead, S, Curtice, L, Beyer, S, McConkey, R, Bogues, S (2008) 'Learning Disability Policy in the UK' *Tizard Learning Disability Review* 13(3), pp 12-15.

Wilkinson, H and Janicki, M P (2002) 'The Edinburgh principles with accompanying guidelines and recommendations' *Journal of Intellectual Disability Research* 46(3), pp 279-84.

Wilkinson, H and Milne, A J (2005) 'Sharing a diagnosis of dementia: earning from the patient perspective' *Ageing and Mental Health* 7(4), pp 300-7.

Wilkinson, H, Kerr, D and Cunningham, H (2006) 'Learning Disability and Dementia: Are we prepared?' *Journal of Dementia Care* 14(3), pp 17-19.

Chapter 14

The Role of Personal Narratives in Addressing Stigma in Mental Health

Neil Quinn, Lee Knifton and Jane Donald

Introduction

Mental health stigma and discrimination serve to reinforce the inequalities experienced by people with mental health problems and are a major issue of concern for social work practice. This chapter introduces the concept of personal narratives and considers their role in addressing stigma and discrimination. The themes that form the basis of this chapter – personal narratives and mental health stigma – are of interest to policy makers, practitioners and researchers concerned with inequalities. Examples from different settings will be used to explore how narratives can influence public and practitioner attitudes and the complexities and paradoxes involved in using this approach are explored. Finally, we will explore the implications of this approach for social work practice and the relevance of narratives for other service user groups.

Personal narratives

A personal narrative is a story told by someone about his or her own life. Cupitt (1991) argues that our lives are constructed and made sense of through stories. We understand our history, ourselves and others through interpreting sets of stories. There has been a long history of using narratives to convey complex ideas. In traditional cultures, before writing existed, stories were used to pass on and reinforce community values and knowledge, shaping how societies and individuals should act. Stories remain an integral part of our daily lives through the arts and media but have been marginalised from public policy and many areas of academic discourse, where rational scientific thought has dominated the agenda.

The use of personal narratives in mental health practice

Within mental health practice, narratives are often used within therapy and research contexts (Bamberg, 2007). Here we will consider how personal narratives can be used to improve public and practitioner attitudes towards people with mental health problems by looking at their use in two areas of practice:

- *Narrative-based workshops*: these equality training workshops are designed to improve practitioner awareness on mental health issues. A one-day workshop was developed by a team comprised of service users, advocacy workers, community development staff and psychologists. It uses didactic and experiential learning approaches to explore mental health, mental illness, stigma and recovery. At the heart of this is the use of a personal narrative, focusing on recovery, delivered by a mental health service user trainer.
- *A mental health arts festival*: the Scottish Mental Health Arts and Film Festival has become a major national cultural event and one of the largest festivals of its kind. Over 600 events have attracted audiences of 40,000 people. Media coverage has been extensive and positive in the press, radio and television, with an emphasis on high-profile artists who appear at the festival. The events are increasingly the culmination of year-round collaborations between artists, artistic organisations, community development groups, mental health groups and practitioners and include theatre, film, concerts, exhibitions, dance, comedy, literature and fusion events. Personal narratives are used in a variety of ways at the festival. They form an essential part of the festival programme within the film, theatre and literary events. Well-known artists have become involved in the festival as curators and performers, sharing their own stories and experiences of mental health issues.

Applying the use of narratives to address stigma

The main focus of this chapter will be to consider how narratives can address stigma and discrimination. First, we will look at the problem of stigma, review existing approaches to addressing stigma and consider the role of narratives in tackling this issue, drawing on the practice examples above.

Mental health problems and stigma

Mental health problems and the associated stigma are major public health and social issues (WHO, 2001). The nature of stigmatising beliefs and attitudes varies according to the nature of the mental health problem and by the cultural context in which it is manifested (Crisp *et al.*, 2000), although some studies acknowledge similar patterns of discrimination across cultures (Van Brakel, 2006). The modern concept of stigma is based on Goffman's (1963) idea of spoiled identity, reflecting social attitudes that discredit and exclude stigmatised people to a position of social disgrace. According to Link & Phelan (2001), stigma comprises four components: (a) A group of individuals is labelled and distinguished from other groups; (b) dominant cultural beliefs result in linking the labelled persons to undesirable characteristics (negative stereotypes); (c) the creation of two distinct categories – 'in-groups' and 'out-groups'; and (d) the labelled persons experience discrimination. For stigma to occur, a fifth component, (e) a power differential, must exist between groups. Not only are people with mental illness trying to cope with managing their symptoms, but the stigma they face, driven by prejudice, results in increased social isolation. Mental health stigma prevents timely access to treatment and can therefore delay recovery and reduce positive outcomes. Further, people with mental health problems have indicated that stigma can often be as devastating and life-limiting as the illness itself (Schulze and Angermeyer 2003). Discrimination is widespread, affecting employment, housing, education and healthcare (Larson and Corrigan 2008).

Existing approaches to addressing stigma and discrimination

The World Health Organization has outlined the importance of addressing stigma and discrimination. In doing so, it advocates two broad approaches: first, addressing discrimination through rights based reforms to mental health services and legislation; second, addressing stigma through public education. Globally there are currently a number of international programmes under way (WHO, 2001). The need to address stigma has been increasingly recognised in recent years across the nations of the United Kingdom (UK), each of whom have prioritised this in policy, programmes and practice.

Public education programmes usually comprise large-scale awareness campaigns whose aims are often to provide 'accurate' information to the public and key groups. This is often medical information and communication uses the methods and assumptions of social marketing. These traditional approaches are positivistic in their worldview (Pilgrim, 2005) in that they assume that there is an objective knowledge about mental health problems that the wider public will respond rationally to. The challenge from this positivistic perspective is therefore to provide accurate information clearly and effectively to the public. This public education approach has largely influenced programmes in the UK to address stigma.

However, emerging evidence on tackling stigma suggests that top-down public education approaches that have been dominated by psychiatric explanatory frameworks (Double, 2002) and information-based campaigns are inadequate. These positivist approaches fail to capture the complexity of mental health and illness (Gergen, 1994), ignore power (Ssasz, 1972; Pilgrim, 2005) and ignore the cultural dimensions of mental health (Fernando, 2002). Standardised approaches fail to consider inequalities in mental health, whereby certain population groups are at higher risk of developing mental health problems based on gender, ethnicity and sexual orientation (Scottish Executive, 2005), and relative deprivation (Wilkinson and Pickett, 2007).

Education interventions only seem to be promising when they are combined with positive personal contact, narratives or dialogue between the public and people who have experienced mental health problems (Pinfold et al., 2005; Quinn & Knifton, 2005). They seem to be more effective when they use social models of mental health, framing symptoms as responses to circumstances rather than bio-medical education (Read & Law, 1999; Byrne, 2000; Corrigan et al., 2001) and when they involve people who have experienced mental health problems in the design and delivery of initiatives (Angermayer & Matschinger, 1996; Penn and Martin, 1998).

An alternative 'constructionist' approach

Consequently, a constructionist approach (Gergen, 1999; Pilgrim and Rogers 1999) offers a more appropriate framework for addressing stigma and discrimination. A constructionist approach acknowledges multiple perspectives, validates the views of a range of stakeholders, including practitioners, policy makers and academics, and acknowledges the realities of those experiencing inequalities. It validates the personal narratives of people with mental health problems within their cultural and social context (Faulkner and Thomas, 2002), narratives that have informed the emergence of the recovery movement and service user research.

Gergen and Gergen (2003) argue that there is something particularly effective about listening to others' narratives that crosses boundaries of meaning and fosters mutuality. Narratives are particularly influential in three ways: (1) they create an atmosphere of receptivity; (2) they are familiar as a major common way of communicating throughout the life course, having a recognizable structure; (3) they create trust and empathy because there is a known storyteller. In relation to tackling stigma, stories or narratives about people have been powerful. These narratives give marginalised groups a voice and produce an alternative view. Harding (1993), in relation to gender, proposes the concept of 'strong objectivity', which starts from the standpoint of recognising the 'lived experience' of traditionally excluded groups to generate more relevant knowledge. Telling tales from such experience generates alternative perspectives that can widen and inform our understandings. For example, Gergen (2003) suggests moving away from male-dominated narratives, and advocates refocusing on women's life stories to influence an understanding of what can and cannot be achieved by women. As we become part of a network of sharing and listening to personal narratives, perspectives, values and understandings are co-created and reconstructed. Personal narratives have the potential to challenge the dominant discourse by allowing knowledge to be generated by those who are traditionally excluded from power, in various aspects of society, including by those who are marginalised due to mental ill-health. By adopting a social constructionist approach we can re-engage with narratives as a valid way of engaging with the community on complex and contested issues.

Using narratives to address stigma

Within an anti-stigma context, it is important to consider how personal narratives have an impact on the individual, on the stigmatised community and on wider society. Personal narratives blend knowledge with emotional engagement. Sharing evocative personal narratives can bring the listener closer to the experiences of the teller. They connect people by discovering shared experience, and common ground in our emotional reactions to these experiences. Tillmann-Healy (1996) illustrates this in relation to her own eating disorder, a condition that is particularly stigmatised. If stigma and discrimination rely on people being described as identifiably different, then narratives are a way of overcoming barriers. By engaging with people about shared experience, we remove the perception that people are different, which we have identified as a key criteria in maintaining stigma.

The particular forms of stigma and commonly held myths associated with mental health problems, such as lack of capability or social ability, may lend themselves to being addressed not only by 'what' is said within a narrative, but also particularly by the presentation of story-telling itself. If it is personally delivered, the narrative has a role in promoting positive personal contact between a stigmatised person and the audience, which helps remove the perception of difference. We also need to consider how playing an active part in telling a narrative may be an empowering experience and promote recovery. This emphasis on recovery makes the role of narratives in tackling mental health stigma distinct from other disempowered groups. There is emerging evidence from a number of evaluations of anti- stigma projects that the personal narrative of service users was the key factor that had the most lasting impact on participants (Knifton et al., 2008).

Narratives have played a central role at a regional level within the UK. For example, in Glasgow an approach to tackling stigma has been developed that is based on a narrative approach. This is a partnership that combines local, regional and national partners, bringing together over a hundred diverse organisations, including health and social care agencies, universities, arts institutions, community organisations, mental health groups and private sector business. This 'community of practice' (Wenger, 1998) uses constructivist principles, such as valuing community knowledge and service user involvement in both the framing of anti-stigma programmes and the evaluation of the success of the initiatives, which use a combination of protest, education and contact. In most cases this has led to the use of community development approaches in tackling stigma and discrimination. Central to this approach is: a focus on face-to-face approaches; an emphasis on community-led developments; and service users influencing the planning and delivery of programmes. Most of this work links research and practice and draws on personal narratives as a core aspect of tackling stigma and discrimination.

Practice examples

We will now explore how personal narratives have been utilised to address stigma and discrimination. The challenges and strengths of this approach will be illustrated by looking at their use in two areas of practice: narrative-based workshops and an arts festival shaped by personal narratives.

Narrative-based workshops

The rationale behind this approach was to tackle stigma and discrimination experienced by mental health service users within key services, workplaces and community groups, targeted towards organisations that service users had consistently identified as major sources of stigma and discrimination, for example benefits agencies, housing agencies and health and social services.

Over a four year period, workshops have been delivered to 2,500 people. In order to explore their impact, we used a combination of qualitative and quantitative research approaches to assess knowledge, personal experience of mental health problems and attitude measures including dangerousness, recovery optimism and social distance (Quinn and Knifton, 2005; Knifton et al., 2008). A number of key findings emerged, including a positive shift in attitudes overall, with a significant improvement in relation to perceived dangerousness and also to limited social contact, such as spending an evening socialising with someone with a mental health problem. Feedback from workshop participants suggested that significant engagement with the narrative, in conjunction with positive personal contact, were the most important parts of the workshop. It was interesting to note that participant demographics, such as gender and experience of mental health problems, did not influence the impact of the narratives. Evaluation further showed that involvement in the process contributed to the development of confidence and skills amongst the service user group and promoted their own recovery.

Arts festival

There was emerging evidence that a national anti-stigma campaign using public education and social marketing had failed to reach diverse communities (Knifton et al., 2010) or increase positive reporting about people with mental health problems (Knifton et al., 2008). A national arts festival was developed to counter these issues, to support the national anti-stigma campaign to have greater reach and impact, allowing narratives to be shared more widely at a public level through arts events, within mainstream arts settings.

An ongoing evaluation has been undertaken over a three-year period. Hundreds of organisations have collaborated to develop over 600 events, which have attracted 40,000 members of the public. A study of audience impact with over 400 attendees in 2007 found that events increased positive attitudes, including positive representations of people's contributions, capabilities and potential to recover (Quinn et al., 2011). In particular, personal narratives delivered through the arts can change stigma by constructing shared meanings and engaging audiences on an emotional level. An analysis of the extensive media coverage of the festival demonstrated that reporting of people with mental health problems was overwhelmingly positive, including representations about recovery, talent, contribution, recovery and mental health (Quinn *et al.*, 2011). Media articles particularly focused around the narratives and experiences of artists who had experienced mental health problems (Anderson, 2009). By validating narratives, the festival has stimulated new projects, which are based on narratives and the arts and which bring together diverse organisations. An example of this is a storytelling project, which aimed to capture the experiences of stigma and discrimination of women from minority ethnic communities.

Complexities and challenges in using narratives

We argue that personal narratives should play a central role in addressing stigma. However, we acknowledge that there are a number of ethical issues and uncertainties that make their use complex and challenging.

Service users are often given guidance as to how to formulate their narratives. These are often elicited stories identified and selected by people funding programmes. It may be that a narrow range of stories are sought and used, often positive recovery narratives, which are often at the expense of more holistic personal narratives. While this may be effective at achieving an impact on the audience, do these 'despair to recovery' narratives distort our perceptions of the reality of people's lives? Given that service users are often approached to share their narratives, one potential problem is that more 'vocal' service users will elect to tell their stories. In seeking to achieve positive change to attitudes and beliefs, we risk the audience assuming that the experiences of the narrator apply more generally to all people with mental health problems.

There are signs from the research that being involved in narrative approaches can promote recovery and self-esteem when people are adequately supported and reimbursed for their time. However, this raises issues concerning the narrator. There may be formal or subtle pressure to share their narrative. Support must be available when people share their experiences, that they are aware of potential consequences, and that they feel prepared to deal with potential hostility. There should be adequate support and safeguards before, during and after events to allow people to withdraw without feeling that they are letting others down. There is a challenge around the issue of informed consent, for example what if people change their minds after the narrative has entered the public domain? Also, we know very little about the long-term impact on the narrator. This presents a challenge for therapeutic work and the extent to which involvement in public education may alleviate or worsen mental health difficulties, depending on the nature and quality of the support and consent discussed above.

The process of sharing a personal narrative on an ongoing basis creates a potential paradox. While reducing stigma among the audience, it may be reinforcing the narrator's negative self-identity based on their label as part of a stigmatised minority group. It is perhaps more useful to consider the multiple, temporal and fluid nature of identities that all narrators have (for example, loving parent, creative writer and so on). This raises the question of whether it is potentially damaging for narrators to be identified and introduced as 'service users' as their primary identity. Those who elicit the stories should present and acknowledge narrators' different identities. It raises the question of whether we can work towards a different approach to narratives and mental health where perhaps the audience engages in dialogue about their own mental health identities: more of a public conversation approach than a listening audience approach.

Implications for social work practice

Social work practice has much to learn from the use of narratives. Social work service providers need to play a much more prominent role in tackling mental health stigma and discrimination. This requires a policy framework backed up by a set of practice initiatives, which help to create an alternative model of mental health that directly counters mental health stigma and discrimination (Beresford and Croft, 2004). Such a practice model would be informed by a recovery approach, that would seek to empower service users and provide the opportunity for growth and imparting hope (Scheyett, 2005). This could take the form of gathering the personal narratives from service users on their experience of stigma and discrimination through community care and other mental health assessments; service users delivering training to mental health officers, which draws on the personal narrative of mental health service users in highlighting the experience of stigma and its impact within the context of Mental Health Act assessments; and engaging service providers through arts events. Personal narratives therefore have the potential to play a key role in the context of anti-discriminatory and anti-oppressive practice.

Conclusions

A number of questions emerge for the reader:

- How can you effectively build the use of narratives into your social work role?
- What support would you offer to service users to ensure that this was done in an ethical way?
- What wider initiatives (for example, arts events performed by service users) could you support to ensure that the service user 'voice' is more prominent in social work practice?

Narratives are complex, which makes understanding their impact challenging. We do not know if it is merely positive contact that has an impact (Corrigan *et al.*, 2007), or the process of sharing a personal narrative, or the content of the story itself. Further research is needed to understand how narratives work according to who is in the audience, who is telling the narrative, and the format that the narrative is told in (for example, directly delivered or through arts, film or other media).

However, we have argued that personal narratives are a promising ingredient in addressing public stigma and awareness and an essential component of anti-discriminatory practice within mental health social work. Furthermore, given their success within the mental health arena, this suggests that there may be potential for using personal narratives in other areas of social work practice. Many other social work client groups are similarly stigmatised and personal narratives could potentially be used to improve public and practitioner attitudes towards young people in care or criminal justice service users, for example.

In conclusion, we return to the issue that stigma and discrimination are linked power and equity. To fundamentally address stigma and discrimination, while playing a key role, personal narratives can only be part of a strategy that seeks to challenge institutional and structural oppression.

References

Anderson, L (2009) 'The media profile of a mental health arts and film festival and the implications for social work practice', MA in Social Work dissertation, University of Strathclyde unpublished.

Angermeyer, M C and Matschinger, H (1996) 'The effect of personal experience of mental illness on the attitude towards individuals suffering from mental disorders' *Social Psychiatry and Psychiatric Epidemiology* 31(6), pp 321-26.

Bamberg, M (ed) (2007) *Narrative: State of the art* Amsterdam: John Benjamins.

Beresford, P and Croft, S (2004) 'Service users and practitioners reunited: The key component for social work reform' *British Journal of Social Work* 34(1), pp 53-68.

Byrne, P (2000) 'Stigma of mental illness and ways of diminishing it' *Advances in Psychiatric Treatment* 6(1), pp 65-72.

Corrigan, P W, River, L P, Lundin, R K and Penn, D L (2001) 'Three strategies for changing attributions about severe mental illness' *Schizophrenia Bulletin* 27(2), pp 187-95.

Corrigan, P W, Mueser, K T, Bond, G R, Drake, R E and Solomon, P (2007) *Principles and Practice of Psychiatric Rehabilitation: An empirical approach* New York: Guilford Press.

Crisp, A H, Gelder, M G, Rix, S, Meltzer, H I and Rowlands O J (2000) 'Stigmatisation of people with mental illnesses' *British Journal of Psychiatry* 177(1), pp 4-7.

Cupitt, D (1991) *What Is A Story?* London: SCM Press.

Double D (2002) 'The limits of psychiatry' *British Medical Journal* 324, pp 900-4.

Faulkner, A and Thomas, P (2002) 'User-led research and evidence based medicine' *British Journal of Psychiatry* 180, pp 1-3.

Fernando, S (2002) *Cultural Diversity, Mental Health and Psychiatry: The Struggle Against Racism* London: Routledge.

Gergen, K J (1994) *Realities and relationships* Cambridge, MA: Harvard University Press.

Gergen, K J (1999) *An invitation to social construction* London and Thousand Oaks, CA: SAGE Publications.

Gergen, M (2003) 'Life Stories: Pieces of a Dream' in Gergen, K J and Gergen, M M (eds) *Social Constructio: A Reader* London and Thousand Oaks, CA: SAGE Publications.

Goffman, E (1963) *Stigma: Notes on management of spoiled identity* Upper Saddle River, NJ: Prentice Hall.

Harding, S (1993) *Whose Science? Whose Knowledge?: Thinking from Women's Lives* Ithaca, NY: Cornell University Press.

Knifton, L, Walker, A and Quinn, N (2008) 'Workplace interventions can reduce stigma' *Journal of Public Mental Health* 7(4), pp 40-50.

Knifton, L, Gervais, M, Newbigging, K, Mirza, N, Quinn N, Wilson, N and Hunkins-Hutchison, E (2010) 'Community Conversation: Addressing Mental Health Stigma with Ethnic Minority Communities' *Social Psychiatry and Psychiatric Epidemiology* 45(4), pp 497-504.

Larson, J E and Corrigan, P (2008) 'The stigma of families with mental illness' *Academic Psychiatry* 32(2), pp 87-91.

Link, B G and Phelan, J C (2001) 'Conceptualising stigma' *Annual Review of Sociology* 27, pp 363-85.

Penn, D L and Martin, J (1998) 'The stigma of severe mental illness: some potential solutions for a recalcitrant problem' *Psychiatric Quarterly* 69(3), pp 235-47.

Pilgrim, D (2005) *Key Concepts in Mental Health* London: Sage Publications.

Pilgrim, D and Rogers, A (1999) *A Sociology of Mental Health and Illness* (2nd edition), Buckingham: Open University Press.

Pinfold, V, Thornicroft, G, Huxley, P and Farmer, P (2005) 'Active ingredients in anti-stigma programmes in mental health' *International Review of Psychiatry* 17(2), pp 123-31.

Quinn, N and Knifton, L (2005) 'Promoting recovery and addressing stigma: mental health awareness through community development in a low income area' *International Journal of Mental Health Promotion* 7(4), pp 37-44.

Quinn, N, Shulman, A, Knifton, L and Byrne, P (2011) 'The Impact of a National Mental Health Arts and Film Festival on Stigma and Recovery', *Acta Psychiatrica Scandinavica* 123(1), pp 71-81.

Read, J and Law, A (1999) 'The relationship of causal beliefs and contact with users of mental health services to attitudes to the "mentally ill"' *International Journal of Social Psychiatry* 45(3), pp 216-29.

Scheyett, A (2005) 'The mark of madness: Stigma, serious mental illnesses, and social work. Social Work in Mental Health' *The Journal of Behavioral and Psychiatric Social Work* 3(4): pp 79–97.

Schulze, B and Angermeyer, M C (2003) 'Subjective experiences of stigma: a focus group study of schizophrenic patients, their relatives and mental health professionals' *Social Science and Medicine* 56, pp 299-312.

Scottish Executive (2005) *Equal Minds: Addressing Mental Health Inequalities in Scotland* Edinburgh: Scottish Executive.

Szasz, T (1972) *The myth of mental illness: foundations of a theory of personal conduct* London: Paladin.

Tillmann-Healy, L (1996) 'A Secret Life in a Culture of Thinness: Reflections on Body, Food, and Bulimia' in Bochner, A P and Ellis, C (eds) *Composing Ethnography: Alternative Forms of Qualitative Writing*: Lanham, MD: Altamira Press, pp 76-108.

Van Brakel, W H (2006) 'Measuring health-related stigma: A literature review' *Psychology, Health and Medicine* 11(3), pp 307-34.

Wenger, E (1998) *Communities of Practice: Learning, Meaning and Identity* New York: Cambridge University Press.

Wilkinson, R G and Pickett, K E (2007) 'The problems of relative deprivation: Why some societies do better than others' *Social Science and Medicine* 65(9), pp 1965-78.

WHO (World Health Organization) (2001) *World Health Report 2001: New understanding, new hope* Geneva: WHO.

Chapter 15

Making Sense of Partnership Working

Andrew Eccles and Alison Petch

Introduction

This chapter will explore the policy and practice of partnership working, examining the various partnerships that social workers are encouraged to pursue but focusing in particular on that between health and social care. It will look at the reasons behind the strong push for partnerships over the past decade and the way in which emphasis has been put primarily on procedures, often at the expense of dealing head on with the complexities of implementation on the ground. This provides the context for the contemporary shift in focus to outcomes, where the chapter explores user- and carer-defined outcomes and considers the extent to which a range of partnerships succeed in delivering the outcomes that users are seeking.

A burgeoning literature has developed around the importance of partnership working as a central feature of government thinking and – more recently – has examined its organisational features and operation in practice. This literature will be drawn on here to inform three areas of discussion. First, some reflection on the wider policy agendas in which interprofessional working has come to the fore. These agendas include the more competitive and managerialist cultures that have become such a central feature of public services in recent years (Clarke *et al.*, 2000) as well as the discourse that has underpinned collaborative practice. Second, policy implementation is considered, looking at processes of interprofessional practice and research on outcomes for service users. Third, the chapter broaches the question of power in partnership relationships and considers how this might impact on the role to be played by social work.

Any discussion of partnership working needs to clarify what is meant by the term. There are a range of overlapping terms underpinned by a common concern with partnership working: collaboration; joint working; co-location; inter-professional working; inter-agency working; multidisciplinary working and integration. What might nominally appear to be umbrella organisations will have a variety of professions working inside them. Health will have doctors in both hospital and community settings, nurses, physiotherapists and podiatrists. Occupational therapists have long been employed in social care as well as health settings. So there is a need for inter-professional working within the same agency, as well as for co-operation across agency boundaries. Perhaps partnership working can be viewed along a continuum, with partnership considered as the model of working and greater integration the ultimate goal. Any discussion of partnership working should also clarify the level at which it is being discussed: strategic, middle management or operational; formal or informal. Among all these considerations, a major debate that underpins the practical achievement of partnership working is whether what is being sought among key workers is a new culture, whereby professional identity is subsumed within a new role, or whether the aim is for retained identities but mutual understanding of these identities.

Policy drivers

Despite much recent emphasis on the concept, inter-professional working and partnership working are nothing new. There have been various attempts over the past half-century to bring agencies closer in communication and organisation. In recent years these have ranged from Health Action Zones and the 1999 Health Act flexibilities in England to the initiatives of the Joint Future Agenda and the development of Community Health Partnerships in Scotland (see Petch, 2008a, for an overview).

There has been a commonsense assumption that partnership working must be a positive development if it enhances communication and the exchange of ideas, especially if it leads to decision-making processes that are quicker and engage more effectively with service users. The term 'partnership', however, has had a wider purchase over the past decade and the reasons for this are more complex than simply better practice. The incoming Labour government in 1997 was keen to move beyond the rhetoric of market-based solutions to public service reform that had characterised preceding Conservative administrations. The marketisation agenda had not necessarily ceased, but the language in which reforms were to be couched had changed.

There was an equal determination not to return to the organisational arrangements familiar under previous Labour governments whereby a strong public sector devised and delivered services. There was therefore a shift in the direction of partnership working and the concept of 'modernisation'. The broader partnership agenda in which inter-professional working sits therefore carries ideological meaning beyond organisational arrangements or common agendas; it served as part of a design to square the desire to move beyond both the Conservative years and Labour's traditional identity. While there may be excellent examples of inter-professional working in practice, the underpinning logic behind the ideas should not be ignored. That it carries this ideological freight can lead to the difficulties of definition and interpretation highlighted above. Partnership working has become something of a catch-all phrase, so lacking in precision that analysis of its impact and outcomes also becomes difficult (Ling, 2001). Perhaps that is no policy accident; but public bodies that are not seen to be engaging in collaborative working of some sort in the current policy climate risk the charge of being iconoclastic.

In addition to its inclusion on many policy agendas, the *absence* of collaborative working has emerged as a key feature in a number of official inquiries into failures in the public services - for example the Laming Report (Laming, 2003). As Barrett *et al.* (2005, p 13) note: 'The lack of collaborative practice between agencies and professions is seen as being responsible for individual tragedies as well as for the failure to tackle general social problems such as social exclusion, homelessness, and crime and disorder'. What has emerged is the development of a discourse about failure in public agencies in which lack of collaboration commands centre stage and becomes the salient feature. However, further scrutiny of these inquiries often points to a more complex picture. For example, while the first Laming Report made 108 recommendations which were primarily organisational, Laming's subsequent enquiry in 2009 noted that frontline staff were 'overstretched' and caseloads often 'very high' in an 'under-resourced' profession where 'front line social workers and social work managers are under an immense amount of pressure' (Laming, 2009, p 44).

This is not to challenge the notion that better communication and collaborative understanding across agencies will make a difference to outcomes. But improvements in communication and organisation should not shift attention away from perhaps equally important social and resource issues, the answers to which are more conceptually complex and politically difficult to address than organisational change. The concern here, then, is that too much expectation will come to be invested in the partnership agenda as a panacea for shortcomings in the sphere of public service delivery. That such expectations arise is, of course, of some benefit to central government, as the solutions effectively are seen to lie locally and organisationally.

Do partnerships work?

The imprecision around what is meant by partnership working also becomes problematic when it comes to evaluation (Taylor and Balloch, 2005). In the absence of a clear understanding of the terms of reference of partnership working, what is it that is to be evaluated? The mantra of 'what works', which drove New Labour policy agendas (Page, 2007) was predicated on evidence-based research. The lack of precision around definitions, however, together with difficulties in measuring the impact of partnerships on actual policy outcomes, means that 'what works' is hard to test. The specifics of testing performance across organisations have been discussed and researched in some detail. El Ansari et al. (2001) point to the numerous variables present in the evaluation of collaborative working. Evaluations of partnership working have concentrated on the development of the process of partnership working, with, as both Cameron et al. (2000) and Dowling et al. (2004) highlight, little evidence of impact in terms of outcomes for service users. Indeed, Heenan and Birrell (2006, p 64) argue that 'the unrelenting drive towards the integration of health and social care in Britain has been largely politically driven with scant evidence to support the view that it will result in significant improvements'. Recent research that sought to explore the extent to which partnership working delivered the outcomes sought by service users will be explored below in the section on implementing partnership working.

A particular difficulty in evaluation lies in the question of attribution (Tett et al., 2003;

Dickinson, 2008; Petch, 2008b). Since organisations in the public sector have become subject to a much more competitive agenda in recent years (witness league tables and star ratings), collaboration brings its own difficulties. Performance indicators and inspection regimes designed to assess outcomes *within* sectors do not easily lend themselves to a cross-sector analysis, while organisations that have become more infused with a managerialist culture are predominantly concerned with meeting internal targets to the detriment of strategic thinking looking across the broader picture of integrated service delivery.

There is, then, something of an irony that the more managerialist culture has in itself produced greater levels of bureaucratic behaviour in response to the culture of inspection (Miller, 2005). Organisations have retreated into themselves in the face of growing levels of audit and the climate in which partnership working has been expected to take hold has not been conducive to particularly creative or open thinking. Recent recognition of this problem (Crerar, 2007) suggests that a better environment for successful inter-professional working will emerge; in the meantime, social work staff who have been working in these less than optimal arrangements will need to maintain their energy – or re-engage – with the elements of partnership working that do actually work well.

One approach to partnership working has seen the development of integrated teams. A substantial study tracking the experience of older people, who were served by either integrated teams or provision that remained organisationally separate, noted no significant differences in outcome across the two approaches (Brown *et al.*, 2003). Indeed, such are the variables and the unpredictability of changes in well-being in the very service area where much of the collaborative agenda has been introduced – older people's services – that some qualitative measures might better serve for an understanding of the differences afforded by more integrated approaches. Such accounts, based on researching the experiences of frontline staff in collaborative settings, do exist (Molyneux, 2001) and stress the importance of developing good working relationships and mutual understanding as well as processes. However, this type of research needs to contend with a dominant paradigm in organisations of 'measuring the measurable', which does not lend itself to the subtleties of a more qualitative inquiry.

Moreover, qualitative approaches, while routinely adopted in social care research, are more likely to be viewed sceptically from a medical research perspective. Evaluation of partnership approaches needs to be innovative if it is to tackle the clear limitations posed by problems of methodology and this type of innovation needs to be accepted by the partner organisations themselves. This is not straightforward, and it is only several years into the push for partnership working that new approaches are being explored (Dickinson *et al.*, 2009).

Implementing partnership working

This section tries to understand why many of the key aims of partnership working have not developed as fully or as quickly as policy makers might have expected. Much has been written about the 'implementation gap' between policy making and actual delivery (Pressman and Wildavsky, 1973; Bergen, 2005). There is a conundrum here. Implementation carried out according to the express designs of policy makers risks being unworkable. This is because discretion, flexibility and the ability to adapt to changing circumstances may best be the preserve of knowledgeable frontline professionals. On the other hand, allowing this level of discretion risks the policy being hijacked by professional vested interests and organisational inertia (see Lipsky, 1980; and a rejoinder from Evans and Harris, 2004).

A compounding problem here is the different governance arrangements of the various partners involved in implementing collaborative agendas. Social services, for example, are subject to local democratic mandate through local government (which in itself may give rise to a patchwork of potentially different approaches to policy implementation). Governance in health is not subject to the same arrangements of accountability, nor geographical boundaries. Equally, territorial arrangements across the United Kingdom (UK) are dissimilar. Partnership thinking appears to be better developed in Scotland than in the rest of the UK (Hudson, 2007; Petch 2008b). Two reasons stand out as an explanation here. First, Scotland's public services – in particular health – have been subject to less competitive organisational arrangements than in England. Surveying the scene of foundation hospitals in England, Kerr notes that it resembles 'pre-Machiavellian Italy with warring Italian city states' (Kerr, cited in Hudson, 2007, p 4). Second, while pursued in a particularly top-down fashion in England (with elements of mandated collaboration as noted by Glendinning et al., 2002), the impetus towards partnership working was subject to more detailed scrutiny pre-implementation in the post-devolution committee arrangements of the Scottish Parliament (as also in the Welsh Assembly).

Successful policy implementation is more likely if there is adequate time for policy changes to bed in. Public policy is strewn with initiatives that required time but were rarely afforded it. Partnership working deals with a particularly difficult area in which to expect rapid progress. The culture of greater flexibility and speed of delivery of consumer goods does not easily lend itself to the complexities of services dedicated to human need, particularly where the organisations required to collaborate have their own longstanding organisational arrangements and working cultures. In this respect, the implementation of partnership working has been flawed as the timetables have often been too ambitious, relegating the crucial aspect of joint training across professions and understanding of working cultures behind protocols and processes.

In practice, the inadequacies of information technology systems have bedevilled development; initially information sharing often meant additional burdens on staff time, creating disenchantment with the practicalities of partnership working for some staff from the outset. This issue is crucial. As El-Ansari and Phillips (2005) note, there needs to be demonstrable benefits for frontline staff engaged in partnership working for the project to take root. A further influence on the success of policy is the common use and understanding of language. Again, the different approach to understanding and expressing issues impacting on service users across professions is well documented (Dalley, 1989), and there is some evidence from evaluations of joint working in practice that professionals are apt to retreat into their own enclaves when faced with this unfamiliarity (Eccles, 2008).

Two further aspects of the implementation process are worth noting here. First, is the question of adherence by professions to particular values. Cooper (2009) deftly explores the underlying reasons why staff are attracted to working in particular professions in the first instance, with the result that they may be more or less willing to work outside the boundaries of certain value bases. Policy advocates and 'change managers' might well imagine that the interprofessional tasks they envisage being undertaken offer no threat to these value bases, but this is not necessarily a view shared by frontline staff. Second, the organisational arrangements for some of this successful interprofessional working have often been ad hoc or informal. It is perhaps the formalisation of arrangements, sometimes headed up by managers imported for the task and operating in a performance indicator framework, which can undermine good working procedures that have developed more organically over time. None of this understanding about the complexities of implementation is an argument against collaboration *per se*. Much of it, however, offers cautionary guidance about a reliance on overly rigid structures. Looser arrangements may work better, as more recent research looking at networks in Scottish health and social care arrangements would suggest (Hudson, 2007).

The impact of partnership working

The complexities of evaluating the outcomes of partnership working have already been noted, as has the preference among policy makers for evaluations to be based on examining structural arrangements and processes rather than the impact in terms of outcomes for service users. That notwithstanding, there is a developing literature that has started to examine the detail of how frontline staff have responded to the inter-professional working agenda (Tett *et al.*, 2003; McNamara, 2006; Eccles, 2008). These studies resonate with the difficulties of policy implementation that have been discussed above and illustrate the micro politics of everyday working: workload equity, challenges to identity and access to resources. The research on collaborative working between health and social care in particular has several recurring themes. These include the predominance of training in collaborative processes but not in the further understanding of working cultures, the equity of workloads across disciplines, the different approaches to understanding ways of working with service users (for example over the issue of consent) and assessment of needs.

These accounts of the practices of partnership working emphasise the procedural way in which collaboration has been implemented, largely through the creation of protocols, alignment of budgets across agencies and statements of commitment to the partnership agenda. In part this reflects a genuine attempt by organisations to work together, but there is also an element here of organisations simply responding to the demands and tight timetables of implementation set by central government. It is in managing the day-to-day operation of collaborative working that the problems arise, with inconsistent commitment by middle managers to achieving the outcomes required of the often aspirational rubric of protocols.

Stewart *et al.* (2003) outline some of the drivers and barriers to partnership working, discussing, for example, planning contexts, operational culture and staff attitudes to change. These barriers might indeed be put in place through resistance to change by professionals who unreflectively adhere to existing patterns of working. But equally some may arise from situations that are less about the processes of change and are instead centred on professionals having concerns about how collaboration might impact adversely on the experience of service users. This takes the discussion beyond simply the mechanics of better working through collaboration into territory that deals with value bases, ethical approaches and different working cultures.

These complexities of implementation are borne out in social work practice. One of the first products of recent partnership thinking in community care, for example, was the idea of a shared assessment tool that could be used across different agencies, involving the gathering of a common dataset to avoid duplication of assessment and aid information sharing across professions. A number of features emerge from research about shared assessment in practice (Eccles, 2008). Its use has been inconsistent; the assessment tool was designed to be handled with equal ease across professional disciplines, but frontline staff have noted discrepancies in its use, most particularly in areas such as personal narrative or gathering information about services users' financial circumstances. This raises a clear dilemma: not duplicating service user assessments may expedite matters more efficiently, but if the quality of assessment is lessened in the process, would this necessarily constitute a gain for the service user? Equally, if these assessments are incomplete or of poor quality and have to be done again (a routine event based on the testimony of staff themselves), is this not in itself another form of duplication?

Prioritisation of resources is of course a key issue in all areas of service delivery and was identified in this same research of partnership working in practice. This, the study suggested, has a different impact on professionals in health and in social work (where the rationing of service delivery is more explicit). As part of the collaborative approach, staff – regardless of background – may have been designated key workers following on from making an assessment and are thus, nominally, responsible for tracking service delivery for service users. This has introduced health staff more clearly to rationing in social services and a world of uncertainty over service delivery which some found discomforting. Thus, assessment for service users may be made more *quickly* using a single process – surely a welcome gain – but this is no guarantee that these same service users will subsequently be recipients of actual service delivery.

Partnership working and user-defined outcomes

The propensity for evaluations of partnership working based around procedures and processes rather than actual outcomes has already been noted. As discussed above, work looking at outcomes by Brown *et al.* (2003), which tracked the experiences of older people, some supported by integrated teams and others by service provision that remained organisationally separate, had noted no significant differences in outcomes across the two approaches. The current focus on the impact of service support in terms of the outcomes for individuals reiterates the need for such a focus. It is manifest in policy, for example, through the fifteen national outcomes reported in the Single Outcome Agreements in Scotland and for health and social care in England by the five outcomes of *Every Child Matters* and the seven outcomes of *Our Health, Our Care, Our Say.* For practice the challenge is to ensure that the support being accessed achieves the desired outcomes – and is changed if it is not doing so.

Research conducted under the Department of Health Modernising Adult Social Care (MASC) programme (Petch *et al.*, 2007) made an initial attempt to shift the balance in the evaluation of partnership working from process to outcomes. The MASC study built on earlier work by the Social Policy Research Unit (Qureshi, 2001; Glendinning *et al.*, 2009) which had explored the outcomes that were valued by older people. With minor modifications, following a validation exercise with a range of user groups, the set of outcomes valued by older people and by people with learning disabilities or mental health problems was confirmed. These are listed in Table 15.1 and indicate the areas that they hope support from health and social care will assist them to achieve.

Table 15.1
Outcomes valued by older people and people with learning disablities

Quality of Life	Process	Change
Feeling safe	Listened to	Improved confidence and skills
Having things to do	Choice	
Seeing people	Treated as and individual	Improved mobility
Staying well		Reduced symptoms
Living life as you want	Reliability	
Living where you want	Responsiveness	
Dealing with stigma		

The extent to which partnership working was delivering on these outcomes was explored in interviews conducted in partnership with three teams of user researchers across fifteen services delivered in partnership for older people, mental health service users and people with learning disabilities. In-depth interviews revealed that service users valued:

- holistic services that met social, emotional and physical needs and built confidence;
- easy access to support when needed, including out of hours and at weekends;
- support from specialist services;
- a say in the nature, timing and location of service provision;
- good relationships with individual staff;
- good communication between staff/agencies.

There were additional comments specific to different service user groups. For those with mental health problems, interviewees reported that responsive, accessible services were vital in an emergency and helped people feel safe, while social contact with staff and other service users was important for emotional and social support and for dealing with stigma. People with learning disabilities noted that integrated services generally met the health needs of users, relationships with staff were very important to quality of life, while carers appreciated the one-stop shop and improved communications and responsiveness of their services. For older people, fluid interventions paced to service users worked best, services played a vital role in reducing social exclusion but home care was problematic in all sites.

This study suggests that the key aspects of partnership working valued by service users are a single point of contact, improved communication, holistic care, responsiveness of services, non-discriminatory practice, having a say and reduced social isolation. Barriers were perceived as discontinuity of staff, lack of available information, lack of transport, time-limited services and inequities in support provision.

The challenge of attribution in partnership working has already been discussed. Nonetheless, this study identified some tentative associations between the different models of partnership working in the different case studies and the particular outcomes that were achieved. The suggestion is that established partnerships of different types may be expected to have a particular impact on certain outcomes. For example, from Table 15.2 it can be seen that specialist partnerships appear particularly likely to lead to individuals feeling that they have been treated with respect.

Table 15.2 Different models of partnership working

Key features of partnership	Related features of services	Outcomes delivered
Co-location of staff	Providing a single point of contact, improving access and communication	Process outcomes especially responsiveness Quality-of-life outcome: feeling safe
Multidisciplinary team	Providing holistic care	Change outcomes Quality-of-life outcomes Process outcomes
Specialist partnership	Providing specialist, non-discriminatory treatment	Process outcomes, especially being treated with respect
Extended partnership	Providing access to other agencies, and partnership with service users	Quality-of-life outcomes including activity and contact with other people Process outcome: having choices

Over a decade into the current push for partnership working, evidence-based outcomes are clearly coming to the fore but using methods of enquiry that are more qualitative. In part this is an acceptance that the clinical-based outcome approaches are so complex in their variables that they have limited utility. It is, equally, a welcome acceptance in an era of performance measurement that less clear-cut, but nonetheless meaningful, qualitative enquiry itself has an important place in evaluations around partnership working. Importantly also, this study (Petch *et al.*, 2007) has started to unpack the numerous arrangements that come under the broad heading of 'partnership' to tease out which particular models of working across professions impact on specific outcomes.

Power and partnership working

This final section looks at the issue of power relations in partnership working. The notion of partnership implies at least some consensus over objectives, but this can underplay significant differentials in power across organisations. Whereas both medicine and education can lay claim to having been influential historically in policy making, based on the weight of expertise or political clout, social work has rarely enjoyed the same position. Some of this is about simple electoral arithmetic, where the public prioritises health and education spending. But equally, the various disciplines have different professional standings. Traditionally, by dint of expert knowledge or the power of organisational foreclosure, social work has been viewed as a semi-profession (Toren, 1972). This is changing, with recent developments in the expansion of its educational foundations, post-qualifying strategy, and the proposal for a Royal College of Social Work. But beneath the protocols about partnership, historic power differentials remain and early work on the current round of health and social services collaboration (Wilkin *et al.*, 2000) notes ways in which the agenda of health services is more likely to prevail where there are joint working arrangements. Even where there has been long-established organisational collaboration – for example, in Northern Ireland – the health agenda will tend to emerge as more powerful in practice (Heenan and Birrell, 2006).

There is a well-rehearsed debate about the power of 'agenda setting' in organisations (see Lukes, 2005, for an overview), and it is precisely this area which would merit enquiry about how the dynamics of policy agendas in partnerships are being played out in practice. With the advent in some localities of single management structures (such as Community Health Care Partnerships in Scotland) across health and social care – a logical response to the problems of joint working arrangements that had been subject to the tensions of bifurcated management – the setting of the policy agenda assumes increasing importance. On the face of it, a plurality of ideas coming from health and social care, which feed into a common agenda, is a welcome development.

So too with partnership: the term embodies a central plank of a policy discourse that has tried to square public services within the circle of a continuing market-driven agenda, but leaves in its wake much imprecision over power relations, value bases and working practices. That forms of partnership working seem better placed to work in Scotland says something about a more distinctive – and perhaps in parts collectivist – Scottish policy identity within the UK. But even here there is still a need to disentangle the various layers of political power and organisational structures that simultaneously promote, and in practice detract from, the partnership agenda. Like 'community', partnership comes with the potential for unheralded but significant changes in professional relationships.

Conclusions

Partnership working straddles a range of underpinning issues. It is complex not only in itself, but also as part of a wider set of political and ideological complexities that need to be recognised in any understanding of how, and on what terms, it now proceeds. There are examples of collaborative inter-professional practice that, for all the difficulties involved in evaluation, can be deemed to have been successful and appear in the new partnership regimes to have led to better communication and swifter attention for service users. But unpacking these benefits from the partnership elements that make up wider agendas in public sector reform – some of which are clearly incongruent with improved collaboration – is a difficult task. It is these wider tensions that have the capacity to impact on implementation of collaborative working procedures and which may – not unreasonably – underpin elements of caution by social workers to the inter-professional working agenda.

Key questions for consideration and reflection for those working in partnership

- What are the motivations for partnership working – and what is sought in terms of both process and outcomes?
- What are the key drivers and barriers that are shaping how things are operating?
- Have key areas such as training and information systems been addressed?
- To what extent do organisational structures support the aspirations for partnership working?
- Do professional value bases continue adequately to be recognised in partnership arrangements?
- Are professions equally well represented in the organisational arrangements of partnership working?

NB: An excellent resource for those working in partnership is *Integrated Working: A Guide*. This is published by the Integrated Care Network whose website at www.dhcarenetworks.org.uk/icn/ provides other valuable resources.

References

Barrett, G, Sellman, D and Thomas, J (2005). *Interprofessional working in health and social care*. Basingstoke: Palgrave.

Bergen, A (2005) '"Implementation deficit" and "street level bureaucracy": policy practice and change in the development of community nursing issues' *Health and Social Care in the Community* 13(1), pp 1-10.

Brown L, Tucker, C and Domokos, T (2003) 'Evaluating the impact of integrated health and social care teams on older people living in the community' *Health and Social Care in the Community* 11(2), pp 85-94.

Cameron, A, Lart, R, Harrison, L, Macdonald, G and Smith, R (2000) *Factors promoting and obstacles hindering joint working: a systematic review* Bristol: University of Bristol: School for Policy Studies.

Clarke, J, Gewirtz, S and McLaughlin, E (2000) *New managerialism new welfare?* London: Sage Publications.

Cooper, A (2009) 'Where do our organisations begin and end? What are the boundaries in the fluid, networked, world of public service?', paper presented at ESRC Research Seminar Series: 'The effects of professionals' human and cultural capital for interprofessional social capital'. 30 January, University of Strathclyde.

Crerar, L (2007) *The Report of the Independent Review of Regulation, Audit, Inspection and Complaints Handling of Public Services in Scotland.* Edinburgh: Scottish Government.

Dalley, G (1989) 'Professional ideology or organisational tribalism? The health service-social work divide' in Taylor, R and Ford, J (eds) *Social Work and Health Care* London: Jessica Kingsley Publishers, pp 32-9.

Dickinson, H (2008) *Evaluating Outcomes in Health and Social Care* Bristol: The Policy Press.

Dickinson, H, Glasby, J, Miller, R and McCarthy, L (2009) 'Whose outcomes are they anyway? Report of the Pilot Evaluation of a Joint Service' *Journal of Integrated Care* 17(1), pp 37-44.

Dowling, B, Powell, M and Glendinning, C (2004) 'Conceptualising successful partnerships' *Health and Social Care in the Community* 12(4), pp 309-17.

Eccles, A (2008) 'Single shared assessment: the limits to 'quick fix' implementation' *Journal of Interprofessional Care* 16(1) pp 22-30.

El Ansari, W and Phillips, C (2005) 'The costs and benefits to participants in community partnerships: a paradox?' *Health Promotion Practice* 5(1), pp 35-48.

El Ansari, W, Phillips, C J and Hammick, M (2001), 'Collaboration and partnerships: developing the evidence base' *Health and Social Care in the Community* 9(4), pp 215-27.

Evans, T and Harris, J (2004) Street level social work, bureaucracy and the (exaggerated) death of discretion *British Journal of Social Work* 34(6), pp 871-95.

Glendinning, C., Colman A., and Rummery K. (2002). Partnerships, performance and primary care. *Ageing & Society*, 22, 185-208

Glendinning, C, Clarke, S, Hare, P, Kotchetkova, I, Maddison, J and Newbronner, L (2006) *Outcomes-focused Services for Older People* SCIE Knowledge Review 13, London: Social Care Institute for Excellence.

Heenan, D and Birrell, D (2006) 'The integration of health and social care: the lessons from Northern Ireland' *Social Policy and Administration* 40(1), pp 47-66.

Hudson, B (2007) 'Partnering through networks: can Scotland crack it?' *Journal of Integrated Care* 15(1), pp 3-13.

Laming, H (2003) *The Victoria Climbié Inquiry* London: The Stationery Office.

Laming, H (2009) *The protection of children in England: a progress report* London: The Stationery Office.

Ling, T (2001) 'Unpacking partnership: the case of health care' in Clarke, C, Gewirtz, S and McLaughlin, E (eds) *New managerialism, new welfare?* London: Sage Publications.

Lipsky, M (1980) *Street Level Bureaucracy* New York: Russell Sage Foundation.

Lukes, S (2005) *Power: A radical view* (2nd edition), Basingstoke: Palgrave.

McNamara, G (2006) 'Implementation of single shared assessment in Meadowbank, Falkirk: a joint future' *Journal of Integrated Care* 14(4), pp 38-44.

Miller, D (2005) 'What is best "value"? Bureaucracy, virtualism and local governance' in Du Gay, P (ed). *The values of bureaucracy*. Oxford: Oxford University Press, pp 233-54.

Molyneux, J (2001) 'Interprofessional team working: what makes teams work well?' *Journal of Interprofessional Care* 15, pp 29-35.

Page, R (2007) *Revisiting the Welfare State* Maidenhead: Open University Press.

Petch, A (2008a). *Health and social care: establishing a joint future?* Edinburgh: Dunedin Academic Press.

Petch, A (2008b) 'Delivering health and social care: do partnerships deliver for users and carers?', available as audio at www.iriss.ac.uk/search/node/petch

Petch, A, Cook, A, Miller, E, Alexander, H, Cooper, S-A, Hubbard, G and Morrison, J (2007) *Users and carers define effective partnerships in health and social care* Edinburgh: Scottish Executive Joint Improvement Team.

Pressman, J and Wildavsky, A (1973) *Implementation* Berkeley, CA: University of California Press.

Qureshi, H (ed) (2001) 'Outcomes in Social Care Practice, Outcomes in Community Care Practice, No. 7', York: Social Policy Research Unit ,University of York.

Stewart A, Petch A and Curtice, L (2003) 'Moving Towards Integrated Working in Health and Social Care in Scotland: From Maze to Matrix' *Journal of Interprofessional Care* 17(4), pp 335-50.

Taylor, D and Balloch, S (eds) (2005) *The politics of evaluation* Bristol: The Policy Press.

Tett, L, Crowther, J and O'Hara, P (2003) 'Collaborative partnerships in community education' *Journal of Education Policy* 18(1), pp 37-51.

Toren, N (1972) *Social Work: the case of a semi-profession* Beverly Hills, CA: Sage Publications.

Wilkin, D, Gillam, S and Leese, B (2000) *The national tracker survey of primary care groups and trusts*, London: King's Fund.

Chapter 16

Adult Protection in the UK: Key issues for early career social workers

Ailsa Stewart

Introduction

As workers in adult care, recently qualified or not, it can often be frustrating that the perceived procedural stricture of child protection systems are not immediately translated into the protection of adults (Leslie and Pritchard, 2009). Systems and procedures in adult protection have traditionally been drawn together from across a range of statutes covering both civil and criminal law. This lack of clarity and consistency over exactly how to support and protect adults has resulted in those at risk of harm often being failed (Parsons, 2006). That is not to say that contemporary child protection systems are without their challenges; they have, for example, often been criticised for being overly bureaucratic and ultimately for failing children, for example in the *Victoria Climbié Inquiry Report* (House of Commons Health Committee, 2003).

It is perhaps obvious that adult protection will involve balancing rights, risks and duties that often appear to be in conflict. As adults we assume that, as long as we remain within the law, we have the right to live our lives as we choose and to make decisions on a day-to-day basis about who we see, how we spend our money and if or when to enter into relationships (Patrick and Smith, 2009). However, as a society we also assume that for those individuals who are, for whatever reason, unable to protect themselves and their own best interests, protection will be provided by the state. It is not difficult to foresee therefore that tensions will arise in meeting these broadly contradictory aims. Perhaps because of this tension and the prospect that all adults could potentially require protection at some stage in their life, the scope of adult protection is difficult to define. In the main, adult protection work is likely to encompass those considered within the broad community care umbrella. However, it could also include those subject to domestic violence or bullying and harassment where the adult's ability to protect themselves is compromised, for example by a learning disability or mental health problem, and they are consequently determined to be vulnerable as defined by statute or policy.

Adult protection is consequently an ethically challenging area of practice that requires considerable skill from practitioners who understand the complex interaction of factors that may render any adult in need of support and protection. In addition, it should be acknowledged that adult protection may be required at one time or another for all adults (Penhale and Parker, 2008), including those who have, and those who lack, capacity as defined in law. The impact of working within this challenging area of practice can be significant for practitioners, particularly for those early in their career. For example, in common with staff in child protection work, practitioners in adult protection may find it difficult to cope emotionally, particularly with incidences of sexual abuse (see, for example, Morrison 1990).

This chapter aims to broadly outline the history of the state's attempts to protect adults who require protection in the United Kingdom (UK). In addition, a brief outline of the current policy and legislative framework is provided. Finally, consideration is given to a framework for using the concept of significant harm and assessing seriousness when planning interventions to protect adults at risk of harm as well as potential interventions. The case studies provided aim to illustrate the central ethical and practice dilemmas for social workers, regardless of the policy framework within which they work and could be used as case studies in training exercises.

The scale of the problem

The evolution of the community care agenda and the increasing numbers of adults with support needs living within the community, has ensured that the need for effective adult protection procedures and processes has become more insistent. However, the history of the abuse of adults and the state's attempts to prevent harm and afford protection stretches back much further with perhaps a re-emergence taking place in the 1970s (Scottish Government, 2007). Much activity has taken place since the 1980s with a number of high-profile inquiries across health and social care and the beginning of an extensive public debate on how to tackle adult protection at legislative and policy levels.

However, the legislative and procedural framework to support and protect adults at risk of harm has been largely piecemeal and spread across civil and criminal law. Recently, formal policy and guidance has begun to emerge following a number of high-profile community-based incidents of harm to adults, for example in Cornwall and the Scottish Borders, and influenced by the campaigning work of organisations such as Action on Elder Abuse. Across the UK, guidance to protect adults was initially developed in the late 1980s and early 1990s (see, for example, DoH, 1993). The recognition of adult protection as an area of work requiring significant development is therefore fairly recent and to some extent is still ill defined (Mandelstam, 2009).

Perhaps one of the reasons for the slow-moving policy response to adult protection has been the challenge in establishing prevalence rates. Much like other protection agendas, harm perpetrated against adults often goes unreported due to fear of recrimination and concern about being abandoned (Penhale and Parker, 2008). Prevalence rates are consequently difficult to quantify and there is little robust evidence about the extent of the abuse of adults in the UK. Work that has been carried out to establish prevalence has, in the main, focused on older people; very little is known about levels of abuse and exploitation among adults with learning disabilities or those with mental health problems.

However, Comic Relief and the Department of Health funded a two-year study undertaken by Action on Elder Abuse (2007), which provides some evidence of prevalence rates among older adults. The study found that 4% of older adults in the UK are victims of elder abuse, amounting to 342,000 people, and that 2.6% of the 4% were abused by people considered to be in a position of trust, including family members, neighbours and health and social care staff. The types of abuse perpetrated were found to include: neglect – 105,000, financial – 86,500, psychological – 58,600, physical – 62,400 and sexual – 42,000. While this study was limited to older adults it does provide some baseline data on the types of abuse perpetrated more generally. However, Phillipson and Biggs (1995: p 202) note that "Attempts to define and map the extent of elder abuse indicate that it should not be seen as a single monolithic phenomenon, but that it takes a variety of forms in different settings and in different kinds of relationships".

Language and definitions

The language surrounding adult protection has often been viewed as disempowering and stigmatising, for example, 'vulnerable', 'abuse' and 'exploitation' (Penhale and Parker, 2008). It is important therefore to consider the use of language when referring to adults and the impact this may have upon them as well as the way in which it alters perceptions of those individuals, for example, eroding their rights as citizens.

The term 'safeguarding' is often used with regard to adult protection as it is with the protection of children agenda. It could be argued that by using parallel language and systems this infantilises adults as they have the right to self-determination in a way that children do not.

During the passage of the primary Scottish legislation, the Adult Support and Protection (Scotland) Act 2007 (ASP), much consideration and debate was given to the language contained within it to ensure that it did not further stigmatise or disempower adults who may be subject to its powers (MacKay, 2009). Consequently, the language in the legislation became 'adults at risk of harm'; the terms 'abuse' and 'vulnerable' are deliberately avoided, except as part of the definition of 'at risk of harm'. There is further, detailed guidance in the legislation and the accompanying Code of Practice over who could be considered at risk of harm and this links appropriately to those considered vulnerable in the government's *No Secrets Guidance* (DH, 2000). Indeed in the recent consultation to review *No Secrets*, 90% of respondents wanted the definition of vulnerable adults revised and there was significant support for replacing this term with 'person at risk' (DH, 2009).

It is further appropriate to distinguish between those at risk of harm who have capacity and those who lack capacity as the legislation, policy and procedural frameworks may be significantly different, although there will inevitably be some overlap. In the UK, 'capacity' is a legal term, and thus not only has a legal definition but also is a legal decision (Scottish Government, 2005).

Two concepts may be particularly important to unpack in the adult protection agenda – 'abuse' and 'vulnerability'. First, what do we mean by 'harm' or 'abuse'? There are a number of definitions across the UK, perhaps most formally described in the *No Secrets Guidance* (DH, 2000) and the ASP (Scottish Government, 2007). Examples of definitions from the *No Secrets Guidance* and the ASP are provided below. However, definitions remain a contested area and indeed there has been a suggestion by Bennet *et al.* (1997) that we may need different definitions for different areas, for example for legislation, care management and research.

Abuse

> *Abuse may consist of a single act or repeated acts. It may be physical, verbal or psychological, it may be an act of neglect or failure to act, or it may occur when a vulnerable person is persuaded to enter into a financial or sexual transaction to which he or she has not consented or cannot give consent.*

> *Abuse can occur in any relationship and may result in significant harm to, or exploitation of, the person subjected to it.*

> *Physical, sexual, financial, emotional, discriminatory or psychological violation or neglect of a person unable to protect him/herself to prevent abuse from happening or to remove him/herself from the abuse of potential abuse by others.* (DH, 2000, p 9)

The ASP defines adults "at risk" as:

> *(1) "Adults at risk" are adults who –*
> *(a) are unable to safeguard their own well-being, property, rights or other interests,*
> *(b) are at risk of harm, and*
> *(c) because they are affected by disability, mental disorder, illness or physical or mental infirmity, are more vulnerable to being harmed than adults who are not so affected.*
> *(2) An adult is at risk of harm for the purposes of subsection (1) if—*
> *(a) another person's conduct is causing (or is likely to cause) the adult to be harmed,*
> *or*
> *(b) the adult is engaging (or is likely to engage) in conduct which causes (or is likely to cause) self-harm.* (ASP, Section 4, 2007)

The types of abuse likely to be considered within adult protection are, however, generally agreed upon and these include: physical abuse, sexual abuse, psychological abuse, material abuse (for example, finance), neglect (including self-neglect), institutional abuse and discriminatory abuse.

Brown (2003) has argued that the dynamics of abuse are complex and that the factors to be considered include:

- *The nature (and underlying intent) of the relationship between the potential abuser and the "at risk" adult; for example, the process of 'grooming' in respect to a vulnerable adult*
- *The process used to gain and maintain access to the vulnerable adult; for example, a perpetrator using the workplace to gain access to "at risk" adults*
- *The degree or severity of the harm to the vulnerable adult (including psychological elements)*
- *The degree of continuing risk to the vulnerable adult or other "at risk" adults in the setting; for example, when an accused member of staff continues to have access to the vulnerable adult*
- *Situations where there might be multiple components of vulnerability; for example, sexual abuse between service users.*
- *The need to consider the situation where a conflict of interest might occur; for example, where an attorney may be connected to a family member and have their objectivity compromised.* (Scottish Government, 2007, p 6)

Complete agreement on what constitutes abuse is, however, unlikely to be achieved. Abuse is a socially constructed concept and as societies change and evolve so does their understanding of what is acceptable and unacceptable behaviour, making abuse a fluid concept (Penhale *et al.*, 2000). Therefore to have a fixed definition of abuse could be detrimental, by essentially tagging certain behaviours as abusive within a constrained set of criteria. In addition, our understanding of abuse and abusive behaviour is likely to be affected by local and cultural factors, including existing practice and procedures and consequently a range of definitions are inevitable. It is therefore important that when working in adult protection that the definition of abuse being used is explicit, either legislatively or procedurally.

Vulnerability

'Vulnerability' is a term often used to describe those who require support to ensure their own protection, however all adults could be considered vulnerable at some stage in their adult life. Indeed, vulnerability and what determines it, is itself a contentious concept (Penhale and Parker, 2008). Attributing a label of vulnerable to an individual can consign them to the status of victim, having things done to them rather than helping themselves for example. In addition, the term 'vulnerable adult' can instill the vulnerability within the adult himself or herself, rather than the vulnerability being caused by a particular set of circumstances or societal structures. In this sense, vulnerable adults can be viewed through the same lens as other marginalised groups whose label has disempowered them.

There are, further, often conflicting views concerning an individual's capacity and social situation, which may aid in defining vulnerability. It can, for example, often be an individual's context that makes them at risk of harm and consequently deemed vulnerable. For example, they may be living with someone who is exploiting them financially (see Case Study 1) and if that person were removed they would no longer be deemed at risk or vulnerable. The *No Secrets Guidance* (DH, 2000, p 9) suggests that:

> *A vulnerable adult is a person aged 18 years or over who is or may be in need of community care services by reason of mental or other disability, age or illness; and who is or maybe unable to take care of him or herself, or unable to protect him or herself against significant harm or exploitation.*

However, the guidance goes on to indicate that those adults falling into the above category must be considered on a case-by-case basis as their own situation and context may impact on any decisions regarding intervention.

This chapter will in the main use the terms 'adult protection' and 'adults at risk of harm' as these are viewed as the least stigmatising and most empowering for service users.

Policy and legislative frameworks across the UK

The complexity of adult protection signifies that any legislative or policy responses will need to be flexible, provide a range of detailed responses and be understood across health, social care, education and justice agencies. However, local authorities have a clear lead in the adult protection agenda across the UK, although the details of this vary across the four nations. This inevitably means that social workers in particular are required to balance complex ethical and practice dilemmas within frameworks that rely heavily on inter-agency collaboration to ensure effective outcomes for adults.

The range of legal and procedural measures available to support and protect adults at risk of harm is viewed as considerable, however they are spread across different areas of law (Scottish Government, 2007). However, it is important to acknowledge that there is no consolidating piece of legislation in England, Wales or Northern Ireland, which protects adults deemed at risk of harm.

Finally, it is important as practitioners to establish what the aim of the legislation or policy (for example, to treat, support or protect) is that you may draw on to support or protect an adult as this may impact on the model of intervention engaged. The following provides a brief summary of the current policy and legislative frameworks across the UK

England

The *No Secrets Guidance* (DH, 2000) aims to provide a clear policy framework for adult protection in England. This includes a focus on the development of inter-agency policies and procedures to protect adults at risk of harm. In addition, it offers a structure for the development of local policies and procedures as well as joint protocols. It *does not*, however, place a statutory duty on agencies to comply with the guidance, although there is an expectation that, unless there are very clear reasons for exemption, all agencies comply. The guidance provides details on a range of issues for practitioners and agencies including definitions of abuse, an explanation of how and why abuse occurs, including patterns of abuse, how to respond to various kinds of abuse, consideration of what level of abuse justifies intervention and the development of inter-agency protocols.

In 2008/09, in response to concerns about a lack of clarity in the *No Secrets Guidance* (DH, 2000), the Department of Health reviewed the guidance in consultation with key stakeholders. Included among the recommendations for change in the final report are:

- *Safeguarding should be built on empowerment, without this it is experienced as safety at the expense of other qualities of life, such as self-determination and the right to family life.*
- *To empower individuals safeguarding decisions should be taken by the individual concerned. People wanted help with options, information and support. However, they wanted to retain control and make their own choices.*
- *Safeguarding adults is not like children protection, adults do not want to be treated like children and do not want a system that was designed for children.*
- *The participation/representation of people who lack capacity is also important.*

(DH, 2009)

More recently (January 2010), Phil Hope, the then Care Minister in England detailed the government's response to the review of *No Secrets*, indicating among other measures that safeguarding boards would be made mandatory throughout England, further emphasising the importance of adult protection in both policy and practice terms.

Wales

In Wales, the policy developed to support and protect adults at risk of harm is *In Safe Hands* (NAW, 2000). *In Safe Hands* was issued as guidance in 2000 under Section 7 of the Local Authority Social Services Act 1970. The focus of this policy is on effective inter-agency working and information sharing in particular.

As with the other jurisdictions within the UK, the implementation of the Welsh policy has not been without its challenges. For example, in June 2009, Gary Fitzgerald, chief executive of the charity Action on Elder Abuse, stated that he felt that the impact of the policy 'was an illusion not a reality' and that it had failed to protect older people (*Western Mail*, June 2009). This concern focused on the fact that the policy did not carry the same weight as legislation and that as such local authorities could ignore the guidance with good reason. As with the review of *No Secrets* in England, campaigners are calling for a broad review of the Welsh policy.

Further guidance on the protection of vulnerable adults from financial abuse in their own homes was developed in 2003 and updated in 2009. More detailed information on adult protection in Wales can be found at: www.ssiacymru.org.uk/index.cfm?articleid= 2592.

Northern Ireland

The policy document *Safeguarding Vulnerable Adults: Regional adult protection and policy procedural guidance* (DH, SSPS, 2006) lays out the framework for adult protection in Northern Ireland. This includes discussion of definitions, principles and the importance of inter-agency working. Recent developments have included the Protocol for Joint Investigation of Alleged and Suspected Cases of Abuse of Vulnerable Adults by the Regional Adult Protection Forum, which is a partnership body, with representation from Health and Social Care Trusts and Boards, the Police Service for Northern Ireland, the Regulation and Quality Improvement Authority and the voluntary sector. It outlines roles and responsibilities of the respective agencies and provides guidance about joint working arrangements and investigation. Further information about policy and practice in adult support and protection in Northern Ireland can be found at: www.nhssb.n-i.nhs.uk/ publications/social_services/Safeguarding_Vulnerable_Adults.pdf

Perhaps it could be argued that one of the advantages of having no consolidating legislation in England, Wales and Northern Ireland is that practitioners are empowered to act by more than one piece of legislation such as: Section 47 of the NHS and Community Care Act 1990 and Sections 29 and 47 of the National Assistance Act 1948.

Many practitioners will have used Section 47 of the National Assistance Act 1948, which allows for the removal of someone at risk of harm and to confine them in a more suitable place. However, there are challenges in using this tool for protection in that although it is there to ensure that a person receives appropriate and necessary care and attention there is no power of compulsion. There is, further, little detail available about how effective this statute is in supporting and protecting those at risk of harm.

In addition, practitioners have been able to use the Mental Health Act 2007, the Mental Capacity Act 2005, the Race Relations Act 1976, the Disability Discrimination Act 2005 and the European Convention of Human Rights Act 1998 in various forms to support and protect adults at risk of harm. Hewitt (2009, p 30), however, suggests that "a wide variety of safeguarding powers already exists. If some of them are little used, that may be because they are in unfamiliar places".

However, the clear disadvantage of the above is that the framework is fragmented, inconsistently applied and perhaps overall unclear. Sixty-eight per cent of those who responded to the written consultation on the review of the *No Secrets Guidance* supported the need to develop legislation – the reasons for this were (DH, 2009):

- *Safeguarding adults should be given the same priority as child protection*
- *Legislation would make safeguarding a priority*
- *Scotland has the ASP, that made adult protection statutory*
- *The government's choice agenda needed to be balanced with a safeguarding agenda.* (DH, 2009)

Scotland

In Scotland there is specific primary legislation, the Adult Support and Protection (Scotland) Act 2007 (ASP), to protect those who are deemed at risk of harm. This legislation importantly places a duty on local authorities and their key partners, health boards, police, education and voluntary organisations to work together to support and protect adults at risk of harm. The legislation is also based on a set of principles, which aims to provide the means to intervene and prevent harm continuing – consistently, to put in place strengthened measures to give greater protection for those at risk from harm and to improve inter-agency co-operation and promote good inter-disciplinary practice.

However, the ASP is only one part of a legal structure, which provides the framework for inquiry, assessment and intervention in the lives of adults in Scotland. The Adults with Incapacity (Scotland) Act 2000 (AWIA) and Mental Health (Care and Treatment) (Scotland) Act 2003 (MHCT Act) are the other two key elements. The AWIA provides for the support and protection of those adults who lack capacity and the MHCT Act provides for the support and protection of those who are experiencing mental health problems.

A number of the policy documents and legislation cited above have as their central aim the co-ordination of effective systems across agencies to best support and protect adults at risk of harm, with associated Codes of Practice and local arrangements providing procedural clarity for practitioners. They also vary in their approach to adult protection and whether or not they allow for treatment, protection and/or support. As such, the policy framework can be confusing unless appropriately clarified at the local level.

Assessing seriousness and risk in adult protection

How do we begin to consider what factors warrant/merit intervention in the life of an adult, with or without capacity? Assessing the seriousness of situations prior to intervention is at the core of practice in the support and protection of adults at risk of harm.

Assessing seriousness is perhaps most closely linked to the concept of 'significant harm'. Significant harm is an important concept as it aids practitioners in determining how serious or extensive abuse must be to warrant intervention (O'Keefe *et al.*, 2007). Again, there are parallels with child protection where significant harm, introduced in the Children Act 1989, is viewed as the threshold after which compulsory intervention is required. The Law Commission in England (1995) makes use of this concept when considering the nature of intervention and defines this as including not only ill-treatment but also impeding and impairing the development of an adult in a number of areas including physical and emotional. Deciding on an intervention may further require consideration of the degree, extent, duration and frequency of harm.

In addition, it is important to define adult protection as broader than physical or sexual abuse, and that it should also include psychological and financial abuse and exploitation (Mantell and Scragg, 2008). The harm that can be perpetuated against an adult can fall into a number of categories although (O'Keefe *et al.*, 2007) found overlapping issues with significant complexity and that where abuse existed it was often incremental.

A further consideration is why people harm adults. A range of triggers have been identified (Mantell and Scragg, 2008) including:

- opportunistic – money, valuables lying around in plain sight;
- long-term – history of abuse, harm within family or situation;
- situational – pressure build-up over time, for example long-term care;
- neglect – withholding of appropriate care;
- unacceptable treatment – punishments for specific behaviours.

Many factors that trigger adults being harmed are the same as those in child abuse, particularly as they relate to situational and opportunistic triggers. Practitioners should be aware of potential triggers when considering intervention to provide support and protection.

Case study 1

Ms B has a mild to moderate learning disability. She has lived in a hostel for homeless people for a number of years during which time she has been subjected to a significant number of assaults (20+), has often been absent overnight and is resistant to additional support being provided.

Staff within her hostel consistently expressed concerns that Ms B was being financially, physically and sexually abused and that over time the level and frequency of abuse was increasing. She often returned to the company of a 'friend' who had been present at and participated in a number of assaults perpetrated against her. (Composite of Mental Welfare Commission Inquiries)

The following questions are provided as a framework for assessing seriousness and significant harm in the above case.

- What level of capacity does Ms B have to protect herself from harm?
- If she does not have capacity – what is the relevant procedural avenue to provide support and protection?
- If she does have capacity – what is the relevant procedural avenue to provide support and protection?
- Has trust been breached in the duty of care or in legal terms?
- In what context has the abuse taken place?
- What are the views and wishes of Ms B?
- Has a risk assessment been undertaken?
- What is the level and frequency of the abuse?
- How long has it been going on?
- What is the risk of significant harm to Ms B and others of non-intervention?

By developing an adult protection framework that considers the context of any alleged abuse, views and wishes of the victim, impact on the person and others, level of capacity/ability to protect themselves, level of threat to their independence and well-being, breach of trust (duty of care/legality of act), likelihood of repeated risks of abuse from the same person and the internal-external factors that may contribute to abuse (Hughes, 2006; Mantell and Scragg, 2008) practitioners can ensure that any response is proportionate to the potential harm in line with the European Convention on Human Rights Act 1998 and that a positive approach is taken to risk assessment and risk management.

There can often be considerable co-ercion within adult protection cases and this must also be given significant consideration in terms of risk of significant harm. In the ASP (Scottish Executive 2007), there is the opportunity for council officers (those staff charged with implementing the legislation) to put aside the lack of consent by an adult to an intervention where it can be evidenced that another party has placed undue pressure on them. It should further be noted that mistreatment prevalence (O'Keefe et al., 2007) increases with being female, declining health status, experiencing loneliness or depression and likely to be in receipt of services.

There will of course be situations where intervention is clearly warranted, for example where an adult lacks capacity and is being sexually or financially abused or exploited. However, there will equally be situations where the course of action is not quite so clear-cut. For example, consider the situation of someone who has legal capacity but also a mild learning disability, whose friend is exploiting him/her financially, so little money is left to live on. While we as professionals and even as individuals may find this unacceptable, the adult at the centre of this example may consider this a fair trade for attention, affection and companionship and be concerned that this relationship continue (Patrick and Smith, 2009). Again the concept of significant harm may be helpful in considering intervention.

Adult protection involves the need to balance choice, rights and associated risks for adults. There should be a clear model for risk assessments for care recipients and others acting in their best interest. A rights-based approach allows a flexible system while at the same time supporting a robust and ethical approach to adult protection and the appropriate sharing of risk across agencies and individuals (Whitelock, 2009).

Interventions

The evidence base regarding the effectiveness of interventions in the lives of adults at risk is fairly limited. It is therefore difficult to establish what works and how transferable interventions are across the range of situations likely to be experienced in adult protection work. However a literature review carried out for the Scottish Executive in 2007 indicated that, in general, interventions are available at three levels – primary, secondary and tertiary – and that they fall into two main categories of intervention – legal and welfare (which includes therapeutic interventions). Examples of interventions examined were the provision of information and advice services, therapeutic interventions (for example, counseling, family therapy), case management and in extreme cases removal to a place of safety. The review also found that preventative work such as raising awareness of the issue in a public education programme, professional education and a zero tolerance approach in society can also be effective.

Case study 2

John Davidson is a retired architect who lives in a rural area, he is frail physically but cognitively very sharp and aware. His son and daughter-in-law live with him. John also has two other daughters. John's son and daughter-in-law do not work neither do they claim benefit, consequently their income is derived solely from John. One of John's other daughters has written to the social work department to raise concerns that her father is being financially exploited by her brother and his wife. Staff from the social work department interview John and it becomes clear that he is frustrated with his son. John has challenged his son about claiming benefits and/or working, he refuses to claim benefits claiming it is beneath him and his wife. He also argues that there are no jobs available. John has asked both his son and daughter-in-law to leave as he feels they are a drain on him financially and emotionally or to secure their own income.

Consider how you would proceed to support John in achieving his stated outcome within the context of the significant harm framework described above and the procedures in your own locality.

As detailed above, the type of intervention used in adult protection may be dependent on the circumstances and of course location of the case. Adult protection work can be required in care homes and other institutional settings as well as in the community and it has been suggested that responses can be grouped under three levels: macro (political/structural), mezzo (community/agency) and micro (individual) (Penhale and Parker, 2008). Most social workers will be able to cite examples of interventions at these different levels from their own practice, however as an illustration consider case study 2 above and how interventions could be planned and implemented at the different levels using your own relevant legislation and procedures. These might include the relevant legislation, media campaigns to raise awareness of rights and responsibilities, promotion of service user involvement in policy development to increase awareness and clarity of procedures and processes including key responsibilities. Finally, seamless multi-agency working including information sharing will be key in effective planning and implementation of any chosen intervention.

In addition, to support effective intervention, it could be argued that raising public awareness of the susceptibility of certain groups of adults to being at risk of harm would be helpful in both prevention and crisis work. In practice in Scotland it has already been noted, anecdotally, that the training and implementation process for the ASP including national and local media campaigns has raised the profile of adult protection in the community.

Perhaps a more central question for consideration in planning and implementing interventions in adult protection is how we move from an intrinsically paternalistic system for adult protection to one that aims to prevent crisis from occurring. In addition, a rights-based approach, which promotes the empowerment of those at risk of harm to protect themselves should be promoted and an examination undertaken of how this can be affected within existing systems.

Conclusion

What is clear from the foregoing is that policy frameworks and legislation are helpful in providing support and protection to adults at risk of harm. In addition, clarity of process is important for workers to be able to achieve effective outcomes for individuals. Further, formal procedures aid in raising awareness of the importance of the issue and in formally recognising the responsibilities to support and protect adults at risk of harm.

However, regardless of the framework within which practitioners approach their adult protection work, there will be considerable ethical challenges. Clarity of purpose, appropriate risk assessment and assessing seriousness tests should aid practitioners through this complex maze of legislative and ethical issues. Significant attention should be paid to the outcomes of the Scottish legislation over the next few years to identify challenges and effective good practice from which others may benefit across the UK.

Finally, it should not be forgotten that the protection of adults at risk of harm is also about providing appropriate support to empower adults to make their own choices about how they live their lives in a safe manner (Hewitt, 2009). Balancing the rights of adults with the requirement to protect is at the heart of adult protection – a clear challenge for all social workers regardless of the stage of their career.

References

Action on Elder Abuse (2007) *Briefing Paper: The UK Study of Abuse and Neglect of Older People* Streatham: Action on Elder Abuse.

Bennett, G, Kingston, P and Penhale, B (1997) *The Dimensions of Elder Abuse and Neglect: Perspectives for the practitioner* Basingstoke: Macmillan.

Brown, H (2003) 'What is financial abuse' *The Journal of Adult Protection* 5(2), pp 3-10.

DH (Department of Health) (1993) *No Longer Afraid: The safeguard of older people in domestic settings* London: HMSO.

DH (2000) *No Secrets Guidance* London: HMSO.

DH (2009) *Safeguarding Adults: Report on the Consultation on the Review of No Secrets Guidance on Developing and Implementing multi-agency policies and procedures to protect vulnerable adults from abuse* London: DH (www.dh.gov.uk/en/Consultations/Responsestoconsultations/DH_102764)

DHSSPS (Department of Health, Social Services and Public Safety) (2006) *Safeguarding Vulnerable Adults: Regional Adult Protection Policy and Procedural Guidance* Ballymena: Social Services Directorate.

Hewitt, D (2009) 'Not Just in the Mental Capacity Act: using the law to protect vulnerable adults' *Journal of Adult Protection* 11(2), pp 25-31.

House of Commons Health Committee (2003) *Victoria Climbié Inquiry Report* London: The Stationery Office.

Hughes, J (2006) *Chairing Multi-disciplinary Adult Protection Meetings* Making Connections, Training and Consultancy.

Law Commission (1995) *Mental Incapacity*, Consultation Paper No. 231, London: HMSO.

Leslie, S and Prtichard, J (2009) 'A Review of Relevant Legislation in Adult Protection' in Pritchard, J (ed) *Good Practice in the Law and Safeguarding Adults: Criminal Justice and Adult Protection* London: Jessica Kingsley Publishers.

Mandlestam, M (2009) *Safeguarding Vulnerable Adults and the Law* London: Jessica Kingsley Publishers.

MacKay, K (2009) 'The Scottish Legal Context of Adult Support and Protection' in Pritchard, J (ed) (2009) *Good Practice in the Law and Safegurading Adults: Criminal Justice and Adult Protection* London: Jessica Kingsley Publishers.

Mantell, A and Scragg, T (2008) *Safeguarding Adults in Social Work* Execter: Learning Matters.

Morrison, T (1990) 'The Emotional Effects of Child Protection Work on the Worker' *Practice* 4(4), pp 253-71.

NAW (National Assembly for Wales) (2000) *In Safe Hands: Implementing adult protection in Wales* Cardiff: NAW.

O'Keefe, M, Hills, A, Doyle, M, McCreadie, C, *et al.* (2007) *UK Study of Abuse and Neglect of Older People* London: Comic Relief and Department of Health.

Parsons, G (2006) 'Setting the Scene for the Protection of Vulnerable Adults (POVA) investigations' *Journal of Adult Protection* 8(2), pp 39-45.

Patrick, H and Smith, N (2009) *Adult Protection and the Law in Scotland* Haywards Heath, Blomsbury Professional.

Penhale, B,and Parker, J with Kingston, P (2000) *Elder Abuse* Birmingham: Venture Press.

Penhale, B and Parker, J (2008) *Working with Vulnerable Adults* Abingdon: Routledge.

Phillipson, C and Biggs, S (1995) 'Elder abuse: a critical overview' in Kingston, P and Penhale, B (eds) *Family violence and the caring professions* Basingstoke: Macmillan.

Scottish Government (2007) *A Review of Literature on Effective Interventions that prevent and respond to harm against adults* Edinburgh: Blackwell (www.scotland.gov.uk/Resource/Doc/203554/0054266.pdf).

Western Mail (2009) 'Protection of Elderly "just an illusion"' *Western Mail*, Retrieved from www.walesonline.co.uk/news/wales-news/2009/06/11/protection-of-elderly-just-an-illusion-91466-23841195/

Whitelock, A (2009) 'Safeguarding in mental health: towards a rights-based approach' *Journal of Adult Protection* 11(4), pp 30-42.

Statutes

National Assistance Act (1948) London: HMSO.

Race Relations Act (1976) London: HMSO.

Children's Act (1998) London: HMSO.

*Human Rights Act (*1998) London: HMSO.

Adults with Incapacity (Scotland) Act (2000) Edinburgh: Blackwell.

Mental Health (Care and Treatment) (Scotland) Act (2003) Edinburgh: Blackwell.

Disability Discrimination Act (2005) London: HMSO.

Mental Capacity Act (2005) London: HMSO.

Adult Support and Protection (Scotland) Act (2007) Edinburgh: Blackwell.

Mental Health Act (2007) London: HMSO.

Chapter 17

Substance Misuse and Social Work: the essential contribution

Joy Barlow

It has been suggested, particularly by Mike Ashton, FEAD[1], a well-known researcher and commentator on drugs and alcohol, that in the substance misuse field we need to select people who are socially skilled, in order to provide a better-equipped workforce. While we would hope that all substance misuse workers are socially skilled, it is in social work, its education, training and Codes of Practice, where the skills of working with people as individuals of worth are most highly identified. Professor Lord Kamlesh Patel, FEAD[2], has also spoken of the importance of his social work training, which helped him 'put oneself in another's shoes', and assisted him in thinking through the act of 'helping'.

Drug and alcohol misuse, which for the purposes of this discussion is defined as problematic to the individual, family and society, impinges on all areas of social work practice and interventions. The growing body of knowledge from the perspectives of medicine, sociology, psychology, justice and ethics continues to frame our understandings of and responses to substance misuse. Social workers need to understand research and its application in the workplace in order to assist their work with people affected by substance misuse, their families and carers. Those social workers who carry responsibility for community care assessments as well as those who work in specialist settings dealing with alcohol and drugs, and related areas such as mental health, criminal justice, and children and families services, need to understand the aetiology of substance misuse, theories underpinning interventions, and how to deliver interventions.

This chapter will examine the role of social workers as part of the substance misuse workforce: their potential contribution; the nature of the links between social work practice and substance misuse; and the benefits to this field of work of the social work discipline and its approach. It will also discuss the nature of education and training for social workers in substance misuse: the importance of early professional development (EPD) in substance misuse and what it should provide for social workers; what works in EPD, and some innovative early professional development in practice. Barriers to good practice will also be identified and how these may be overcome. Finally, some key questions will be outlined.

Before any of this is attempted, however, it is necessary to look at the current policy landscape with regard to drugs and alcohol, upon which the rest of the chapter will be predicated. It should be noted that for the purposes of this chapter the substances under discussion are alcohol and drugs, excluding tobacco. While there is work going on in community development on smoking cessation, which by its very nature involves social services (McKie *et al.*, 2009), significant work in this area is conducted in the health arena.

Recent policy emphasis

In all the recent alcohol strategies across the United Kingdom (UK) and devolved jurisdictions there is a new emphasis on changing our relationship with alcohol. There is recognition that changing a socially embedded behaviour – like alcohol use – requires a radical cultural shift (Lloyd, 2009). The main focus appears to be that of public health, focused on the early identification of alcohol problems and early brief interventions.

It is important to note that alcohol, when set in historical context, has had the most impact on our lives, over the longest period and has caused the most damage, public concern and legislative response (Lloyd, 2009). Yet there has always been a separate policy response to alcohol and drugs. Indeed, in the most recent strategies, which deal with substance misuse across the devolved jurisdictions of the UK, only the Welsh strategy has combined alcohol with drugs. It has been suggested that the 'firewall' between drug and alcohol policy should be breached in order that more cohesive service delivery may be developed (Trace, private communication).

One of the ways in which the Scottish Government had hoped to approach the significant cultural change required in our relationship with alcohol, was to attempt to introduce minimum pricing. The Scottish Parliament rejected this keystone proposal of the Alcohol Bill, although evidence shows that those who are alcohol dependent respond quickly to price increases by buying less. It is also known that young people, especially those who are under-age purchasers, are also price sensitive. It is believed that if the sales of cut-price alcohol were to stop, then we would see a positive change in some drinking behaviour (Law, 2009). Despite the setback on minimum pricing the Scottish Government's Alcohol Bill (which was unanimously approved) does involve measures to ban drinks promotions in shops, and imposes a "social responsibility" tax on licensed premises. Cultural change, assisted by legislation, is making some progress.

Turning to drugs, the most recent drug strategies were published in 2010 for the UK (HM Government, 2010), for Scotland (Scottish Government, 2008), and for Wales (WAG, 2008). The most recent UK strategy marks a significant shift in Government policy. "This strategy sets out a fundamentally different approach to tackling drugs, and an entirely new ambition to reduce drug use and dependence" (UK Drug Strategy, 2010, p 3). It focuses, as did the Scottish Strategy in 2008, on recovery, enabling local communities to support individuals to become free of dependence and make a meaningful contribution.The strategy structures this recovery-oriented approach around three themes: reducing demand, restricting supply and building recovery in communities.

As in all the strategies of the devolved jurisdictions, the emphasis on treatment is to ensure that more people are tackling their dependency and moving towards recovery.

Universal services such as access to accommodation, education, training and employment, are required to provide a greater range of support services.

Another feature of the strategies, particularly that in Scotland, is the emphasis on the children of drug-using parents. These children are given prominence in the framework for integrating children's services, known in Scotland as *Getting It Right For Every Child* (Scottish Government, 2010). As will be described later in this chapter, the welfare and safe-guarding of children of drug-users is seen as a prime responsibility of social work services.

In Scotland's Strategy – *The Road to Recovery* – recovery is the main goal of treatment. The focus is on the integration of treatment services with a wider range of generic services – highlighting social integration, with the emphasis on person-centred care and individual care plans.

In the Welsh strategy there is a strong emphasis on involving service users, putting them at the heart of policy, planning and service design (WAG, 2008, p 31). As with previous strategies, commissioners of services 'should consider wraparound services as a core component of treatment for all substance misusers' (p 36).

In this flurry of strategic activity, significant changes are being wrought – or at least sought. With the involvement of more agencies in treatment and recovery in the drugs field, and on a 'whole-population' approach to alcohol, social work services will be expected to respond in ways not hitherto seen as essential to their social work practice. This essential element will call for different ways of working both within the profession and with others.

There has been considerable debate in recent years about the classification of drugs, and indeed whether the Misuse of Drugs Act 1971 is sufficiently robust for the current situation. The debacle over the classification of cannabis – reduced from a B classification to C, and then re-instated as class B, causes particular confusion in the minds of both users of the drug and those who work with them, particularly in youth work and offending. In addition, the emergence of 'legal' highs – now not legal (for example, mephedrone) – leads one to wonder how the classification systems can remain as they are. The Royal Society of Arts (2007) was the first to suggest an index of harms related to substance misuse, including alcohol, rather than the procedures of control and scheduling of illegal drugs which are carried out under the Misuse of Drugs Act 1971. The Royal Society of Arts report also noted that substance misuse was primarily a health and social issue, and should be better integrated into social policy and health frameworks.

In the recent past it can be said that policy on drugs has been led by health or criminal justice, and the contribution made by social work has been undervalued. In the consultation preceding the UK 2008 drugs strategy, training for social workers in substance misuse was not mentioned, while other groups such as health and youth workers were singled out. The time is now right for recognition of the potential social work contribution to alcohol and drug practice, and an emphasis on the importance of

EPD in this field of practice is required.

Finally, before leaving the policy focus it is perhaps timely to ponder the perceived dichotomy between harm reduction and abstinence, a debate reignited in the discussion about recovery. The United Nations Office on Drugs and Crime put forward this view in 2008:

> *Harm reduction is often made an unnecessary controversial issue, as if there were a contradiction between treatment and prevention on the one hand, and reducing the adverse health and social consequences of drug use on the other. This is a false dichotomy. They are complementary.*
>
> (United Nations Office on Drugs and Crime, 2008, preface)

In the recovery focus it will be important to integrate all outcomes of interventions into a model of recovery defined by the individual. This may be achieved by making recovery, at the earliest opportunity, the focus of all treatment modalities and through the establishment of an expert care management system that is the single integrated gateway to treatment. We need to create a balance between substitute prescribing and abstinence treatments, using care management and case review. Harm reduction can be used as a stepping stone to structured care, and residential rehabilitation will need to be available as a greater option for choice, than has hitherto been experienced. Work on recovery conducted by the Royal Society of Arts, identifies that drug misusers need a personalised package of support with greater control over their individual drug treatment, in order to sustain their road back to recovery. All of this will profoundly affect every social worker's approach to substance misuse in their daily practice.

The links between substance misuse and social work interventions

The links between substance misuse and interventions provided by social work are varied and complex. Simply using illicit or licit substances is not a reason for social work intervention; yet the groups with which social workers interact are at significant risk of using substances in ways that put themselves and others at risk. Research evidence illustrates this point. A few examples will suffice.

Children and families work is significantly affected by issues of substance misuse. Social work childcare teams estimate that for 50 to 90% of parents on their caseload, substance use is a factor[3]. It is reported that 2 to 3% of all children aged under 16 in England and Wales and 4 to 6% in Scotland have one or both parents with serious drug problems (ACMD 2003). Estimates of the number of children currently living with an alcohol-using parent range from 300,000 to 2.5 million (Cleaver *et al.*, 1999; Tunnard, 2002). The number of children in Scotland living with a parent with an alcohol problem is potentially 100,000 (Harwin *et al.*, 2009). More recent research by Manning and Best (2009) indicates that these numbers will be far higher if we consider the impact of hazardous drinking (for example, binge drinking) on the capacity of the parent to provide appropriate care.

Until the end of the twentieth century, little had been written about the effect of substance misuse on parenting capacity, apart from the work of Velleman & Orford (1999). Very little evidence had been accrued from children themselves about the impact of living with a parent with a dependent drug habit. The work of Barnard & Barlow (2003) at the Centre for Drug Misuse Research, University of Glasgow, on children growing up in drug-dependent households heralded an increased focus on the impact of substance misuse on children from pre-conception to young adulthood.

From research we know that parenting capacity is impaired when substance misuse is unstable and chaotic; children experience emotional distance from parents, if not physical distance, which raises the issue of attachment, especially in the very early months and years of a child's life. The risk of abuse and neglect coupled with the disruption of household routines and lack of attention to medical needs will prompt the need for intervention. The unpredictability of parental response and reduced empathy are also problem risk factors of which social workers must be aware (Barnard and Barlow, 2000).

In this particular area of practice and intervention, social workers are often called on to make significant decisions, often ethically fraught: 'for all they did to us 'cos of the drugs, they were still mum and dad and we know they loved us and we were scared of being separated from them and taken into foster care' *(Rachel)* (Barnard, 2007, p 90)

Working with older people affected by alcohol and drug misuse is only just beginning to surface, although practitioners will be well aware of the potential impact on health and well-being; for example, older men and women are more likely to drink every day than younger people and less likely to know about alcohol units. In addition, older men drink more spirits as a larger percentage of their overall consumption than younger men (Lader and Goddard, 2006). The most common misuses of substances by older people are the drinking of alcohol and taking benzodiazepine. The foregoing indicates the importance of social workers having both knowledge and skills in substance misuse. One might say that this is the *'bene esse'* of their professional life.

The benefits of a social work approach

As suggested above, generic social work services have not always been seen as integral to interventions aiding recovery by substance misusers. In an era where recovery is now to be promulgated, the whole person is the focus, and that includes the socialisation or 'habilitation' of substance misusers. This is where the social worker's role is integral to interventions. As Sarah Galvani has suggested 'perhaps the key advantage our profession has is its emphasis on the individual within a particular environment and context[4]'. Relationships are of paramount importance in the progress of individuals towards recovery, and social workers should have an understanding and experience of the development of relationships for individual users of services. This theme of the individual within the context of their social environment emerges in many other chapters of this book.

The other important contribution from social work practice is found in the values and ethics of the profession. The Codes of Practice for social services workers describe the standard of professional conduct and practice required of them as they go about their daily work (SSSC, 2009). These Codes illustrate the importance of the rights and dignity of service-users; of not judging them but being mindful of the harm to themselves and others their behaviour may have. Social work practice is rooted in respect, in supporting informed choice and respecting diversity. A further potential benefit is social work's emphasis on critical self-reflection, on attitudes, on values and on practice. All of these factors are required in work with substance misusers, whether working in treatment agencies or in the more generic areas of social work where substance misuse has an impact. They are brought to bear in a number of basic tasks undertaken by social workers:

- talking to users/services about substance misuse and understanding the effects of use on both client and family;
- discussing the strengths and deficits associated with their substance use;
- assessing risk and if necessary providing brief interventions;
- referral on to specialist services.

To support people in recovery means that workers may be required to work with people over a long period of time. Social workers may have to resist the requirement, due to lack of resources, of closing cases, as current research on recovery indicates the importance of long- term support (White, 2008).

Finally, to turn a benefit of social work practice on its head, one of the disadvantages of a non-judgemental approach is the possibility of the development of a collusive relationship in which a worker takes the side of the client to the detriment of objectivity. The social worker, as with others involved in substance misuse interventions, is often faced with ethical dilemmas. Particularly in the field of safeguarding and protecting children, honesty and transparency of approach is vital to the integrity of the worker's relationship with the substance misuser; and objectivity about potential outcomes has to be at the heart of all social work practice.Awareness of the dangers of collusion is something social workers can contribute to the practice of a range of professions.

The importance of early professional development in substance misuse

As far back as 1992, the inter-ministerial group on alcohol misuse was concerned about 'the inadequate level of professional education and training in relation to alcohol problems' (Harrison, 1992, p 639). Indeed, over the last 30 years there has been no real consensus about how much social workers should learn about alcohol and drugs in their qualifying programmes. Most research concludes that social workers are ill-prepared and receive little training (Galvani 2007). 'Research and practitioners' reports suggest that workers are all too painfully aware of this gap in their knowledge and skills, and feel frustrated that they have not been equipped to respond' (Galvani & Forrester, 2008, p 10).

It is true that social work education has changed dramatically over the recent past. Throughout the UK the creation of the social work degree has provided a rethink about content of the degree, the development of National Occupational Standards and new subject bench-mark statements. Professional registration has also had an impact on post-qualifying awards. Nevertheless, to date there are no mandated substance misuse modules at the qualifying level, although some institutions do have mandatory courses within their individual programmes. Given that individual degree programme teams determine the content of degree courses, and may choose not to address alcohol and drug misuse, one looks to post-qualifying learning and EPD to provide the necessary knowledge and skills in alcohol and drugs work. In post-qualifying pathways specialising in children and young people, mental health, adult services and criminal justice, there is some recognition of the importance of knowledge and skills in the areas of alcohol and drugs. These are small steps, better than before, but require substantial further development.

What social workers should know

A very useful survey undertaken by Galvani & Forrester in 2008 sought the views of social workers who qualified in 2006 and 2007 as to how well they had been prepared for working with people who use alcohol and drugs. In brief, the survey showed that more than 60% of respondents did not feel that they had been adequately prepared to identify either problems or immediate risk. Even fewer felt confident in delivering interventions or offering support, or being able to work with specialist colleagues. Given that most social workers will be working at 'level one' or one-to-one engagement with clients, those are basic competencies that universal/generic staff should be expected to exhibit (NTA, 2006).

The *Models of Care for the Treatment of Adult Drug Misusers* (NTA, 2006) and the *Drugs and Alcohol National Occupational Standards* (Skills for Health, 2003) identify the following competencies for alcohol and drugs workers across the professions:

- advice and information;
- screening (identification) and assessment;
- provision of brief interventions for hazardous and harmful drinkers;
- partnership with specialist treatment services to provide a 'shared care' approach,

that is, to provide specific interventions within the context of generic services.

Nearly three-quarters of the respondents to Galvani and Forrester's survey indicated training needs in assessing risk; and around 60% did not feel confident in talking about alcohol and drug issues to clients. If this survey is in any sense representative, then generic social workers are not able to fulfil the level of competence required to carry out the basics of early identification, assessment and referral necessary in this important area of social work intervention.

STRADA (Scottish Training on Drugs and Alcohol) has conducted training needs analyses in various parts of Scotland over recent years. Findings are far-ranging and not specifically targeted at social work; nevertheless, they are interesting as they reflect those of the Galvani and Forrester survey. In addition to the areas already identified, respondents to the training needs analysis also noted:

- values and attitudes;
- awareness raising, and the role of practitioners in reducing harm;
- understanding the wider context of alcohol and drug misuse;
- skills in recognising the impact of alcohol and drugs on child safeguarding and protection;
- understanding the principles of a person-centered approach to provide a recovery focus to interventions;
- skills in reduction of harm;
- ability to use critical thinking and reflective practice. (STRADA, 2005)

In the new age of recovery embedding the principles of recovery in all relevant services will be vital. Service providers and professional bodies across all sectors both specialist and universal, will need to promote a culture of ambition and a belief in recovery. Work is already beginning on the development of a skills framework, which supports the recovery agenda (UK Strategy, 2010). The 'Models of Care' will be replaced by a more up-to-date evidence base, and a holistic and recovery-focussed model.

Nevertheless, those who work with drug and alcohol misusers will continue to need knowledge and understanding as a basis of skill development, which relates directly to why people use such substances and how they can be helped to change.

Early professional development

If we accept the premise, and indeed to some extent evidence, that qualifying training is not preparing social workers for their essential contribution to at least the early identification and support of individuals experiencing alcohol and drug problems, then how can this be remedied? The answer to that lies with EPD; and the responsibility for making this possible lies to some extent with employers. To return briefly to Galvani and

Forrester's survey, the data would suggest that those social workers working in health and adult mental health settings are better served in training and development than those who work in local authorities and with children and families (Galvani & Forrester, 2008, p 29).

The onus then is on EPD to make up what is not available in qualifying courses. It is unlikely that any of the new more generalist degree courses will ever encompass all that is required in specialist settings of any kind, such as domestic violence, mental health or criminal justice. Nor would such fragmentation be appropriate. EPD provides a basis on which to build. All qualifying courses, however, should provide basic information about alcohol and drug misuse. This basic information, according to Galvani & Forrester (2008, p 31), should include:

- the nature of alcohol and drugs and their effects
- models for understanding use and misuse
- key issues in talking to and assessing people in relation to alcohol and drug misuse.

If the building blocks are available then a curriculum of EPD can focus on key learning points identified by training needs analyses. In EPD, social workers will need specialist knowledge. To quote the former chief executive of the Federation of Drug and Alcohol Professionals, Simon Shepherd:

> There may be an aspiration that general social work training prepares you for dealing with people with substance misuse problems but it does not and cannot. Responding to someone with a crack problem requires knowledge and skills that go beyond general training.
>
> (CommunityCare.co.uk, August 2007)

Another important area of provision is that of 'training for trainers', which helps build the capacity within professions and organisations where essential knowledge and skill should be imparted. However, all this depends on the learning and development programmes being of good quality, and the role of evaluation is critical.

Outcome data indicate that with a comparatively small amount of improvement, social workers feel able to deal better with substance misuse in post-qualifying practice (Galvani & Forrester, 2008).

What works in learning and development in alcohol and drugs?

This is not an easy question to answer as robust, independent evaluations of learning and development courses are few and far between. A Europe-wide survey undertaken in 2006 for the International Think-Tank on Education and Training in Addiction (I-ThETA) found that 'evaluation is mostly done by providers' self-evaluation, and only exceptionally are the effects of education inputs researched.' (Uchtenhagen, 2006)[5].

Forrester (2009, p 119) posits the view that working with families affected by parental drug misuse 'is synonymous with effective work in general'. Among other recommendations for good effective general practice, Forrester identifies the importance of direct observation and feedback using motivational interviewing techniques to their best effect, commitment to evidence-based practice, the importance of reflection and high-quality supervision. All of this is based on evidence that it would work, if it were put into practice. While these are broad areas of effective practice, they resonate particularly in work with alcohol and drug problems.

The following areas of learning and development are seen to have had an impact on practice:

- training and development that is designed in the light of research, of evidence of what works and of policy;
- a recognition of the different learning styles and behaviours of participants;
- relating theory to practice;
- designing of training and development on the basis of identified training needs. (Roche, 2001)

Knowledge of particular areas of practice, such as harm reduction, treatment models, motivational interviewing, brief interventions, drug and alcohol awareness, and the impact of parental problem substance use on parenting, all appear to have impact on more effective practice. Other areas, such as the ability to reflect on attitudes and values, critical appraisal of interventions and practice and service user engagement, are noted as effective (STRADA Evaluation Report, 2008).

Thus, an evidence-based curriculum for EPD for social workers is available in outline. It should be an amalgamation of the learning priorities already identified in this chapter with the practice of critical reflection and self-evaluation from a wider perspective, as well as specialised work on alcohol and drugs.

Examples of innovative early professional development

Of the following examples of innovative practice, two are web-based.

The first is the website 'Social Work, Alcohol and Drugs'[6] set up by Sarah Galvani when she was based at the University of Birmingham. If one takes the view that knowledge can be culled from books and the internet, this is an extremely useful site. Its objective is 'to provide social workers with accessible information on substance use that is geared towards the social work profession, its roles, values and responsibilities'[7].

In Scotland 'The Learning Exchange'[8], provided by the Institute for Research and Innovation in Social Services, is a digital library of learning resources for social services and social work education and training. The reviews include information sheets, official publications, interactive learning resources, video clips, case studies and radio broadcasts, all of which may be used for education purposes. STRADA provides the specialist collection on alcohol and drug resources for this site.

EPD requires a curriculum of both knowledge and skills. Research evidence would indicate that the use of motivational interviewing and brief interventions can be effective in supporting behaviour change (Miller, et al., 2002). Life story book work with both adults and children, particularly those affected by inter-generational drug and alcohol use, can also be effective. It is important to intervene at the appropriate 'tipping point' in working with both adults and young people on issues of substance misuse. Thus, early intervention and prevention are important areas for development. Mentoring, particularly with children and young people seems to be efficacious (Horwath, 2005). The development of attachment by changing parents' working models through increasing insight and reflective capacity should be part of training and development courses on substance misuse and its impact on child neglect (Daniel et al., 1999). Multi-systemic family therapy techniques and courses which help practitioners increase children's sense of achievement and self-worth are all recognised as effective approaches.

Courses that centre upon practitioners' attitudes and values are reported as vital for greater understanding and empathy.

> if you don't have a lot of knowledge about alcohol and drugs and the effects they have, then how can you really make an informed decision ... but that's maybe when these types of multi-agency training help because you get to challenge your attitudes and get more knowledge.
>
> (STRADA Scottish Government Report 2008)

Barriers to good practice and how they might be overcome by early professional development

A lack of training
We have already established that this may be a significant inhibitor towards more effective practice. Recognising that adult learners have a responsibility for their own learning, it is incumbent upon individuals to seek out the training at the level they require it. It also is incumbent on managers to have a continuing understanding of staff training needs and of learning and development opportunities. Supervision and support are critical in the identification and sourcing of appropriate quality training. Learning and development providers also have a responsibility to indicate, for example, specific learning outcomes, for whom the training is appropriate, at what level and to what end.

A lack of knowledge
This will also be an inhibiting factor. Knowledge can be gained from specialist websites

and literature. Drug and Alcohol Findings is an excellent resource[9], along with other resources mentioned in this chapter. Attitudes will also affect practice and as has already been noted, social work values and attitudes must apply when working with alcohol and drug misusers, their families and carers.

A lack of confidence

A lack of confidence in applying information is also a barrier to effective practice. Tim Leighton stresses the importance of confidence, because it is important to evaluate when people need intervention, 'not to meddle if it's not necessary' (FEAD: Film Exchange – Alcohol and Drugs)[10]. The ability of social workers, to listen and assess the need for intervention confidently, and to communicate with others who can contribute to those tasks, are all important.

A lack of partnership working

This can also affect practice. The evaluation of STRADA courses (Barlow, 2009) shows the effectiveness of multi-agency training and the ability to know who to call and when. In multi-agency training, an ability to examine and sometimes contest the roles and responsibility of partners, is developed.

A lack of management ownership for the transfer of training to the workplace

This is an area that might warrant a chapter on its own. Suffice it to say here that managers must recognise their responsibility in promoting the transfer of knowledge to workplace practice. This involves taking an active interest in staffs' careers, providing opportunities to improve and extend their abilities, especially by using day-to-day work tasks, and above all encouraging them to continue learning (Barlow 2009).

Key questions

Knowledge and skills about drugs and alcohol may not find room in qualifying courses for the development described in this chapter as necessary for adequate professional practice. It may be concluded therefore that such training must take place after qualifying and during EPD. A number of key questions to practitioners follow from this:

- What is the knowledge and skills base you already have in working in the area of substance misuse? How has your general undergraduate training contributed to these?
- Where are you able to find access to the knowledge and skills you need to develop?

- How able are you to use supervision effectively to (a) evaluate your current practice with regard to substance misuse and (b) assess your future training and development needs?
- Are you able to assess the nature of the relationship with service users on issues of substance misuse? Can you reflect on your attributes, values and principles of practice in your daily work?
- How will your practice change on the basis of the new recovery focus; can you find appropriate support for this change?

Notes

1   www.fead.org.uk (accessed 26 May 2010)
2   www.fead.org.uk (accessed 26 May 2010)
3   www.swalcdrugs.com (accessed 26 May 2010)
4   www.swalcdrugs.com (accessed 26 May 2010)
5   www.i-theta.org/fileadmin/pdf/reports/summary_countryreports_-_A.Uchtenhagen.pdf (accessed 24 June 2009)
6   www.swalcdrugs.com (accessed 26 May 2010)
7   www.swalcdrugs.com (accessed 26 May 2010)
8   www.iriss.org.uk/learnx (accessed 27 May 2010)
9   www.findings.org.uk (accessed May 27 2010)
10 www.fead.org.uk (accessed 27 May 2010)

References

ACMD (Advisory Council on the Misuse of Drugs) (2003) *Hidden Harm: Responding to the Needs of the Children of Problem Drug Users* London: Home Office.

Barnard, M A (2007) *Drug Addiction and Families* London: Jessica Kingsley Publishers.

Barlow, J (2009) 'Messages for the Workforce' in Barlow, J (ed) *Substance Misuse: The Implications of Research Policy and Practice*, Research Highlights 53, London: Jessica Kingsley Publishers.

Barnard, M and Barlow, J (2003) 'Discovering parental drug dependence: Silence and disclosure' *Children and Society* 17(1), pp 45-56.

Cleaver, H, Unell, I and Algate, J (1999) *Children's Needs – Parenting Capacity: The Impact of Parental Mental Illness, Problem Alcohol and Drug Use and Domestic Violence on Children's Development* London: The Stationery Office.

Daddow, R and Broome, S (2010) *Whole Person Recovery: A User-centred Systems Approach to Problem Drug Use* Royal Society of Arts.

Daniel, B, Wassell, S and Gilligan, R (1999) *Child Development for Child Care and Protection Workers* London: Jessica Kinsley Publishers.

Forrester, D (2009) 'Hidden Harm: What practical drug misuse does to children' in Barlow, J (ed) *Substance Misuse: The Implications of Research Policy and Practice*, Research Highlights 53, London: Jessica Kingsley Publishers.

Galvani, S (2007) 'Refusing to listen: are we failing the needs of people with alcohol and drug problems?' *Social Work Education* 27(7) pp 697-707.

Galvani, S and Forrester, D (2008) *What works in training social workers about drug and alcohol use?*, A survey of student learning and readiness to practice, London: Home Office.

Harrison, L (1992) 'Substance Misuse and Social Work qualifying training in the British Isles: a survey of CQSW courses' *British Journal of Addiction* 87, pp 635-42.

Harwin, J, Madge, N, and Heath, S (2009) *Children Affected by Parental Alcohol Problems (ChAPAPs). A report on research, policy, practice and service development in relation to ChAPAPs across Europe* Brunel University.

HM Government (2010) *Reducing Demand, Restricting Supply, Building Recovery: Supporting People to Live a Drug-free Life* (The Drug Strategy 2010), London: Home Office.

Horwath, J (2005) 'Is this Child Neglect? The influence of differenced in perceptions of child neglect on social work practice' in Taylor, J and Daniel, B (eds) *Child Neglect Practice Issues for Health and Social Care* London and Philadelphia, PA: Jessica Kingsley Publishers, pp 73-96.

Lader, D and Goddard, E (2006) *Drinking Adults' Behaviour and Knowledge*, Survey Report No. 31, London: Drugs Omnibus.

Law, J (2009) 'Is alcohol different? Alcohol: Attitudes, beliefs and practice' in Barlow, J (ed) *Substance Misuse: The Implications of Research, Policy and Practice – Research Highlights 53* London: Jessica Kingsley Publishers

Lloyd, C (2009) 'How we got to where we are' in Barlow, J (ed) *Substance Misuse: The Implications of Research Policy and Practice*, Research Highlights 53, London: Jessica Kingsley Publishers.

McKie, L, Black, M, Bryce A (2009) 'Second Chance Learning: a community development approach to smoking cessation' in Barlow, J (ed) *Substance Misuse: The Implications of Research Policy and Practice*, Research Highlights 53, London: Jessica Kingsley Publishers.

Manning, V and Best, D (2009) *Supporting the Supporters: Families of drug misusers* London: UKDPC (United Kingdom Drug Policy Commission).

Miller, R, Rollnick, S (2002) *Motivational Interviewing: Preparing People for Change* New York: The Guilford Press.

NTA (National Treatment Agency) (2006) *Models of Care for Treatment of Adult Drug Misusers*, Update 2006, London: NTA.

Roche, A (2001) 'What is this thing called workforce development?' in Roche, A M and McDonald, J (eds) *Systems, settings People* Adelaide: National Centre for Education and Training in Addiction (NCTEA), Flinders University of South Australia.

Royal Society of Arts (2007) *Drugs: Facing Facts*, the report of the RSA Commission on Illegal Drugs and Public Policy, London: RSA.

Scottish Government (2008) *The Road to Recovery: A New Approach to Tackling Scotland's Drug Problem* Edinburgh: Scottish Government.

Scottish Government (2010) *Getting it Right for Every Child* Edinburgh: Scottish Government.

SSSC (Scottish Social Services Council) (2009) *Codes of Practice for Social Services Workers and Employers* Dundee: SSSC.

Skills for Health (2003): *Drugs and Alcohol National Occupational Standards (DANOS) Guide* Bristol: Skills for Health.

Tunnard, J (2002) 'Parental Drug Misuse: a review of impact and intervention studies' Research in Practice (www.rip.org.uk, accessed 5 October 2010).

STRADA (Scottish Training on Drugs and Alcohol) (2005) 'Dumfries & Galloway Alcohol and Drug Action Team Learning and Development Needs Analysis', unpublished.

STRADA (2008) 'Evaluation Report to Scottish Government', unpublished.

Uchtenhagen, A (2006) *Continued Education: A cross-national comparison.* I-ThETA (International Think Tank on Education and Training in Addictions) (www.i-theta.org/fileadmin/pdf/reports/summary -communityreports)

Uchtenhagen, A pdf accessed 20 Nov 2009.

United Nations Office on Drugs and Crime (2008) 'Reducing the adverse health and social consequences of Drug Abuse: A Comprehensive Approach', available at www.unodc.org/documents/prevention/Reducing-adverse-consequences-drug-abuse.pdf (accessed 5 October 2010).

Velleman, R and Orford, J (1999) *Risk and Resilience: Adults who were the children of problem drinkers* Newark, NJ: Harwood Academic Publishers.

Watkins, A *et al* (2009) 'Implementation and Evaluation of an Inter-professional Learning Programme for Inter-agency Child Protection Teams' *Child Abuse Review* 18, pp 151-67.

WAG (Welsh Assembly Government) (2008) *Working together to reduce harm* (The Substance Misuse Strategy for Wales 2008-2010), Cardiff: WAG.

White, W (2005) *Materials from Recovery Symposium* Philadelphia PA, May 2.

White, W (2008) *Recovery management and recovery – Oriented systems of care: Scientific rationale and promising practices* Pittsburgh, PA: Northeast Addiction Technology Transfer Centre, Great Lakes Addiction Technology Transfer Centre, Philadelphia Department of Behavioural Health and Mental Retardation Services.

Chapter 18

Social work and the Use of Technology in Social Care

Andrew Eccles

Technology is set to play an increasingly important role across a range of social care activity. There are a number of reasons for this, among which are the increasing sophistication of the technology itself, the potentially liberating effects it might serve for people who use care services and the cost savings that the use of this technology might engender. This raises a number of questions for social work practice. Some of these questions are generated by the new ways of delivering services occasioned by the technological possibilities, but some are raised by other shifts – for example shared assessments across professions – that are occurring in tandem.

This chapter concentrates on particular kinds of equipment that aid daily living under the broad rubric of *assistive technologies* and offers some critical reflection on their introduction. Much has been written on the benefits for social care service users conferred from technology (Fisk, 2003; McCreadie & Tinker, 2005; Poser and Mols, 2009) and the chapter starts with some exploration of these. But it is also concerned with what Mort, *et al.* (2009, p 85) note as a need to address an 'ethical and democratic deficit in this field which has arisen due to a proliferation in research and development of advanced care technologies that has not been accompanied by sufficient consideration of their social context'. To this end, the chapter explores a theme that has resonance across social work practice more generally; that is, how social workers adapt to fast-changing environments and reflect on what these changes might mean for the social work values they hold. More specifically on the topic of the use of technology, four areas of particular interest to social workers will be developed and discussed here. The first is the policy context in which these technologies are being developed and implemented. Second is the ethical dimension to the use of technology, the awareness of which should be at the heart of social work practice. The third area concerns the idea of care in relation to technological intervention in the delivery of services, especially when this results in the absence of human contact with carers. The fourth issue explores the idea of the 'virtuous' social worker and the implications for good practice that arise from interprofessional working and assessment involving the use of technology. Existing arguments about the consistency of assessment across professions (Eccles, 2008) are given added impetus here, as there may be significantly different approaches to technology, or understanding of its ethical implications, across different disciplines, which may be played out in practice settings.

The chapter starts by looking at the use of assistive technologies in settings relevant to social work, before turning attention to the user group most likely to be recipients of assistive technologies, that is, older people, framing the discussion here in the wider policy context around demographic change and service provision. It should perhaps be emphasised again at this point that this chapter does not take issue with the use *per se* of innovative technology in social care settings; technologies can offer additional security, liberation in mobility and greater connectivity that would not otherwise be possible and their availability is a cause for some celebration, not least for carers. The chapter does, however, offer areas for critical reflection (surely an essential aspect of social work practice) and will hopefully stimulate discussion points for readers around what might be an appropriate use of technology in social care settings.

Technologies and their use

Assistive technologies have moved rapidly from 'first generation' detectors and basic sensors to their current use in lifestyle monitoring, surveillance and the development of smart houses. Greater access in people's homes to broadband – sometimes as a direct result of public funding – and a new generation of mobile-based technology is now moving apace. Applications of technology in social work settings are becoming clearer. People with physical disabilities can find technologies that aid mobility, further independence and release them from the routines of relying on care workers. In criminal justice settings, offenders can be 'tagged' and subject to surveillance and monitoring of movement as an alternative to incarceration. Older people who might otherwise be in residential care settings can remain longer in their own homes or, where actually in residential care, have greater freedom of movement. Much of this technology is essentially passive, in the sense that it is activated only when there is deviation from usual patterns of movement or behaviour. Such that there are deviations in behaviour, or when sensors are activated, simple technology can also herald a quick solution; a telephone call to establish that service users are safe and well might suffice. These uses for technology have been well documented and subject to critical reflection (McCreadie and Tinker, 2005; Loader *et al.*, 2009).

Policy objectives in this field are ambitious and reflect the rate of change possible in technological domains. At the forefront of policy – in terms of service user coverage and budgetary investment – is the use of telecare technology for the delivery of social care, and telemedicine technology for the delivery of healthcare. For example, the telecare development programme of the Scottish Government proposes that by 2015:

> *all new homes, public and private, and all refurbished social housing, will be fitted with the capacity for care and health services to be provided interactively via broadband from day one of occupation; telehealth will be widely recognised by service users and their carers as the route to greater*

*independence and quality of life; independent evaluation will confirm that
no care service users in Scotland who could benefit from telecare services
in a home-based setting remain in an institutional environment; remote long
term condition monitoring undertaken from home will be the norm.*

(Scottish Government, 2008, p 6)

Similar objectives exist for other parts of the United Kingdom (UK) and telecare policy has been the recipient of dedicated funding. Clearly, significant change in the way that social care is viewed and delivered is under way. How this change is enacted in a social care world will become a key issue especially as organisational and cultural shifts are likely to operate on timescales longer than technological innovation materialises. Some implications for areas such as criminal justice are discussed in Chapter 20 by Mike Nellis. The focus of this chapter now turns to the major user group of assistive technologies; that is, older people in community care settings. In doing so it addresses the four issues laid out at the start: the policy context, ethical considerations, the meaning of care, and the complexities of interprofessional working.

The policy context

While clearly there are powerfully liberating aspects underpinning the use of technology with older people, discussions on its application are likely also to centre on demographics. Technology providers talk openly of an approaching 'demographic timebomb' (Tunstall, 2009, p 3) where the social and healthcare needs of increasing numbers of very old people will outstrip the resources they require. Similarly, commissioners of technology are apt to talk of the unsustainability of current patterns of care delivery, to the extent that a discourse based on the *necessity* of technological solutions for future service delivery easily emerges. The headline figures are clear; there will indeed be an increasing number of people over the age of 65 as a proportion of the population in years to come. The rate of change in this ratio is unusually rapid, and the age group most likely to be particularly in need of services – people aged 85 and over – is set to increase disproportionately even in this overall shift. Concomitant to this is a relative decline in people of working age, giving rise to an increase in the (perhaps unfortunately constructed notion of) 'dependency ratio' between those who are, at least nominally, economically active and those who are not.

However, this scenario requires all manner of caveats. An understanding of the likely needs of this ageing population is contestable; compressed morbidity – where debilitating illness is confined to shorter periods in the lifespan – may also be a feature of this changing population in future. Equally, future medical advances may mitigate conditions that are currently debilitating or require care services. The evidence around needs in this population change is complex; for example, older people's own assessment of their health needs is consistently more optimistic than that of the medical profession

(Bowling & Dieppe, 2005), while the whole territory of the social construction of old age and the perceived limitations of older people (Townsend, 1981, 2006) presents itself at the centre of these arguments. Tinker (1997) notes this in her discussion of the 'dependency ratio' at different junctures and cautions against over-reaction as indeed did Walker (1993) when he noted the potential for a loss of due consideration around the needs of older people as demographic changes took place. None of this is noted here in a way that underestimates the scale of demographic change. What is important though is that these changes should not be a precursor to technology being used deterministically as a solution to a *perceived* problem based on current patterns of service provision. Perhaps an equally radical paradigm shift – such as a reframing of social obligations to care, or innovative ways of communal living – might reasonably be part of a wider discourse on how society adapts to these challenges. To have an explicit policy objective that 'Telecare services grow as quickly as possible' (Scottish Government, 2008) is perhaps an indicator that technology solutions have become something of an article of faith, and takes us into the territory of wider ethical considerations around the use of telecare.

Ethical issues around the use of technology in social care

The ethical angle is notable mostly by its absence in discussions around the increased use of technology. In social work practice there are codes and guidelines around ethical procedure, although the codes themselves are wide open to interpretation. There may be several reasons for this. Ethics can be a complex topic, not easily approachable or assimilated. A practice world that has been shaped by managerialism and performance indicators (Kirkpatrick *et al.*, 2004; Miller, 2005) may baulk at the uncertainty and imprecision that ethical questions throw up; indeed, in relation to telecare itself, these indicators may encourage less than optimal practice (Beale, 2009). But that does not mean the ethical questions will go away, or that they should not remain, for social workers, central to consideration of the use of assistive technologies. This is not straightforward. Technological solutions clearly have utility and confer substantive benefits for service. But they are perhaps also rather seductive as a way of dealing with complex social changes and their attendant financial implications. It is in the framing of the balance between benefit and risk that social workers and other professionals engaged in the use of technology need to ask questions – some perhaps quite unfamiliar.

The ethical frameworks currently employed by the various agencies engaged in the provision of telecare are for the most part limited in scope. This reflects the practical reality that ethical frameworks have to be understood by practitioners and their terminology has to resonate with the care assessment process. The key framework in wide use is essentially biomedical, with four principles: autonomy, beneficence, non-maleficence and justice (Beauchamp & Childress, 2001). These are powerful and important concepts. They are also limited in their scope, historically shaped, and unevenly relevant across different cultural settings. Moreover, much of the discussion in biomedical ethics centres on hospital treatment, invasive procedures and end-of-life decision-making, which are not features that register prominently in considerations around social care. Even then, within the context of telecare, these concepts are differently interpreted across different agencies.

The 'primacy of autonomy' (Wilmot, 1997) in community care policy sits at the heart of much of the telecare agenda. This importance placed on individual independence may in turn underplay the significance of the interdependence of human affairs, and unpacking arguments around autonomy in any development in community care is rarely straightforward. While the objective of reductions in care home admissions in the telecare agenda may be laudable, a cursory look at the history of the development of community care in United Kingdom over the past twenty years (Malin et al., 2002; Means et al., 2008) suggests that a primary driver in the move from institutional care to 'care in the community' has been fiscal. The ASTRID framework (Frisby, 2000), drafted primarily for dementia care, notes that this autonomy, in its guise of greater independence, might bring with it isolation among service users – what Wilmot (1997) notes as 'unwanted autonomy'. The picture here is complex. There is clear evidence that the use of technology, not least communication technology and virtual communities, can alleviate isolation among older people (Blaschke et al., 2009), but there is also the potential for telecare technology to increase isolation which may manifest itself as an increased risk of depression (Lowe, 2009). Thus, one factor in any method of calculating cost savings through the use of technology might want to include potential attendant costs for healthcare if depression were to increase. An additional consideration here would be the quality of care that any such depression might attract; that any such increase in isolation through depression would be detected, and if detected, adequately dealt within the healthcare system. Current telecare policy recognises this potential for isolation in the development of a system of 'befrienders' to provide human contact, to be developed in tandem as the use of telecare increases. But this is an area that is adversely affected by the fiscal pressures in local care services and the voluntary sector.

Autonomy has a central place in discussions around community care but takes on quite different meanings for different groups of people. In a Confucian tradition, the full worth of being autonomous is only recognised in relation to a more complex array of interdependence and reciprocities with others, akin to the sentiments expressed in an ethic of care, an approach that will be developed below (see Tao and Drover, 1997, for an interesting discussion on this point). To what extent is there space in the consideration of assistive technology for its culturally sensitive application, given that the biomedical four principles that underpin the ethical framework in common use might not carry similar currency across cultural settings? More evidence on how these assessment decisions – balancing care, risk and potential harm – are in fact calculated is needed; all are invariably actions grounded in complex social situations. Two further questions emerge here. Is a biomedical ethical framework adequate for the needs of different telecare user groups and are assessors sensitive enough (for example in assessing risk) in its interpretation? If the policy objective remains a 'rapid expansion' in the use of telecare, but particular constituencies (across age groups or geographical location) have different attitudes to its use, how is sensitivity to this to be realised, particularly when performance targets may be grouped around technology-based budget spend? As Hanson *et al.* (2009, p 111) note in their study of the impact of sensor-based technology: 'In order to make "sense of sensors" alongside the data provided by the devices, one needs rich contextual information that is normally accumulated through social interactions between caregivers and care receivers, a two-way communication process that can best be described as a "dialogue of care".

A further principle derived from the biomedical tradition (Beauchamp and Childress, 2001) centres on justice. In a clinical setting this might involve two patients receiving the same treatment for the same condition (although this decision would likely be tempered by quality-of-life years and perhaps also patient lifestyles). In the wider social context there exists a parallel policy agenda committed to the pursuit of social justice. In this case there may be a sound argument for unequal treatment to address social inequality (for example free installation and access to broadband for particular socio-economic groups). Be that as it may, there are interesting aspects to any discussion of social justice and technology arising through the fast-moving telecare agenda. Key elements of second-generation telecare (monitoring the movement of people in their own homes, for example, prior to deciding on care packages) require at least a telephone landline, while broadband access would offer a clear advantage to allow families of Telecare users to become engaged in this process of monitoring. The trends in some of the UK's socially disadvantaged households is otherwise. However, the cost of telephone landline installation and service has given way to cheaper alternatives such as 'pay as you go' mobiles telephones, the use of which will be self-limiting through cost. This prospect of a digital divide in society has been rehearsed more generally (Steyaert & Gould, 2009); here the specifics need attention, as the ability to access and indeed then use technology with confidence underpins the future of telecare development.

While it is older people who are the main recipients of current telecare policy, telecare itself, as noted earlier, has application across a range of groups of people. It may have a particularly liberating application for people with physical disability, where the argument has been made that traditional care relationships based on human contact may potentially be demeaning (see Phillips, 2007, for a discussion).

Here, the implications of increased autonomy might take on a very different complexion between different recipients of technology (as, indeed, assistive technologies might be viewed in various ways among older people themselves). The point here is that, to date, the ethical framework predominantly being used serves an important but limited function and is open to different interpretations even in their status of guidelines. That it remains essentially a biomedical framework in application to situations of social care prompts the need for other sources of ethical enquiry. It is not suggested that the already complex task of making care decisions should be subject to a further accretion of ethical principles or approaches in dealings directly with telecare; nonetheless, there are ethical approaches grounded in a social care tradition that offer a broader ethical awareness for policy making which involves the use of new technologies.

Technology and human care

This section briefly explores other ethical approaches that may be worth consideration in relation to the use of assistive technologies and links these to wider considerations of what we mean by care in different contexts. These approaches are likely to be more familiar to social workers. While the ethical principles discussed above ideally ought not to be employed in a 'checklist' approach (although such approaches are perhaps more likely in the increasingly managerial world that social work now inhabits), alternative lines of enquiry lend themselves even less to clear-cut application. But these complexities should not preclude proper reflection. A useful alternative approach comes from the tradition of an ethic of care (Gilligan, 1993; Noddings, 1984; Tronto, 1993). This approach does not tend to feature in the frameworks routinely employed by telecare partnerships, and would not lend itself to straightforward use, despite its particular relevance to the field of community-based medicine and social care. Yet its application to the whole question of the use of technology as a *strategy* is certainly relevant. It is precisely in this field of community health and social care that interaction between professions and service users might exist in a relationship developed and sustained over a longer period than in acute medical settings that form the backdrop of the ethical principles that tend to be most in use. Barnes (2006) notes the way in which social care workers go beyond *tasks* to develop relationships over and above contractual obligations, taking the argument into the territory of an 'ethic of care' with its emphasis on relational approaches to care that are, above all, contextual and not necessarily uniform in their approach. This approach posits care as a *moral* activity based on a complex array of obligations and reciprocities. A simple example of this might be care workers going beyond contractual obligations – spending more time to ensure continuity in care recipients' lives, or making additional visits to particular clients with whom the care worker has developed a relationship perhaps over a number of years. This might on the surface raise issues of equity across service users, but some older people value independence highly and might regard being the recipient of care demeaning, a sign of a loss of faculty. Others might welcome human intervention, particularly if they have lost lifelong partners. This relational aspect to care may thus be played out quite differently in different settings. It may also prompt, adversely, a reluctance to engage with technology (on the part of care workers as well as service users) where the relations that have developed are particularly strong and may tend preclude full consideration of technological possibilities.

Equally, in this emphasis on the importance of relationships in social work practice we need to guard against assumptions that technologically based care is axiomatically inferior in the absence of human relationships. As Pols and Moser (2009, p 160) argue, 'In discussions about the use of new technologies in health care, including the most recent versions appearing as "telecare", there is the fear that cold technologies will be implemented at the cost of warm human care'. However, they conclude from their research that 'the opposition between cold technology and warm care does not hold, but that there are different relations between people and technologies within different use practices allowing different affective and social relations' (2009, p 159). So, again, it is the *specific context* here in which decisions are made that is crucial. In a practice world of performance measurement and the need for greater efficiency, is there space for proper contextual consideration? Equally, if service users do *not* want to use technology as an alternative to human-based care services, can this choice be upheld? As households are increasingly being equipped with connectivity as part of government strategy on the future use of telecare, would it be reasonable (and part of an agenda based on choice) for their occupants to allow its potential in health and care provision to be ignored?

Another aspect of the remote delivery of care, through monitoring and surveillance, centres on the qualitative difference to ethical judgements that might arise from the remote monitoring that accompanies the use of some telecare technologies. Intuitionism (Driver, 2007) opens up lines for reflection here. Intuitive responses to right and wrong courses of action in the face of immediate human dilemmas are less likely to be played out when the ethical dilemmas are more abstracted. Intuitionism in itself does not provide an adequately complete ethical framework, nor line of enquiry, but might usefully be employed in wider considerations about the use of technology. Are the care needs of service users who are monitored remotely perceived in the same way as they would be if there was human contact, and will decisions over a course of action be different when the immediacy of care needs is filtered through a process of remote monitoring? There is research that addresses these qualitative differences in the field of telemedicine (Finch *et al.*, 2008), which suggests that physical human engagement involves sensitivity to user conditions that technology may not pick up remotely. Might this approach also facilitate easier decision-making in the resource-limited context of social care for older people and will the contingent resources that may be needed to act on the outcomes of telecare monitoring sufficiently be in place? If the care workforce is reduced with the use of technological-based substitutes, will numbers still be sufficient to address contingencies thrown up by the need to have remote care supplemented by actual physical intervention in the wake of demand?

Of course, if significant expenditure can be saved as a result of employing assistive technology and these savings are then redirected to enhance levels of care or service delivery that are more targeted to those in most need, a strong argument can be made for remote care. This would need to be balanced against questions of equal importance to social work, for example dignity and respect. Care services based on human care delivery are also rationed and not all needs can be satisfied. Even so, the question remains: does the remoteness of the decision-making process make a difference to how care needs can be triaged or perceived? We could make a contrary argument here too. That care workers in regular contact with service users might 'go the extra mile' for particular clients might be laudable but might also impinge on a just allocation of time across all service users. Perhaps the remote monitoring of service users through the use of technology leads to a detached decision-making process over who ought to be prioritised in the event that human intervention is required, which is more *just* than the uneven allocation of time expended, for example, by care workers. But the human approach might not be unjust, as such, but essentially contextual; if clients are perceived to need extra time on occasion this may be an intuitive reaction that might not, in itself, disadvantage others. Indeed, we can extend this argument, perhaps particularly with reference to older people; the generational reticence to be 'a bother' to others may mean that health or social needs go undetected (this was touched upon in the previous discussion about isolation). Noticing that something is amiss with an older person may require a human take on a situation that would escape monitoring or self-reporting facilitated by the use of technology.

The virtuous social worker in social work practice

These different issues which emerge from reflection about an increased use of technology in the field of social care – advantages, weaknesses, questions for the meaning of care and relationships in the care process – should ideally be part of a social worker's awareness in engaging with a world of increased technological possibilities. But such is the complexity (and newness for application) of factors – risk, protection, empowerment – that attend the use of technology that frameworks of ethical practice in themselves may be of limited use and that the virtues associated with being a social worker may have to come to the fore (see Banks & Gallagher, 2009, for a stimulating discussion on the issue). This approach would marry awareness of ethical codes and frameworks (which, in practice, are variously interpreted and variously employed) to the essential *virtuousness* of practitioners that would come by dint not only of professional training but also, hopefully, of vocation. Thus, the difficulties of interpreting contexts for the use of technology might be less problematic in the presence of the virtuous practitioner, who will be more likely to take the morally sound course of action. This might prove more difficult when it comes to assistive technology, however, unless there is a highly developed common understanding of what might constitute a 'virtuous' approach in relation to care in an increasingly technological world.

The inter-professional context

The increasingly fluid world of assessing care needs across professional boundaries (where there may be different ethical codes – or at least understanding of these codes

– in play) may mean that recourse to virtue *per se* by dint of professional training or vocational calling is open to query. There is now a substantial body of literature that discusses the greater incidence of inter-professional working that has been a hallmark of health and social care policy over the past decade (Clarke & Glendinning, 2002; Leathard, 2003; Petch, 2008) with a more recent literature looking at the frontline practice of interprofessional working where shared assessment tools are in use (Eccles, 2008). The latter research has noted inconsistencies in, for example, understanding of consent issues and in obtaining agreement from service users, but the thrust of recent policy has been to assume that common data sets are sufficiently straightforward to collect, such that inconsistencies across professional disciplines will be minimal. The interest here then is in the consistency of assessment that recommends the use of assistive technology. Professional attitudes to care, ethical frameworks and the use of these frameworks, and vested interests in the status quo, all suggest inconsistency of approaches to the use of technology. This is not, in itself, surprising; the impact of professional domains has long been recognised (Daley, 1991). How assessments are made and how older people have their care managed in the context of the use of technology across these different domains would merit further enquiry. Decision-making may well be virtuous, but consistency of understanding of what constitutes virtue is open to question, as is how virtuous decision-making can be, not only across professions, but also in the wider context of a culture of different performance indicators across these professions. Decisions on the appropriateness of technology may embrace discussion across professionals from social work, housing, health as well as technology. Within social work there may be debates about what care means in the context of telecare technologies – for instance, is it a reconfiguration of relationships between social workers and service users or an empowerment of service users through the possibilities for greater independence? Are care relationships viewed differently across different professions, such that assessments for the use of technology are inconsistent – and does this matter? If it does matter, then the task of social workers is to have their voice heard in the process; a voice that is anchored in a particular value base and ethical awareness.

Conclusions

The foregoing discussion leaves us with some questions that might be asked of social work as it engages with technology in its various practice settings:

- Are the ethical frameworks in use sensitive enough to embrace a contextual appreciation of a service user's situation?
- Are these frameworks understood and employed across different professions which may be engaged in assessing for the use of technology?
- Assuming that local ownership of policy is important for successful

implementation, do the policy drivers and outcome measures allow local telecare partnerships autonomy and flexibility?

- Is this technology able to contribute to outcomes that are compatible with social justice?

Finally, consideration is necessary about alternatives in the policy discourse, in that the challenges of demographic change may serve as a basis for paradigm shifting ways in which to reconfigure what care and caring relationships might look like in the twenty first century. For all the clear benefits of an increased use of technology, there needs to be reflection and debate by social workers on how it can best be used with service users, especially in what is likely to be a coming period of fiscal restraint.

Note

This is a revised version of an article by the author, 'Ethical considerations around the use of assistive technologies', which first appeared in the *Journal of Technology in Human Services*, 28 (2010), pp 44-59.

References

Banks, S and Gallagher, A (2009) *Ethics in professional life: Virtues for health and social care* Basingstoke: Palgrave Macmillan.

Barnes, M (2006) *Caring and social justice* Basingstoke: Palgrave MacMillan.

Beale, S (2009) 'Evaluation of the Scottish government's telecare programme', Paper presented at the Human Services in the Network Society: Changes, Challenges and Opportunities, Institute of Advanced Studies, University of Strathclyde, UK, September 2009.

Beauchamp, L and Childress, A F (2001) *Principles of Biomedical Ethics* (5th edition), Oxford: Oxford University Press.

Blaschke, C, Freddolino, P and Mullen, E (2009) 'Ageing and technology: A review of the research literature' *British Journal of Social Work* 39(4), pp 641-56.

Bowling, A and Dieppe, P (2005) 'What is successful aging and who should define it?' *British Medical Journal* 331, pp 1548-51.

Clarke, J and Glendinning, C (2002) 'Partnership and the Remaking of Welfare Governance' in Glendinning, C, Powell, M and Rummery, K (eds) *Partnerships, New Labour and the Governance of Welfare* Bristol: The Policy Press.

Dalley, G (1991) 'Beliefs and behaviour: Professionals and the policy process' *Journal of Aging Studies* 5(2), pp 163-180.

Driver, J (2007) *Ethics: The Fundamentals* Oxford: Blackwell.

Eccles, A (2008) 'Singe shared assessment: The limits to "quick fix" implementation' *Journal of Integrated Care* 16(1), pp 22-30.

Finch, T, Mort, M, Mair, F S and May, C (2008) 'Future patients? Telehealthcare, roles and responsibilities' *Health and Social Care in the Community* 2008 16(1), pp 86-95 (www.guardian.co.uk/commentisfree/2009/dec/22/loneliness-at-christmas-public-services).

Fisk, M (2003) *Social Alarms to Telecare* Bristol: The Policy Press

Frisby, B (2000) *ASTRID: A guide to using technology in dementia care* London: Hawker.

Gilligan, C (1993) *In a Different Voice* Cambridge MA: Harvard University Press

Kirkpatrick, I, Ackroyd, S and Walker, R (2004) *The new managerialism and public service professions* Basingstoke: Palgrave.

Leathard, A (ed.) (2003) *Interprofessional Collaboration* Hove: Brunner-Routledge.

Loader, B, Hardey, M and Keeble, L (eds) (2009) *Digital welfare for the third age* London: Routledge.

Lowe, C (2009) 'Beyond telecare: The future of independent living' *Journal of Assistive Technologies* 3(1), pp 21-3.

McCreadie, C and Tinker, A (2005) 'The acceptability of assistive technology to older people' *Ageing and Society* 25, pp 91-110.

Malin, N, Wilmot, S and Manthorpe, J (2002) *Key Concepts and Debates in Health and Social Policy* Maidenhead: Open University Press.

Means, R, Richards, S and Smith, R (2008) *Community care* (4th edition), Basingstoke: Palgrave.

Miller, D (2005) 'What is Best Value? Bureaucracy, Virtualism and Local Governance' in Du Gay, P (ed) *The Values of Bureaucracy* Oxford: Oxford University Press.

Mort, M, Roberts, C and Milligan, C (2009) 'Ageing, technology and the home: A critical project' *European Journal of Disability Research* 3, pp 85-9.

Noddings, N (1984) *Caring: A feminine approach to ethics and moral education* Berkeley, CA: University of California Press.

Petch, A (2008). *Health and social care: Establishing a joint future?* Edinburgh: Dunedin.

Phillips, J (2007) *Care* Oxford: Polity.

Pols, J and Moser, I (2009) 'Cold technologies versus warm care? On affective and social relations with and through care technologies' *European Journal of Disability Research,* 3, pp 159-78.

Scottish Government (2008) *Telecare in Scotland: Benchmarking the present, embracing the future.* Edinburgh: Crown Copyright.

Steyaert, J and Gould, N (2009) 'Social work and the changing face of the digital divide' *British Journal of Social Work* 39(4), pp 740-53.

Tao, J and Drover, G (1997) 'Chinese and western notions of need' *Critical Social Policy* 17, pp 5-25.

Tinker, A (1997) *Older people in modern society* London: Longman.

Townsend, P (1981) 'The Structured Dependency of the Elderly: A Creation of *Social* Policy in the Twentieth Century' *Ageing and Society* 1, pp 5-28.

Tronto, J (1993) *Moral boundaries: A political argument for an ethic of care* London: Routledge.

Tunstall (2009) 'Support for carers: Solutions for independent living' www.tunstall.co.uk/assets/literature/carers%20guide.pdf, retrieved 2 February 2010)

Walker, A. (1993) *Age and Attitudes* Brussels: EC Commission.

Wilmot, S (1997) *The Ethics of Community Care* London: Cassell.

Part 4

Themes and Issues in Criminal Justice

Chapter 19

Changing Lives, Changing Work:
Social work and criminal justice

Fergus McNeill

Introduction

In Chapter 14, the personal and social significance of narratives of and about social work service users was discussed in some depth. Partly in response to that chapter, and partly prompted by two recent literature reviews commissioned by the Scottish Government (McNeill, 2009a; McNeill *et al.*, 2010b), this chapter tries in a provisional and tentative way to connect up two types of narratives that are highly important to social work in criminal justice systems – whether we call it forensic social work, probation work, offender management or community corrections (see McNeill *et al.*, 2010a). The first of these concerns the personal stories of once active 'offenders' who manage to desist from crime and move on constructively in their lives. Obviously this is the kind of developmental narrative that social work in criminal justice exists to support. But the second developmental narrative is, in some respects, just as important and just as neglected. This is the story of the changing character of criminal justice social work itself – focused specifically on the Scottish experience, but drawing on evidence from other jurisdictions within and beyond the United Kingdom (UK). In the conclusion, I try to draw some parallels between these two stories about changing identities and to consider the implications of each for the other.

Changing lives, changing 'offenders'[1]

How and why do people who have offended, and people who have been labelled as 'offenders', go about changing their lives? What can social workers – including newly qualified social workers – do to prompt, support and sustain such change? What kind of research evidence exists that can, in turn, support social workers in this task? These are the questions with which this first section of the chapter aims to engage.

Figure 19.1 presents the three necessary and sufficient pre-conditions for people to change, at least as argued in social casework theory over four decades ago (Ripple *et al.*, 1964). First, the person doing the changing needs to be motivated. Second, they need to have the capacity to change – meaning in this context the requisite set of skills. 'Human capital' is another term for these personal resources that inhere within individuals. But, third, people who want to change also need to have access to opportunities. The term 'social capital' refers to the resources that inhere within social networks and relationships. In terms of the practice of supervision, these three preconditions entail three roles or tasks for probation staff: they need to be counsellors who can develop and deploy motivation; they need to be educators who can develop and deploy human capital; and they also need to be advocates who develop and deploy social capital. Or at least, if they cannot be all of these things themselves, they need to be able to help the offender to access them. By way of illustration, think of the diagram as a cross-section of a rope. The rope will not be strong enough to pull the person towards change unless the strands are woven together. Someone needs to do the weaving and keep hold of the rope – especially when there is a strain in the process or an obstacle that the person needs to be pulled over (see McNeill *et al.*, 2005).

Figure 19.1: The preconditions for change

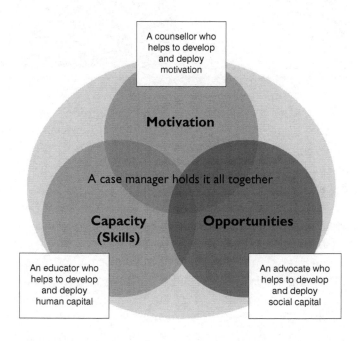

But before thinking further about these three preconditions and the roles they imply for social workers, it makes sense to think about the change process they exist to support; the process of desistance from offending. Figure 19.2 represents the criminal career of a very persistent offender. The person in question commits their first crime at the age of 8, the offending escalates during adolescence, it peaks at 18 and plateaus until 25 after which it tails off, eventually ending at age 30. The area under the curve represents the volume of offending for which this person is responsible. Obviously, there are only two ways that criminal justice interventions can, in theory, reduce this volume. They can push the curve towards the horizontal axis, thus reducing the volume of crimes committed in each year; or, they can push the curve towards the vertical axis, thus reducing the length of the criminal career. Better still, they can do both.

Figure 19.2: The criminal career of a very persistent offender

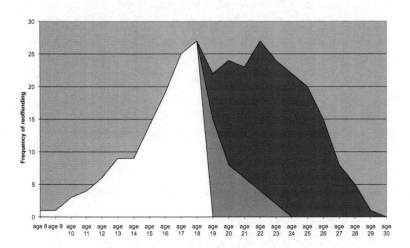

In an ideal world, the effect of a perfect social work intervention – and with it perfect public protection – is represented by the white area under the curve. The offender gets probation at age 18 and by age 19 his or her rate of offending has reduced to 0. In the real world however, protection through change looks more like the light grey area under the curve. The offender stays active until 25, but the volume of offending tails off much more rapidly than it would have without intervention – the volume of offending without any intervention is represented in the dark grey area under the curve. Even in this less perfect midway scenario, the dark grey area shows the significant volume of offending that can be produced by interventions that support change and slow down an offending career.

So, what do we know from those studies that have explored the ending of criminal careers, the process of desistance that we are trying to accelerate? In this chapter, only the briefest of summaries can be offered (see Maruna, 2001; Farrall and Calverley, 2006; McNeill, 2006; Weaver and McNeill, 2010). First of all, some have suggested that there is a difference between primary desistance, meaning a lull or crime-free gap in a criminal career, and secondary desistance, meaning a change in the way that an ex-offender seems him or herself (Maruna and Farrall, 2004). Essentially, secondary desistance is about ceasing to see yourself as an offender and finding a more positive identity; it is about successfully peeling off the criminal label that criminal justice systems are so effective at applying. Although not all researchers concur that this kind of reconstruction of identity is a necessary aspect of desistance (see Laub and Sampson, 2003; Bottoms *et al.*, 2004), it is at least more likely to be necessary for those whose offending has been persistent and who have deeply entrenched criminal identities, but not for those whose engagements with crime and justice have been more transitory. With respect to persistent offenders, it can be argued that secondary desistance should be the holy grail of probation services because secondary desistance is about the internalisation of change and the fundamental redirection of the ex-offender's life. As such it also represents the most secure basis of public protection because the ex-offender has changed in a lasting way, a way that will endure long after short-term controls and constraints have been removed.

Getting there, however, is very difficult. Taken together, the research suggests that the process of desistance, again focusing on those who have developed persistent offending patterns, is typically characterised by ambivalence and vacillation (Burnett, 1992, 2000, 2004). It is not an event, it is a process; a process of 'to-ing' and 'fro-ing', of progress and setback, of hope and despair.

Theories of desistance tend to focus on the significance of ageing, on related life events and social bonds, or on related narrative changes in the offender and their sense of self (Maruna, 2001). Most scholars now tend to stress the interplay between these three factors (Farrall and Bowling, 1999); it is not just getting older, getting married or getting a job, it is about what these kinds of developments mean and signify to offenders themselves and whether they represent compelling enough reasons for and opportunities to change the pattern of one's life.

Given the significance of these subjectivities, it is interesting, but perhaps not surprising, that hope plays a key part in these processes (Burnett and Maruna, 2004; Farrall and Calverley, 2006). Desistance can, it seems, be provoked by someone believing in the offender; someone who perhaps carries hope and keeps it alive when the offender cannot do so for themselves. Of course, the brutal reality is that the social circumstances of the lives of many repeat offenders suffocate hope.

Against this backdrop, Maruna (2001) describes the prognosis for many persistent offenders as 'dire' (precisely because of the criminogenic backgrounds, environments and traits that they experience). Perhaps because of their experience of adversity, we know from research and practice experience that persistent offenders are very often highly fatalistic; or to use psychological terms, they have 'low self-efficacy' and an 'external locus of control'. They do not feel that they determine the direction of their own lives. Rather, life happens to them. Yet Maruna (2001) discovered that, despite this background and previous outlook, desisters somehow manage to acquire a sense of 'agency' – of control over their own lives.

But desistance is not just about the acquisition of new personal narrative and a new sense of personal empowerment; far less it is simply about the acquisition of the new understandings and skills that offender programmes typically focus on. Desistance requires social capital as well as these forms of human capital (Farrall, 2002, 2004); social capital is about networks of relationships, trust and reciprocity, and the opportunities for participation and inclusion that these resources represent (see McNeill and Whyte, 2008, ch. 9). Important ongoing studies of desistance in both Sheffield and Tübingen have suggested that, for young men involved in persistent offending, returning home and rebuilding ties with their parents and families is an important aspect of desisting from crime (see www.scopic.ac.uk/SPOOCS.html).

Finally, there is some evidence that for many ex-offenders, desistance is about personal redemption, not necessarily in the spiritual or theological sense but rather in the sense of finding a way to 'make good' on a troubled and troubling past by making a positive contribution to families or communities now (Maruna, 2001). Psychologists refer to this as 'generativity'; it takes little imagination to see the generative potential that resides in community penalties and indeed generativity may provide one hypothesis about why reparative community penalties sometimes outperform rehabilitative ones in terms of reducing reoffending (McNeill and Maruna, 2007).

These findings have wide-ranging implications for probation work, but there are some quite specific central messages. First, if desistance is an inherently individualised and subjective process, then we need to make sure that our approaches can accommodate and exploit issues of identity and diversity. One-size-fits-all interventions will not work. As Chapter 22 by Gill McIvor in this volume illustrates, both our understandings of pathways to desistance and the means of supporting desistance need to be gender-sensitive. Second, the development and maintenance not just of motivation but also of hope become key tasks for probation workers, more of which below. Third, desistance can only be understood within the context of human relationships; not just relationships between workers and offenders (talhough these matter a great deal) but also between offenders and those who matter to them. Fourth, although we tend to focus on offenders' risk and needs, they also have strengths and resources that they can use to overcome obstacles to desistance – both personal strengths and resources and strengths and resources in their social networks. We need to support and develop these capacities. Fifth, if desistance is about discovering agency, then interventions need to encourage and respect self-determination; this means working with offenders, not on them. Finally, interventions based only on human capital – what a Dutch colleague recently described to me as 'between the ears' interventions – will not be enough. Probation needs to work on social capital issues with communities and offenders – we need to work 'beyond the ears' if you will.

But there is a more revolutionary implication of the desistance perspective that we need to confront and consider. Figure 19.3 represents – admittedly somewhat harshly – the type of approach to offender intervention programmes that has come to the fore in the UK of late.

Figure 19.3: Offender Interventions

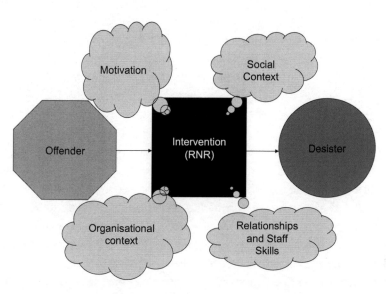

RNR = Risk-Needs-Responsivity Model of Offender Rehabilitation

In simple terms, the idea is that the offender is put through a programme that conforms to the principles of effective practice (more of which below) and emerges as a desister; the rough edges get smoothed off in the process. It is the offender who is changed by the intervention – and much of the focus has been on how to make the intervention or programme more effective. A number of complicating factors have emerged in the practical experiences of this general approach and in the evaluation research that has sought to account for the sometimes limited impact of such programmes. First, researchers have learned – not only through desistance research but also through programmes research – that more attention needs to be paid to the offender's motivation and to the impact of their social context on the outcomes of the intervention (Farrall, 2002). Second, it is now well understood that there is more to effective programmes than designing them well: they also need to be run well – this requires the right organisational arrangements, the right staff skills and the qualities of relationships between offenders and probation staff – both within programmes and beyond them (Raynor, 2004a, 2004b, 2008).

Arguably, the delay in recognising the significance of these sorts of additional ingredients in the recipe for effective practice is a result of thinking too much about interventions or programmes and too little about the change processes that they exist to support. Desistance research, if taken seriously, would invert our priorities – recognising the change process as our central concern and considering offender programmes as but one aspect of the many means of supporting the process:

> *Treatment was birthed as an adjunct to recovery, but, as treatment grew in size and status, it defined recovery as an adjunct of itself. The original perspective needs to be recaptured. Treatment institutions need to once again become servants of the larger recovery process and the community in which that recovery is nested and sustained.*
>
> (White, 2000, cited in Maruna *et al.*, 2004, p 9).

To use education as an analogy, one might ask the question whether it is more important that teachers understand how children learn and develop and how they can support these processes or that they know what currently seems to be the best way to teach them? While we may want the answer to this question to be 'Both!', the former seems to be more of a priority than the latter.

Figure 19.4 seeks to simply convey the relationships between desistance, case management and programmes. Services, systems and practitioners need to begin by understanding the desistance process and how best to support it, then embed the overall intervention or case management process in this understanding, and then embed within case management the role that specific programmes may play. As a member of an accreditation panel for such programmes, I am often troubled to find programme designers making submissions on the basis that the programme *is* the change process. It is not; it is merely one aspect of the service required to support the change process.

Figure 19.4: Programmes in context

Rather than developing these arguments any further here (see McNeill, 2009a), I want to change tack and review the evidence about a different change process – the development of criminal justice social work itself. This is also a story about motivation, capacity and opportunity, ALthough in the context of practice, we might be more likely to discuss professional values, knowledge/skills and resources.

Changing lives, changing social workers[2]

In this part of the chapter, I am drawing on a second literature review (McNeill, *et al.*, 2010b), which provides an analysis of the evidence about cultural change in community justice. The main body of evidence reviewed in that publication highlights a range of issues and problems linked to the pace, scale and management of change, as well as the extent to which it is centrally driven and/or practitioner owned. The review points to the importance of practitioners and their values in change processes, as well as to the degree of clarity of, coherence within and feasibility of change objectives. To borrow language from the discussion of desistance above, problems arise where there is external pressure for change, but where social workers, for whatever reason, lack the motivation, the capacities or the opportunities to practice differently. Where change initiatives fail to engage with them, to motivate them, to equip them and to resource them to change, change cannot happen. But just as we need to see an offender's journey towards desistance as being rooted in their history, so too we need to understand the historical identities of criminal justice social work before we can assess its development and its emerging character in the twenty-first century. To do this, I draw in this part of the chapter not on analysis of policy developments in criminal justice social work (see McNeill, 2005; McNeill and Whyte, 2007) but rather on those few empirical studies that have engaged with practice narratives and cultures – that is, with the way that social workers understand and explain what they do. For those readers outside Scotland, this might seem less relevant, given that, as we will see, the professional trajectories of criminal social work and probation in England and Wales diverged in 1968 and grew further apart when the Diploma in Probation Studies replaced the Diploma in Social Work as the professional qualification for probation work in the late-1990s. However, as will become obvious, although the organisational contexts have diverged, many of the practical challenges are similar, so there is much to learn from the Scottish case study.

Scottish probation

Although probation and criminal justice social work *practices* have been studied a number of times in Scotland in recent years, there has been very little work directly focused on understanding the *cultures* of criminal justice social work. A recent (and not yet published) oral history of Scottish probation in the 1960s (conducted by the author and involving interviews both with ex-probation officers and with ex-probationers) suggests that the probation services from which criminal justice social work emerged were themselves complex and contested organisations[3]. Probation officers' accounts of their pathways into probation work reveal a little about the ideologies and values that shaped these services. Their accounts stress not only the significance of the types of religious and political values that one might expect to find associated with humanitarian endeavour, but also of more mundane needs in the post-war years to find meaningful work that carried a degree of social status. Their accounts of their selection and recruitment suggest a preoccupation (among the selectors) with the creation of a workforce capable of engaging with people in adversity but unlikely to disrupt established hierarchies within the criminal justice system. Probation officers were often ambivalent about the power and status of courts and judges; although they sometimes experienced this as marginalising and even oppressive, they were also attracted to the associated status lent them as officers of the court.

Although they recollected their formal training to varying degrees, probation officers learned the job principally from their peers – a recurring finding in probation research. Such processes of professional socialisation may have had a conservative effect on Scottish probation's cultures, ensuring continuities with earlier eras and diminishing the practical impact of new strategies and techniques. Perhaps partly for this reason, the approaches to practice that they described were much less imbued with theories of 'social casework' than might be expected from a reading of official and academic sources of the time (see Vanstone, 2004; McNeill, 2005; McNeill and Whyte, 2007). Routine practice, most of it with young people, was focused principally on diversion and containment, with casework or 'treatment' approaches reserved for the small number of adults on probation, particularly those with mental health problems. In the course of their work, Scottish probation officers were also highly conscious of their engagements with local communities, working in a patch-based system to build ties to informal sources of social control and support (families, churches, employers, youth organisations, former probationers). They actively used such ties to try to bind probationers; 'binding' them sometimes in the sense of healing but also often in the sense of restraining. This engagement with and utilisation of community resources perhaps reflected Scottish probation's distinctively local character; Scottish services were always aligned to local council areas rather than to courts, despite occasional criticisms of this model (see Morison, 1962).

Unfortunately, there has been no study to date of how the cultures and practices of the various social work agencies and workers came together in the forging of the generic social work departments. What does seem clear is that probation work somehow moved from being a higher-status form of social work to being a lower-profile and lower-status activity within those departments, perhaps largely because of the gendering of and gender dynamics within these new organisations. Many male probation officers quickly became managers of the generic social work teams, and their interests in probation may have been diminished by their recognition of the need to develop other services.

Social work with offenders

Just as the 1970s and 1980s were a fallow period for probation development in Scotland, they were also a fallow period for probation research. The next significant Scottish study of probation – Ford and Ditton's *Probation in Scotland* – was not published until 1992 (see also Ditton and Ford, 1994), although the fieldwork was conducted between 1985 and 1989, before the introduction of the National Objectives and Standards (SWSG, 1991). This study was described as a 'formal ethnography' but it was based mainly on interviews with social workers, judges and probationers and on case records, rather than on observational methods. Ford and Ditton discerned differences in general approaches among the social workers – describing some as 'befrienders', some as 'rehabilitators' and some as 'supervisors' – but also noted that social workers varied their approaches to suit the nature of the case in question. They identified some variations between generalist and specialist workers and found an association between 'court agent-based approaches' and better levels of service. For persistent offenders at least, the most positive outcomes seemed to be achieved by workers who combined a court-agent approach with a rehabilitative focus, especially where such workers were more experienced, more specialised and better supervised. Interestingly, and much in line with the oral history study referred to above, Ditton and Ford found that:

> the ability to carry authority easily, showing firmness and control in a relaxed way ... is important, as is the ability to confront the probationer in a straightforward way. 'Pushy' social workers, who consistently demand real effort and change, are seen as showing genuine interest and concern, helping to create and maintain the motivation of the probationer ... in general, persistent offenders need persistent social workers.
>
> (Ditton and Ford, 1994, p 189).

Leaving aside the question of the effectiveness of social work with offenders in the 1980s, what these findings perhaps reveal is some heterogeneity within criminal justice social work's evolving occupational or professional cultures. It appears that the variations in role construction may have reflected a range of professional ideologies and values. Certainly it seems that the practical and ideological embedding of probation work within the emergent cultures of the generic social work departments was far from straightforward and far from uniform.

The impact of National Standards

The extensive research programme that evaluated the impact of the introduction in 1991 of the National Objectives and Standards (SWSG, 1991) found evidence that these ambiguities survived the creation of criminal justice social work as a separately funded specialism. Paterson and Tombs (1998) reported that while the reforms had ensured that the necessary organisational and managerial changes were effectively put in place, the success of the reforms also required a major shift in the professional culture, evidence of which was much more qualified. Essentially, they suggested that it would take time for social workers committed to a welfare model of practice (if indeed that is what they were) to adapt to the 'responsibility model' implicit in the national standards. In their view, the success of criminal justice social work in reducing the risk of custody and reducing the risk of reoffending – the 'new' policy objectives – depended precisely on this kind of longer-term cultural change 'from social workers as experts in welfare to the production of a new kind of social work expertise – an expertise in risk assessment to assist with the targeting of organisational resources and to indicate their potential to impact on criminal behaviour' (Paterson and Tombs, 1998, p 61). As various chapters in this volume have suggested, this shift from welfare to risk has affected not just criminal justice social work, but also many other kinds of human or social services.

Contemporary criminal justice social work

By the early 2000s, some research evidence was emerging that this longer-term cultural shift was indeed becoming evident. Robinson and McNeill (2004), for example, report the findings from a qualitative study conducted (by McNeill) in 2001-2002, which involved in-depth interviews and focus groups involving about 20 social workers. They found that the social workers tended to accept public protection as an overarching aim, but that they typically insisted that protecting communities *required* helping offenders; that the social work relationship was their primary vehicle for change; and that both offending behaviour and their efforts to bring about change had to be located in their wider social contexts. These ways of linking public protection and social welfare concerns perhaps reflect the Scottish policy context in suggesting a broader concept of rehabilitation connected with social inclusion agendas. However, they also illustrate how, at the front line, ideological change can be negotiated, mediated and managed in practice by individual penal professionals finding differing ways to re-inscribe existing purposes and practices with evolving ideologies. Perhaps unsurprisingly in this regard, it was apparent in Robinson and McNeill's (2004) study that the ways in which public protection came to be interpreted and operationalised in practice was primarily governed by risk, and in particular, risk of harm. Workers and others moved more clearly towards public protection as a super-ordinate or governing purpose and, correspondingly, towards assisting individuals *primarily* as an instrumental rather than an intrinsic good, in cases where the risk of serious harm to the public was seen as significant.

The final, and most fully developed, ethnographic study of criminal justice social work was conducted by a team based at the Universities of Strathclyde and Glasgow between 2003 and 2005 (Halliday *et al.*, 2008, 2009; Tata *et al.*, 20008; McNeill *et al.*, 2009). Rather than relying on interviews, and thus on *accounts* of practices, this study included two lengthy periods of participant observation, in two different criminal justice social work (CJSW) teams, focused on the routine production of social enquiry reports (SERs). Leaving aside the specific findings about SER practice, this study paints a detailed picture of the impact on CJSW of the wider social changes affecting the field of penality so well articulated by Garland (2001) in his account of the emergence of the 'culture of control'. The criminal justice social workers evidenced an enduring role tension between their responsibilities as justice professionals towards the courts, and their responsibilities as social work professionals towards their clients or service users. In their discourses and practices, they also revealed a sense of 'double-marginalisation'; both from generic social work (or more specifically generic social managers) and from the law-profession-dominated world of the courts.

The insecurities of this double-marginalisation, underpinned by their awareness of the changing social and political climate, meant that, on some level, they recognised that those welfare discourses and techniques that previously provided the capital in and through which they had historically traded had lost their political and cultural purchase (see also McCulloch and McNeill, 2007). Policy discourses and public debates seem to have led social workers to believe that their welfare affiliations are a liability that must be offset by adapting to a risk management and protection ethos. Thus, criminal justice social workers have come gradually to invest, some more reluctantly than others, in new discourses and techniques of risk assessment, management and reduction; discourses and techniques that represent new forms of capital through which some of them perhaps sense that they might maintain or acquire influence from their marginal position within criminal justice. Nonetheless, this strategy sits uneasily with their existing habituses (meaning 'durable dispositions'), in many cases framed in earlier eras. Their individual and shared histories at the intersections between the fields of justice and welfare seem to produce habituses that predictably retain much more than a residualised commitment to penal welfarism; thus, even where the need to trade or invest discursively in risk and protection is recognised, the meanings of risk and protection are themselves reframed; existing practices are re-legitimated in new ways. In this, there may be a significant degree of 'resignation' about and 'adaptation' to the risk agenda in relation to purposes and objectives, but there is also 'misadaptation' and 'revolt' in relation to techniques and practices. That this finding was evidenced not only among experienced social workers but also among relatively recently qualified staff members (who had been educated both about the emergence of risk and its associated technologies *and* about criminal justice social work's welfare traditions) underlines the durability of the latter influence on the profession and its practices – or at least it suggests that the eclipse of welfarism might require the passage of considerable time, or some more violent rupture in the development of the profession[4].

Conclusions: lives in transit

So what lessons can we take from these two accounts of the struggles involved in change or the difficulties of lives in transit? First of all, it is clear that living in transit between two places or states is often very uncomfortable. One famous Scottish desister expressed it thus:

> I am finding out a great deal about myself. I am making new relationships and living in a world totally unknown to me. I love it yet there are times when I hate it. I am torn between two worlds – alienated from the old one and a stranger in this new one. (Boyle, 1985, p 80)

Although it may be stretching the analogy somewhat, it is clear that the double-marginalisation of criminal justice social workers discussed above leaves them lost in the badlands between social work and criminal justice and perennially uncertain about their territories and mobilities. Despite its rapid advances in terms of scale, specialism and resourcing, criminal justice social work continues to struggle with fundamental issues of identity and purpose; the increasingly febrile nature of Scottish penal politics creates a difficult climate within which to address these uncertainties but, at the same time, renders their resolution all the more important. The extent to which similar tensions imbue probation work, offender management or community corrections in other jurisdictions is best judged by others, but it would not be surprising to see these problems reflected to varying extents elsewhere (see McNeill, et al., 2010a).

The evidence about desistance suggests that 'offenders' are most likely to move through this liminal or marginal state successfully where they are powerfully motivated, where they have or are developing the new skills that they need, and where the new social worlds, new networks and new opportunities they are trying to access are genuinely open to them. Developing a new sense of self – acquiring a new habitus (or disposition) – becomes more possible when these conditions are met.

Might it be much the same for criminal justice social work itself? If criminal justice social work services are to adapt and develop to the social and political context of twenty-first century Scotland, the professional social workers at the heart of the enterprise need to be engaged and motivated to do so. The same is probably true of probation or correctional workers in other jurisdictions. The change process needs to be one to which practitioners can normatively subscribe; one that is consistent with their values and motivations. They also need support in developing the skills and knowledge required for twenty-first century criminal justice practice. Finally, they need access as equals to the social and professional worlds of criminal justice. Indeed, it seems that, to some extent at least, the recent Scottish Prisons Commission recognised this in its proposal to establish a National Community Justice Council:

'[W]e have identified a need for renewed vision, visibility and leadership of these services. Community justice and criminal justice social work services are pivotal to making the reforms proposed above work; these services need to be credible and to enjoy the confidence and support of Scottish judges and Scottish communities. This requires the proper resourcing of community justice and criminal justice social work – not just in financial terms, but in terms of boosting the specialist knowledge and skills of the workforce, their integration and standing within the criminal justice system, and their standing and status within local authorities and local communities too ... [W]e need to find ways to release their key professional skills in helping troubled and troubling people comply with supervision and helping them tackle their underlying problems. That way, social workers can play their vital part centre-stage in a joined-up justice system that is more immediate, more efficient and more effective.

(Scottish Prisons Commission, 2008, paragraph 3.50).

Clearly, both for offenders and for criminal justice social workers, it is hard to live a life in transit – but it helps to be clear about where you are going and why, to have the skills, resources and support to get there, and to travel in the hope that a welcome awaits.

Notes:

1 This section of the chapter draws both on McNeill (2009a) and on an article recently published in the European Journal of Probation (see www.ejp.ro)(McNeill, 2009b). I am grateful to the editor for permission to use the material here.
2 I am grateful to my co-authors for their permission to use this material here.
3 The study is entitled 'Oral Histories of Scottish Probation' and was funded by the British Academy (Award no: SG48403). One written account of some of the study's findings is available (McNeill, 2009c).
4 There are, of course, jurisdictions where such 'violent ruptures' have been manufactured precisely to shift professional cultures that were seen to be too wedded to welfarist ideals. The abandonment of social work training and qualifications for probation officers in England and Wales in the mid-1990s is one such example.

References

Bottoms, A, Shapland, J, Costello, A, Holmes, D and Muir, G (2004) 'Towards Desistance: Theoretical Underpinnings for an Empirical Study' *Howard Journal of Criminal Justice* 43(4), pp 368-89.

Boyle, J (1985) *The Pain of Confinement: Prison diaries* London: Pan Books.

Burnett, R (1992) *The Dynamics of Recidivism* Oxford: University of Oxford, Centre for Criminological Research.

Burnett, R (2000) 'Understanding criminal careers through a series of in-depth interviews', *Offender Programs Report* 4(1), pp.1–16.

Burnett, R (2004) 'One-to-one ways of promoting desistance: In search of an evidence base' in Burnett, R and Roberts, C (eds) *What Works in Probation and Youth Justice.* Cullompton: Willan Publishing.

Burnett, R and Maruna, S (2004) 'So "prison works" does it? The criminal careers of 130 men released from prison under Home Secretary, Michael Howard' *Howard Journal*, 43(4), pp 390-404.

Ditton, J and Ford, R (1994) *The Reality of Probation: A formal ethnography of process and practice* Aldershot: Avebury.

Farrall, S (2002) *Rethinking What Works with Offenders: Probation, Social Context and Desistance from Crime* Cullompton: Willan Publishing.

Farrall, S (2004) 'Supervision, Motivation and Social Context: What Matters Most When Probationers Desist?' in Mair, G (ed) *What Matters in Probation* Cullompton: Willan Publishing.

Farrall, S and Bowling, B (1999) 'Structuration, Human Development and Desistance from Crime' *British Journal of Criminology* 17(2), pp 252–67.

Farrall, S and Calverley, A (2006) *Understanding Desistance from Crime: Theoretical Directions in Rehabilitation and Resettlement* Maidenhead: Open University Press.

Ford, R and Ditton, J (1992) *The Reality of Probation: A formal ethnography of process and practic.* Aldershot: Avebury.

Garland, D (2001) *The Culture of Control: Crime and Social Order in Contemporary Society* Oxford: Oxford University Press.

Halliday, S, Burns, N, Hutton, N, McNeill, F and Tata, C (2008) 'Shadow writing and participant observation: A study of criminal justice social work around sentencing' *Journal of Law and Society* 35(2), pp 189-213.

Halliday, S, Burns, N, Hutton, N, McNeill, F and Tata, C (2009) 'Street-level Bureaucracy, Interprofessional Relations and Coping Mechanisms: A Study of Criminal Justice Social Workers in the Sentencing Process' *Law and Policy* 31(4), pp 405-28.

Laub, J and Sampson, R (2003) *Shared Beginnings, Divergent Lives: Delinquent Boys to Age Seventy* Cambridge, MA: Harvard University Press.

Maruna, S (2001) *Making Good* Washington, DC: American Psychological Association.

Maruna, S and Farrall, S (2004) 'Desistance from crime: A theoretical reformulation' *Kvlner*

Zeitschrift fur Soziologie und Sozialpsychologie 43, pp 171-94.

Maruna, S, Immarigeon, R and LeBel, T (2004) 'Ex-offender reintegration: theory and practice', in Maruna, S and Immarigeon, R (eds) *After Crime and Punishment: Pathways to Offender Reintegration* Cullompton: Willan Publishing.

McCulloch, P and McNeill, F (2007) 'Consumer Society, Commodification and Offender Management' *Criminology and Criminal Justice* 7(3), pp 223-42.

McNeill, F (2005) 'Remembering probation in Scotland' *Probation Journal* 52(1), pp 25-40.

McNeill, F (2006) 'A desistance paradigm for offender management' *Criminology and Criminal Justice* 6(1): pp.39-62.

McNeill, F (2009a) *Towards Effective Practice in Offender Supervision* Glasgow: Scottish Centre for Crime and Justice Research (www.sccjr.ac.uk/documents/McNeil_Towards.pdf).

McNeill, F (2009b) 'What Works and What's Right' *European Journal of Probation* 1(1), pp 21-40 (www.ejprob.ro/index.pl/what_works_and_whats_just).

McNeill, F (2009c) 'Helping, Holding, Hurting: Recalling and reforming punishment', the 6th annual Apex Lecture, at the Signet Library, Parliament Square, Edinburgh, 8 September (www.strath.ac.uk/media/departments/glasgowschoolofsocialwork/Apex_Lecture_2009_f m.pdf).

McNeill, F and Maruna, S (2007) 'Giving Up and Giving Back: Desistance, Generativity and Social Work with Offenders' in McIvor, G and Raynor, P (eds) *Developments in Social Work with Offenders* London: Jessica Kingsley Publishers.

McNeill, F and Whyte, B (2007) *Reducing Reoffending: Social Work and Community Justice in Scotland* Cullompton: Willan Publishing.

McNeill, F, Batchelor, S, Burnett, R and Knox J (2005) *21st Century Social Work: Reducing Re-offending: Key Practice Skills* Edinburgh: Scottish Executive.

McNeill, F, Burns, N, Halliday, S, Hutton, N and Tata, C (2009) 'Risk, responsibility and reconfiguration: Penal adaptation and misadaptation' *Punishment and Society* 11(4), pp 419-42.

McNeill, F, Bracken, D and Clarke, A (2010) 'Social Work and Criminal Justice' in Shaw, I, Briar-Lawson, K, Orme, J and Ruckdeschel, R (eds) *The Sage Handbook of Social Work Research* London and New York: Sage Publications.

McNeill, F, Burnett, R and McCulloch, T (2010) *Culture, Change and Community Justice* Glasgow: Scottish Centre for Crime and Criminal Justice (www.sccjr.ac.uk/documents/SCCJR%20report%20No_02:2010.pdf).

Morison, R P (1962) *Report of the Departmental Committee on the Probation Service*, Cmnd 1650, London: Her Majesty's Stationery Office.

Paterson, F and Tombs, J (1998) *Social Work and Criminal Justice: Volume 1 – The Impact of Policy* Edinburgh: Scottish Office Central Research Unit.

Raynor, P (2004a) 'Rehabilitative and Reintegrative Approaches' in Bottoms, A, Rex, S and Robinson, G (eds) *Alternatives to Prison: Options for an Insecure Society* Cullompton: Willan Publishing.

Raynor, P (2004b) 'Opportunity, Motivation and Change: Some Findings from Research on Resettlement' in Burnett, R and Roberts, C (eds) *What Works in Probation and Youth Justice* Cullompton: Willan Publishing.

Raynor, P (2008) 'Community penalties and Home Office research: On the way back to "nothing works"?' *Criminology and Criminal Justice* 8(1), pp 73-87.

Ripple, L, Alexander, E and Polemis, B W (1964) *Motivation, Capacity and Opportunity: Studies in Casework Theory and Practice* Chicago, IL: School of Social Service Administration, University of Chicago.

Robinson, G and McNeill, F (2004) 'Purposes Matters: The Ends of Probation' in Mair, G (ed) *What Matters in Probation Work.* Cullompton: Willan Publishing.

Scottish Prisons Commission (2008) *Scotland's Choice* Edinburgh: Scottish Prisons Commission.

Social Work Services Group (1991) *National Objectives and Standards for Social Work Services in the Criminal Justice System* Edinburgh: Scottish Office.

Tata, C, Burns, N, Halliday, S, Hutton, N and McNeill, F (2008), 'Assisting and Advising the Sentencing Decision Process: the Pursuit of "Quality" in Pre-Sentence Reports' *British Journal of Criminology* 48(6), pp 835-55.

Vanstone, M (2004) *Supervising Offenders in the Community: A History of Probation Theory and Practice* Aldershot: Ashgate.

Weaver, B And McNeill, F (2010) 'Travelling Hopefully: Desistance Research and Probation Practice' in Brayford, J, Cowe, F and Deering, J (eds) *What Else Works? Creative Work with Offenders* Cullompton: Willan Publishing.

White, W (2000) 'Toward a new recovery movement: historical reflections on recovery, treatment and advocacy', Paper presented at the Center for Substance Abuse Treatment, Recovery Community Support Program Conference, Alexandria, Virginia, April.

Chapter 20

The 'Complicated Business' of Electronic Monitoring

Mike Nellis

Introduction

If one counts the short-lived 1989/90 electronically monitored bail pilots established by the-then Conservative government, 2009 was the twentieth anniversary of electronic monitoring (EM) in Britain – and the tenth anniversary of its roll-out as a fully national scheme in January 1999 under New Labour. No great fanfare was attached to this anniversary, and government no longer speaks of EM in the portentous and transformative terms that accompanied its inception or its national roll-out: curfewing offenders in their own homes for up to 12 hours per day for a period of several months has not reduced reliance on imprisonment to any significant extent nor, in itself, altered the fundamental nature of the community supervision of offenders. That said, EM has added a new dimension to and become a somewhat commonplace feature of such supervision – some 550,000 people have been tagged since 1999. Approximately 80% of EM cases have been stand-alone sentences, requirements in a broader sentencing package or measures of early release from prison (the Home Detention Curfew [HDC] scheme). EM has also been used as a condition of bail and a number of post-release orders, including parole, and as a component of intensive supervision schemes for young offenders. Such uses have slowly come to be accepted by probation and social work in Britain – more so in England and Wales than in Scotland – but EM has never really been embraced with enthusiasm or, arguably, used to best effect.

One reason for this is that the administration of EM is contracted out on behalf of government to private sector organisations. The existence of these organisations has long given cause for concern to liberal penal reform organisations, who rightly question the ethics of 'profits from punishment', and worry that crime control is turning into an 'industry' and that the prevalence of crime in society – usually understood as a social problem to be managed or eradicated – is becoming a business opportunity. It has even been suggested that EM is an intrinsically commercial form of crime control, a distinct tool for the private sector to encroach on the traditional territory of state-based probation services (Lilly, 1992; Paterson, 2007a). This is exaggerated – EM has more complex origins than this, in the affordance of remote location monitoring offered by information and communication technology developed and deployed in the first instance to enable capital transfer in the global economy, and to accelerate transnational decision-making.

It is true, however, that commercial organisations in the security and telecommunications field were best placed to exploit and customise this technology for crime control purposes, but they did so at the behest of governments whose law and order policies (and deeper regulatory impulses) signalled the emergence of a 'market' for tougher measures of community supervision than those traditionally associated with social work (Nellis, 2006).

This chapter will take for granted that an ethical and practical case can (or could) be made for EM as an alternative to custody – both the kind that is used to monitor curfews and in certain instances satellite tracking (which was piloted in England and Wales in 2004-06, but not pursued further at the time), preferably as an integrated element in more humanistic forms of supervision aimed at rehabilitating offenders rather than simply punishing them. It will, however, accept that, in the words of a recent joint report from the probation, police and court inspectorates in England and Wales (Criminal Justice Joint Inspection, 2008), the relationship between the government (specifically the National Offender Management Service [NOMS]) and the private contractors is 'a complicated [vastly bureaucratic] business', which, paradoxically, after twenty years of experimenting with it, still leaves EM with much 'unrealised potential'. Consistent with earlier legislative and policy developments, and with ideas about 'partnership' and 'mixed economies' of provision, the Criminal Justice Joint Inspection (CJJI) report encouraged a more integrated use of EM (Nellis and Goodman, 2009; Nellis, 2010). This, in turn, was seemingly consistent with steps that NOMS was already taking to make 'offender management' – the increased coordination of multi-component community sentences – into a more coherent experience for individual offenders. In practice, with EM, precisely because it is administered by the private sector, integration may be more problematic than it may at first appear.

Electronic monitoring and the private sector

The decision to use private sector service delivery in the original three-site EM bail pilot in 1989-90 in England and Wales was primarily ideological, reflecting the-then Conservative government's explicit desire to open public services up to the influence of market forces – having already committed itself to a preliminary programme of contracting out prisons. The technology manufacturers involved in this pilot were security company Chubb and telecommunications company Marconi, with Securicor subcontracted to both to do installations and fitting in offenders' homes. The probation service, which was deeply critical of this development, but at the same time aloof from it because bail was not an integral part of its work, was never seriously considered as a provider, and never considered itself as such. The pilot was not particularly successful – numbers were low and the probation service prematurely assumed that tagging was being dropped. A new three-site pilot was resumed in 1996, however, with Securicor itself running two of them, and Geografix, a small Norwich-based company specialising in vehicle tracking, running the third. These pilots segued into national EM provision under New Labour in 1999. Given this government's desire to 'modernise' an allegedly moribund public sector, there was no hint once it was in office of turning away from the private sector as a service provider (Nellis, 1991; 2004a).

The first five-year contracts in England and Wales were split between three security companies – Securicor, Premier (which had bought up Geografix) and Reliance, covering the north, the Midlands (and London) and the south respectively, from company monitoring centres in Manchester, Norwich and Swindon. In the retendering exercise in 2005, Reliance lost out, and the contracts went to G4S (formerly Securicor, now merged with Group 4) and Serco (Premier's parent company, using its own name since separating from its United States [US] partner Wackenhut). The Manchester and Norwich monitoring centres remained, dividing the country in two. Scotland, which piloted EM in 1998, and rolled it out nationally (only as a sentence) in 2002, was by contrast a single EM jurisdiction, originally administered by Reliance but after their retendering exercise, by Serco, from a monitoring centre in East Kilbride. Northern Ireland, which only began EM in April 2009, is similarly single, but monitored by G4S from its Manchester centre. Each of the monitoring centres is staffed on a 24/7 basis by shifts of workers who watch computer screens to ascertain if curfews are being abided by; seek to contact offenders by telephone if they are not; deal (again by telephone) with problems that offenders or their families have with the tag; and liaise with relevant agencies about recall and enforcement. The majority of field monitoring officers work from home or from their company's regional offices across the country where kit is stored. Much of their work does not begin until after 3pm, when new court orders for curfews are faxed to the monitoring centre and allocated to them. All drive cars and have to undertake installations in offenders' homes within a requisite timescale, whether in dense conurbations or remote rural locations. These monitoring officers constitute a new criminal justice occupation in Britain about whose working practices little is known, although former employees of Premier and Securicor have both written insightfully on their experience (Jones, 2005; Paterson, 2007b).

Now that these companies are established contributors to contemporary criminal justice, it is difficult to recall just how much hostility there initially was to them. Writing in the second edition of their influential penology textbook, Cavadino and Dignan (1997, p 306) spoke for many when they demanded 'immediate abandonment of such misguided projects as new mandatory and minimum sentences, electronic "tagging", "boot camps" and secure training orders, and an end to further privatisation in the prison service'. The National Association of Probation Officers and the Association of Chief Officers of Probation both opposed EM at the start, although the latter's lead officer was eventually instrumental in generating a more favourable view, as well as pointing out that if EM failed, it would be the private sector, not probation, that took the blame (Whitfield, 1997, 2001). Partly because the Home Office never wavered in its determination to use EM, probation and youth justice staff in England gradually accepted that EM had some legitimate uses.

There was an element of Hobson's choice in this, but a younger generation of frontline officers, genuinely more attuned to the emerging public protection ethos of their agencies, and to the potential of technology in human services, replaced the probation veterans among whom EM was thought incommensurate with 'social work values'. In addition, the experience of HDC, more so than curfew orders, brought probation officers into contact with offenders and families who appreciated the early release from prison that EM made possible. In Scotland, where a stronger welfare ethos has survived (although EM has been embedded within a probation order), criminal justice social workers remain more sceptical of it, and have only experienced HDC since 2006. Scottish local authorities (where criminal justice social work is based) were surprisingly sanguine about the initial involvement of the private sector in EM provision, but this may have been because social workers did not want to be tainted with the 'stigma' of EM – especially if it failed – preferring it to be seen as different and separate from them (Nellis, 2006). Thinking about the division of labour between public and private in this way has a certain 'common sense' appeal, but in reality the relation of the private sector and the state is more complex.

Incorporating the private sector into the state

For all that they have an established presence in criminal justice now – providing private prisons, prisoner escort services, secure units for young people and detention centres for asylum seekers, as well as EM – these companies are better known as brands than tangible business entities and do indeed have histories and traditions very different from the voluntary and statutory organisations that emerged in the twentieth century to rehabilitate and resettle offenders. Securicor, for example, which nowadays operates in 40 countries, originated with Night Watch, a small private security firm started in 1935 in Mayfair and Hampstead to protect the homes of the affluent. It employed only ex-military personnel, and grew steadily, leading to persistent accusations that it was becoming a private army. For this reason the Home Office objected to its changing its name to Security Corps – Securicor was the compromise in 1953. Under this name it took up daytime guarding, armoured cars/cash in transit, and data transit, and slowly won the respect of the police, as a partner rather than a rival in crime prevention. In the 1960s it opened the Harmondsworth [immigration] detention centre at Heathrow airport, a forerunner of the custodial services it has developed in conjunction with the Home Office (Underwood, 1997, p 28). In the 1990s it entered the telecommunications market, setting up Cellnet (a mobile communications network) with British Telecom, initially using it to set up a stolen car tracking service, then tracking its own security vehicles and developing Datatrak, a means of guiding emergency vehicles to specified locations. With this history and accumulated expertise it was a relatively small step to tender for contracts involving the management of prisons and EM.

Serco, a company now operating in 30 countries, has very different roots. It can trace its history back to the creation of Radio Corporation of America (RCA), set up to exploit the potential of the-then wireless technology in the entertainment and communications industries, whose subsidiary in the United Kingdom (UK) was established in 1929. In the Second World War, RCA became involved in developing military communications technology, including radar, sonar and aircraft electronics, returning to UK and US defence markets in the 1960s. Over the next two decades it worked in civil aviation, urban and motorway transport control, weapons testing ranges and satellite monitoring. Following the merger of RCA's American parent company with General Electric in 1985, and uncertainty about the UK company's future, RCA's 'facilities management' work (contracts for government departments) was the subject of a management buy-out, creating a new company, Serco (short for 'service company') in 1988. It branched out into facilities management for other private companies, the health services and local government – and in the 1990s (when it was also expanding globally), after some boardroom anxiety about things that might go wrong – the prison service. Serco formed a partnership with the US Wackenhut Corporation, (branding themselves as Premier Prison Services [PPS]) winning contracts to run both prisons and EM (Blum et al., 2002).

The partnership between Serco and Wackenhut ended somewhat acrimoniously, after which Serco dropped their joint name and pursued prison and EM contracts on its own. Inevitably, all the private contractors suffered bad publicity at some time or other in respect of the 'justice' aspects of their business. Serco was publicly excoriated for its failings in respect of a tagged young man who was involved in a murder, although in this instance the Youth Offending Team, which was jointly responsible for him, was equally at fault (Her Majesty's Inspectorate of Probation, 2004; Nellis, 2004b). In March 2007, poor staff training and failure to follow procedures were exposed by undercover television reporters in one of G4S's regional offices, causing the company considerable public embarrassment (www.bbc.co.uk/insideout). In both cases, the companies' ostensibly arm's length relationships to the Home Office usefully deflected criticism away from it.

Yet for all their entrepreneurial origins and histories, the EM providers do not operate as independent commercial entities. They are governed by tightly drawn, highly prescriptive contracts and their own performance – on 37 criteria in the 1999-2005 period – is itself subject to detailed monitoring. These still include fitting the tag in the requisite time, checking equipment regularly, following up potential violations and notifying the Home Office when breaches of curfew have occurred. Fines have been levied for failures of performance – in 2004 these amounted to £58,260 from Securicor, £66,370 from Premier and £262,000 from Reliance (0.2%, 0.2% and 1.5% of their expected income in that year). Failure to follow up violations on time was the commonest performance failure. In the original contracts the Home Office kept track of performance via data supplied by the contractors themselves, in the second contract the Home Office (and later the Ministry of Justice, which split off from it in 2007) acquired 'real time access to the contractors management information databases' (National Audit Office, 2006, p 12), enabling ongoing remote assessment of specific performance times – arguably a rather striking example of 'watching the watchers'.

The tightness of the contracts and the closeness of the scrutiny to which the commercial suppliers are subject does indicate that EM is ultimately controlled by government and that policy and practice is primarily shaped by the regulatory ethos of 'the managerial state' rather than by purely commercial imperatives. The contractors are well networked into wider global developments in security technology and telecommunications, can act as powerful advisers to government in terms of what is feasible and possible in EM, and can even stimulate innovation, but they are not running the show. 'Contracting-out' does involve the commodification (and in the case of EM, reinvention) of hitherto public sector tasks, but it is not in itself full 'privatisation'; it may be a stage on the road to it, or, if government wishes to remain in control of the process, an end in itself (Coyle *et al.*, 2003). EM contractors in Britain are not operating as independent competing businesses in a free market: they are, in effect, a duopoly functioning as part of the state. It is not uncommon for this arrangement to be referred to as 'sub government', but, arguably, a richer and more complex conceptual framework is needed to fully understand it. Notwithstanding the difficulty of generating data about it, Lilly and Knepper's (1992) concept of 'the commercial-corrections complex' is long overdue for elaboration, updating and refinement.

Social work/probation in the network society

To a greater or lesser degree, historically, technology has always affected the available forms of penal control and EM must be understood, not as a 'new punishment' that arose in a social and cultural vacuum, but as an expression of what Castells (1996) calls 'the network society', and what Bogard (1996) calls 'the telematic society'. These are different ways of registering the character of societies that are infused with – whose everyday functioning depends on – information and communication technology and the expectation that computer-mediated knowledge of remote events (a blip on the Tokyo stock market, a man arriving home for curfew in Edinburgh) will be instantly available. EM was a consequence – a politically determined one – of the affordances offered by this pervasive technology, customised to meet the needs of crime controllers (just as similar technology can be customised for health carers, to remotely monitor the life signs of older or disabled people). In Britain, government has used commercial organisations with established twentieth-century traditions of exploiting new technological opportunities to develop and deliver EM in criminal justice – a tradition that public sector organisations did not have – but EM was not in itself a purely commercial development. It reflected a pre-existing governmental desire for the intensification of control over – the ever-more meticulous regulation of – the lives of offenders in the community, which in turn reflected the influence of managerial ideologies on government itself. The emerging technology first enabled the political desire for control to be realised, then sustained, deepened and embedded. It continues to run the risk of inflating the focus on control at the expense of other legitimate considerations in the community supervision of offenders unless these are actively affirmed and set in place. Therein, still, lies the challenge for social work.

It is unlikely that EM would have developed in the way it has other than in a political context concerned to reduce the use, and costs' of imprisonment. Professionally, social work ought to have no problem with reducing prison use; it is absolutely not within its gift to accomplish this on its own, but the supportive and caring services it has traditionally offered to offenders indisputably have a part to play. At the same time, if it accepts the challenge of penal reduction, it must also address the question of control – the types and intensity of control it is prepared to impose on offenders in the interests of reducing reoffending and protecting victims, as well as the forms of control it wishes to reject, and the grounds for doing so. It was arguably social work and probation's own diffidence on the question of control in the 1990s that made it so easy for government to undermine their credibility as means of supervising offenders in the community, and to turn to new experts and new technologies. Given the way that both EM and the private sector were used by government as sticks with which to beat social work/probation, it is understandable that social work initially rejected both, but had social work been more criminologically sophisticated in its understanding of what crime control required, and better informed about the history and potential of EM, it may have been less easy for the private sector to make headway, despite the ideological climate that favoured its involvement. Structural arrangements were set in place then, which, despite probation's eventually more emollient attitude towards EM, still shape the way that it can be imagined and used.

In England and Wales the prison population has not reduced – not even stabilised – and these are dark times for penal reformers in which to promote strategies of penal reduction (less so in Scotland, where this is government policy). The National Audit Office (2006) confirmed that the use of EM achieves value for money both as a sentence and as a form of early release, but perhaps the best that can be said for it, penally, is that it stops the prison population being larger than it would otherwise be, if EM were not in play. The National Audit Office (2006) in fact suggested that a further £9.3 million (in prison places) could be saved if all prisoners eligible for HDC were granted it on time (which they were not, because of delays in getting home assessment reports to the prison). It is not clear that this has happened, because since then, the use of HDC has declined, the combined result of adverse publicity, increased risk aversion on the part of prison governors and the availability of an alternative form of early release that does not involve tagging - the End of Custody Licence - which some prisoners clearly prefer. This may signal a change in the fortunes of EM, the end of its heyday, the beginning of its decline, but in theory at least the offender management strategy currently being pursued by NOMS implies both that there should be greater use of it, and that it should be more integrated into other elements of community supervision, becoming part of a rehabilitation package rather than a stand-alone punishment. In reality, the outcome of the offender management strategy in respect of EM may simply be its increased use as a stand-alone sentence with low-risk offenders and as a bail condition. Integration with other aspects of community supervision may be too difficult, or too costly, to achieve, in part because of the sheer difficulty of bridging the public/private divide and working together.

Conclusions

The Criminal Justice Joint Inspection's (2008) view that the relationship between government and its EM contractors was 'a complicated business' was a huge understatement, and that very choice of name for its report may have been an oblique way of signalling concern about the immense overbureaucratisation of contemporary criminal justice processes more generally, not just in relation to EM. The sheer number and immense length of the electronic documents that govern (and constitute) communication between NOMS and its regions, NOMS and probation areas and Youth Offending Teams, NOMS and the EM contractors (to name only a few lines of transmission) – and the pace at which they are updated, upgraded and replaced – is so vast that no single operative or manager could fully understand even the ones that relate to their specific tasks. Knowledge is ceasing to be something that resides in people's heads, informing understanding and shaping one's practical actions, and is becoming information that resides in computerised systems, to be consulted for guidance whenever action is required. As Richard Sennet (2006) notes, information overload is an inalienable feature of 'the managerial state', a feature of contemporary statecraft, part inadvertent (reflecting the technical capacity of communication systems), part deliberate (reflecting a desire to regulate, to overwhelm, to dominate):

> the glut of information generated by modern technology ... threatens to make its receivers passive. Overload prompts disengagement... large amounts of raw data create a political fact; control becomes more centralised as volume increases ... the receiver can react less to it, indeed disengages from it interpretively.
>
> (Sennett, 2006, p 172)

Information overload has been a major reason why local probation managers and practitioners have failed to think creatively about the uses of EM: all the thinking has been done in the centre and handed down, reinforcing the sense that prevailing patterns of use are inviolate and that there is nothing more to be said. There is no likelihood that in the near future the government will cease using commercial organisations to deliver EM – the information flow will not lessen – and some possibility, if the NOMs strategy of 'contestability' is pursued assiduously that those self-same organisations will be tendering for other aspects of the probation service's work. Whatever lingering mistrust probation officers have towards the private sector in respect of EM, it is magnified considerably by this anxiety, increasing the difficulty of working across the divide, and reducing the likelihood of creative thought about the integrated uses to which EM might be put. Yet if EM is to have any future other than a purely punitive one, its 'unrealised potential' must be tapped by social workers and progressive penal reformers, attuned to the realities of 'the network society' but grounded in the humanistic values to which they have always laid claim.

References

Blum, S, Tromans, J, Turner, T and Williams, F (2002) *Serco: The family history 1929-1999* London: Serco Group.

Bogard, W (1996) *The Simulation of Surveillance: Hypercontrol in telematic societies* Cambridge: Cambridge University Press.

Castells, M (1996) *The Rise of the Network Society* (2nd edition), Oxford: Blackwell.

Cavadino, M and Dignan, J (1997) *The Penal System* (2nd edition), London: Sage Pubications.

Coyle, A , Campbell, A and Neufeld, R (2003) *Capitalist Punishment: prison privatisation and human rights* London: Zed Books.

Criminal Justice Joint Inspection (2008) *A Complicated Business: A joint inspection of electronically monitored curfew requirements, orders and licences* London: HMI Probation, HMI Court Administration and HMI Constabulary.

Her Majesty's Inspectorate of Probation (2004) 'Inquiry Into the Supervision of Peter William's by Nottingham City Youth Offending Team', London: Her Majesty's Inspectorate of Probation.

Jones, A (2005) 'A tagging tale: the work of the monitoring officer, electronically monitoring Offenders in England and Wales' *Surveillance and Society* 2(4), pp 581-88.

Lilly, J R (1992) 'Selling Justice: Electronic Monitoring and the Security Industry' *Justice Quarterly* 9(3), pp 493-503.

Lilly, J R and Knepper, P (1992) 'An International Perspective on the Privatisation of Corrections' *Howard Journal of Criminal Justice* 31(1), pp 174-91.

National Audit Office (2006) *The Electronic Monitoring of Adult Offenders* London: The Stationery Office.

Nellis, M (1991) 'The Electronic Monitoring of Offenders in England and Wales: recent developments and future prospects' *British Journal of Criminology* 31(2), pp 165-85.

Nellis, M (2004a) 'The Electronic Monitoring of Offenders in Britain: a critical overview' in Bottomley, K, Hucklesby, A , Mair, G and Nellis, M (eds) *Electronic Monitoring of Offenders: Key Developments.* London: Napo.

Nellis, M (2004b) 'The Limitations of Electronic Monitoring. The case of Peter Williams' *Prison Service Journal* 164, March, pp 3-12.

Nellis, M (2006) 'NOMS, Contestability and the Process of Technocorrectional Innovation' in Hough, M, Allen, R and Padel, U (eds) *Reshaping Probation and Prisons: The new offender management framework* Bristol: The Policy Press.

Nellis, M (2010) 'Electronic Monitoring: towards integration in offender management?' in McNeill, F, Raynor, P and Trotter, C (eds) *Offender Supervision: New Directions in Theory, Research and Practice* Cullompton: Willan Publishing.

Nellis, M and Goodman, A (2009) 'Probation and Offender Management' in Hucklesby, A and Wahidin, A (eds) *Criminal Justice* Oxford: Oxford University Press.

Paterson, C (2007a) 'Street Level Surveillance: human agency and the electronic monitoring of offenders' *Surveillance and Society* 4(4), pp 314-28.

Paterson C (2007b) 'Commercial Crime Control and The Electronic Monitoring of Offenders in England and Wales' *Social Justice* 34(3-4), pp 98-110.

Sennett, R (2006) *The Culture of the New Capitalism* New Haven, CT: Yale University Press.

Underwood, S (1997) *Securicor: The people business* Oxford: Capstone Publishing.

Whitfield, D (1997) *Tackling the Tag: The electronic monitoring of offenders* Winchester: Waterside Press

Whitfield, D (2001) *The Magic Bracelet: Technology and offender supervision* Winchester: Waterside Press.

Chapter 21

Criminal Justice Social Work in Three Countries: Scotland, Ireland and Canada

Denis C. Bracken

Introduction

Depending on where one is taking a programme of studies leading to a social work qualification, it may be possible to find course work on criminal justice social work as a regular part of the curriculum, an optional part of the curriculum, or not a part of social work education and training at all. One would perhaps be more likely to find a placement in a criminal justice agency than to find course work that went some way towards preparing a soon to be qualified social worker for contemporary criminal justice practice. espite this variation in preparation, social workers are employed in criminal justice work, most frequently with offenders and victims, throughout North America, the British Isles, Ireland, Australia, New Zealand and elsewhere. How social workers in the criminal justice system view their preparation for practice and the contexts in which they practice is what this chapter is about. It is based on research in three countries each with different frameworks for social work education and practice in criminal justice: Scotland, Ireland and Canada.

The evidence of a move away from social work in criminal justice exists both in some practice contexts and in the social work academic literature. For example, a formal social work role in criminal justice has been significantly reduced in recent years in England and Wales where there was a specific rejection of social work as a lead discipline in criminal justice work with offenders in the mid-1990s. A part of social work training designed especially for probation work ceased (Smith, 2005) and a new training regime without social work was established. Reamer (2004), arguing in the American context, suggests that the problem was with the social work profession, in that social work 'abandoned' criminal justice as an area of practice. While both these examples no doubt have merit in their respective countries, ideas about how to work with offenders in a manner that provides a measure of protection for society by identifying the potential risk to reoffend, and addresses issues that lead to reoffending, have moved to the forefront of correctional practice. This is true both for places where social work has a strong role in work with offenders and for those where it does not.

In the 1990s there emerged what has become known as the 'What Works' agenda. It has produced a similarity in the structure of working with offenders, based on practice using risk assessment as a key organising principle, with the identification of criminogenic needs to focus supervision and/or programme development. The principle of responsivity, also part of What Works, is intended to direct offenders to programmes based on individual learning styles. The What Works context for dealing with offending behaviour is heavily influenced by social learning theory and individual psychology (Andrews, 1995). It has been criticised by some for minimising the impact of poverty, racial discrimination and unemployment and for suggesting that tackling these issues is a relatively minor aspect of working with offenders either in custody or in the community (see, for example, Atkinson, 2004; Vanstone, 2004 and Ward 2008). Some suggest that this implies a return to a medical model of offending behaviour (Mair, 2004). More broadly, Webb (2006) has been critical of social work practice grounded in the assessment of risk, raising the issue of both deskilling and the rationing of resources based on apparently objective actuarial assessment of need.

The development of risk assessment methods has gone through various evolutions (Bonta and Wormith, 2008) resulting in a continuous refinement of the process for identifying factors influential in leading an individual to crime. For the person working with offenders using this approach, it is important to elicit information from the offender to develop an accurate assessment of the offender's risk of reoffending, the identification of those factors that are subject to 'treatment', and the appropriate programme to which the offender can be referred which matches their learning style. In many instances, it is assumed that cognitive-behavioural programmes are the best to address criminogenic factors. The intent of this approach is two-fold: to identify those offenders with the highest level of criminogenic need (and therefore at greatest risk of reoffending) and who therefore merit sufficient resources to promote change; and to identify those offenders with lower levels of need, and therefore lower levels of risk of reoffending, for whom correctional intervention should be minimal. Identification of those at highest risk of reoffending can also mean the mobilisation of resources to provide increased surveillance and public safety. What might be termed 'traditional welfare issues' (homelessness, lack of education, poor family dynamics, etc) would not be addressed by a correctional worker (beyond a possible referral to another agency) if these welfare issues were not themselves identified through the risk assessment process as factors contributing to offending behaviour.

For social work, then, the question is where do social work skills, knowledge and values fit with this model for working with offenders? Are social work skills necessary to complete a risk assessment, to differentiate between 'needs' as defined in a traditional social work sense from 'criminogenic needs' (those which are identified through actuarially-based risk assessment instruments), and to assess the ability/responsivity of offenders to benefit from what have become largely cognitive-behaviourally based group treatment programmes? Where do the debates in social work on 'care and control' come into the discussion?

Criminal justice social work in Scotland, Ireland and Canada

The three countries under consideration here each have a history of social work involvement in criminal justice. Scotland, Ireland and Canada have all been influenced by the What Works agenda, the development of risk assessment as a key organising principle, and all have systems of social work education, training and qualification. But there is considerable divergence among the three concerning how social work as preparation for work with offenders is viewed and how important social work skills seem to be for working in criminal justice.

The linkages between the social work profession and criminal justice in *Scotland* are strong, and one might say, particularly in comparison with other jurisdictions, there is a commitment to each other. Both the history of social work in Scotland and the links to criminal justice work are well told elsewhere (e.g. McNeill and Whyte, 2007; Brodie *et al.*, 2008), so what follows is a brief summary heavily reliant on other works. Much of contemporary social work in Scotland including the strong link between social work and criminal justice starts with the Kilbrandon Report of 1964 and the subsequent Social Work (Scotland) Act of 1968. Probation services at that time became part of local generic social work departments. This is not to suggest that social workers had not been involved in probation before 1968, but the prominence of social work in criminal justice was solidified after 1968 (McIvor and McNeill, 2007; McNeill and Whyte, 2007). In 2003, social work training was revised and social work qualifications began to be awarded by the Scottish Social Services Council. Nine universities in Scotland provide honours degree courses leading to a social work qualification.

Criminal justice social work continues to be a recognised area of professional practice. The Association of Directors of Social Work considers the social work honours degree programme 'as an essential qualification for social workers who work within the Criminal Justice system and we are committed to assisting in the development of a core Criminal Justice Curriculum within the honours degree programme' (ADSW, 2004, p 4). Most criminal justice services are delivered by qualified social workers, although some unqualified workers are also involved in service delivery. Recent job advertisements specify that a social work qualification is required. Despite this, the influence of the What Works approach to working with offenders, combined with an emphasis on community safety and/or punishment in the community has resulted in challenges to a more traditional role for social work generally, and in criminal justice in particular (for example, see Section 1 of McNeill and Whyte, 2007). For a case in point, one has only to read the Scottish Government's (2006) *21st century social work review*.

> *Evidence to the review has demonstrated how social workers can use their distinctive knowledge and skills to change the behaviour of those who are motivated to change and to control those who are not. The use of such*

> *skills in personalising work with offenders has to be balanced with the*
> *strong enforcement required for public protection.*
>
> (Scottish Executive, 2006, 25)

This balance between care and control has a long history in social work (Parsloe, 1976; and more recently Barry, 2000), and its restatement here by the Scottish Government demonstrates how it continues to be a topic of discussion.

One might argue that, for *Ireland*, criminal justice and social work are areas of mutual interest, and even of mutual acceptance. The profession sees it as an important area of practice, and the criminal justice system recognises its value. But, Ireland has always hired non-social workers into the criminal justice system including as probation officers, and continues from time to time to do so.

The development of social work as a profession in Ireland has been described as moving through four phases (Skehill, 1999, quoted in Christie, 2005) and it is the introduction of social science degree courses in the 1950s and 1960s combined with the expansion of the profession after 1970 and the passage of the Health Act which has relevance to the relationship between social work and probation/community corrections.

The rapid expansion in the number of social workers was provided for by the development of new social legislation. The Child Care Act 1991, the Children Act 1997 and the Children Act 2001 (replacing the Children Act 1908) have all required the employment of additional social workers. Increasing numbers of social workers have also been employed in adult mental health services, probation services and, to a lesser extent, in social work with older people (Christie, 2005, p 115).

The number of probation officers began to expand in the 1970s and went from six in 1970 to 207 in 2003 (Christie, 2005, p 116). Professional social work qualifications gradually became a requirement for being what was originally termed a 'welfare officer', although a social science degree did not become a requirement until 1975 (McNally, 2007). The establishment of the National Social Work Qualification Board (NSWQB) in the early 1990s to replace the accreditation process of social work qualifications by the British Central Council for Education and Training of Social Workers helped to solidify the place of the profession. Probation officers have been and continue to be active in the NSWQB, thus keeping a clear connection between probation officers and social work. The latest available employment data is from 2005. Probation posts are considered by the NSWQB as social work posts, and these make up 12.7% of the social work posts nationally (Health Service Executive [which includes child protection] makes up 59.3% and the voluntary sector 13.8%) The number of people without social work qualifications in probation posts is not calculated, but estimates from interviews suggest that approximately 20% of probation officers (about 30) are not qualified as social workers. Job postings for probation officer positions in the past few years have included the requirement of a Bachelor of Social Science degree or equivalent qualification recognised for entry to an National Qualification in Social Work (NQSW)/Masters in Social Work and one year's relevant experience or NQSW/Masters in Social Work. In the past, provision has been made for unqualified probation officers to complete the NQSW.

With respect to education and training, University College Cork, University College Dublin, NUI-Galway & Trinity College Dublin all provide social work training, including criminal justice placements and a criminal justice module. Probation officers have been involved in the development and delivery of these modules, as well as in supervising students in placements.

Criminal justice social work in *Canada* might be characterised as a case of benign neglect leading to indifference. In general, the social work profession does not place particular emphasis on criminal justice as a major area of practice, and provincial criminal justice bureaucracies see social work as simply one of a range of possible preparatory courses prior to employment.

Canada has a history of social work as a discipline in corrections, and more simply as one of several disciplines that might have a role to play in work with offenders although not one with any particular advantage over others. In 1969, the *Report of the Canadian Committee on Corrections* (Canada, 1969, p 278), highlighted the importance of rehabilitation through the use of 'knowledge gained from social and behavioural sciences as well as accumulated correctional experience'. It also emphasised the need for 'professionally trained staff' in corrections and included social work along with psychiatry and applied psychology as examples of these professions. Through the 1980s and 1990s, the involvement of social work as a profession in criminal justice declined to the extent that the *Canadian Social Work Review*, the principal journal for social work in Canada, rarely if ever publishes articles related to criminal justice.

Where there is a mention of social work practice as it relates to criminal justice in official or scholarly work on social work in Canada, the discussion would appear to be quite generic and possibly somewhat distant from the realities of contemporary practice. For example, the Canadian Association of Social Workers' Guidelines for the Development of Professional Practice Legislation (CASW, 2009 in the section on professional practice in corrections does not mention risk assessment or cognitive behavioural-based groupwork with offenders. A recent chapter in a text on social work practice (Evans, in Turner & Turner, 2005) has a short section on criminal justice, but again any connection to the realities of contemporary approaches to practice is absent.

Social work training programmes in Canada (which are university-based degree programmes) do not appear to place a heavy emphasis on criminal justice. Criminal justice social work as a required module is non-existent, although most programmes have field placements in criminal justice government and voluntary sectors. Many have optional courses on criminal justice, although most of these are cursory introductions to policy and systems.

In a recent survey (Bracken, 2005), the provincial/territorial heads of probation were surveyed and stated that all probation services require a social science degree for work in probation. Social work was mentioned along with psychology, criminology and sociology. A 1996 study of the national social work labour force in Canada (CASSW, 1996, p 56) found that 18% of probation officers had a social work degree (mostly a Bachelor of Social Work), compared to 26% with a sociology degree and 18% with a degree in psychology. The result therefore might be described as indifference. Criminal justice bureaucracies see a social work qualification as one of a range of possible credentials necessary to work as a probation officer or in provincial correctional settings. The same is true for the federally-run Correctional Service of Canada, which includes parole (throughcare) officers and correctional staff in federal penitentiaries. The social work profession pays lip service to corrections as an area of practice but appears to be considerably behind in understanding the realities of contemporary practice. It is not a priority in social work education across the country.

Research on criminal justice practice

Within these three national contexts, social workers who are practitioners in the criminal justice system were asked questions related to issues in contemporary social work practice in criminal justice: Did their social work training for prepare them for what they would face in practice? How important are traditional 'welfare' issues in contemporary work with offenders, particularly if there is an emphasis on public safety? What is the impact of risk as an organising principle for practice? And finally, what might be an ideal preparation for social work in criminal justice?

To explore the research questions further, nine different focus groups were held throughout Scotland, with participation from qualified social workers and, in a few cases, other unqualified staff including social work students on placement. The overwhelming majority of participants were qualified social workers. In Ireland, four focus groups were held, with participants from all areas of the Irish Republic except the northwest. The Canadian data is based on a combination of research projects with probation officers in the province of Manitoba (about 20% of whom have a social work degree), along with survey research with nine of the ten provincial probation directorates and one of the three territorial probation offices. In all, the provinces and territories involved represented over 90% of the Canadian population.

Preparation for Practice

Not surprisingly, those trained prior to the introduction of the What Works agenda in the early 1990s found that there was little of direct relevance to contemporary practice in their early training. Most of that would have been training in 'generic' social work. The following quote from a Scottish social worker puts this into context.

> "When I did my training at Jordanhill [then a college of education with a social work training course, now part of the University of Strathclyde] I don't remember doing anything about criminal justice but equally I don't think

we did anything, say about child abuse or whatever, it was very generic in terms of the training." (Scotland)

There have, however, been opportunities for placements in criminal justice agencies for some time. An Irish probation officer explained it this way:

"I remember people doing placements in Mountjoy [Prison] for example. So people were coming back talking about it, that it was a very interesting [thing] to be doing. They were chatting about it. It [criminal justice] wasn't from the lectures, it was from actually [the] placements." (Ireland)

Generic training has since moved on and at least in Scotland and Ireland there are opportunities to take course modules in criminal justice in addition to placement experiences although, as is indicated in the quote below, not everyone may appreciate the value of these modules:

"... we had an elective – a choice of three and you had to pick two out of the three – criminal justice was the one that I chose. There wasn't a lot of information; it was more like how do you a write a report and how do you work out what their offences are." (Scotland)

In Canadian social work education, most university-based social work degree programmes have a generic base, but will have optional courses in a range of practice or policy contexts, including criminal justice. Criminal justice options are most frequently about policy development with adult or youth offenders. Two university-based social work programmes[1] have an optional practice course, although only one of those introduces students to the elements of What Works. Nearly all Canadian social work programmes have criminal justice field placements as part of the range of placement options, particularly at the Bachelor of Social Work (BSW) level.

Best education for practice

Subjects from both Scotland and Ireland spoke specifically about risk assessment as part of social work training, and also more broadly as to what might constitute best preparation for criminal justice practice.

A question on exposure to the theory of risk along with its application in criminal justice decision-making as part of educational preparation elicited limited discussion in all focus groups. It would appear that what people learn about risk in Scotland was reported as what they experience through in-service training and preparation for proper completion of the assessment forms. In Ireland where focus group participants did mention risk assessment as part of a degree programme or another qualification course, it was usually in the context of various practice areas including child protection and criminal justice.

Risk as it relates to social work practice is a common theme in Canadian social work education, although consideration of how it applies to practice is focused on child protection and possibly mental health.

Answers to questions pertaining to the broader question about what might constitute a good foundation for criminal justice practice were that a combination of educational preparation and experience, through a supervised placement or work in some other related area, were considered in general the ideal. Since nearly all focus group participants were social workers in both Scotland and Ireland, the emphasis on social work training is hardly surprising. Positive comments were made about training received once people had come into the service. Generic social work training, including criminal justice placements, work experience in other areas of social services, and focused in-service training, were all seen as important contributors to being prepared for practice.

Although Canadian probation officers were not asked the question specifically, heads of probation made it clear that their idea of who to hire was social science graduates in a range of disciplines. However, in some cases, particularly Ontario, job advertisements[2] for probation officers continue to mention the importance of social work skills, although a social work qualification is not a requirement.

Welfare issues in contemporary criminal justice practice

Some concerns were expressed in the research in Scotland and Ireland about offenders' problems that did not 'fit' the category of criminogenic need, but which nevertheless were recognisable in a more traditional sense of 'need' (Doyal & Gough, 1991) and the fear that these needs may be left behind or ignored in contemporary practice. Regardless of whether or not these fears are/were well founded, it was clear from the responses that the participants in the focus groups in both Scotland and Ireland were aware of this as an issue. Another common theme related to this was that contemporary practice (as perhaps had been true before) necessitated a careful balancing of the care and control aspects of practice (Barry, 2000). Many saw the What Works approach as driven by a community safety agenda with politicians and the media pushing a very populist and at times very punitive ways of dealing with offenders, thus emphasising the 'control' aspect at the expense of broader welfare type issues. While not opposed to holding offenders to account, many in the focus groups felt that an over-emphasis on punishment minimised the work that social workers are capable of doing. An emphasis on control and surveillance, possibly made easier by actuarially based risk assessment, was thought to come from a community safety agenda promoted by the media and politicians. These sentiments can be seen in the brief comments made during research focus groups given below"

"[W]ay back when I was a young one, one of the issues that was part of the paradigm that I spoke about was, the issue of care versus control, and grappling with sort of the social control elements of social work and the sort of therapeutic support and welfare elements, so that's there as one of those bedrock ideas, so it's nothing new." (Scotland)

"I think that that balance is important and I ... because I'm seeing [a] change in the service. What I think we might be concerned with ... is looking at what's happening in England in the probation service there, and looking at things coming in our own service like national standards which you can see, the box ticking, you see the influence of politicians and what's going to look good in the public eye, and public interest and that, and how that's going to be served in that way." (Ireland)

"... perhaps a person while they may be low risk, they have a lot of needs, now that does not mean to say that you drag them into criminal justice system, but you don't just send them on their merry way, I think professionally." (Ireland)

"I think there has been a fairly significant shift in this country [Ireland] and from kind of, you know, if you take the two kinds of paradigms, of two ideal paradigms, of a welfarist kind of approach which we had, towards more a correction, which we chose the Canadian model of corrections services, I think." (Ireland)

In Canada, the views of most of the heads of probation across the country were clear that probation services were seen as a correctional service. On the issue of providing welfare-type services that do not necessarily focus exclusively on identified criminogenic needs, one provincial probation service (Quebec) made it clear that it did not see its role as risk management but more as providing rehabilitative services. Others easily identified risk management as a core objective, but three stated that risk management also meant that more traditional 'welfare' issues had to be addressed to manage risk successfully. Manitoba probation officers who were participants in a research project on ways of supervising the conditional sentence (a form of house arrest) spoke of trying to balance the care and control aspects of the job in comparing a punitive sentence (conditional sentence) with a probation order.

I think it comes down to discretionary power. I feel far less discretionary power with a conditional sentence than I do with a probation order, and I tend to be more of a drill sergeant, which is what I've been called, when I'm supervising conditional sentences as opposed to more of a social worker. (Canada)   (Bracken, 2007, p 77)

Risk-based practice

More recent descriptions of What Works have suggested that work with offenders can move beyond the control/surveillance aspects of the 'static risk subject' of earlier generations of risk assessment. The offender is now perhaps the 'transformative risk subject' of later generations of risk assessment technologies (Hannah-Moffat, 2005), and therefore amenable to interventive (mostly cognitive-behavioural) strategies. Social workers involved in criminal justice practice in Scotland, Ireland and Canada did not appear to deny the value of risk-based practice.

Objections to risk-based practice from the data tended to be around the apparent rejection of the value of social work skills and the emphasis placed on the control/surveillance aspects of contemporary practice. A concern expressed in the literature on risk assessment in social work (Webb, 2006) has been the potential for 'deskilling' in the sense that basic social work skills such as developing a relationship with a client/offender, working on a plan towards individual change, use of advocacy skills, and community work, were of limited value within a What Works practice framework. With risk assessment identified as a major organising principle for practice, the completion of a risk assessment form seemed to many who participated in the research as either a good way to help structure one's work with offenders, or part of a de-skilling process, which denigrated their skills beyond information gathering and form completion (or 'ticking boxes' as many of the participants said).

There has been much discussion in the literature on this particular issue, focused in three areas: what kind of skill is needed to gather the right information to complete successfully a risk assessment form and is there the time to gather the information to do it; what if anything does one do with the information so collected in terms of integrating it into a plan; and does this mean that other skills are not really necessary?

Barry (2000) identified this as a concern in the early days of the What Works implementation in Scotland. McNeill et al. (2005) reviewed the practice literature and suggested that most offenders have high levels of need (beyond criminogenic needs), and regardless of how these are connected to criminogenic need and offending behaviour, they are issues that must be dealt with by practitioners using a variety of social work skills. Robinson's (2003) work suggested that de-skilling was not necessarily the issue with her sample of probation officers in England. Rather, 'the fact that the LSI-R (a standard risk assessment instrument) proved to be of limited use as a "decision technology" was due less to active resistance on the part of the practitioner than to the complexity of the offender population, which defied actuarial classification' (Robinson, 2003, p 608). Fitzgibbon (2007) located concerns about de-skilling as being a part of the organizational context within which risk assessment takes place. When there are pressures to complete assessments in an atmosphere of 'resource constraints and lack of training in traditional casework skills [the situation] is conducive to all manner of subjective judgements creeping into assessments' (2007, p 96).

Comments by probation officers and criminal justice social workers reflect the general view that there are some distinct advantages to using risk as a way of organising practice, but that it also has its dangers.

"I find the whole idea of risk assessment a bit of a mixed blessing, but one of the good things I liked about it was, it put a sort of a shape on the social control bit, it was always a bit foggy, it put a bit of shape on that and I appreciated that." (Scotland)

"... in the end, your output, your result, your positive outcome is you write a court report and you get on with it, and you do that, and you complete the risk assessment. You've written a standardised report that at times I do feel really, nearly anyone if given the formula could possibly have worked out how to write in six months. 'Cause it is the formula." (Ireland)

"Now I find it [the LSI-R] a very useful thing because I think it gives me a very easy way of organising my information and analysing the information. But in the end, I decide what the risk is. The piece of paper doesn't, and I suppose I fear that down the road we might decide ... that we will put the LSI-R in the place of developing our clinical judgement." (Ireland)

A Canadian probation officer, interviewed almost ten years ago, articulated the following sentiment about risk assessments, seeing it as a tool but also expressing some skepticism. 'There is a subjectivity to it. They [the risk assessments] can change quickly. It's a tool but I don't worship at the altar of them' (Bracken, 2003, p 107).

These comments can be seen as reflecting points along a continuum. At one end is the probation officer from Ireland commenting on how useful she found the LSI-R for organising the information and helping her to make a decision as to the risk level of the offender. Although there was some concern about the professional judgement piece being left behind, at present it was a useful tool. The Scottish and Canadian probation officers were in the middle, appreciative of the utility of risk assessment, but perhaps only as one of may 'tools' that are there to be used. The scepticism about risk assessment (a 'mixed blessing', they are not something to be worshiped) is readily apparent. Lastly, at perhaps the other end is the second Irish probation officer who saw the assessment of risk as part of the 'formula' that virtually anyone could do if given some brief training. In his perspective, there would appear to be limited room for professional judgement.

Conclusion

What Works provides a framework within which to practice, especially with respect to the identification of issues involved in offending (criminogenic need) and what approach may be useful in terms of intervention strategies and with which offenders (responsivity). The data from the practitioners suggests broad agreement with this approach.

However, the What Works agenda is perceived by some as distrustful of social work, because it sees social work's commitment to the person in environment as giving license to 'wander off the track' and lose the focus on reducing offending behaviour within a framework based largely in an individualistic perspective of crime causation.

There were early concerns that social work might disappear as a discipline in criminal justice, particularly as What Works became very much the organising principle for work with offenders. This now seems less likely, given research on desistance (McNeill et al., 2005), the continuing recognition that social work skills are important for work within a What Works framework (Raynor, 2007), and the persistence of social work as a lead discipline in work with offenders, at least in Scotland (ADSW, 2003) and Ireland (Probation Service, 2008). The data would suggest that those surveyed are most concerned about how what they as social workers have learned can be a part of contemporary practice and not to have the What Works approach (especially an emphasis on surveillance) crowd out what social work does. Arguably, early versions or 'generations' of risk assessment looked as if social work had no place in practice derived from What Works. Later generations at least seem to recognize that the findings of actuarial assessments should be integrated into broader case management plans (Bonta & Wormith, 2008). It is difficult to generalise with the Canadian experience, given that data was not collected from focus groups across the country. However, it does seem clear that the attitude of 'indifference' is likely to continue, with criminal justice social work represented primarily in field placement settings for social work training and not as a significant part of a degree curriculum. Provincial criminal justice bureaucracies provide limited acknowledgement of what social work may have to offer.

More recent reviews of social work and criminal justice (McIvor and Raynor, 2007; Ward, 2008) point to the continuing need, and gradual recognition of this need, for the kinds of things social work had been doing for years – promoting skills, values, theories, etc related to personal change. Some of the proponents of What Works appear to have caught up with social work by explaining the importance of 'core correctional practices' (CCP) (Dowden and Andrews, 2004), or more narrowly, 'positive interpersonal skills' (Bonta & Wormith, 2008). CCP are identified as using authority in a firm, fair manner, reinforcing anti-criminal behaviour, teaching problem-solving skills, effective use of community resources and finally good interpersonal skills. It could be said that some or all of these are strongly related to the social work literature on working with involuntary clients (eg Rooney, 1992; Trotter, 1999). As Raynor (2007, p 335) has remarked, 'Others might well define some or all of these "Core Correctional Practices" as social work skills'.

Notes

1 The University of Manitoba and the University of Windsor.
2 A recent posting describes the skills required in the following terms: 'Job requires a sound knowledge of social work theories including analytical skills to prepare reports for the courts to assist in disposition and enforcement; to interact and exchange client information with professionals and judicial officials; to interview clients and assess client needs to establish a plan for rehabilitation'
(www.gojobs.gov.on.ca/PDR.aspx?JobID=21821, downloaded 17/10/09).

References

Andrews, D (1995) 'The Psychology of Criminal Conduct and Effective Treatment' in McGuire, James (ed) *What Works: Reducing Reoffending Guidelines from Research and Practice* Chichester: John Wiley, pp 35-62.

Atkinson, D (2004) 'The What Works Debate: Keeping a human perspective' *Probation Journal* 51(3), pp 248-52.

ADSW (Association of Directors of Social Work) (2003) *ADSW Policy Statement on Criminal Justice Social Work* Edinburgh: ADSW.

Barry, M (2000) 'The Mentor/Monitor Debate in Criminal Justice: "What Works" for Offenders' *British Journal of Social Work* 30(5), pp 575-95.

Bonta, J and Wormith, S (2008) 'Risk and need assessment' in McIvor, G and Raynor, P (eds) *Developments in Social Work with Offenders* London: Jessica Kingsley Publishers, pp 131-52.

Bonta, J, Rugge, T, Scott, T, Bourgon, G and Yessine, A (2008) 'Exploring the Black Box of Community Supervision' *Journal of Offender Rehabilitation* 47(3), pp 248-70.

Bracken, D (2003) 'Skills and knowledge for contemporary probation practice' *Probation Journal* 50(2), pp.101-14.

Bracken, D (2005) 'Developments and Trends in Canadian Probation' *Vista* 10(2), pp 99-108.

Bracken, D (2007) 'Risk Management and/or Punishment in the Community: Supervising Conditional Sentences' *British Journal of Community Justice* 5(2), pp.71-82.

Brodie, I, Nottingham, C, and Plunkett, S (2008) 'A Tale of Two Reports: Social Work in Scotland from Social Work and the Community (1966) to Changing Lives (2006)' *British Journal of Social Work* 38(4), pp 697-715.

Canada (1969) *Report of the Canadian Committee on Corrections Towards Unity: Criminal justice and corrections* Ottawa: Queen's Printer.

CASSW (Canadian Association of Schools of Social Work) (1996) *In Critical Demand: Social Work in Canada* Ottawa: CASSW.

CASW (Canadian Association of Social Workers) (2009) *Guidelines for the Development of Professional Practice Legislation* (www.casw-acts.ca/canada/guidelines_e.pdf).

Canton, R and Hancock, D (eds) *Dictionary of Probation and Offender Management* Cullompton: Willan Publishing.

Christie, A (2005) 'Social Work Education in Ireland: Histories and Challenges' *Portularia* 5(1), pp 111-30.

Dowden, C and Andrews, D A (2004) 'The importance of staff practices in delivering effective correctional treatment: A meta-analysis of core correctional practices' *International Journal of Offender Therapy and Comparative Criminology* 48, pp 203-14.

Doyal, L and Gough, I (1991) *A Theory of Human Need* Basingstoke: Macmillan.

Evans, D G (2005) 'Adult Custodial & Community Corrections' in Turner, J and Turner, F (eds) *Canadian Social Welfare*, (2nd Edition), Toronto: Pearson Education Canada, pp 394-403.

Fitzgibbon, D W (2007) 'Risk analysis and the new practitioner: Myth or reality?' *Punishment Society* 9(1), pp 87-97.

Gelsthorpe, L & Morgan, R (eds) (2007) *Handbook of Probation* Cullompton: Willan Publishing.

Hannah-Moffat, K (2005) 'Criminogenic needs and the transformative risk subject' *Punishment & Society* 7(1), 29-51.

Mair, G (2004) 'Introduction: What Works and What Matters' in Mair, G (ed.) *What Matters in Probation* Cullompton: Willan Publishing.

McGuire, J (ed) What *Works: Reducing Reoffending Guidelines from Research and Practice* Chichester: John Wiley.

McIvor, G and McNeill, F (2007) 'Probation in Scotland: Past Present & Future' in Gelsthorpe, L & Morgan, R (eds) *Handbook of Probation* Cullompton: Willan Publishing.

McIvor, G & Raynor, P (eds) (2007) *Developments in Social Work with Offenders* London: Jessica Kingsley Publishers.

McNally, G (2007) 'Probation in Ireland: A Brief History of the Early Years' *Irish Probation Journal* 4(1), pp 5-24.

McNeill, F & Whyte, B (2007) *Reducing Reoffending: Social Work & Community Justice in Scotland.* Cullompton: Willan Publishing.

McNeill, F, Batchelor, S, Burnett, R & Knox, J (2005) *21st Century Social Work: Reducing Re-offending: Key Practice Skills.* Edinburgh: Scottish Executive.

Parsloe, P (1976) 'Social Work and the Justice Model' *British Journal of Social Work* 6(1), pp 71-89.

Probation Service (2008) 'Currently Recruiting Probation Officers Jun 08' (www.probation.ie/pws/websitepublishing.nsf/Content/News~New+Developments+in+PWS~Currently+Recruiting+Probation+Officers+Jun+08)

Raynor, P (2007) 'Postcript: Opportunities and Threats' in McIvor, G & Raynor, P (eds) *Developments in Social Work with Offenders* London: Jessica Kingsley Publishers, pp 332-38.

Reamer, F G (2004) 'Social work and criminal justice: the uneasy alliance' *Journal of Religion and Spirituality in Social Work* 23(1/2), pp 213-31.

Robinson, G (2003) 'Technicality and Indeterminancy in Probation Practice: A Case Study' *British Journal of Social Work* 33(5), pp 593-610.

Rooney, R (1992) *Strategies for Work with Involuntary Clients* New York: Columbia University Press.

Scottish Executive (2006) *The Framework for Social Work Education in Scotland* Edinburgh: Scottish Executive.

Scottish Government (2006) *Changing Lives: Report of the 21st century social work review* Edinburgh: Scottish Government.

Skehill, C (1999) *The Nature of Social Work in Ireland: A Historical Perspective* Lewiston, ID: Edwin Mellen Press.

Smith, D (2005) 'Probation and Social Work' *British Journal of Social Work* 35(5): pp 621-37.

Trotter, C (1999) *Working with Involuntary Clients: A Guide to Practice* London: Sage Publications.

Turner, J & Turner, F (eds) (2005) *Canadian Social Welfare* (2nd Edition), Toronto: Pearson Education Canada.

Vanstone, M (2004) *Supervising Offenders in the Community: A History of Probation Theory & Practice* Aldershot: Ashgate.

Ward, D (2008) 'BJSW Critical Commentary: What Works in Probation Offender Management: evidence for a new direction?' *British Journal of Social Work* 38(2), pp 395-405.

Chapter 22

What Works with Women who Offend?

Gill McIvor

Introduction

The supervision of offenders in the United Kingdom (UK) and other western jurisdictions has been increasingly characterised by structured programmes of intervention using cognitive-behavioural methods. However, the contemporary landscape of 'what works' with offenders has been shaped almost exclusively by theoretical and empirically based understandings of offending by men. Because there are important differences in male and female offending (and its antecedents), the resulting models of practice, aimed at reducing 'risk factors' associated with offending, are of questionable relevance to women. This chapter provides an overview of what is known about the nature of women's offending and how it is responded to by the criminal justice system. Based predominantly on experiential accounts of practitioners and female offenders and reference to the literature on female desistance, it considers how policy and practice might better engage with and address women's often complex needs. While our understanding of 'what works' with women who offend is still limited, there is growing consensus that services need to be women-focused, accessible, holistic and capable of offering women longer-term support.

The nature of female offending

Perhaps the most striking feature of offending by women is its relatively low incidence in comparison with offending by men. While the gap between male and female offending – the 'gender gap' – is smaller when self-reported offending is considered (e.g. Graham and Bowling, 1995; Flood-Page et al., 2000) boys are more likely than girls to report having committed all but the least common offences (Jamieson et al., 1999), to report more frequent offending and to report committing more serious offences (Jamieson et al., 1999).

Across different jurisdictions, women represent a relatively small proportion of those convicted and sentenced by the courts (McIvor, 2007). In England and Wales, for instance, women represented only 19 per cent of defendants who were convicted of an offence in 2005 (Home Office, 2006) while men accounted for 85% of all convictions in Scotland in 2007/08 (Scottish Government, 2009a). In both jurisdictions, men are more likely than women to be convicted of almost all categories of offence, with the exception of 'other' crimes of indecency (offences mainly related to prostitution) in Scotland and neglect of children, 'offences by a prostitute', Education Act offences and non-payment of a television licence in England and Wales. In Scotland, other categories where women formed a higher than average proportion of those convicted included 'other' non-sexual crimes of violence (including neglect or maltreatment of children), fraud, shoplifting and 'other' miscellaneous offences (McIvor, 2007).

In England and Wales in 2005 the most common offences for which women were convicted were failure to pay for a television licence, driving while disqualified, shoplifting, non-payment of fares on public transport, common assault, offences under the Education Act and failing to surrender to bail (Home Office, 2006). Scottish data for 2004/05 indicated that women were most likely to have been convicted of failure to pay for a television licence, shoplifting, breach of the peace, assault (including resisting arrest), driving while disqualified and speeding (Scottish Executive, 2006a).

Taken together, this data indicates that women's offending is less common, less frequent and less serious than offending by men, suggesting that women's pathways into offending may be different and that different theoretical explanations for male and female involvement in crime are required.

Pathways to offending, criminogenic needs and risk

Women's offending challenges traditional theoretical explanations of crime that were developed essentially to explain offending by men. This has resulted in the development of theoretical explanations for women's offending that have focused on a range of biological, psychological and sociological factors and which increasingly have incorporated feminist analyses to locate women's offending within patriarchal structures and wider socio-structural influences (Gelsthorpe, 2004). Increasingly, attention is being paid to identifying the factors that appear to be associated with women's pathways towards crime, reflecting the recognition, from qualitative studies that privilege women's understandings of their experiences, that women's needs and pathways into crime are different from those of men (Kendall, 2002). Women's own accounts of their offending suggest that is often rooted in structural inequalities such as poverty and deprivation (for example, stealing to provide for children) or problems relating to substance misuse. Female offenders frequently have experiences of abuse, psychological problems (including depression and low self-esteem) and past or present involvement in abusive personal relationships (Chesney-Lind, 1997; Rumgay, 2000; Loucks, 2004), although how these latter experiences may contribute to women's offending is less well understood.

It is now recognised that women are likely to have different 'criminogenic needs' (ie. 'needs' that are associated with an increased risk of offending) from men (Hedderman, 2004a) because their routes into offending and reasons for offending are often different (Jamieson et al., 1999). Some needs – such as experiences of physical and sexual abuse – appear to be more specific (although not necessarily unique) to women (Hollin and

Palmer, 2006). Others – such as criminal history, unemployment and substance misuse – appear to be associated with offending among both women and men. However, even if certain factors appear to be *associated* with both male and female offending, how these factors intersect with offending may be different, reflecting gendered experiences, motivations and opportunities (Shaw and Hannah-Moffat, 2004). For example, in a study of young people and offending in Scotland, Jamieson *et al.* (1999) found that young women often reported having been initiated into drug-use by their male partners and having subsequently begun committing offences to finance their (and often their partner's) use of illicit drugs. This is consistent with Australian research that suggests that drug use may play a different role in the development of male and female offending (Makkai and Payne, 2003; Johnson, 2004), with men more likely than women to report involvement in offending *prior to* their first use of drugs.

Despite the evidence of different pathways and explanations for female crime, programmatic interventions with women who offend have tended to be based on the assumption that men and women have broadly similar needs and that interventions that have been developed for men need only be modified slightly to make them suitable for women. However, the limited research on patterns of female offending means that the ability to develop gender-appropriate assessment tools and related interventions is inherently constrained. The technology of risk assessment has been derived from research involving samples principally of (young, white) men with the result that "the literature and subsequent practices ignore and dismiss the effect of gender and diversity, or the social and economic constraints on offenders' lives" (Shaw and Hannah-Moffat, 2004, p 91). Risk assessment, according to Shaw and Hannah-Moffat, redefines 'needs' as risk factors related to recidivism rather than as a statement of entitlements, limiting the scope of interventions to those factors for which a direct link to recidivism can be found. The result is that risk assessment practices "decontextualise, individualise and pathologise offending in accordance with gendered and racialised norms" (Shaw and Hannah-Moffat, 2004, p 91) by failing to identify and encourage a focus on the structural barriers that contribute to women's involvement in crime (Kendall, 2002). It has further been argued that the redefining of 'welfare needs' as 'psychological needs' related to risk of recidivism (Hudson, 2002) has contributed to an increase in the imprisonment of women because risk assessment practices result in women – who tend to have more 'needs' than men – being construed as 'riskier' than they actually are (Carlen, 2003).

The sentencing of women

Imprisonment
Female offending is less frequent, less serious and more transient than offending by men and women who offend therefore represent a relatively small proportion of those imprisoned by the courts. However, the use of imprisonment with women has increased in recent years, resulting in female prison populations reaching unprecedented levels.

For example, in England and Wales the average number of women in prison increased by 173 per cent between 1992 and 2002 (compared with an increase of 50 per cent in the average male prison population over the same period) while the percentage of women in the prison population increased from 3.4 per cent to 6.1 per cent over the same period. In 2002, women were most likely to be imprisoned for drug offences (41%), violence against the person (16%) and theft and handling (14%), with 71 per cent receiving sentences of less than one year (Home Office, 2004a). More recent data reveals a continuing trend, with 4,370 women in custody in England and Wales in December 2005. Between December 2004 and December 2005, the female prison population increased by 3 per cent, with the highest increases among young women under 18 years of age (20 per cent) and those aged between 18 and 20 years (16 per cent) (NOMS, 2006).

A similar picture is found in Scotland, where the daily sentenced female prison population increased by 73 per cent between 1996/97 and 2004/05 and the percentage of women in the daily prison population increased from 3 per cent to 5 per cent (Scottish Executive, 2006a). In 2004/05 adult female prisoners (ie, those aged 21 years and over) were most likely to have been imprisoned for other thefts (primarily shoplifting), drug offences, petty assaults and breaches of the peace and more than two-thirds of adult women who received a prison sentence (71 per cent) were sentenced to less than six months in custody (Scottish Executive, 2006b).

The reasons for the increase in women's imprisonment are likely to be complex (Gelsthorpe, 2006), although there is little evidence that it reflects marked changes in levels or patterns of female crime. In Scotland, for instance, there is no evidence that women were proportionately more likely to be convicted of crimes and offences during the period when the female prison population rose and the *number* of women given custodial sentences did not increase to any significant extent over this period. However, the average length of sentence imposed on women rose sharply (from 172 days in 1996/97 to a high of 276 days in 2002/03) suggesting that *some* women who were convicted were being dealt with more harshly by the courts (McIvor, 2007).

In England and Wales, the number of women convicted *did* increase between 1992 and 2002, but this appears to be because fewer of those who were arrested were cautioned rather than having their case taken to court (Home Office, 2004a). Hedderman (2004b) has concluded from her analysis of sentencing trends that while *some* of the increase in the numbers of women imprisoned in England and Wales might be accounted for by the fact that more women were appearing before the courts, the scale of the increase, coupled by a lack of evidence that women were committing more serious offences and the observation that the use of custodial sentences was increasing across all offence types, suggested instead that sentencing by the courts – especially the Magistrates Courts – was becoming more severe. Research by Patel and Stanley (2008) on the use of the community order and suspended sentence order in England and Wales suggests that these disposals are often replacing other non-custodial sentences (such as fines) and that this, combined with a relatively high breach rate, is likely to result in even more women going to prison.

Although the types of offences for which women are imprisoned and the lengths of sentences they receive would suggest that most in fact present little 'risk' to society, the personal and social costs of being imprisoned – and the economic costs to society – can be immense. The backgrounds of women in prison tend to be characterised by experiences of abuse, drug misuse, poor educational attainment, poverty, psychological distress and self-harm. While men often share many of these characteristics, problems among female prisoners are generally much more acute and their offending presents less of a threat to public safety (Loucks, 1998). Female prisoners are more likely than male prisoners to have a history of physical or sexual abuse (Stermac et al., 1991) and are more likely to self–harm (Leibling, 1992). Imprisonment often serves to weaken or destroy women's existing ties to the community, including ties with their children (Caddle and Crisp, 1997; Sheehan and Flynn, 2007). An independent inspection of Cornton Vale prison in Scotland, while commending the progress that had been made in improving the physical estate and opportunities for prisoners, concluded that much still had to be done and questioned what the prison could do for the very damaged women who were sent to it by the courts (HM Inspectorate of Prisons, 2005).

Despite clear evidence that female prisoners have a range of social and personal problems and are likely to require significant amounts of support on release (Wilkinson, 2004), relatively little research has focused on the services accessed by and support available to women following a prison sentence. There is, however, evidence that female ex-prisoners have considerable needs (Morris et al., 1995; Gelsthorpe and Sharpe, 2007) and that they have more needs than similarly sentenced men (Blanchette and Dowden, 1998). Despite this, women often have limited information about services that are available in the communities to which they return and little attention appears to be paid to women's need for access to the structural determinants of social justice (such as appropriate housing and employment) when they are released (Carlen, 2003; Hannah-Moffat, 2003; McIvor et al., 2009).

Carlen (2003) has argued that the proliferation of prison programmes and in-prison reforms may persuade sentencers that imprisonment can be beneficial in its effects, especially for those who are deemed to be 'at risk' and prisons may be viewed by the courts as a means of providing women with a period of 'respite' from long-standing drug misuse and associated problems. Yet, as Carlen and Tombs (2006) have argued, the resources that have been introduced into prisons, such as anti-addiction programmes, would be much more effective if implemented in a community setting.

Women and community sentences
Given the differences in the pattern and nature of offending by men and women, it is of little surprise that there are important gender differences in the use and experience of community sentences. More specifically, the use of community sentences with women

raises important questions about *distribution* and *delivery*. The delivery of community sentences – and, more specifically, consideration of what effective intervention (what works) with women might look like – is considered shortly. First, however, some brief commentary on the distribution of community sentences is required.

There are important gender differences in how often community sentences are used and in the characteristics of men and women made subject to different community disposals. For example, traditionally, women have been under-represented on community service orders and over-represented on probation (e.g. Worrall, 1996). While disparities in the use of different disposals with men and women are not as great as they previously were, notable gender differences remain. For example Mair *et al.* (2007) found that women made up just under 14 per cent of all offenders given a community order in England and Wales and were most likely to receive additional requirements of supervision and unpaid work. However, Patel and Stanley (2008) found that women were more likely than men to receive supervision and drug treatment requirements while women were less likely than men to receive requirements involving unpaid work and participation at accredited programmes.

In Scotland, women represented 18 per cent of those given probation orders and drug treatment and training orders (DTTOs) in 2006/07: that is, they were as likely as men to receive these disposals. However women were more likely than men to receive additional probation requirements relating to medical/psychiatric/psychological treatment or drug treatment and were more likely than men to have their probation order or DTTO breached (in the case of probation, as a result of non-compliance as opposed to the commission of a further offence) (Scottish Government, 2007). The issue of women's compliance with community penalties is returned to later in this chapter.

By contrast, women remain under-represented on community service in Scotland, making up only 10 per cent of those given orders in 2006/07. Despite the longstanding perception of community service as a 'young man's punishment' (Worrall, 1996), women given community service tend to do better than men, being slightly more likely to complete their orders or have them revoked for reasons other than breach (Scottish Government, 2007) and reconviction rates are lower for women than for men (Scottish Government, 2009b). This may, however, be partly a result of differences in the prior criminal histories of men and women sentenced to community service, with women tending to be less heavily convicted and more often first offenders than men (McIvor, 1998).

Supervising women in the community

Having considered how the *use* of community sentences differs between men and women, attention is now turned to the question of *delivery*, including the content of effective intervention and issues surrounding enforcement and compliance. The acknowledgement of gender differences in pathways to crime requires the development of approaches to supervision that are capable of meeting female offenders' needs: applying or adapting interventions that have been developed for use with male offenders is unlikely to 'work' with women who offend. The development and shaping of gender-appropriate interventions (e.g. Bloom *et al.*, 2003) has been premised on this recognition of difference and aimed at ensuring that the services women receive and the way in which they receive them are appropriate to their circumstances and needs. In Scottish research into women and probation, social work practitioners identified a number of ways in which female probationers differed from men. For example, women were considered more likely to be in a state of crisis and to present a range of problems. They were more likely, as a consequence, to be demanding of workers' time and to require more extensive intervention and emotional support (McIvor *et al.*, 2000; Barry and McIvor, 2008). Women were thought more likely than men to have committed offences that did not in themselves require detailed attention and discussion and were considered more responsive to informal contact (such as phoning or 'dropping in' should the need arise). Despite women who offend being acknowledged to have complex needs, social workers believed that existing community services were compartmentalised and unsuited to women with multiple problems (Barry and McIvor, 2008).

What women want

Interviews with women on probation provide helpful pointers towards understanding what women want from and value about supervision. For instance, female probationers in Scotland apparently valued the emphasis that their social workers placed on their problems rather than on the offence and receiving both practical and emotional support. Above all, however, the benefit of having someone to talk to about and understand their problems was stressed. As one woman who was interviewed explained: "It was like a therapy to be able to talk about my feelings, about the way things had been. That was basically what we did. We talked and talked and talked". The importance to women of talking over problems should not be underestimated. It is consistent with Gilligan's (1982) feminist theory of psychological development, which emphasises its relational dimension for women. Talking over issues with their supervisor appears to be important for women as a means of gaining increased self-understanding, exploring feelings that have previously been unacknowledged, re-assessing their self-worth and, by being empowered through gaining a fresh perspective, starting to rebuild their lives.

In McIvor *et al.*'s (2000) study, women appreciated supervisors who were caring, understanding, interested in them and easy to talk to. Female probationers also appeared to respond positively to their supervisor's accessibility (being there to turn to when problems arise), commitment and 'professionalism': striking an appropriate balance between friendliness and authority and avoiding creating dependence. Another important aspect of the supervisory relationship – which contributed to reported improvements in women's sense of self-worth – was being treated with respect. Being treated by their supervisor in a manner that signified lack of respect, by contrast, could increase the likelihood of women resisting engagement and failing to comply.

The apparent importance attached by women to their relationship with their social worker raises interesting questions about supervisors' gender. Horn and Evans (2000) found that female probation officers in England were allocated more female probationers and male workers more male probationers. Case allocation policies typically result in female probationers being supervised by women and research suggests that women have a preference for a female supervisor (Wright and Kemshall, 1994) although this is also true of men (Mair and May, 1997). While around one half of the female probationers interviewed by McIvor et al. (2000) did not express a preference regarding the sex of their supervisor, those who did opted mostly for a woman because they found it easier to discuss personal issues with women, thought that other women were better able to empathise with them by drawing on their own personal experiences or had difficulty trusting men as a result of past experiences of abuse.

It is important to recognise that the experiences and needs of women who offend are also structured by other dimensions of diversity such as ethnicity (Chigwada-Bailey, 2003), age (Wahidin, 2005) and cultural or religious practices that may intersect in ways that remain relatively poorly understood. Nonetheless, attending to and addressing diversity in social work practice with women who offend is necessary to ensure that services and interventions provided can be as effective as possible and to meet demands for equality of treatment that are now enshrined in law. As Gelsthorpe and McIvor (2007) have argued, equality of treatment need not be equated with the same treatment: although it is important that negative discrimination is avoided, it is equally important that dimensions of diversity are appropriately accommodated as a means of promoting both procedural justice and social justice.

Compliance and enforcement

Practitioners supervising women in the community need to take account of the practical and other constraints that often make it difficult for them to comply with the requirements of their orders. These include the chaotic lifestyles of some women, linked to mental health difficulties and/or the misuse of alcohol and drugs, however women's willingness to engage may also be affected by perceptions of unfair (i.e. unduly harsh) treatment by the courts or by their attitudes towards authority derived from experiences of social work involvement as a parent or as a child (McIvor et al., 2000). Studies of DTTOs and Drug Courts in Scotland have also indicated that women's partner's – who are likely themselves to be involved in drug misuse – may have an adverse impact upon their ability to comply (Eley et al., 2002; McIvor et al., 2006).

Women under supervision are also more likely than men to have responsibility for the care of children and other dependants which raises additional questions regarding the timing and location of appointments. Home-based appointments may be more convenient for women with children, although some women may prefer office-based appointments because they are better able to offer privacy and 'space'. For example, some women interviewed by McIvor *et al.* (2000) were critical of the time, cost or effort involved in attending office appointments. Others, on the other hand, reported that attending office appointments was a source of embarrassment and stigma.

Women are likely to value some flexibility in the timing and location of appointments both on practical grounds and to facilitate a more responsive approach to their needs. The key issue, as Wright and Kemshall (1994) have argued, is ensuring that women have been consulted with respect to these matters. However, it is also important that practitioners are able to exercise some flexibility with respect to how orders are *enforced* to avoid women being penalised for non-compliance as a result of circumstances that are often beyond their control.

The limitations of cognitive-behavioural interventions

From the preceding discussion it will be clear that women tend to attach considerable importance to the relational aspects of supervision. This is consistent both with Gilligan's (1982) feminist theory of psychological development and with research that suggests that women and men have different learning styles, and has implications for the types of interventions that are likely to engage women successfully in the process of change (Gelsthorpe and McIvor, 2007). In particular, despite being the approach associated with accredited programmes in the UK, the appropriateness of cognitive-behavioural programmes for women who offend has been called into question on empirical, methodological and theoretical grounds. Cognitive-behavioural interventions – derived from social learning theory, cognitive theory and behaviourism – are premised on the relationships between thoughts, feelings and behaviour and assume that offending is a result of offenders having failed to acquire particular cognitive skills.

At the empirical level, few evaluations of cognitive-behavioural interventions with female offenders have been carried out and where they have there is little evidence of an effect on recidivism (Lart *et al.*, 2008). For example, Cann (2006) found no evidence of lower reconviction rates among female prisoners who had participated in accredited cognitive skills programmes (Enhanced Thinking Skills and Reasoning and Rehabilitation) than among matched prisoners who had not. Cann suggests that there was no evidence that the programmes targeted appropriate criminogenic needs among female prisoners, possibly because they were designed to address male criminogenic needs using methods compatible with the learning styles of men.

It has also been argued that having been developed from research conducted on young men, cognitive-behavioural programmes have limited relevance for women and even when adapted for use with women (or developed specifically for women) this tends to be constrained by a narrow focus on factors that are predicted to bring about reductions in crime (Shaw and Hannah-Moffat, 2004). Moreover, by positing a link between cognitive deficits and offending, cognitive-behavioural programmes have been accused of teaching women that their problems are a result of their own deficient thinking, holding women responsible for their own oppression and attempting to regulate their conduct by drawing attention away from the structural inequalities of their lives (Kendall, 2002; Shaw and Hannah-Moffat, 2004).

This is not to suggest that women who offend *never* make inappropriate choices with respect to their decisions to offend. Some women may benefit from a relatively structured exploration of how their attitudes and beliefs may have contributed to their offending but this may be more effective if it seeks to build on women's existing strengths and competencies (Porporino and Fabiano, 2005) and it needs to be understood in the context of severely constrained choices. As Worrall (2002, p 144) notes, "important as enhanced thinking skills are, they can only be, at best, a prerequisite to empowering women to make better choices, if the choices genuinely exist". It needs to be recognised that many woman commit crime in response to deep-rooted and enduring socio-economic conditions that are difficult to change. Drawing both on the views and experiences of women and on theoretical and methodological critiques of the appropriateness of the 'what works' approach to effective supervision of women, the foregoing analysis points clearly to the importance of engaging with female offenders in ways that acknowledge and aim to address the structural context of their offending. Thus, according to Gelsthorpe (2004, p 29):

> Criminal justice practice needs to focus on not just the immediate lead up to the crime of an individual female offender (the psychological processes involved) but on the broad social and individual factors. [...] Far from being irrelevant to an understanding of women's offending, personal difficulties and welfare problems are inextricable from it.

This conclusion receives support from the growing body of literature on desistance from crime, which provides additional pointers to effective practice with women who offend.

Supporting female desistance

In recent years, increasing attention has been paid to the processes associated with desistance from offending: how and why people eventually stop committing crimes (e.g. Graham & Bowling, 1995; Rex, 1999; Maruna, 2001; Farrall, 2002). Understanding the processes that accompany or promote the cessation of offending may inform the development of more effective interventions with offenders (McNeill, 2003, 2006). Research on desistance has concentrated primarily on men, although some studies have explored female desistance. There is evidence that young women desist sooner than young men (Graham & Bowling, 1995; Jamieson et al., 1999; Flood-Page et al., 2000) and that there are important gender differences in the process of desistance from crime (McIvor et al., 2004). The process of desistance may be similar in some respects for young men and women, with the familiar themes of maturation, transitions, changed lifestyles and relationships being pertinent for both groups (e.g. Jamieson et al., 1999; Giordano, et al., 2002). However, Jamieson et al. (1999) found that young women were more likely than young men to cite moral as opposed to utilitarian rationales for stopping offending and were more likely to emphasise the importance of relational aspects of this process, including parental attitudes, experiences of victimisation, the assumption of parental responsibilities and dissociation from offending peers. The relational aspects of female desistance have also been highlighted by Giordano et al. (2002) Barry (2007) and McIvor et al. (2009).

In the latter study of women leaving prison in Victoria, Australia there were clear differences in the experiential accounts of women who had successfully desisted since leaving prison and those who had continued to offend. Many women attributed their desistance to their success in avoiding drug use since leaving prison, in some cases prompted by self-reflection about how they had been affected by drugs. This enhanced self-awareness was in some cases linked to personal resolve to achieve and sustain a 'better' or 'normal' life and often involved women taking active steps to dissociate from former lifestyles and associates and find new interests and friends. Supportive family and other relationships were identified by several women as having contributed to their desistance while concerns about the impact of continued offending on women's children also emerged as a dominant theme (McIvor et al., 2009). In comparison with women who had continued to offend (most often as a result of resumed drug use and financial difficulties), the accounts of desisters' post-prison experiences were characterised by a sense of personal agency and self-efficacy, which has also been highlighted by Hannah-Moffat (2003) and Rumgay (2004) as being central to successful desistance among women.

Practice aimed at supporting women's desistance should, therefore, focus on promoting self-efficacy and facilitating the creation of positive social and family networks that provide women with alternative opportunities for personal development and self-fulfilment (Rumgay, 2000) while avoiding stereotyped assumptions about the significance for women of caring and other relational responsibilities (Weaver and McNeill, forthcoming). Equally, however, it is important to heed the lessons from studies in which desistance has eluded women and be aware of the likely barriers to positive change. These include drug use (often initiated by a partner or friend), unsuitable and unstable accommodation, boredom, mental health issues (such as anxiety and depression) and a range of stressful experiences such as bereavement, redundancy, homelessness and relationship breakdown (Jamieson et al., 1999; McIvor et al., 2009). In short, promoting and supporting desistance involves enabling women to access both social supports and the structural requirements of social justice. The challenges in doing so are evidenced by the reported lack of appropriate services and resources for women who offend including education and employment opportunities, affordable social housing, mental health provision and drug services (McIvor et al., 2000; Barry and McIvor, 2008).

Developing holistic approaches to women who offend

The recognition that women have different pathways into (and out of) offending from men resulted in the development, in the 1990s, of gender-appropriate approaches to the supervision of women. For example, Bloom and Covington (1998) argued that effective intervention with women should build on women's strengths and competences and focus on developing their coping and decision-making skills, promoting independence and self-reliance and dealing with specific women's issues such as substance misuse, domestic violence, sexual abuse, pregnancy and parenting and relationships. Bloom and Covington stressed that services needed to be tailored to the needs of women and not simply adapted from services that have been developed for men and that they needed to be provided in a safe, trusting and supportive women-focused environment.

Growing awareness of the need for gender-appropriate services for women who offend prompted the establishment in England and Wales in 2004 of a cross-departmental Women's Offending Reduction Programme (WORP), aimed at developing a more co-ordinated response to the characteristics and needs of female offenders (Home Office, 2004b; NOMS, 2005). The key priorities for the programme were making community interventions more appropriate and accessible for women; meeting women's mental health needs; dealing with substance misuse; building the evidence base to identify what work best with female offenders; and communicating, training and providing guidance on gender issues (Home Office, 2004b). More recently, the independent review of vulnerable women in the criminal justice system conducted by Baroness Corston (Corston, 2007) called for a more focused and gender-specific approach to women who offend and those at risk of offending. The government accepted the majority of the 43 recommendations in the Corston Report and established a cross-departmental Criminal Justice Women's Strategy Unit to implement its response.

As Gelsthorpe (2007) notes, an outcome of the WORP was the establishment of pilot Women's Offending Action Teams in two regions to provide a multi-agency response to female offenders' needs. A key recommendation of the Corston Report was the development of women's centres for women involved in offending or at risk of offending, drawing on lessons learned from the operation of existing initiatives for women such as the Asha Centre in West Mercia (formerly the Hereford and Worcester groupwork programme for female probationers) (Roberts, 2002; Gelsthorpe and Sharpe, 2007) and aiming to provide an integrated, holistic and accessible service for women at different stages of the criminal justice system. The development of 'one-stop shop' services for women has been identified by the government as a priority under its Diverting Women from Custody project (Ministry of Justice, 2008) and is being taken forward in the Together Women Programme, introduced in five centres in the North West of England and Yorkshire and Humberside in late 2006/early 2007. The centres offer a range of services and supports to women through service providers holding surgeries and through a drop-in facility where women can access a range of activities. Together Women taps into existing community services or aims to establish additional services where gaps exist. An initial evaluation suggested that women valued having access to women-only provision and appreciated the helpfulness and interest shown by staff (Hedderman *et al.*, 2008).

In Scotland, the 218 Time Out Centre in Glasgow was established in late 2003, managed by a voluntary agency (Turning Point). 218 provides a range of residential and non-residential services offering a holistic, gender-appropriate approach to women who are at risk of imprisonment (Loucks *et al.*, 2006; Malloch and Loucks, 2007). In delivering a programme specifically designed for women, 218 makes available a variety of in-house services provided by a range of health and criminal justice agencies in a safe environment. It also aims to link women into a range of external services, connecting them to their communities as advocated by Rumgay (2000) as a means of providing longer-term support. The establishment of 218 was recommended by a Ministerial Group on female offenders, which also advocated shifting the penal culture more broadly away from punishment and towards rehabilitation and 'treatment', with a particular emphasis on the development of gender-responsive provision (Scottish Executive, 2002).

An evaluation of 218 identified reported reductions in drug use and offending and reported improvements in health and well-being among women who had made use of the service. Women appeared to value having access to drug services, the relationships established with Centre staff and being linked into other relevant services (Loucks *et al.*, 2006) although the focus on 218 as a *criminal justice* service (rather than a service for socially excluded women) may have placed important constraints on the impact it could make (Malloch *et al.*, 2008). A key challenge for policy and practice, of course, lies in identifying how aspects of best practice that have evolved through services such as 218 and other women-centred initiatives can be rolled out to areas where such dedicated facilities are not considered feasible in terms of capacity and cost. In the absence of dedicated provision, robust case management and effective advocacy by supervisors is all the more important to ensure that women are able to access the range of services they require.

Conclusions and implications

Despite some evidence from Scottish data that women given probation are slightly less likely than men to be reconvicted within two years (Scottish Government, 2009b) there is still little 'hard' evidence of what works with women who offend and why. A recent review of interventions for female offenders commissioned by the Ministry of Justice for England and Wales concluded that there was a dearth of research into 'what works', despite the growing policy attention to women who offend in the UK and elsewhere and the recognition that women's criminogenic needs are likely to be different from those of men (Lart *et al.*, 2008). However, as Kendall (2002, p. 191) observes "the 'what works' research is informed by an epistemology rooted in traditional notions of the scientific method which devalues subjectivity, assumes a linear causality and emphasises universality". The growing body of *qualitative* research that seeks to give a voice to women in the criminal justice system provides important pointers to what women themselves find helpful about supervision and what may help support their efforts to desist from crime.

Despite our somewhat limited evidence of 'what works' in reducing offending among women, it is possible, based on a contemporary understanding of female offending and response to it, to identify emerging lessons for effective service provision (Gelsthorpe *et al.*, 2007). The starting point for effective policy and practice has to be an acknowledgement of women's distinctive pathways into crime and the implications this has for the types of services and interventions that may be required. Women who offend are likely to have complex problems and needs and, compared to men, to require more intensive support. Flexibility with respect to patterns of contact and enforcement will also be necessary to ensure that services are appropriately responsive (particularly in times of crisis) and to avoid unnecessary breach. Effective services should be women-friendly (providing a safe environment in which their problems can be addressed), accessible and holistic, with appropriate provision to meet women's childcare needs. The 'one-stop shop' model offers much promise in this respect but is dependent on effective multi-agency co-operation at the local level, supported by integrated social policies that enable women to access the services and support they need to achieve a sense of social justice and self-efficacy through an improved quality of life.

Developing effective practice with women who offend raises a number of questions for policy and for practice. What services are women likely to need and how can they be made more accessible? How might practice with female offenders and its organisational context need to differ to ensure that it engages with women and meets their needs? How can services be better co-ordinated to provide a more holistic response? What, if any, role should cognitive-behavioural programmes play? What potential does groupwork offer in providing support for isolated and excluded women? How can women be linked into services and resources that will provide them with longer-term support? Finally, what additional consideration should be given to addressing wider questions of diversity to promote social inclusion and citizenship and facilitate desistance from crime? The answers to these questions about how best to develop services and enhance justice for women can only be found in dialogue between policy-makers, practitioners, researchers and, most importantly, women themselves.

References

Barry, M (2007) 'The transitional pathways of young female offenders: Towards a non-offending lifestyle' in Sheehan, R, McIvor, G and Trotter, C (eds) *What Works with Women Offenders*, Cullompton: Willan Publishing.

Barry, M and McIvor, G (2008) *Chaotic Lives: A Profile of Women in the Criminal Justice System in Lothian and Borders* Edinburgh: Lothian and Borders Community Justice Authority (www.cjsw.ac.uk/cjsw/files/ChaoticLivesReport09.pdf).

Blanchette K & Dowden C (1998) 'A profile of federally sentenced women in the community: Addressing needs for successful integration',*Forum on Corrections Research* 10(1), pp 40-43 (www.csc-scc.gc.ca/text/pblct/forum/e101/e101i-eng.shtml, accessed 17 May 2010).

Bloom, B and Covington, S (1998) 'Gender-Specific Programming for Female Offenders: What is it and Why is it Important?', Paper presented at the Annual Meeting of the American Society of Criminology, Washington, DC

Bloom, B, Owen, B and Covington, S (2003) *Gender-Responsive Strategies: Research, practice and Guiding Principles for Women Offenders* Washington DC: National Institute of Justice.

Caddle, D and Crisp, D (1997) *Imprisoned Women and Mothers*, Home Office Research Study 162, London: Home Office.

Cann, J (2006) *Cognitive Skills Programmes: Impact on reducing reconviction among a sample of female prisoners* Home Office Research Findings 276, London: Home Office.

Carlen, P (2003) 'A strategy for women offenders? Lock them up, programme them ... and then send them out homeless' *Criminal Justice Matters,* 5, pp 36-7.

Carlen, P and Tombs, J (2006) 'Reconfigurations of penality: The ongoing case of the women's imprisonment and reintegration industries' *Theoretical Criminology* 10(3), pp 337-60.

Chesney-Lind, M (1997) *The Female Offender: Girls, Women and Crime* Thousand Oaks, CA: Sage Publications.

Chigwada-Bailey, R (2003) *Black Women's Experiences of Criminal Justice* (2nd edition), Winchester: Waterside Press.

Corston, Baroness (2007) *The Corston Report: A Review of Women with Particular Vulnerabilities in the Criminal Justice System* London: Home Office.

Eley, S, Gallop, K, McIvor, G, Morgan, K and Yates, R (2002) *Drug Treatment and Testing Orders: Evaluation of the Scottish Pilots* Edinburgh: Scottish Executive Social Research.

Farrall, S (2002) *Rethinking What Works With Offenders: Probation, Social Context and Desistance From Crime* Cullompton: Willan Publishing.

Flood-Page, C, Campbell, S, Harrington, V and Miller, J (2000) *Youth Crime: Findings from the 1998/99 Youth Lifestyles Survey* Home Office Research Study 209, London: Home Office.

Gelsthorpe, L (2004) 'Female offending: A theoretical overview' in McIvor, G (ed) *Women who Offend* London: Jessica Kingsley Publishers.

Gelsthorpe, L (2006) 'Women and criminal justice: Saying it again, again and again' *The Howard Journal* 45(4), pp 421-4.

Gelsthorpe, L (2007) 'Sentencing and gender' in Sheehan, R, McIvor, G and Trotter, C (eds) *What Works with Women Offenders* Cullompton: Willan Publishing.

Gelsthorpe, L and McIvor, G (2007) 'Difference and diversity in probation', in L Gelsthorpe and R Morgan (eds.) *Handbook of Probation*, Cullompton: Willan Publishing.

Gelsthorpe, L and Sharpe, G (2007) 'Women and resettlement', in A Hucklesby and L Hagley-Dickinson (eds.) *Prisoner Resettlement: Policy and Practice*, Cullompton: Willan Publishing.

Gelsthorpe, L, Sharpe, G and Roberts, J (2007) *Provision for Women Offenders in the Community* London: The Fawcett Society.

Gilligan, C (1982) *In a Different Voice* Cambridge, MA: Harvard University Press.

Giordano, P C, Cernkovich, S A and Rudolph, J L (2002) 'Gender, crime, and desistance: Toward a Theory of Cognitive Transformation' *American Journal of Sociology* 107, pp 990-1064.

Graham, J & Bowling, B (1995) *Young People and Crime* London: Home Office.

Hannah-Moffat, K (2003) 'Getting women out: The limits of reintegration reform' *Criminal Justice Matters* 53, pp 44-5.

Hedderman, C (2004a) 'The 'criminogenic' needs of women offenders' in McIvor, G (ed) *Women Who Offend* London: Jessica Kingsley Publishers.

Hedderman, C (2004b) 'Why are more women being sentenced to custody?'in McIvor, G (ed) *Women Who Offend*, London: Jessica Kingsley Publishers.

Hedderman, C, Palmer, E and Hollin, C (2008) *Implementing services for women offenders and those 'at risk' of offending*, action research with Together Women, London: Ministry of Justice.

HM Inspectorate of Prisons (2005) *HM and YOI Cornton Vale – Inspection 2-3 February 2005* Edinburgh: Scottish Executive.

Hollin, C and Palmer, E (2006) 'Criminogenic need and women offenders: A critique of the literature', *Legal and Criminological Psychology* 11(2), pp 179-95.

Home Office (2004a) *Statistics on Women and the Criminal Justice System* London: The Stationery Office.

Home Office (2004b) *Women's Offending Reduction Programme: Action plan* London: Home Office

Home Office (2006) *Criminal Statistics 2005 England and Wales* London: Home Office.

Horn, R and Evans, M (2000) 'The effect of gender on pre-sentence reports' *The Howard Journal* 39(2), pp 184-97.

Hudson, B (2002) 'Gender issues in penal policy and penal theory' in Carlen, P (ed) *Women and Punishment: The Struggle for Justice* Cullompton: Willan Publishing.

Jamieson, J, McIvor, G and Murray, C (1999) *Understanding Offending Among Young People* Edinburgh: The Stationery Office.

Johnson, H (2004) *Key Findings from the Drug Use Careers of Female Offenders Study* Canberra, ACT: Australian Institute of Criminology.

Kendall, K (2002) 'Time to think again about cognitive behavioural programmes' in Carlen, P (ed) *Women and Punishment: The Struggle for Justice* Cullompton: Willan Publishing.

Lart, R, Pantazis, C, Pemberton, S, Turner, W and Almeida, C (2008) *Interventions Aimed at Reducing Re-offending in Female Offenders: A Rapid Evidence Assessment* London: Ministry of Justice (www.justice.gov.uk/publications/docs/intervention-reduce-female-reoffending.pdf, last accessed 16 October 2009)

Leibling, A (1992) *Suicides in Prison* London: Routledge.

Loucks, N (1998) *HMPI Cornton Vale: Research into Drugs and Alcohol, Violence and Bullying, Suicides and Self-Injury, and Backgrounds of Abuse* Scottish Prison Service Occasional Paper 1/98, Edinburgh: Scottish Prison Service.

Loucks, N (2004) 'Women in prison' in McIvor, G (ed) *Women Who Offend* London: Jessica Kingsley Publishers.

Loucks, N, Malloch, M, McIvor, G and Gelsthorpe, L (2006) *Evaluation of the 218 Centre* Edinburgh: Scottish Executive Social Research.

Mair, G and May, C (1997) *Offenders on Probation* Home Office Research Study 167, London: Home Office.

Mair, G, Cross, N and Taylor, S (2007) *The Use and Impact of the Community Order and the Suspended Sentence Order* London: Centre for Crime and Justice Studies.

Makkai, T and Payne, J (2003) 'Key findings from the drug use careers of offenders (DUCO) study' *Trends & Issues in Crime and Criminal Justice No. 237*, Canberra, ACT: Australian Institute of Criminology.

Malloch, M and Loucks, N (2007) 'Responding to drug and alcohol problems: Innovations and effectiveness in treatment programmes for women' in Sheehan, R, McIvor, G and Trotter, C (eds) *What Works with Women Offenders* Cullompton: Willan Publishing.

Malloch, M, McIvor, G and Loucks, N (2008) '"Time Out" for Women: Innovation in Scotland in a context of change' *The Howard Journal of Criminal Justice* 47(4), pp 383-99.

Maruna, S (2001) *Making Good: How Ex-convicts Reform and Rebuild their Lives* Washington, DC: American Psychological Association.

McIvor G (1998) 'Jobs for the boys? Gender differences in referral for community service' *The Howard Journal* 37(3), pp 280-91.

McIvor, G (2007) 'The nature of female offending' in Sheehan, R, McIvor, G and Trotter, C (eds) *What Works with Women Offenders* Cullompton: Willan Publishing.

McIvor, G, Westmarland, N, Jamieson, J and Moodie, K (2000) *Women on Probation: The Effectiveness of Different Models of Supervision* Stirling: Social Work Research Centre, University of Stirling.

McIvor, G, Murray, C and Jamieson, J (2004) 'Is Desistance from Crime Different for Women and Girls?' in Immarigeon, R and Maruna, S (eds) *After Crime and Punishment: Ex-offender Reintegration and Desistance from Crime* Cullompton: Willan Publishing.

McIvor, G, Barnsdale, L, Malloch, M, Eley, S and Yates, R (2006) *The Operation and Effectiveness of the Scottish Drug Court Pilots* Edinburgh: Scottish Executive Social Research.

McIvor, G, Trotter, C and Sheehan, R (2009) 'Women, resettlement and desistance' *Probation Journal* 56(4), pp 347-61.

McNeill, F (2003) 'Desistance-Focused Probation Practice' in Chui, W-H and Nellis, M (eds) *Moving Probation Forward: Evidence, Arguments and Practice* Harlow: Pearson Longman.

McNeill, F (2006) 'A desistance paradigm for offender management' *Criminology and Criminal Justice* 6(1), pp 39-62.

Ministry of Justice (2008) *Delivering the Government Report to the Corston Report* London: Ministry of Justice (www.justice.gov.uk/publications/docs/delivering-the-government-response-to-the-corston-report-web.pdf, last accessed 19 October 2009).

Morris A, Wilkinson C, Tisi, A, Woodrow, J and Rockley, A (1995) *Managing the Needs of Female Prisoners* London: Home Office.

NOMS (National Offender Management Service) (2005) *Women's Offending Reduction Programme: Annual Review 2004-2005* London: Home Office.

NOMS (2006) *Offender Managemnt Caseload Statistics Quarterly Brief: October to December 2005 England and Wales* London: Home Office.

Patel, S and Stanley, S (2008) *The Use of the Community Order and the Suspended Sentence Order for Women* London: Centre for Crime and Justice Studies.

Porporino, F and Fabiano, E (2005) 'Is there an evidence based supportive of women-centred programming in corrections?' *Corrections Today* October, pp 26-8.

Rex, S (1999) 'Desistance from offending: Experiences of probation' *The Howard Journal of Criminal Justice* 38(4), pp 366-83.

Roberts, J (2002) 'Women centred: The West Mercia community based programme for women offenders' in Carlen, P (ed.) *Women and Punishment: The Struggle for Justice,* Cullompton: Willan Publishing.

Rumgay, J (2000) 'Policies of neglect :Female offenders and the Probation Service' in Kemshall, H and Littlechild, R (eds) *Improving Participation and Involvement in Social Care Delivery* London: Jessica Kingsley Publishers.

Rumgay, J (2004) 'Scripts for Safer Survival: Pathways Out of Female Crime' *Howard Journal of Criminal Justice* 43(4), pp 405-19.

Scottish Executive (2002) *A Better Way: The Report of the Ministerial Group on Women's Offending* Edinburgh: Scottish Executive.

Scottish Executive (2006a) *Criminal Proceedings in Scottish Courts 2004/5* Edinburgh: Scottish Executive.

Scottish Executive (2006b) *Prison Statistics Scotland 2005/06,* Edinburgh: Scottish Executive.

Scottish Government (2007) *Criminal Justice Social Work Statistics 2006-7* Edinburgh: Scottish Government.

Scottish Government (2009a) *Criminal Proceedings in Scottish Courts, 2007/08* Edinburgh: Scottish Government.

Scottish Government (2009b) *Reconviction Rates in Scotland: 2005-06 and 2006-07 Offender Cohorts* Edinburgh: Scottish Government.

Shaw, M and Hannah-Moffat, K (2004) 'How cognitive skills forgot about gender and diversity' in Mair, G (ed) *What Matters in Probation* Cullompton: Willan Publishing.

Sheehan, R and Flynn, C (2007) 'Women prisoners and their children' in Sheehan, R, McIvor, G and Trotter, C (eds) *What Works with Women Offenders* Cullompton: Willan Publishing.

Stermac, L, MacLean, H and Loucks, A (1991) *Treatment Needs of Female Offenders* Ottawa: Correctional Service of Canada.

Wahidin, A (2005) 'The needs of older men and women in the criminal justice system: An international perspective' *Prison Service Journal,* 160, (www.hmprisonservice.gov.uk/assets/documents/10000FA4483_needs_of_older_men_and_women.doc).

Weaver, B and McNeill, F (forthcoming) 'Travelling Hopefully: Desistance Research and Probation Practice' in Brayford, J, Cowe, F and Deering, J (eds) *What Else Works? Creative Work with Offenders* Cullompton: Willan Publishing.

Wilkinson, C (2004) 'Women's release from prison: The case for change' in McIvor, G (ed) *Women Who Offend* London: Jessica Kingsley Publishers.

Worrall, A (1996) 'Gender, criminal justice and probation' in McIvor, G (ed) *Working with Offenders* London: Jessica Kingsley Publishers.

Worrall, A (2002) 'Missed opportunities? The probation service and women offenders' in Ward, D, Scott, J and Lacey, M (eds) *Probation: Working for Justice* Oxford: Oxford University Press.

Wright, L and Kemshall, H (1994) 'Feminist probation practice – making supervision meaningful' *Probation Journal* 41(2), pp 73-80.

Conclusion

Malcolm Hill, Raymond Taylor and Fergus McNeill

Introduction

Social work is generally seen as operating at the interface between the individual and the social. This has two main aspects. First, social workers aim to work with service users in relation to their social circumstances. Second, specific legislation and policy documents authorise and guide social work practice, especially in the statutory sector, although in some arenas the responsibilities are vague or diffuse (Chapter 16). Such powers and responsibilities reflect the interests and wishes of society at large. According to Wilson *et al.* (2008), the configuration of service users within their social settings and workers in their policy/organisational context requires social workers to acquire and develop a reflective understanding of individuals; their family and social circumstances; the worker's own agency and inter-organisational context; and the broader social, political, cultural and economic environment. The chapters in this book have sought to illuminate all of these domains, with most addressing the interaction between two or more, thereby highlighting the desirability of recognising and embracing multiple inter-relatedness in assessments and interventions undertaken by social workers.

In this concluding chapter we shall review the main themes emerging from the book, especially those that cross-cut different settings and client groups, and discuss trends likely to impact on social work practice in the future. We consider first of all the developing nature of social work itself, much influenced by its wider policy contexts, and then consider challenges arising from societal and technological changes.

Changes and continuities in the nature of social work

In the early 1980s, the Barclay Report (1982) reviewed the current social work scene and provided a template for training and practice in succeeding years. The report clarified that there were two distinct elements and traditions in social work, the first concerned with individualised relationship-based work (counselling) and the second with more strategic deployment of resources (social care planning). Both aspects remain relevant, although care planning has come to be applied mainly in relation to individuals and families, whereas Barclay also included neighbourhood working as carried out in the-then fashionable local or patch teams.

Ironically, perhaps, work with groups and neighbourhoods, as well as the notion of influencing policy, have become more marginal to social work just at the time that it has grown in the fields of health promotion and public health. Reflecting this, relatively little attention has been given in the book to work with groups, neighbourhood networks and organisations, although these remain potentially vital for a holistic approach to marshalling resources and social capital for addressing needs and deeds, problem-solving and social care (Chapters 9, 12, 14 and 19). Collective action by neighbourhood organisations remains an important strand in measures to reduce poverty and alleviate its impact (Chapter 7; see also Holman, 1998, 2001).

Elements of challenging local and societal attitudes have perhaps featured more strongly in the book. These are prominent in anti-oppressive practice whose continuing relevance has been discussed in Chapter 5. Similarly, other chapters have called for social workers to adopt awareness-raising measures and seek to alter public and official attitudes, for example in relation to mental health and learning disabilities (Chapters 6, 13 and 14), old age (Chapters 12 and 16) and residential childcare (Chapter 10). This includes enhancing understanding of risk and harm, as well as showing the pitfalls of stereotyping and assumptions about appropriate interventions (Chapters 2 and 6).

Walker (2004) argues for both the continuation of a community work strand within social work and its integration with psychosocial practice. He describes the resulting dual role of social work as 'addressing the external community of injustice and inhumanity as well as the internal community of conflicts and contradictions' (2004, p 163). He notes, for instance, how the Framework for the Assessment of Children adopts an ecological approach as described by Aldgate in Chapter 9, which requires understanding of resources and stresses in the local environment as well as within the child and family. Walker also recognises that engaging with service users as resource people, whether as volunteers, mentors, carers or community activists, can enhance their identity, self confidence and skill repertoire in addition to increasing network support locally and helping tackle wider social problems. Conversely, psycho-social skills assist with challenging racism, mental health stigma and other forms of discrimination (Chapters 5, 6 and 14).

In the past, working at the neighbourhood level has often been associated with radical and mainly left-wing perspectives (Chapter 5). However, in recent years, interest has been shown across the political spectrum in such notions as strengthening civil society and promoting social capital, whether as intermediaries or as alternatives to state action. As we write, a former community activist occupies the White House and the newly elected Conservative-Liberal Democrat government in the United Kingdom (UK) plans to empower local volunteer associations to provide services. If this is to be linked with the goal of social justice, then it is important that the poor, less articulate or less well connected are enabled to take action as well as those who are more affluent and influential (Chapters 7 and 19; Holman, 2001).

Most of the chapters in the book reflect the general trend for social workers to concentrate on work with individuals and possibly their families. Several assert the central relevance of developing and sustaining close positive relationships as the key basis for deploying more specific methods as in counselling and promoting behaviour change (e.g. Chapters 8, 16, 19, 21 and 22). In Chapter 18 Eccles points to the danger that the human qualities of face-to-face support and care for frail or disabled older people may be attenuated if technological aids replace interpersonal contact. In the context of criminal justice, Nellis in Chapter 20 also points to the difficulties in connecting new technologies with human services. In Chapter 10 Kendrick *et al.* describe how, despite diverse approaches to residential childcare and associated training in different countries, a shared core theme involves relationship-based work within the everyday life-space. To work well, this requires careful reflection and supervision, which Green Lister in Chapter 8 also highlights as a necessity in the different context of (alleged) serious abuse and neglect at home. As argued by MacKay and MacIntyre, in Chapter 6 on personalisation, this may also require a significant change in the relationship between social worker and service user and a shift in the way that services are currently delivered.

Human experience, engagement skills and intuition are all essential ingredients of relationship-based practice (Chapters 3, 9 and 21). Recruitment and initial training should ensure that new practitioners have these qualities. However, they need to be honed and reinforced in teams and agencies that are supportive of professional development and reflection. Wilson *et al.* (2008) identify aspects of relationships that should be understood and constantly re-evaluated, including the balance between the cognitive and affective, conscious and unconscious, professional and personal. It is also vital that relationship-based social work includes a comprehensive ethical framework (Chapters 3 and 18).

Arguably, a shift has occurred within all areas of social work practice, where there is greater concentration on the 'front end' of interaction with service users and reduced emphasis on longer-term support, although clearly exceptions to this occur, perhaps especially in the voluntary sector. Across a range of client groups, emphasis has been placed on assessment and investigation (Chapters 8, 16, 19 and 21), not always followed by appropriate intervention. An opposite danger is that we too readily resort to institutional alternatives for want of intermediate supports and accommodation, as in relation to older people, those with mental health problems and women involved in the justice system (McIvor; Roberts; Bates and Lymbery). While autonomy and choice usually favour 'least restrictive environments' whenever possible, it is important not to stereotype residential care, as Kendrick *et al.* argue with respect to young people in Chapter 10. In the UK, residential childcare no longer has many of the characteristics associated with institutionalisation and can be a preferred and helpful option in certain circumstances.

The so-called 'mixed economy' of welfare provision has always been present in the British welfare state, but in their different ways, governments from the 1980s onwards have sought an enhanced role for the voluntary and/or private sectors (Dickens, 2010). It is common now to think in terms of commissioners of services (usually local authorities in relation to social work services) and providers (which are often independent or non-statutory). This trend has been justified in terms of choice, freedom and efficiency (best value), but has been seen by some as diluting basic services and commodifying or depersonalising social care (Chapter 2; Wilson *et al.*, 2008).

Chapters 11 and 20 by Sellick and Nellis respectively describe in very different contexts the growing influence of private for-profit agencies in social welfare and youth/criminal justice. Traditionally, social workers in the UK (although less in North America or Hong Kong for example) have tended to see the private sector as inimical to social work values. However, Sellick has observed a shift in attitudes among local authority social workers towards acceptance that certain kinds of private organisation can provide a valued and innovative service. This is particularly so where privatisation is what Dellgran and Hojer (2005) describe as professionally driven rather than policy driven. In other words, experienced social workers themselves set up or run agencies in order to gain the freedom of self-employment and ability to offer a more selective service. Similarly, with respect to residential childcare, independent providers have sometimes led positive innovation (Chapter 10).

'Managerialism' and professional independence

A key policy trend apparent before 1997 but extended considerably under new Labour has been the use of a number of centrally directed mechanisms aimed at improving the quality and consistency of services. These have come to be known collectively and pejoratively as managerialism, that is, seeking to control or micro-manage local service delivery by such means as target setting, common assessment frameworks and guidance, performance indicators, National Standards and inspections. Each of these has distinct functions of course, but collectively they embody an emphasis on following rules and procedures towards centrally defined goals (Dickens, 2010).

In defence of such measures it can be said that unless there is a framework of regulation the quality of service delivery is likely to be very uneven and poor practice will occur (as in banking!). On the whole, though, the social policy community and many academics and practitioners have been rightly critical of these developments, for their threats to professional autonomy and discretion, narrow focus, and imposition of time-consuming procedures at the expense of direct helping activities. Similar criticisms have been made in relation to education, health and criminal justice services. In Chapter 3, Stevens argues that this approach cannot ensure sensitive and ethical practice, which at the end of the day relies on the personal qualities and training of the practitioner. In Chapter 9, Aldgate discusses how measures intended to improve practice and co-operation with regard to assessment in children's services have become over-prescriptive and complex, although less so in Scotland and Wales than in England or Northern Ireland. Similarly, Eccles suggests in Chapter 18 that new forms of technology are best applied not simply as an instrumental means of meeting the requirements of short-term performance indicators, but also within a reflexive paradigm shift about the best ways to provide social care. Nellis develops a somewhat similar argument in Chapter 20 in the context of his discussion of the electronic monitoring of offenders.

Specialism

The structure of this book, like that of most statutory social work services and voluntary agencies, has been mostly organised around three broad groupings of social work clients (children; adults in need of social support and care; and adults involved in the criminal justice system). Nearly all agencies employing social workers are to a greater or lesser extent specialist, which, depending on their viewpoint, represents either an advance or retreat from the heyday of generic social work in the 1970s and 1980s. In the field of criminal justice, social work has become marginalised in England and Wales, although not to the same extent in Ireland and Scotland (Chapter 21).

One of the main rationales for specialisation is that detailed expertise is required. Despite the extended length of social work education and the raising of standards to degree level (Chapters 1 and 17), courses do not have the time to prepare social workers adequately with the knowledge and skills necessary to operate across the whole lifespan or to develop a full grasp of the multiple policy, legal and organisational contexts (for example, in health, education or justice) which frame social work practice. Hence, this book contains chapters that expose professionals to up-to-date thinking, research and practice development in relation to specific domains.

However, we hope that readers will not confine themselves to matters in their chosen specialism. It remains the case that social workers in nearly all contexts will not only need to deploy generic skills informed by shared values, but will also deal with individuals, families and communities with mixes and interactions of life stages, problem types and system contacts. The reciprocal relationships of older people with younger generations are critical to the care and well-being of both. Relationships with partners, children and parents are crucial in desistance from offending, although in different ways and with different timing for males and females (Chapters 19 and 22). The care and behaviour problems of children and young people are often closely connected to, for instance, parents' substance misuse or mental health problems (Chapter 17), while children are deeply affected when a parent is in custody or hospital. Therefore, in many cases, collaboration between adult and children's services is required and, arguably, a family approach. Hence, assessments and interventions frequently require some degree of awareness of the issues and underpinning knowledge affecting other specialisms within social work, as well as across disciplinary boundaries.

Of course, social work is not alone in having age- or issue-related divisions. These can pose particular difficulties for service users with long-term difficulties. Discontinuity and disruption of support face disabled young people and their parents at school-leaving, while problems can arise when young people with health problems no longer fall in the ambit of paediatrics or Child and Adolescent Mental Health Services.

Orientation to service users

Several chapters note how services should be founded on internationally agreed human rights (for example Chapters 7 and 12). Particularly highlighted in this book have been the rights to respect and to autonomy, which are closely related to the notion of empowerment (Chapters 2, 6 and 13). This is a central part of one internationally agreed definition of social work, namely it 'promotes social change, problem-solving in human relationships and the empowerment and liberation of people to enhance well-being' (IASSW, 2001).

Although 'client self-determination' was a core principle of early social work and user participation has been a strong strand in recent decades (Chapters 2 and 14; Beresford and Croft 1993; Kemshall and Littlechild, 2000), in practice social workers and social service organisations have often acted in a top-down way. The growth in professional confidence may have contributed to a tendency to substitute workers' judgements for service users' wishes. In some respects, this is required by legislation. For instance, social workers in all UK jurisdictions are required to take into account children's views, but their primary responsibility is to make and contribute to decisions in the child's best interests (Chapter 8). In Chapter 2, Bates and Lymbery suggest that with adults too, concern about potential harm and about potential public criticism for exposing people to risk has led to suspicious and over protective approaches (see also Chapters 19, 20, 21 and 22). They argue instead for a person-centred ethos to risk management, which includes paying careful attention to people's own views about safety and a positive approach to risk-taking. This view is echoed by MacKay and MacIntyre in Chapter 6.

Closely linked to this is the notion of understanding and treating service users as whole human beings (Chapters 5 and 17). This is critical not only out of respect for them as individuals and to better understand the context of their presenting problems, but also to avoid stigma. Further, this lends itself to recognising people's strengths (in themselves and their networks), which can be resources for dealing with the difficulties at hand (Chapters 2, 19 and 22; Saleeby 2002).

Assessment

It is commonly agreed that assessment is not simply the accumulation of information or even a thorough review of evidence. Workers need to bring to bear their own professional knowledge and apply relevant theory and research knowledge (Chapters 1, 19 and 21). Assessments should take account of expressed needs and available informal resources in addition to expert-defined needs and risks (Chapters 2 and 8).

In Chapter 9, Aldgate points out the value of Common Assessment Frameworks for providing guidance to individual practitioners and facilitating shared communication across agencies and professions. However, she also highlights that these cannot substitute for in-depth professional understanding and discretion, a point echoed by

Green Lister in Chapter 8. Similarly, Crisp *et al.* (2007) concluded that thorough training and supervision are vital for practitioners to be able to make accurate and comprehensive assessments.

Evidence-based practice (EBP)

Both social work education and most areas of social policy have witnessed an emphasis on evidence-based practice (or policy). There is a spectrum of ways of interpreting what is meant in this context by 'evidence-based', although it tends to be commonly accepted that it is research evidence being referred to, rather than, say, practice experience. A broad view of EBP indicates that it is desirable for policies and interventions to be based as far as possible on research findings, which ideally bring together a range of forms of information and multiple perspectives. At the other end of the spectrum, 'evidence-based' is taken to mean much more specifically that interventions should be mainly or only undertaken when they have been 'proved' to be effective through quasi-experimental studies, ideally involving randomised control-led trials. This is particularly the stance taken by some supporters of 'What Works' within criminal and youth justice or of cognitive-behavioural programmes for parents or children (Chapters 8, 19, 21 and 22). A useful caution comes from the experience of evidence-based medicine, sometimes portrayed as committed only to experimental evidence, but where attention has also been given to patients' experiences, the personal qualities of doctors and nurses, and ethics (Gilgun, 2005).

A key term in EBP is that of 'outcomes', that is, that services should be judged by their presumed effects. There are dangers with this approach. First, it is easy to be trapped by the old fallacy that because something follows a particular action, it has been caused by that action. For instance entry to custody or residential care may follow social work contact and hence be seen as an outcome of it, but the causal chain will usually have been long and complex. Second, there is a risk that the processes involved in intervention and even the basic rights of individuals will be neglected in the pursuit of 'outcomes' defined by professionals or policy-makers, however laudable (Chapter 3). That said, it is clearly important that services do produce good outcomes in the sense of changes that services users want and that professionals think they need (Chapter 6).

Nevertheless, research evidence about the differential effects of different courses of action can and should inform decision-making and contingency planning, for instance when placing a looked-after child or deciding on the best ways to recruit foster carers. However, it must be borne in mind that any particular case may be one of the exceptions that almost invariably are present among the generalisable findings of research (Hill, 2009).

Most of the chapters have taken account of evidence in the wider sense. In Chapter 1, McIntyre and Orme highlight the difficulty of giving sufficient attention to research within qualifying training. Hence, practitioners should be alert to opportunities to fill gaps in their understanding and to gain access to up-to-date research findings. Supervisors and, where they exist, agency research staff can play a vital role in making available review findings and identifying the implications of recent research for practice. In Chapter 8, Green Lister reviews a range of interventions to safeguard children and improve parenting. She notes the unevenness of the evidence available, but also describes how research has shown which kinds of programme do normally have a positive impact. Just as important, some evaluations indicate the kinds of person or behaviour likely to be more or less responsive. Similarly, McIvor in Chapter 22 demonstrates how women tend to be less responsive than men to the standard forms of cognitive-behavioural programmes that have become common for seeking to modify offending and other behaviours. They tend to prefer and react better to more individualised approaches focusing on relationships. Drawing on research about desistance from offending, McNeill, in Chapter 19, reviews the influences that can assist positive change. Rather than focusing on EBP rooted in evaluation research, his suggestion is that interventions must be designed around the developmental processes they exist to support, and must pay heed to their social contexts. In many respects, his argument implicitly reasserts the importance of practitioners' understandings of human development and ecological (or systems) perspectives, which have featured regularly throughout the history of social work education.

Promotion of collaboration with other professions and agencies

If a systems perspective is important in understanding service users' problems and change processes, it is equally important to understanding and developing social work itself. More than most, social work as a profession cannot function in isolation from others. The need for better collaboration across agencies and professions has been a recurrent theme in health and welfare policies for a long time. This can be seen as part of a wider process in which the edges of organisations have become more diffuse and there is greater emphasis on networks of expertise distributed across a range of locations (Cooper and Dartington. 2004; Edwards et al., 2009).

Co-operation can occur across a number of boundaries, in different ways and to different extents (Chapter 15), so it is important to be clear about language and expectations. Different considerations apply when seeking to work together:

- among professions within the same organisation (e.g. doctors, nurses and social workers in hospital);
- with the same profession in a different agency (e.g. between social workers in a local authority and in a voluntary or private agency: see e.g. Chapters 11 and 20);
- across both professional and agency boundaries, as in case conferences or Youth Offending Teams.

Despite widespread adherence to the ideal of co-operation, problems in working together have been regularly identified too (Chapters 8 and 15). This highlights that social work in particular relies on other agencies to fulfil its aims to the full, and also that there are many barriers, including differences in training, values, priorities, geographical coverage and time schedules (Chapter 15). It also has to be recognised that alongside gains, co-operation brings costs – of time devoted to communication and joint planning and potentially of threats to professional identity. It is now generally agreed that the most fruitful partnerships occur when core identities are retained, but there is openness to the expertise of others and preparedness to understand others' viewpoints (Chapter 15; *Edwards et al.*, 2009). There is evidence that rigid perceptions of other professions have diminished, but nevertheless 'quite entrenched characterisations' persist alongside a greater commitment to joint working (Reynolds, 2007). With its shorter history and more precarious claims to professional status compared with medicine, teaching and law, social work tends to have less power at strategic and sometimes case levels (see Chapter 19). On the other hand, the interdisciplinary mix of social work education tends to heighten understanding of different theoretical perspectives and knowledge bases.

Probably the earliest efforts to produce what Birchall and Hallett (1995) called 'mandated collaboration' (i.e. directed by government) came in the community care field, prompted by the Griffiths Reports about financial and quality problems affecting the social and healthcare of older people in the context of a rapidly expanding number of frail older people with chronic illness (Holloway and Lymbery, 2007). Eccles and Petch have reviewed recent policy, research and practice (see Chapter 15). They conclude that it is vital for practitioners to clarify the use of language and expectations when setting up co-operative arrangements. In particular, it is valuable to explore what degree of partnership is desirable and what needs to be put in place at different levels to attain it.

In child and family social work, problems in inter-agency communication and joint working were identified at least as early as the Maria Colwell inquiry in 1973 and repeated in many subsequent child abuse inquiries (Munro, 2002). Over the last ten years a more concerted and positive attempt to promote 'integrated working' has occurred, culminating in the creation of Children's Trusts in England. Aldgate (Chapter 9) believes that collaboration works best when it is rooted in the practice and language of each of the main professional groups (health, education and social work). Practical, ethical and civil rights issues have affected attempts to link information systems across agencies, which accounts in part for the decision of the incoming 2010 government to abandonment the Contactpoint system developed in England for this purpose. The need remains to reconcile children's and parents' rights to privacy and consent with safeguarding children, in light of evidence that multiple referrals are a key indicator of risk to children's welfare (Chapter 8).

Social workers have worked in co-located multi-disciplinary teams for a long time, as in child guidance clinics, but the range and number of these has grown, for instance in Youth Offending Teams (Bottoms and Kemp, 2006) and in community mental health teams (Dickens 2010), as well as looser networks. These can help improve mutual understanding and communication, but can also lead to tensions and conflicts, as Eccles and Petch (Chapter 15) also observe. It is helpful if there is an opportunity to reflect on tensions and differences in language, routines, expectations and so on, especially if dialogue is assisted by external support (Edwards *et al.*, 2009).

Societal changes

Social work has always responded to wider political and social changes, as befits its roles in ameliorating the negative consequences of socio-economic development with the assistance of available informal and formal resources. The pace of change has been accelerating in living memory and shows little sign of slowing down. A Scottish review of twentieth-first century social work concluded that 'increasing demands, greater complexity and rising expectations mean that the current situation is not sustainable'. Hence 'doing more of the same won't work' (Scottish Executive, 2006, p 10). In other words, social work needs to keep changing too, holding on to the core and the good, but adapting in significant ways. Several chapters have stated that responses to intensive concerns about risk in present-day society have distorted practice, so that now a new approach is required that is more in tune with service users' own perspectives and with 'natural' recovery processes, for instance (Chapters 2, 8, 12 and 19).

For decades the UK has had an ageing population, with multiple consequences. To a considerable degree the growth in the proportion of the population who are aged over 65 has been offset by general improvement in health and fitness in later life. But a significant recent development has been the growing numbers of the 'very old' and increased incidence of dementia, which have resulted in higher demand for both residential and domiciliary social care services (Chapter 12). It is important to bear in mind, however, that demographic changes can be used as a rationale for decisions made on financial grounds, whereas in Chapter 18 Eccles suggests that they can provide an opportunity for a paradigm shift to reconfigure the nature of care and caring relationships.

The impact of the population structure is also felt through changes in the employment ratio that have led to pressures to raise the official ages of eligibility for retirement and a pension. This blends with the wishes of some older people to remain economically active for longer. The shift in the electorate towards fewer young adults and a larger 'grey' vote also gives more prominence to the needs and wishes of older people. Some have suggested that, as a result, children will have a lower profile from now on, although arguments about the importance of investing in the next generation as the basis for society's future remain strong (Jensen *et al.*, 2004).

In the later part of the twentieth century, the general standard of living rose, but inequality also inreased. The government of the 1980s and 1990s believed that disadvantage was best dealt with by market mechanisms and a minimal state safety net, but the New Labour government from 1997 introduced policies and a special interdepartmental unit to combat 'social exclusion'. It also espoused ambitious goals of reducing and eventually removing child poverty, through such mechanisms as tax credits, increased child benefit and support for parents to work. As Hamilton (Chapter 7) observes, considerable progress occurred, although less impact was made in relation to families living with serious and persistent poverty. Contrasts in health and life expectancy between the more and less affluent remain very high (Scottish Executive, 2006). This reinforces the need for social workers' awareness of financial benefits and advocacy in relation to material and accommodation needs, while a range of services should be mindful of the potentially discriminatory effects of indirect costs as well as direct charges (Chapter 7).

Immigration to the UK has increased during the last ten years, but with a very different pattern compared with earlier inward movement. The largest number of new residents has come from Eastern Europe, some on a quite temporary basis. Another important group has comprised refugees, mostly coming from places with violent conflict in Africa and Asia. Many of both groups are young and resourceful, so may need little help except as regards language and adapting to different systems and a way of life. Some, however, do need concerted support, notably asylum-seekers, who are not allowed to work until or unless they are granted leave to stay in the country. Unaccompanied minors have a wide range of social, legal, health and educational needs, although often also a striking degree of optimism and resilience (Kohli, 2007; Hill and Hopkins, 2009).

During the 1960s and 1970s, in contrast, many people came from the Commonwealth, Ireland and the United States (US). Although significant communities with their origins around the world had been established long before, the number of black and minority ethnic British people rose markedly. Most are now at least second or third generation. This spread the cultural traditions rooted in South Asia, China and the Caribbean and created significant groups within the UK adhering to Buddhism, Hinduism, Islam and Sikhism. One related and concerning development is the expression of racism, but arguably a stronger movement has been that of anti-racism, which soon became incorporated as a central tenet in social work education. There have been many twists and turns in terminology and ethos affecting social work in a multi-cultural society, with even the term 'multiculturalism' itself subject to different positive and negative interpretations. The new millennium has seen a merging of anti-discriminatory legislation and organisations across race, religion, gender, disability and sexuality, reframed more positively in terms of equalities. Dominelli (Chapter 5) has pointed to the continuing relevance of anti-oppressive practice, which takes account of global trends and influences. Stevens (Chapter 3) highlights that the spiritual dimension of human experiences is often neglected and needs to be seen in the light of the range of religious beliefs represented in Britain. Spirituality, she argues, is important for everyone and social workers should be alert to ways in which this may shape and influence the lives of service users. This may be most apparent when dealing with people who are recently bereaved or anticipating their own imminent death or that of a loved one, and hospice and hospital-based social workers are normally well attuned to the importance of spirituality. However, questions about the purpose of life and what happens after death impinge in many other circumstances, particularly when reflections are prompted by major life events or separations.

Technological developments

Technological innovation has been an aspect of human evolution for millennia, but developed rapidly during the Industrial Revolution. It is commonly agreed that the rate of change in recent years has in some respects been unprecedented, with novel objects like floppy disks and CDs becoming obsolete after a couple of decades. In particular, developments in communication have transformed most people's working and private lives, so it is only to be expected that this has had a major impact on social work, for which interpersonal and written recording have always been central elements. One very obvious consequence has been the use of electronic media for case records and sharing information. Combined with the emphasis on assessing outcomes, this has led to concerted efforts by central government and local agencies to align their communication systems. Garrett (2005) refers to this as the 'electronic turn' in social work. He criticises the way in which this has taken place for increasing bureaucratic activity. Green Lister and Aldgate (Chapters 8 and 9) support the need for better assessment, inter-professional sharing of information and planning assisted by new technology, but argue for a light touch in the development of new processes and systems.

A distinctive application of new technology has been in the field of surveillance with regard to criminal and anti-social behaviour. The growth in public surveillance (via CCTV and speed cameras for instance) has the potential for improving both physical and emotional security as well as helping with the identification of law breakers, but the risks and effects of infringing civil liberties are also substantial. Whereas public surveillance is mainly about prevention, deterrence and detection, individualised surveillance has been applied with convicted people notably through 'tagging' (electronic monitoring) (Moore 2004; Nellis 2004, 2006). In North America, this approach has sometimes been used as the sole or primary court disposal, but in the UK it has normally been combined with intensive supervision or probation (Moore, 2004). This has occurred in recognition that, as with custody, a purely deterrent method is unlikely to work and needs to be accompanied by intervention to alter the circumstances and context in which crimes are committed (Chapter 19). The division of responsibility between an often private agency handling the electronic instrument and a statutory agency carrying out interpersonal work has been an uneasy one (Chapter 19).

A further important development in the application of technology has been in relation to mobility, communication and alarm systems for older and disabled people, particularly those living alone. In Chapter 18, Eccles acknowledges that benefits that have included, for example, an increase in independence and a reduction in isolation. However, he also notes that innovation has often been driven at least partly by a concern with economic efficiency. He also states that inadequate thought has been given to ethical considerations and points to the risk of losing touch with the human need for direct personal contact.

Next steps for professionals at an early career stage

Within the context of such rapid and complex social change, our learning is necessarily lifelong. Professionals are particularly beholden to improve and update their knowledge and understanding through both early and continuing professional development (Chapters 1 and 17). A corollary has been the increasing tendency for agencies to commit themselves to being or becoming 'learning organisations'. As Bates and Lymbery note in Chapter 2, ideally this is not simply about bureaucratic measures. Both informal and formal processes are necessary, with subtle mechanisms created by agencies and teams for adapting in the light of successes and failures. It is vital that practitioners constantly re-assess their work and identify information and understanding, narrow and broad, which they need to enhance. At times, consultation with colleagues, managers or specialists will suffice and may be the only feasible option in a crisis. In the longer run, this can be supplemented by accessing in-service and external training in the form of short courses or perhaps more extended part-time programmes. Busy practitioners often have little time or energy for a lot of reading. While books (like this one!) may be the ideal, journal articles are often easier to find time for and these are increasingly available online. Similarly, a growing number of websites are excellent sources to keep abreast of policy developments and research (see, for instance, the Social Care Institute for Excellence's website at www.scie.org.uk and Research in Practice at www.rip.org.uk).

Several chapters have noted the crucial significance of reliable, supportive and challenging supervision to help practitioners learn, reflect and question their assessments and actions (e.g. Chapters 1, 4 and 8). Moreover, managers have a responsibility to afford their workers the time to attend training and 'become familiar with research relevant to their practice' (Gilgun, 2005, p 52). It is part of a manager's role to ensure that staff have adequate induction, guidance and help with stress (Chapter 4). Supervisors should be competent and available to aid practitioners with the emotional and psychological aspects of working with people (Chapter 4; Huffington et al., 2004). Just as 'managerialism' has proceduralised relationships between workers and service users in an attempt to manage risk and uphold standards, so management has sometimes come to be seen mainly in terms of checking, comparison and compliance (Kirton, 2009). Hence, special efforts and on occasion external consultancy may be necessary to ensure that adequate attention is given to the well-being and self-esteem of workers and to create a sense of trust and autonomy (Cooper and Dartington, 2004). In Chapter 2, Bates and Lymbery point to the importance of creating a supportive team climate. They also describe the merits of a systematic approach to assessing how person-centred a service is in order to reframe thinking about risk and its management.

Practitioners as individuals and collectively should seek to make the most of their managers, by such means as seeking help, advocating on behalf of services users, contributing to agency policy formulation and identifying ways to improve service delivery. Many frontline staff have no inclination to become managers themselves, but some are motivated to do so and with time others come to see it as desirable or necessary. Hence, it is important to understand the qualities required in management and the steps practitioners can take in preparation for management roles (Chapter 4).

Final remarks

We hope this book has stimulated you not only to think, but also to test out possible changes or additions to your practice informed by the concepts and details presented in the volume. If a collection of this nature can have a single conclusion or a straightforward message, it is probably this: our capacity to adapt positively to changing circumstances, whether as service users or as social workers, depends on our willingness and capacity to learn. In both cases, change is a social and cultural project as well as an interpersonal and individual project. It requires us to learn both about the external changes that affect us, and about ourselves – how we have developed in the past, how we are responding to challenges now and what we might do to secure our future development. More fundamentally, it raises moral and political questions about what and who we value, about what changes we want to support and about what changes we must resist. We hope that the chapters in this collection will assist practitioners in struggling with these complex and challenging – but also endlessly fascinating and engaging – questions.

References

Barclay Report (1982) *Social Workers: Their Role and Tasks* London: Bedford Square Press.

Beresford, P and Croft, S (1993) *Citizen Involvement* London: Macmillan.

Birchall, E and Hallett, C (1995) *Working Together in Child Protection* London: HMSO.

Bottoms, A and Kemp, V (2006) 'The relationship between youth justice and child welfare in England and Wales' in Hill, M, Lockyer, A and Stone, F (eds) *Youth Justice and Child Protection* London: Jessica Kingsley Publishers.

Cooper, A and Dartington, T (2004) 'The vanishing organization: organizational containment in a networked world' in Huffington, C, Armstrong, D, Halton, W, Hoyle, L and Pooley, J (eds) (2005) *Working Below the Surface* London: Karnac.

Crisp, B, Anderson, M R, Orme, J and Green Lister, P (2007) 'Assessment frameworks: A critical reflection' *British Journal of Social Work,* 37(6), pp 1059-77.

Dellgran, P and Hojer, S (2005) 'Privatisation or professionalization: Attitudes, motives and achievements among Swedish social workers' *European Journal of Social Work* 8(1), pp 39-62.

Dickens, J (2010) *Social Work and Social Policy* London: Routledge.

Edwards, A, Daniels, H, Gallagher, T, Leadbetter, J and Warmington, P (2009) *Improving inter-professional collaborations: multi-agency working for children's well-being* London: Routledge.

Garrett, P M (2005) 'Social work's "electronic turn": notes on the deployment of information and communication technologies in social work with children and families' *Critical Social Policy* 25(4), pp 529-53.

Gilgun, J F (2005) 'The four cornerstones of evidence-based practice in social work' *Research on Social Work Practice* 15(1), pp 52-61.

Griffiths, R, Sir (1988) *Community Care: Agenda for Change* (Griffiths Report) London: HMSO.

Hill, M (2009) 'The place of child placement research in policy and practice' in Schofield, G and Simmonds, J (eds) *The Child Placement Handbook* London: BAAF.

Hill, M and Hopkins, P (2009) 'Safeguarding children who are refugees or asylum-seekers' in Broadhurst, K, Grover, C and Jamieson, J (eds) *Critical Perspectives on Safeguarding Children* Chichester: Wiley.

Holloway, M and Lymbery, M (2007) 'Caring for people: Social work with adults in the next decade and beyond' *British Journal of Social Work,* 37(3), pp 375-86.

Holman, B. (1998) 'Neighbourhoods and exclusion' in Barry, M and Hallett, C (eds) *Social Exclusion and Social Work* London: Russell House Publishing.

Holman, B (2001) 'Neighbourhood projects and preventing delinquency' *Youth Welfare* 1(1), pp 45-52.

Huffington, C, Armstrong, D, Halton, W, Hoyle, L and Pooley, J (2004) *Working Below the Surface* London: Karnac.

IASSW (International Association of Schools of Social Work) (2001) *Definition of the Social Work Profession* London: IASSW (www.iassw.aiets.org)

Jensen, A-M, Ben-Arieh, A, Conti, C, Kutsar, D, Phadraig, M and Neilsen, H (2004) *Children's Welfare in Ageing Europe* Trondheim: Norwegian Centre for Child Research.

Kemshall, H and Littlechild, R (eds) (2000) *User Involvement and Participation in Social Care* London: Jessica Kingsley Publishers.

Kirton, D.(2009) *Child Social Work Policy and Practice* London: Sage Publications.

Kohli, R (2007) *Social Work with Unaccpmpanied Asylum-seeking Children* Basgingstoke: Palgrave Macmillan.

Moore, R (2004) 'Intensive supervision and surveillance programmes for young offenders' in Burnett, R and Roberts, C (eds) *What Works in Probation and Youth Justice* Cullompton: Willan.

Munro, E (2002) *Effective Child Protection* London: Sage Publications.

Nellis, M (2004) 'The tracking controversy' *Youth Justice,* 4(2), pp, 77-99.

Nellis, M (2006) Electronic monitoring of offenders: The Scottish experience', *Scottish Journal of Criminal Justice Studies,* 12, pp 74-96.

Reynolds, J (2007) 'Discourses of inter-professionalism' *British Journal of Social Work* 37(3), pp 441-57.

Saleeby, D (2002) *The Strengths Perspective in Social Work Practice* Boston, Ma: Allyn and Bacon.

Scottish Executive (2006) *Changing Lives: Report of the 21st Century Social Work Review* Edinburgh: Scottish Executive.

Walker, S (2004) 'Community work and psychosocial practice – chalk and cheese or birds of a feather' *Journal of Social Work Practice* 18(2), pp 161-65.

Wilson, K, Ruch, G, Lymbery, M and Cooper, A (2008) *Social Work: An introduction to Contemporary Practice* London: Pearson Longman.

Index